Marketing and Resource Management for Green Transitions in Economies

Jean-Vasile Andrei
Petroleum-Gas University of Ploiesti, Romania

Mile Vasić
European Marketing and Management Association, Banja Luka, Bosnia and Herzegovina

Luminita Chivu
National Institute of Economics Research, Romanian Academy, Romania

Boris Kuzman
Institute of Agricultural Economics, Serbia

A volume in the Advances in Marketing, Customer Relationship Management, and E-Services (AMCRMES) Book Series

Published in the United States of America by
IGI Global
Business Science Reference (an imprint of IGI Global)
701 E. Chocolate Avenue
Hershey PA, USA 17033
Tel: 717-533-8845
Fax: 717-533-8661
E-mail: cust@igi-global.com
Web site: http://www.igi-global.com

Library of Congress Cataloging-in-Publication Data

CIP Pending
ISBN: 979-8-3693-3439-3
EISBN: 979-8-3693-3440-9

British Cataloguing in Publication Data
A Cataloguing in Publication record for this book is available from the British Library.

Advances in Marketing, Customer Relationship Management, and E-Services (AMCRMES) Book Series

Eldon Y. Li
National Chengchi University, Taiwan & California Polytechnic State University, USA

ISSN:2327-5502
EISSN:2327-5529

MISSION

Business processes, services, and communications are important factors in the management of good customer relationship, which is the foundation of any well organized business. Technology continues to play a vital role in the organization and automation of business processes for marketing, sales, and customer service. These features aid in the attraction of new clients and maintaining existing relationships.

The Advances in Marketing, Customer Relationship Management, and E-Services (AMCRMES) Book Series addresses success factors for customer relationship management, marketing, and electronic services and its performance outcomes. This collection of reference source covers aspects of consumer behavior and marketing business strategies aiming towards researchers, scholars, and practitioners in the fields of marketing management.

Coverage

- Social Networking and Marketing
- Mobile CRM
- Mobile Services
- Web Mining and Marketing
- Database marketing
- Ethical Considerations in E-Marketing
- Telemarketing
- CRM and customer trust
- Customer Relationship Management
- Electronic Services

IGI Global is currently accepting manuscripts for publication within this series. To submit a proposal for a volume in this series, please contact our Acquisition Editors at Acquisitions@igi-global.com or visit: http://www.igi-global.com/publish/.

The (ISSN) is published by IGI Global, 701 E. Chocolate Avenue, Hershey, PA 17033-1240, USA, www.igi-global.com. This series is composed of titles available for purchase individually; each title is edited to be contextually exclusive from any other title within the series. For pricing and ordering information please visit http://www.igi-global.com/book-series/advances-marketing-customer-relationship-management/37150. Postmaster: Send all address changes to above address.

Titles in this Series

For a list of additional titles in this series, please visit: www.igi-global.com/book-series

Ethical AI and Data Management Strategies in Marketing
Shefali Saluja (Chitkara Business School, Chitkara University, India) Varun Nayyar (Center for Distance and Online Education, Chitkara University, India) Kuldeep Rojhe (Center for Distance and Online Education, Chitkara University, India) and Sandhir Sharma (Chitkara Business School, Chitkara University, India)
Business Science Reference • copyright 2024 • 303pp • H/C (ISBN: 9798369366608) • US $215.00 (our price)

AI and Data Engineering Solutions for Effective Marketing
Lhoussaine Alla (Sidi Mohamed Ben Abdellah University, Morocco) Aziz Hmioui (Sidi Mohamed Ben Abdellah University, Morocco) and Badr Bentalha (National School of Business and Management, Sidi Mohammed Ben Abdellah University, Morocco)
Business Science Reference • copyright 2024 • 527pp • H/C (ISBN: 9798369331729) • US $395.00 (our price)

Improving Service Quality and Customer Engagement With Marketing Intelligence
Mudita Sinha (Christ University, India) Arabinda Bhandari (Presidency University, India) Samant Shant Priya (Lal Bahadur Shastri Institute of Management, India) and Sajal Kabiraj (Häme University of Applied Sciences, Finland)
Business Science Reference • copyright 2024 • 399pp • H/C (ISBN: 9798369368138) • US $255.00 (our price)

Compelling Storytelling Narratives for Sustainable Branding
Paula Rodrigues (Lusíada University Porto, Portugal & Research Centre in Organizations, Markets and Industrial Management (COMEGI), Porto, Portugal) Ana Pinto Borges (ISAG European Business School, Portugal) Elvira Vieira (ISAG European Business School, Portugal & Research Center in Business Sciences and Tourism (CICET-FCVC), Portugal) and Victor Tavares (ISAG – European Business School, Portugal & Research Center in Business Sciences and Tourism (CICET - FCVC), Porto, Portugal)
Business Science Reference • copyright 2024 • 443pp • H/C (ISBN: 9798369333266) • US $345.00 (our price)

IGI Global
PUBLISHER of TIMELY KNOWLEDGE

701 East Chocolate Avenue, Hershey, PA 17033, USA
Tel: 717-533-8845 x100 • Fax: 717-533-8661
E-Mail: cust@igi-global.com • www.igi-global.com

Table of Contents

Preface xv

Chapter 1
Environmental Issues and Globalizing World: An Overview 1
Abdullah Karataş, Niğde Ömer Halisdemir University, Turkey
Mustafa Talas, Niğde Ömer Halisdemir University, Turkey

Chapter 2
Advancing Sustainable and Green Development: Unlocking the Potential for Better Tomorrow. 13
Edosa Getachew Taera, Hungarian University of Agriculture and Life Sciences, Hungary
Zoltan Lakner, Hungarian University of Agriculture and Life Sciences, Hungary

Chapter 3
Green Transformational Leadership: A Systematic Literature Review and Future Research Suggestion 47
Zeinab Afsharbakeshlo, Kharazmi University, Iran
Mohammadsadegh Omidvar, Kharazmi University, Iran
Iza Gigauri, St. Andrew the First-Called Georgian University, Georgia

Chapter 4
Green Hotels Between Circular Economy Objectives and Sustainable Development Goals 75
Katica Radosavljevic, Institute of Agricultural Economics, Belgrade, Serbia
Branko Mihailovic, Institute of Agricultural Economics, Belgrade, Serbia

Chapter 5
Mapping Green Infrastructure Harnessing OSM Data for Sustainable Development 105
Munir Ahmad, Survey of Pakistan, Pakistan

Chapter 12
Descriptive Analysis of Maize Characteristics 291
Biljana Grujić Vučkovski, Tamiš Research and Development Institute, Pančevo, Serbia
Irina Marina, Institute of Agricultural Economics, Belgrade, Serbia

Compilation of References 317

About the Contributors 370

Index 376

Detailed Table of Contents

Preface xv

Chapter 1
Environmental Issues and Globalizing World: An Overview 1
Abdullah Karataş, Niğde Ömer Halisdemir University, Turkey
Mustafa Talas, Niğde Ömer Halisdemir University, Turkey

The world is getting smaller and turning into a global village. For this reason, we are faced with a phenomenon called globalization. This phenomenon emerges as a result of the electronic communication revolution. In this new era, societies, cultures, social structures, economic structures—in short, all social systems are undergoing transformation. Fundamental changes are occurring in the fabric of societies. There are also different ways of expressing the phenomenon of globalization. This process, which is also called postmodernism, post-structuralism, new capitalism, clash of civilizations, information society, is actually nothing new for humanity. We can talk about an extension of the history of globalization dating back thousands of years. However, its effect in recent periods, called the period of speed and pleasure, is much more evident. In this study, the relationship between globalization and global environmental issues was examined. In this regard, firstly globalization was emphasized in the conceptual framework, and then global environmental issues were discussed.

Chapter 2
Advancing Sustainable and Green Development: Unlocking the Potential for Better Tomorrow. 13
Edosa Getachew Taera, Hungarian University of Agriculture and Life Sciences, Hungary
Zoltan Lakner, Hungarian University of Agriculture and Life Sciences, Hungary

This chapter explores sustainable and green development, integrating environmental, social, and economic issues for a brighter future. It defines these concepts, examines their evolution, and discusses various approaches for implementing sustainable practices across industries. The chapter also addresses issues, laws, regulations, and obstacles related to these concepts, emphasizing the complex connection between environmental preservation and economic growth. It presents case studies and policy proposals to promote a sustainable and green future, emphasizing the need for holistic approaches in designing policies and practices.

Along with environmental concerns and sustainability trends, green transformational leadership (GTL) has gained the attention of scholars and practitioners. In response to the increasing environmental challenges, the need for companies to adopt responsibility strategies and management systems is growing. Therefore, this chapter presents a comprehensive and integrated review of research on GTL. A systematic literature review explores various definitions and theories of GTL, explains its behavioral, attitudinal, and performance outcomes, and illuminates the future of green transformational leadership. The conducted analysis covers all the relevant works indexed in the Scopus and Google Scholar databases throughout the period from 2013 to 2023. The research results demonstrate an emergent interest in GTL. The research contributes to leadership and sustainability literature by completing the theory of green transformational leadership. It provides a practical implication to introduce green transformational leadership in organizations to respond to environmental challenges effectively.

The goal to be achieved through the implementation of the concept of sustainable development is to limit pollution. In most European Union countries, sustainable development is one of the key strategies that will be implemented in the coming years in order to achieve satisfactory economic growth and aid the stabilization process. Achieving sustainability in the Republic of Serbia requires a strategic approach that is long-term and integrates and unifies various development processes, in order for them to be as sophisticated as the challenges of development are complex. The European Union has recognized the importance of the circular economy concept and has devoted considerable attention to it in recent years. The hotel industry has direct and indirect impacts on the environment. The pollution generated by this industry has attracted attention in recent years, and consumers are becoming more aware of the importance of environmental protection. As a result, green hotels have become a new industry trend.

The chapter provides a comprehensive analysis of global studies on urban green spaces (UGS), highlighting their diverse methodologies and findings. Spanning countries such as the USA, Kenya, Germany, Finland, Portugal, China, Brazil, Belgium, Ukraine, Norway, Spain, South Africa, and many more, these studies underscore the pivotal role of UGS in enhancing urban quality of life, addressing socio-economic disparities, and mitigating environmental challenges. Utilizing approaches such as citizen science mapping, spatial analysis, and socio-economic assessments, the research emphasizes the importance of equitable UGS access, efficient urban planning, and community engagement. Furthermore, the findings offer policy recommendations aimed at optimizing UGS provision, enhancing accessibility, and integrating green infrastructure into urban development strategies. This research highlights the worldwide importance of UGS and provides crucial insights for policymakers, planners, and communities aiming for healthier, more sustainable cities.

This chapter critically examines the alignment of green human resource management (Green HRM) practices—specifically in recruitment, training and development, and performance management—with legal standards, focusing on privacy protection, personal data security, and anti-discrimination laws. It also explores the potential to integrate sustainability features into established workplace systems and practices, such as near miss management systems, to enhance environmental responsibility within organizations. This method is advantageous as it utilizes existing tools and procedures familiar to employees, ensuring smoother implementation while leveraging prior legal evaluations.

This research investigates the challenges and opportunities for fostering green entrepreneurship among women in Azerbaijan and Georgia, post-Soviet republics grappling with transitioning economies. Employing qualitative data from interviews with nine female entrepreneurs and green policy experts, alongside legislative analysis and descriptive statistics, the study illuminates a significant gap in understanding and utilization of green economy practices among these entrepreneurs. Despite their successes, participants faced hurdles in incorporating green principles, including regulatory complexities and resource limitations. Collaboration between government, civil society, and the private sector emerges as crucial for supporting women entrepreneurs in embracing sustainability initiatives. The findings underscore the need for enhanced awareness and educational efforts to promote green practices and facilitate collaboration, thereby advancing sustainable development goals in the region.

Despite China's impressive success in increasing domestic agricultural production in recent decades, the country has yet to ensure self-sufficiency in some food staples. Against the backdrop of the increasing volatility of climate conditions, the degradation of agricultural land, and the depletion of water resources endanger the sustainable development not only of agriculture, but also of rural communities. China's efforts in building a so-called ecological civilization involve curbing greenhouse gas emissions and prioritizing principles of green development. While converging in understanding the need to sustain development, the food security and the green development doctrines differ in a way that increasing the agricultural output is hardly possible without aggravating anthropogenic pressure on ecosystems. In this chapter, the authors use the example of China trying to find common ground between ensuring food security for everyone and the important task of greening the agricultural sector.

The scope of the study is the examination of impact of ESG scores on the top 800 ESG-scored listed companies globally that may reflect supply chain performance. This study aims to shed light on how corporate governance issues affect supply chain processes. To this end, 800 globally listed companies are leveraged and assessed based on their ESG performance by incorporating Thomson Reuters environmental, social, and governance (ESG) scores into these models. The main objective of this study is to assess the extent to which environmental, social, and governance practices influence supply chain performance. To measure supply chain performance, the authors consider various indicators, including supply chain management score, monitoring score, and partnership termination scores. These metrics allow us to evaluate the effectiveness of supply chain processes over our sample period of ten years. To analyze the relationships between ESG scores and supply chain performance, the authors use partial least square (PLS) regression modeling.

Since the damage to the environment in the production of goods and services to meet human needs has emerged as a threat to global sustainability, it becomes critical to examine and reduce the environmental impacts of each activity undertaken. While this necessity forces all sectors to green transformation, it is of great importance that the aviation sector, which has a significant impact on all aspects of sustainability, is also addressed within this framework. In line with this necessity, the aim of this study is to identify the practices that reflect the green image of airline companies within the scope of green transformation. For this purpose, the information declared on the corporate websites of four selected airline companies were compared using content analysis methodology. It is aimed that the findings obtained will contribute to all businesses operating within the scope of green transformation together with the stakeholders in the sector.

This study examines the interrelationship between English language, social psychology, and global economics. In this sense, through the present study, it is aimed to highlight their joint impact on behavior and societal norms. As the global lingua franca, the role of English in cultural adaptation and economic decision-making is investigated in order to reveal how linguistic proficiency and psychological factors influence economic behaviors and trends in a global context. The research delves into the effects of globalization and technology on language use and psychological well-being, suggesting that the synergy among these elements shapes economic resilience as well. By integrating insights across various disciplines, the findings propose a number of effective strategies for promoting economic growth and social cohesion by offering valuable implications for policymakers and business leaders aiming at inclusive global development and economic resilience.

Chapter 12
Descriptive Analysis of Maize Characteristics 291
Biljana Grujić Vučkovski, Tamiš Research and Development Institute, Pančevo, Serbia
Irina Marina, Institute of Agricultural Economics, Belgrade, Serbia

In this chapter, the authors followed the trend of the movement of maize according to selected variables: harvested area (in ha), production (in t), and the value of maize exports (thousand USD). The movement of these variables was observed in the example of twenty-seven European countries that have available data in the period from 2010 to 2022. The aim of the research was to determine the changes that occurred in the analyzed countries during the observed time period and according to the variables in terms of growth and/or reduction of average indicator values. The basic source of data was the FAOSTAT database, but also other relevant scientific and professional literature. The results of applying descriptive statistics showed that the greatest deviation from the arithmetic mean was recorded in the value of maize exports (Cv = 209.3493), while the Pearson correlation coefficient showed that the strongest correlation was between production and area harvested of maize (.955). Finally, a conclusion was given according to the graphic presentation in the form of a trend line of maize production.

Compilation of References 317

About the Contributors 370

Index 376

Preface

In the face of an ever-evolving global economy, marked by environmental changes, shifting markets, and intricate resource management challenges, the necessity for a cohesive strategy that promotes sustainable growth and resilience has never been more critical. This book, *Marketing and Resource Management for Green Transitions in Economies*, emerges as a timely and essential resource that addresses these pressing issues head-on.

As editors, we have sought to bring together a comprehensive collection of insights that reflect the dynamic interplay between environmental imperatives, market evolutions, and resource management strategies. The contemporary economy is navigating through uncharted waters, where green transitions are not just desirable but essential for the longevity and health of our planet and economies. This transition, driven by a shift towards renewable energy, sustainable agriculture, and eco-friendly manufacturing, is redefining global trade and investment landscapes.

The growing environmental awareness and its impact on market dynamics cannot be overstated. The demand for sustainable products is rising, green finance is gaining momentum, and Environmental, Social, and Governance (ESG) criteria are becoming integral to investment decisions. These trends underscore a critical realization: long-term profitability is inextricably linked to sustainable practices. Yet, this evolution also brings about challenges, such as the need for new skills, adaptation to green technologies, and navigating ever-changing policy frameworks.

Our book explores the synergies and trade-offs between these elements, emphasizing the importance of a unified approach to steering the global economy toward sustainable development. This work is not only relevant to academics but also to practitioners and policymakers. By presenting complex concepts in an accessible manner and underscoring practical implications, we aim to influence current and future practices in business and governance.

Chapter 1

In this chapter, we explore the intricate relationship between globalization and global environmental issues. The concept of globalization is dissected through various lenses, including postmodernism, post-structuralism, and new capitalism. The chapter outlines how the rapid advancements in electronic communication have effectively turned the world into a global village, leading to significant transformations in societies, cultures, and economic structures. This process, although not new, has been accelerated in recent times, creating both challenges and opportunities. By examining globalization within a conceptual framework, the chapter sets the stage for a deeper understanding of its impact on global environmental issues, emphasizing the need for integrated approaches to address these challenges.

Chapter 2

This chapter delves into the multifaceted concepts of sustainable and green development, integrating environmental, social, and economic dimensions. We define and trace the evolution of these concepts, exploring various approaches to implementing sustainable practices across different industries. The chapter highlights the complex relationship between environmental preservation and economic growth, addressing relevant issues, laws, and regulations. Through case studies and policy proposals, the chapter underscores the importance of holistic strategies in designing sustainable policies and practices, aiming to promote a greener future.

Chapter 3

Green transformational leadership (GTL) has become a focal point in addressing environmental challenges within organizational contexts. This chapter presents a comprehensive review of GTL research, analyzing various definitions, theories, and outcomes related to this leadership style. By conducting a systematic literature review of works indexed in Scopus and Google Scholar from 2013 to 2023, the chapter illuminates the emerging interest in GTL and its practical implications. It provides valuable insights for introducing GTL in organizations to effectively respond to environmental challenges, contributing significantly to the literature on leadership and sustainability.

Chapter 4

Focusing on sustainable development strategies within the European Union and the Republic of Serbia, this chapter discusses the integration of these strategies to achieve economic growth and environmental stability. The chapter highlights the importance of the circular economy, particularly in the hotel industry, which has significant environmental impacts. The discussion includes the growing trend of green hotels and the increasing awareness among consumers regarding environmental protection. By emphasizing the need for a sophisticated, long-term strategic approach, the chapter provides insights into achieving sustainability in complex developmental contexts.

Chapter 5

Urban green spaces (UGS) play a crucial role in enhancing urban quality of life and addressing socio-economic and environmental challenges. This chapter offers a comprehensive analysis of global studies on UGS, spanning various methodologies and findings across different countries. The research highlights the importance of equitable access to UGS, efficient urban planning, and community engagement. Policy recommendations are provided to optimize UGS provision, enhance accessibility, and integrate green infrastructure into urban development strategies, underscoring the worldwide importance of UGS.

Chapter 6

This chapter critically examines the alignment of Green Human Resource Management (Green HRM) practices with legal standards, focusing on privacy protection, personal data security, and anti-discrimination laws. It explores the integration of sustainability features into established workplace systems, such as Near Miss Management Systems, to enhance environmental responsibility. By utilizing familiar tools and procedures, the chapter highlights the advantages of smoother implementation and leveraging prior legal evaluations to promote green HRM practices effectively.

Chapter 7

This chapter investigates the challenges and opportunities for fostering green entrepreneurship among women in Azerbaijan and Georgia, two post-Soviet republics with transitioning economies. Using qualitative data from interviews with female entrepreneurs and green policy experts, along with legislative analysis, the study reveals a significant gap in understanding and utilizing green economy practices. The chapter emphasizes the need for collaboration between government, civil society, and the private sector to support women entrepreneurs in adopting sustainability initiatives, thereby advancing sustainable development goals in the region.

Chapter 8

China's efforts in building an ecological civilization involve balancing food security with green development principles. This chapter examines the challenges posed by climate change, land degradation, and water resource depletion on China's agricultural sustainability. By exploring the tensions between increasing agricultural output and mitigating environmental impacts, the chapter seeks to find common ground between ensuring food security and promoting green development. The discussion provides insights into China's strategies for sustaining agricultural development while curbing greenhouse gas emissions and prioritizing green practices.

Chapter 9

This chapter provides an in-depth analysis of how Environmental, Social, and Governance (ESG) scores impact the supply chain performance of the top 800 globally listed companies. By incorporating ESG performance data from Thomson Reuters, the study assesses the influence of corporate governance on supply chain processes. Using Partial Least Square (PLS) regression modeling, the chapter evaluates various supply chain performance indicators, offering valuable insights into the relationship between ESG practices and supply chain efficiency over a ten-year period.

Chapter 10

The aviation sector, with its significant environmental impacts, is a critical area for green transformation. This chapter aims to identify practices that reflect the green image of airline companies by comparing information declared on the corporate websites of four selected airlines. Using content analysis methodology, the chapter provides findings that contribute to the broader understanding of green transformation in the aviation industry, offering practical implications for businesses and stakeholders aiming to adopt sustainable practices.

Chapter 11

This chapter explores the interconnectedness of the English language, social psychology, and global economics. As the global lingua franca, English plays a crucial role in cultural adaptation and economic decision-making. The chapter investigates how linguistic proficiency and psychological factors influence economic behaviors and trends in a global context. By examining the effects of globalization and technology on language use and psychological well-being, the chapter proposes strategies for promoting economic growth and social cohesion, offering valuable implications for policymakers and business leaders.

Chapter 12

In this chapter, the authors followed the trends in maize movement according to selected variables: harvested area (in hectares), production (in tonnes), and the value of maize exports (thousand USD). These variables were observed across twenty-seven European countries with available data from 2010 to 2022. The aim of the research was to determine the changes that occurred in these countries over the observed period, specifically in terms of growth and/or reduction of average indicator values.

The insights and strategic guidance provided within these pages offer valuable tools for businesses seeking to transition to sustainable practices, adapt to evolving market conditions, and manage resources more efficiently. For researchers, educators, students, business leaders, and policymakers, this book serves as a crucial resource for understanding and implementing innovative solutions to the challenges posed by market transformation and resource management.

We hope that this book will contribute significantly to both academic research and practical applications in the fields of green transition, market resilience, and resource management. By highlighting the viability and benefits of green business models, we aim to inspire a new wave of sustainable practices that will shape the future of our global economy.

Jean-Vasile Andrei
Petroleum-Gas University of Ploiesti, Romania

Mile Vasic
European Marketing and Management Association, Banja Luka, Bosnia and Herzegovina

Luminita Chivu
National Institute of Economics Research, Romanian Academy, Romania

Boris Kuzman
Institute of Agricultural Economics, Serbia

Chapter 1
Environmental Issues and Globalizing World:
An Overview

Abdullah Karataş
Niğde Ömer Halisdemir University, Turkey

Mustafa Talas
Niğde Ömer Halisdemir University, Turkey

ABSTRACT

The world is getting smaller and turning into a global village. For this reason, we are faced with a phenomenon called globalization. This phenomenon emerges as a result of the electronic communication revolution. In this new era, societies, cultures, social structures, economic structures—in short, all social systems are undergoing transformation. Fundamental changes are occurring in the fabric of societies. There are also different ways of expressing the phenomenon of globalization. This process, which is also called postmodernism, post-structuralism, new capitalism, clash of civilizations, information society, is actually nothing new for humanity. We can talk about an extension of the history of globalization dating back thousands of years. However, its effect in recent periods, called the period of speed and pleasure, is much more evident. In this study, the relationship between globalization and global environmental issues was examined. In this regard, firstly globalization was emphasized in the conceptual framework, and then global environmental issues were discussed.

DOI: 10.4018/979-8-3693-3439-3.ch001

INTRODUCTION

Environment has a great meaning for every living thing because every living thing needs its environment to survive. This need is the main determinant and driving force of the sustainability of life. This need has led every living thing to live in harmony with its environment throughout the historical process. However, humans have disrupted this order. "*Human civilisation and globalisation are the dominant culprits of constant change in the global environment in present scenario*" (Singh & Singh, 2017, 13). Only humans have changed the adaptation process and paved the way for the formation of unavoidable environmental issues.

"The environment has provided habitation for humans and numerous organism but the insatiable needs of humans have driven them to devise strategies for survival and adaptation." (Akintunde, 2017, 121). Science and technology have guided man in these strategies. Although living creatures other than humans survive by adapting to the environment they live in, humans have made tremendous changes in the environment with the help of technology and science. By relying on science and technology, humans have caused a lot of damage on the environment and still continue to do so. Today, human-origin environmental issues that cannot be prevented have reached global dimensions. By overconsuming and polluting nature, humans actually destroy their own future. However, human well-being requires the following three important criteria to work together in harmony (Holdren, 2008, 424):

"Economic conditions and processes, *such as production, employment, income, wealth, markets, trade, and the technologies that facilitate all of these;*

Sociopolitical conditions and processes, *such as national and personal security, liberty, justice, the rule of law, education, health care, the pursuit of science and the arts, and other aspects of civil society and culture; and*

Environmental conditions and processes, *including our planet's air, water, soils, mineral resources, biota, and climate, and all of the natural and anthropogenic processes that affect them."*

As can be seen from the above criteria, human welfare does not seem possible without the environment, so humans cannot ignore the environment and nature for the sake of more profit and savings. It would not be realistic to say that people's commercial activities are not the main cause of environmental issues that cannot be prevented today. While increasing industrial facilities pollute the air, soil and water, deforestation for the sake of urbanization makes living creatures deprived of their homes. Mass extinction of species, depletion of the ozone layer, increasing air, water and soil pollution around the world is directly related to human activities. Along with other global environmental issues, climate change continues to exist as a serious problem that endangers future generations. All these bad and big effects cause great changes and deteriorations in the environment. "*Human induced environmental change appears to be taking place on the planet on a scale and speed never seen before*" (Aponen, 2014, 131). The phenomenon called globalization accelerates this process.

The world is getting smaller and turning into a global village. For this reason, we are faced with a phenomenon called globalization. This phenomenon emerges as a result of the electronic communication revolution. In this new era, societies, cultures, social structures, economic structures; In short, all social systems are undergoing transformation. Fundamental changes are occurring in the fabric of societies. There are also different ways of expressing the phenomenon of globalization. This process, which is also called postmodernism, post-structuralism, new capitalism, clash of civilizations, information society, is actually nothing new for humanity. We can talk about an extension of the history of globalization dating back thousands of years. However, its effect in recent periods, called the period of speed and pleasure, is much more evident. In this study, the relationship between globalization and global environmental issues was examined. In this regard, firstly globalization was emphasized in the conceptual framework, and then global environmental issues were discussed.

GLOBALIZATION

Globalization as a word emerged in the early 1980s. Its involvement in academic life dates back to the early 1990s. This important phenomenon attracted attention in Turkey in the second half of the 90s.

Today, globalization has become a topic that occupies the agenda on radio, television or in any meeting or opening. Therefore, it has become a fashion. As such, it has created an atmosphere of intense debate. 'Globalization', which is at the center of the discussions, has not been slow to create passionate supporters on the one hand and allergic opponents on the other, like every wind of fashion. While those who are in favor of it point to globalization as the reason for all kinds of positive developments, those who are against it consider it as the cause of all kinds of negativities (Timur, 2000, 7-8).

Globalization, which has managed to be a key concept in cultural analysis, has completely affected cultural textures, from cinema to new trends in music, to art, from people's consumption habits to their attitudes. Globalization, which makes itself felt in every aspect of life, has gained great popularity. According to some numerical data, it is thought that globalization is economy-centered. For example, according to the UN Human Development Report, more than 1.5 trillion dollars change hands daily. According to these data, globalization is largely economic. However, despite all this, explaining globalization only with the increase in the efficiency of financial markets would represent an incomplete perspective. Because globalization is a social phenomenon as a whole. It is a phenomenon that has economic, cultural, political and technological dimensions (Baştürk, 2001).

This process, which aims to direct the world economically, socially, culturally, politically and to homogenize societies, is also called "new world order-or disorder". The current process is also named as "the end of history", "clash of civilizations", "increasing radicalization of the consequences of modernity", "the emergence of the conditions of post-modernity as the cultural dimension of multinational capitalism" and "increasingly radicalized breaks between homogeneity and heterogeneity" (Keyman, 2002, 51-53). This new reality of the world, which can also be considered as the "trauma" experienced by societies, is based on two foundations: economy and communication. Due to revolutionary changes in the field of communication, there are serious problems in the cultural field. Societies are affected by different cultures both positively and negatively. While positive effects are considered as "gains", negative effects are seen as factors that constantly take away something from the "essence of culture".

Today, globalization has gained a very different meaning and structure from the above explanations. The rules of globalization are determined as respect for human rights, absolute loyalty to the market economy, global peace and stability. These determined rules created a new world power. This world power has also been institutionalized as an official ideology. Countries and understandings that shake or are assumed to shake any of the three rules mentioned will be excluded from globalization. Being pushed out of the New World Order is presented as the main sanction of this new ideology called "global official ideology". What is then presented is the idea that these concepts and values consist of the traditions and interests of the North-West (Öz, 2001, 13).

As a result, whatever its name is, globalization is a phenomenon that must be accepted as a lived reality with its aspects that surround the world and affect everyone. As a different approach, only according to the interests of the society in which we live, social and cultural planning activities can be undertaken to benefit from the positive aspects and eliminate the negative aspects as much as possible.

Globalization in the Conceptual Framework

The word origin of globalization is English. The root of the word "globalization" comes from "globe". While "Globe" is an adjective meaning ball-shaped, it is also a noun meaning world model. The word "The Globe" means world, sphere, earth. Derived from the word "globe", "global" means affecting the whole world, that is, worldwide. It can be exemplified as "Global effects of pollution, global warning".

Another meaning of the word "global" is "affecting events and possibilities as a whole" (Oxford Wordpower Dictionary, 1993). Accordingly, the word globalization derives from the adjective global and means that an event or an object has a worldwide impact.

Although the adjective global (in the strong sense of worldwide or in the sense of the whole) has been in use for a long time, its use has become widespread with the current interest in globalization. The Oxford Dictionary of New Words also defines global as a new word. The same dictionary defines 'global consciousness' as part of a culture's evaluation of other cultures. The dictionary states that such usage is based on Marshall Mc. He claims that he was influenced by the 'global village' idea put forward by Luhan in his book Studies in Communication (1960). The understanding of downsizing or 'contraction' is found in this influential book that considers the collective simultaneity of today's media, especially televisual, experience." (Robertson, 1999, 22).

The concept of globalization was first used in a widespread and modern sense in 1961. After Italy announced that it increased the quota on car imports, Webster's Dictionary used "global" and "globalization" (Gürlek, 2001, 27). According to a publication of the OECD (Organization for Economic Co-operation and Development), the term was first used as "Globalization of Markets" by Theodore Levit in 1983 (Kantrow, 1985, 53). Levit used it to characterize the major changes that have occurred in the last two decades in the international economy, covering the rapid and massive production, consumption and investment of goods, services, capital and technology (Levit, 1983, 92-102).

Although the term global literally refers to the world we live in, globalization as a phenomenon actually refers to subjects. In other words, the globalization process that has affected the world is not a phenomenon that every nation, every society and every person living in the world decides to realize together. Globalization is the phenomenon of those who design and implement globalization as an intellectual, cultural and economic project (Erkızan, 2002, 65-66).

Globalization in Historical Process

Nineteenth-century sociologists such as Comte, Saint-Simon, and Marx centered their works (including their political work) on what many of us these days call globalization. This situation became particularly complicated on the sociological front during the last period of classical sociology, mainly due to the strengthening of nationalism. Thus, classical sociologists faced the problem of the simultaneity of "nationalization" and "globalization" (Robertson, 1999:32-33).

Some social scientists, while evaluating globalization in the historical process, stated that globalization is not new and that waves of globalization have been experienced before:

"When we look at the history of world capitalism in the last two hundred years, it can be seen that two separate phases of globalization have occurred. We see that the first of these phases continued to influence the world goods and financial markets between roughly 1870 and 1914, after the technological developments of the 18th century industrial revolution. The main feature of this first wave of globalization that left its mark on the years in question is that the gold standard was accepted as the norm in money markets and trade relations. "After the 1914-1960 interim period, which was shaped by the First and Second World Wars and the relatively independent development and trade policies of nation states, it is seen that a new globalization period has entered the world scale" (Yeldan, 2002, 8-9).

Albrow states that there were four stages before globalization, but there are five stages with globalization. Albrow also took current interest into account when making this classification. According to him, there are five phases in the history of sociology: Universalism, national sociologies, internationalism, localization and globalization (Albrow & King, 1990, 6-8).

When we look at some historical facts, the idea that globalization is not new gains importance. However, it is impossible to claim that the last wave of globalization is the same or similar to the previous ones in terms of its effects, prevalence and tools used. These revolutionary changes, which are based on impacts and innovations that are incomparably greater than previous waves, reorganize social life with the support of significant technological changes and developments in communication techniques and their shaping in the course of history. One of the most affected by these revolutionary changes was undoubtedly the environment.

GLOBAL ENVIRONMENTAL ISSUES

Human influence is great in bringing environmental issues to their current state. Especially after the Industrial Revolution, with the help of developing technological opportunities and science, incredible damage was done to nature, and the relationship between humans and nature began to develop only under the guidance of materialist philosophy. As a reflection of this materialist philosophy, environmental issues which cannot be prevented anymore, have reached such a level that these issues have begun to threaten even future generations (Weiss, 1990, 7).

"With the accelerated industrialization after the Second World War, production also increased, and this increase in production brought about the need for raw materials. During this development and transformation process in industrialization, the pollutants released into the environment and the excessive use of resources have led to the destruction of the environment to a degree never seen before" (Sipahi, 2010, 333).

Global environmental issues affect everyone in the world, rich or poor, educated or uneducated. Not only humans, but also all other living things breathe, eat and survive in the environment they live in. But only humans change and pollute the environment in which they live, damage natural areas, and take away the right to life of all living things other than themselves. These selfish behaviors of humans cause global environmental issues. According to Kain (2023) global environmental issues can be briefly listed as follows:

"Pollution: *Pollution is the unwanted addition of substances to water, land, or air that have a negative impact on human existence, other animals, living circumstances, and our natural resources.*

Waste Disposal: *The collection, processing, and dumping of human society's waste materials are known as waste disposal.*

Desertification: *Desertification is a form of land degradation that occurs in dry places where biological production is lost as a result of biotic processes or as a result of human activity, making fertile areas more and more arid.*

Water Scarcity: *Water scarcity is the absence of adequate water resources to meet regional water usage demands.*

Global Warming*: The extremely quick rise in the planet's average temperature over the past century is known as global warming, and it is mostly caused by greenhouse gases that are emitted when people burn fossil fuels.*

Ocean Acidification: *The continuing lowering of the pH of the seas due to the absorption of carbon dioxide (CO_2) from the atmosphere is known as ocean acidification.*

Acid Rain: *Any type of precipitation that contains acidic elements, like sulfuric or nitric acid, that falls from the atmosphere in wet or dry forms on the ground is referred to as acid rain, also known as acid deposition.*

Ozone Layer Depletion:*The upper atmosphere's ozone layer gets thinned due to ozone layer depletion. This occurs when ozone molecules come into an interface with chlorine and bromine atoms in the atmosphere and are broken down." (Kain, 2023).*

When we look at the global environmental issues listed above, it is possible to see human traces in all of them. However, humans, like all other living creatures, need clean air and water to live. It can be said that polluting and destroying the environment just for the sake of economic gain, triggered by globalization, is actually the greatest evil that humans do to themselves. Despite this, unconscious behaviors towards the environment continue and are likely to continue in the future.

HUMAN IMPACT ON TODAY'S GLOBAL ENVIRONMENTAL ISSUES

The place a person lives in is directly related to his lifestyle (Aytan, 2021, 979). Humans lived in caves and tree holes ages ago and chose the hunter-gatherer lifestyle to survive. Today, with the help of science and technology, they have made incredible changes in their environment and have literally exploited natural resources and brought them to the point of exhaustion. Industrialization and the resulting increasing urbanization activities have been important determinants in this process. *"Industrialisation is the period of social and economic change that transforms a human group from an agrarian society into an industrial society. This involves an extensive reorganisation of an economy for the purpose of manufacturing"* (Anderson, 2023). Especially with the industrial revolution, industrialization and urbanization have become the main cause of environmental issues.

"Established national and universal values have been replaced by a tendency towards activities that are based on increased consumption and increase the profitability of global capital. In search of profit, the conversion of culture, history, nature, architecture and art values into money is almost a rule, and their protection is almost an exception. Filling cities with five-star hotels, skyscrapers, unnecessary shopping malls, bridges, underpasses and overpasses that destroy natural values are among the results of the passion for globalization reflected in cities. Under these conditions, not only cities lose their identities, but also the balance of ecology is disrupted" (Keleş, 2010, 30).

Never-ending human consumption, industrial activities, traffic and pollution affect heat emissions in a city. This situation triggers climate change. Climate change brings with it other challenges, floods, high temperatures, heavy rains, abnormal climatic events, inefficiency in agriculture, respiratory diseases and skin problems for humans (Idowu, 2013, 88). *"The level of world urbanization has crossed the 50% mark, and nearly all future population growth is projected to occur in cities"* (Liddle, 2017, 1). With urbanization, natural areas are opened to construction and the natural balance is disrupted. Creatures living in nature are either forced to migrate or become extinct because their environment is taken away from them. *"Urbanization is one of the leading causes of species extinction"* (McKinney, 2006, 248). Emissions from traffic and transportation cause serious air pollution, and the air, which becomes more polluted day by day, poses a serious threat to all living things. It should not be ignored that air pollution is caused not only by transportation but also by homes. *"Each year, 3.2 million people die prematurely from illnesses attributable to the household air pollution caused by the incomplete combustion of solid fuels and kerosene used for cooking"* (WHO, 2023). Along with air pollution, water and soil pollution seriously affects all people without any borders.

"Various natural imbalances, such as the depletion of the ozone layer, the greenhouse effect caused by the increase in the amount of carbon dioxide in the air, and drought that has been going on for many years, are all problems created by humans. Such environmental problems are no longer problems that concern a single country or region; it has become a common problem for more than 6.7 billion people living on earth"(Baykal & Baykal, 2008, 13).

Humans actually change their own future negatively with the environmental issues they cause and cause these issues to grow more and more. In the face of environmental issues accelerated by the cycle of globalization, nature's carrying capacity has now been exhausted. Despite this, humans do not give up their greed and ambition. However, as an Indian proverb emphasizes, people will sooner or later clearly realize that money is something that cannot be eaten. Without confronting this painful reality, harmonious unity with nature should be established in society and environmental awareness should be spread among society members.

Figure 1. Behavioural change model

(Akintunde, 2017, 122)

As seen in Figure 1, knowledge should be a key concept in increasing social environmental awareness. In order to create such an awareness in society, spreading educational activities and teaching environmental education as a compulsory course in school curricula at all levels will provide great benefits.

CONCLUSION

The impact of globalization all over the world is undeniable. Globalization, as a process, has affected all world societies. With globalization, the focus has been on economic development and capital accumulation, and nature has been relegated to the background. This situation has caused enormous environmental issues. "Air pollution has crossed the borders of one country and polluted another country and still continues to pollute. *"In recent decades, air pollution has become one of the most important problems of megacities. Initially, the main air pollutants of concern were sulfur compounds, which were generated mostly by burning coal"* (Molina & Molina, 2004, 644). With the contamination of water resources by human activities such as air pollution, the pollution problem has crossed borders and the pollution of oceans, lakes and streams has affected not only humans but all living things.

It is clearly seen that global environmental issues now threaten the human race. It would be wiser for the future to seek solutions to these issues rather than focusing only on economic interests. *"Throughout the world, demographic, economic, and technological trends have accelerated our ability to knowingly and unknowingly modify the environment we live in and that sustains us. We humans have become the principal driver of environmental change"* (Cosgrove & Loucks, 2015, 4823). Unfortunately, the globalization thesis, which focuses on the circulation and increase of capital along with social interaction, has failed because it cannot see the real truth. Members of society with environmental awareness will value not only globalization focusing on capital but also the environment and will act responsibly to protect it.

It should not be forgotten that not only having environmental awareness but also taking action with this awareness is of great importance. For environmental awareness, environmental education should be considered as a key concept in every segment of society. Providing such training to people of all ages and professions will support the creation of a society with high environmental awareness in the future.

REFERENCES

Akintunde, E. A. (2017). Theories and concepts for human behavior in environmental preservation. *Journal of Environmental Science and Public Health*, 1(2), 120–133. 10.26502/jesph.96120012

Albrow, M., & King, E. (1990). *Globalization, Knowledge and Society*. Sage Publications.

Anderson, K. (2023). *What was the Industrial Revolution's environmental impact?* Greenly. https://greenly.earth/en-us/blog/ecology-news/what-was-the-industrial -revolutions environmental-impact Accessed 01.01.2024

Arponen, V. P. J. (2014). The cultural causes of environmental problems. *Environmental Ethics, Volume*, 36, 131–147.

Aytan, O. A. (2021). Hareketli avcı-toplayıcı grupların yaşam biçimiyle yerleşik çiftçi toplulukların yaşam biçimi arasındaki insan-mekan ilişkisinin mukayesesi. *Kahramanmaraş Sütçü İmam Üniversitesi Sosyal Bilimler Dergisi*, 18(2), 979–1012. 10.33437/ksusbd.780605

Baştürk, Ş. (2001). Bir olgu olarak küreselleşme. *İş-Güç Endüstri İlişkileri ve İnsan Kaynakları Dergisi, 3*(2).

Baykal, H., & Baykal, T. (2008). Küresel Dünya'da çevre sorunları. *Mustafa Kemal Üniversitesi Sosyal Bilimler Enstitüsü Dergisi*, 5(9), 1–17.

Cosgrove, W. J., & Loucks, D. P. (2015). Water management: Current and future challenges and research directions. *Water Resources Research*, 51(6), 4823–4839. 10.1002/2014WR016869

Erkızan, H. N. (2002). Küreselleşmenin tarihsel ve düşünsel temelleri üzerine. *Doğu Batı Dergisi*, 5(18), 65–66.

Gürlek, S. (2001). *Küreselleşme ve milli devletin geleceği bağlamında Türk milliyetçiliğini yeniden düşünmek.* Türkiye ve Siyaset, Küreselleşme ve Milliyetçilik Özel Sayısı, Kasım-Aralık, 27.

Idowu, O. O. (2013). Challenges of urbanization and urban growth in Nigeria. *American Journal of Sustainable Cities and Society*, 2(1), 79–95.

Kain, T. (2023). *What Are The Biggest Environmental Problems?* Sigma Earth. https://sigmaearth.com/the-biggest-environmental-problems/

Kantrow, A. M. (1985). *Sunrise-sunset which changes the mhytos of the industrial becoming old.* New York, John Wiley and His Sons.

Keleş, R. (2010). Türkiye'de kentleşme kime ne kazandırıyor? İdeal Kent Kent Araştırmaları Dergisi. *Sayı*, 1, 28–31.

Keyman, E. F. (2002). Kapitalizm-oryantalizm ekseninde küreselleşmeyi anlamak: 11 Eylül, modernite, kalkınma ve öteki sorunsalı. *Doğu Batı Dergisi*, 5(18), 31–53.

Levit, T. (1983). The globalisation of markets. *Harvard Business Review*, 61(3), 92–102.

Liddle, B. (2017). Urbanization and inequality/poverty. *Urban Science (Basel, Switzerland)*, 1(35), 1–7.

McKinney, M. L. (2006). Urbanization as a major cause of biotic homogenization. *Biological Conservation*, 127(3), 247–260. 10.1016/j.biocon.2005.09.005

Molina, M. J., & Molina, L. T. (2004). Megacities and Atmospheric Pollution. *Journal of the Air & Waste Management Association*, 54(6), 644–680. 10.1080/10473289.2004.10470936 15242147

Robertson, R. (1999). *Küreselleşme Toplum Kuramı ve Küresel Kültür (Çev. Ümit Hüsrev Yolsal)*. Bilim ve Sanat Yayınları.

Singh, R. L., & Singh, P. K. (2017). Global Environmental Problems. In: Singh, R. (eds) *Principles and Applications of Environmental Biotechnology for a Sustainable Future* (p. 13-41). Springer, Singapore. 10.1007/978-981-10-1866-4_2

Sipahi, E. B. (2010). Küresel çevre sorunlarına kolektif çözüm arayışları ve yönetişim. Selçuk Üniversitesi Sosyal Bilimler Enstitüsü Dergisi. *Sayı*, 24, 331–344.

Timur, T. (2000). *Küreselleşme ve Demokrasi Krizi*. İmge Kitabevi.

Weiss Brown, E. (1990). In fairness to future generations. *Environment*, 32(3), 6–31. 10.1080/00139157.1990.9929015

WHO-World Health Organization. (2023). *Household air pollution*. WHO. https://www.who.int/news-room/fact-sheets/detail/household-air-pollution-and-health

Yeldan, E. (2002). *Küreselleşme Sürecinde Türkiye Ekonomisi*. İletişim Yayınları.

Chapter 2
Advancing Sustainable and Green Development: Unlocking the Potential for Better Tomorrow.

Edosa Getachew Taera
Hungarian University of Agriculture and Life Sciences, Hungary

Zoltan Lakner
Hungarian University of Agriculture and Life Sciences, Hungary

ABSTRACT

This chapter explores sustainable and green development, integrating environmental, social, and economic issues for a brighter future. It defines these concepts, examines their evolution, and discusses various approaches for implementing sustainable practices across industries. The chapter also addresses issues, laws, regulations, and obstacles related to these concepts, emphasizing the complex connection between environmental preservation and economic growth. It presents case studies and policy proposals to promote a sustainable and green future, emphasizing the need for holistic approaches in designing policies and practices.

INTRODUCTION

Our planet is now confronting several critical difficulties, such as resource depletion, fast population growth, and climate change's growing and deadly impacts. These interconnected challenges threaten our future and the well-being of generations to come. Yet, within this crisis, there exists a chance for profound and revolutionary transformation. Recognizing this allows us to unleash the promise of a brighter

DOI: 10.4018/979-8-3693-3439-3.ch002

future (Gakh, 2023). As Al Gore aptly stated, "The future will either be green or not at all" (Erdős, 2019). This highlights the critical importance of sustainable and green development.

Sustainable and green development go beyond mere environmentalism. It is a multifaceted concept that recognizes the interconnectedness of economic prosperity, social equity, and environmental protection (Simon, 1987; Attfield, 2023). It acts as the linchpin for a future that is more resistant, promoting fair allocation of resources, comprehensive economic development, and a strong commitment to environmental conservation. Thus, it is not a choice; it is a necessity.

This chapter delves into the power of advancing sustainable and green development as the key to a more resilient future for all. It is critical to achieve a balance between social fairness, economic advancement, ecological responsibility, and environmental preservation. Failure to achieve this balance will have dire consequences. Thus, through responsible resource use, innovation, and inclusivity, fostering social inclusivity and sustainable development promotes social fairness, economic prosperity, and environmental responsibility, addressing climate change and resource scarcity.

By utilizing a combination of desk review (Moore, 2018) and thematic analysis (Anderson, 2007), the study explores the importance, principles, and challenges of advancing sustainable development while also showcasing approaches to unlocking the potential and best practices. Collaborative efforts, multidisciplinary research, and accelerating transformative change are crucial for unlocking a brighter future. Individuals' actions also play a part. Studies show that sustainable choices in everyday life, from purchases to home habits, contribute to a more sustainable society (Pinho & Gomes, 2023). Policymakers are increasingly recognizing this and implementing behavioral interventions to promote such actions (Krefeld-Schwalb & Gabel, 2023). However, the effectiveness of these interventions hinges on tailoring them to individual motivations and responsiveness.

SUSTAINABLE AND GREEN DEVELOPMENT

Sustainable and green development pertains to the practice of fulfilling the requisites of the current generation with no concessions to the forthcoming generations' capability to satisfy their requirements. This strategy is to be developed in an environmentally friendly and sustainable manner. Xiaoyi (2023) and Darvishi et al. (2023) vowed that this concept entails combining conservation and development, addressing fundamental human needs, promoting social fairness and cultural variety, and safeguarding ecological integrity. According to the United Nations General Assembly (1987), achieving sustainable development entails addressing current requirements while safeguarding the capacity of future generations to satisfy their own needs (Imperatives, 1987).

Scholars from several disciplines have offered multiple viewpoints on sustainable development. Biologists have concentrated on enhancing the production and regeneration capacities of ecosystems and the environment (Pandey & Ghasiya, 2023). Sociologists prioritize improving human living standards while remaining within the boundaries of natural systems (Fischer, 2023). Economists consider sustainable development an ongoing enhancement of societal welfare while safeguarding the environment (Malik et al., 2023). Sources of renewable energy, including wind and solar power, are essential for attaining sustainable development by conserving the environment and natural resources (Kumar & Rathore, 2023). Generally, sustainable development acknowledges that the pursuit of economic progress must be accompanied by measures to rectify social disparities and environmental harm (Kamakia, 2015). Thus, the notion of sustainable development is vital for harmonizing economic growth with the preservation of natural resources and concentrating on the current and future requirements of human beings.

On the other side, the term "green development" describes a strategy for social and economic advancement that places an emphasis on ecological health and environmental sustainability. It provides lucid insights into the difficulties associated with social and economic growth as well as environmental sustainability (Adams, 2008). Green development promotes clean technology advancement and finance new business opportunities through green economic principles, addressing climate change challenges and promoting adaptation methods, especially for marginalized populations like women (Setiawan & Wismayanti, 2023).

Briefly, understanding sustainable and green development is crucial due to environmental degradation and climate change concerns (Bansode, 2022). Sustainable practices, considering all environmental, economic, and social factors, can improve life for current and future generations, ensuring a higher standard of living for the present and generations to come.

Importance of Sustainable and Green Development From Business and Social Perspectives

It is of the utmost importance that present and future generations benefit from the implementation of green and sustainable practices, which also serve to foster economic expansion and augment human welfare. The significance of sustainable development from both business and social standpoints is clearly illustrated in the associated visual representation.

Figure 1. The importance of sustainable and green development from the perspective of businesses and society

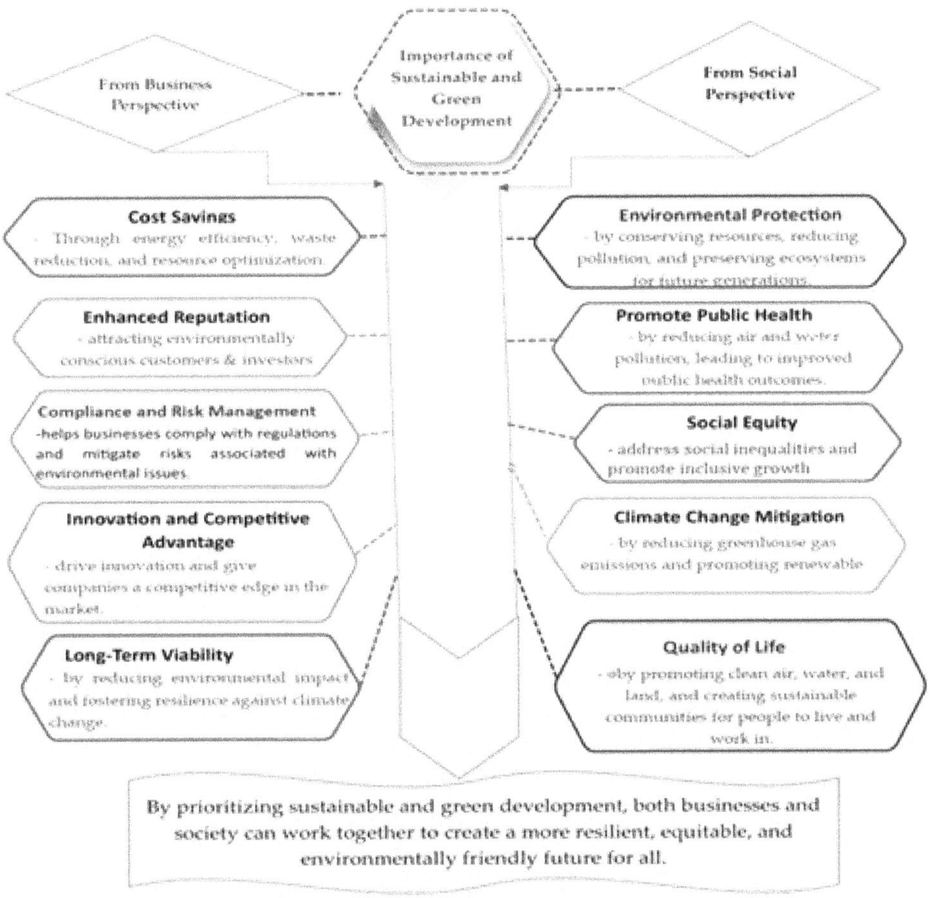

compiled by the authors

Sustainable and green development is a complex concept that requires a shift in thinking and values (Xing-ling, 2005). It involves improving human life without harming the environment and demands the constant replenishment of nutrients necessary for life (Osipov, 2019). To recap, sustainable and green development is crucial for maintaining peaceful coexistence, addressing social injustice, and promoting financial stability, making the world more resilient, egalitarian, and ecologically sensitive.

Principles of Sustainable and Green Development

Sustainable and green development are based on the idea of balancing social progress, environmental preservation, and economic advancement.

1. **Intergenerational Equity**: Intergenerational equality is a sustainable development strategy that balances current needs with future sustainability, but it poses challenges to environmental preservation and responsible resource management (Cross, 2023).

Sustainable development's key tenet is intergenerational equality, encompassing both interests and non-interests' equity (Dong, 2002). Spijkers (2018) links this notion to the SDGs and the necessity to balance them with intragenerational fairness. However, the application of this principle in sustainable development policies is often limited by the influence of neoclassical environmental economists, which can exacerbate existing inequities (Beder, 2000). To address these limitations, it is crucial to consider future generations' rights and incorporate them into economic evaluation and management, as well as establish an institutional network to enforce these rights (Padilla, 2002).

2. **Protection of the Environment**: Environmental protection is a crucial element of ecologically friendly and sustainable development. Its main goal is to reduce and avoid any adverse consequences that a variety of human activities may have on the environment (Ziaul & Shuwei, 2023). Environmental conservation aims to preserve Earth's biodiversity through laws, cutting-edge technology, and eco-friendly human behavior. It emphasizes reducing air and water pollution, promoting renewable resources as alternatives to fossil fuels, and promoting sustainable practices. To mention a few of these resources, they include solar, wind, and hydropower. Because of the decreased carbon footprint, this encourages a more ecologically friendly and sustainable future (Malik et al., 2023).

Sustainable and green development, especially for environmental preservation, is complex. Dumitriu (2021) stresses the necessity of institutional frameworks in resolving the climate problem and reaching global objectives, while Caldwell (2007) stresses the need for sustainable development to prioritize environmental preservation and future generations. Isopescu (2018) examines how eco-innovative design conserves natural resources and reduces energy consumption in the built environment. Arntzen (2000) emphasizes the interconnectedness of environmental protection, sustainable development, environmental conservation, and human well-being, highlighting the deliberate maintenance of environmental quality through management.

3. **Social inclusivity**: A comprehensive approach called sustainable development seeks to build a society in which every individual has equal access to opportunities and essential resources. The goal of eradicating poverty, according to Darvishi et al. (2023), is to support underprivileged and marginalized people by addressing the underlying causes of poverty and putting workable solutions into place. Eco-friendly practices emphasize healthcare and educational system improvement, promoting social justice, and ensuring everyone's potential for health and education while fostering a warm, peaceful community (Zilincikova & Stofkova, 2022).

Agyeman et al. (2002) and Sharma & Ruud (2003) both emphasize the need for governments and organizations to integrate the principles of environmental justice and equity into sustainable development policies and practices. This is echoed by Been et al. (2016), who discuss the potential tensions and synergies between environmental sustainability and social inclusivity in the context of sustainable communities. Haase et al. (2017) highlight the need for a holistic approach to greening initiatives, considering both social and environmental aspects and emphasizing the importance of social inclusion.

4. **Economic efficiency**: Economic efficiency promotes sustainability by maximizing resource efficiency, supporting environmentally friendly companies, and fostering green job creation, aiming to balance environmental preservation and economic progress. This will provide a prosperous and sustainable future for future generations (Malik et al., 2023).

The fundamentals of sustainable and green development, particularly in relation to economic efficiency, are explored in several studies. According to Ayres et al. (2007), although cutting greenhouse gas emissions is critical for long-term sustainability, boosting energy prices through a carbon tax may not be the most effective option. Midilli et al. (2006) underscore the prominence of green energy strategies, particularly in maintaining a constant sectoral impact ratio, in order to accomplish sustainable development. Mikhno et al. (2021) discuss the role of a "green economy" in improving resource efficiency and reducing environmental risks, highlighting the use of indicators such as the Pigouvian tax. Trotter (2012) advocates for a green economy, highlighting the need for inventive solutions to real-world challenges. These studies collectively underscore the potential of green energy and a green economy to promote sustainable development and economic efficiency.

Sustainable and Green Development Initiatives Around the World

Numerous nations worldwide are promoting a balanced approach between environmental preservation and economic growth through various sustainable and green development initiatives. The "Our Common Future" study of the World Commission on Environment and Development emphasizes the need for a worldwide strategy for sustainable growth (Imperatives, 1987). Action-centered networks, as suggested by Jordan (1994), are seen as a means to address environmental challenges, with examples such as the Business Council for Sustainable Development and local Groundwork Trusts. Green technologies are emphasized as a key driver for sustainable development, promoting a balance between economic and environmental aspects (Shaikh, 2017). Lafferty and Meadowcroft's (2000) comparative analysis of sustainable development approaches in high-consumption populations reveals varying levels of engagement and progress across different countries.

The European Green Deal is one such plan that aims to make history on the continent by 2050 by being the first carbon-neutral policy ever (Yusif Asgarov, 2022). The roadmap outlines a comprehensive strategy for a sustainable, inclusive economy, emphasizing biodiversity preservation, a circular economy, and renewable energy (Hasewend & Jokic, 2020). The bargain too points to reshaping the EU into a moral society with effective asset utilization and a cutting-edge, competitive economy. Be that as it may, it faces challenges in lessening territorial and social disparities and requires significant open speculation to accomplish its objectives (Wolf et al., 2021). Asian nations like Japan and South Korea prioritize sustainable development for economic growth, investing in clean energy, reducing emissions, and focusing on innovation, R&D, and technology transfer. In order to achieve sustainable development in Asian nations, Ale et al. (2009) highlight the importance of innovation, R&D, and technology transfer. Hordofa et al. (2021) provide more evidence highlighting the significance of green investment and technological advancements in mitigating $CO2$ emissions. Gorkina (2023) underlines the efforts of Asian nations, especially Japan and South Korea, in transitioning towards sustainable renewable energy sources.

Rwanda and Morocco are two African nations that have made great strides toward sustainable development, particularly in the domains of renewable energy, sustainable agriculture, and ecotourism (Ahenkan & Osei-Kojo, 2014; Mubera & Jules, 2018). For instance, ecotourism, sustainable agriculture, and renewable energy are supported by rules in Rwanda (Ronald et al., 2019). Among the significant renewable energy initiatives in which Morocco has invested is the Noor Solar Power Plant, which is among the largest concentrated solar power plants globally (Terrapon-Pfaff et al., 2019).

Green and sustainable development is achievable through international cooperation, political resolve, and strategic planning, but challenges like climate change, population growth, and job shortages hinder progress (Ahenkan & Osei-Kojo, 2014). The degree of sustainable development in African nations has improved, but there is still room for growth (Bartniczak & Raszkowski, 2018). Establishing sustainable development bodies and implementing poverty-reduction strategies and environmental impact assessment methods have been identified as major successes in Southern Africa (Mutangadura, 2005).

When it comes to green city initiatives, cities in Europe are leading the way in green urbanism, implementing a wide variety of initiatives led by municipal planners and governments. These initiatives, encompassing greenways, enhanced public transportation, energy saving, and sustainable land use (Turok, 2013), aim to promote sustainable development and address climate change at the urban level. Urban sustainability rankings and indices, such as the European Green Capital Award, serve as tools to evaluate and promote environmental performance and sustainable practices among cities (Rosol et al., 2017). The Award incentivizes cities to improve urban environments across various environmental parameters, including climate change mitigation, sustainable transport, and waste management (Beretta, 2014). However, some argue that green city indices need a more holistic approach, incorporating socio-economic factors and acknowledging the interdependencies between different urban policy areas (Venkatesh, 2014). Recognizing these limitations, the European Union's Green Deal aims to involve cities in achieving climate neutrality by 2050, focusing on clean energy, a circular economy, biodiversity restoration, and pollution reduction (Messina, 2021).

APPROACHES FOR UNLOCKING THE POTENTIAL OF SUSTAINABLE AND GREEN DEVELOPMENT FOR A BETTER TOMORROW

Business schools are focusing on green development, preparing future managers with sustainability skills, and enhancing curriculum intellectual rigor through collaborations between institutions and corporations (Martins et al., 2023). A range of approaches have been proposed to unlock the potential of sustainable and green development. According to Yıldırım & Yıldırım (2020), the green economy plays a vital role in attaining sustainable development objectives, and according to Omer (2021), green energy like wind, solar, and biomass should be promoted and put into practice. Ilic et al. (2022) advocate for the advancement of eco-innovation within the corporate and industrial sectors, emphasizing technology and information. Behera (2023) highlights that to enhance sustainability, consider environmental legislation, green technology, and efficient waste management. These methods emphasize the importance of a comprehensive, sustainable, and green development plan, discussing various methods for unlocking its potential.

Green Growth Strategies

Green growth strategies aim to enhance the economic value of natural resources with ecological growth-focused attention in sustainable development. Economic development tactics are based on careful monitoring and identifying the gaps in protecting our environment from long-term hazards and ensuring sustainable economic growth (Fedotova et al., 2023). Nations can create a prosperous and ecologically sound society by incorporating 'green growth' concepts and considering environmental concerns in their economic development plans (Hidayati et al., 2022). In short, harmonious coexistence of environmental protection and economic improvement will be possible only if those measures are provided their due.

Both Morssy (2012) and Hallegatte et al. (2012) stress the significance of green growth tactics in attaining sustainable development. Hallegatte's framework focuses on the short-term and long-term advantages of green policies, while Morssy highlights the position of innovation while transitioning to a green economy. Mathews (2013) emphasizes the potential of green development initiatives to improve social, economic, and environmental well-being, even in the world's poorest nations.

Nexus Approach

The nexus approach is an integrated approach through which a synergistic approach to resource utilization is adopted to achieve coherence and policy efficiency, as it will be good for the growth of the economy under the blue growth concept (Brouwer, 2023 May). The study focuses on analyzing dependencies in various fields like agriculture, energy production, and water to promote sustainable development through synergistic change (Ioannou & Laspidou, 2023). Adopting a comprehensive plan by all stakeholders can ensure correct resource reduction, fair allocation, environmental conservation, and social progress while addressing resource scarcity and unfair allocation.

According to Liu et al. (2018), the nexus method has promise in addressing sustainability issues and advancing integrated planning and governance due to its consideration of the interconnectivity of many sectors. This approach is particularly important in managing resources in resilient urban areas and multipurpose land-use schemes, where participatory approaches and knowledge transfer are crucial (Hülsmann & Jampani, 2020). Green finance, a key component of sustainable green growth, can be leveraged to reduce environmental risks in developing economies (Mohsin et al., 2023). However, the enactment of the nexus approach in sustainable urban design and regeneration projects is influenced by existing planning frameworks, which can either enable or constrain community participation (Tubridy, 2021).

Innovations and Emerging Technologies

Innovation is crucial for sustainable practices and can be encouraged through regulations and incentives to unlock potential in emerging technologies (Chatjuthamard et al., 2023). This will propel green development at historically unheard-of speeds, in addition to efficiently addressing the urgent environmental concerns that require our attention.

Innovations and emerging technologies play a crucial role in unlocking the potential of sustainable and green development for a better tomorrow (Pociovălişteanu et al., 2016; Majerník et al., 2023; Grosclaude et al., 2014; Islam, 2023). The aforementioned breakthroughs, including electric automobiles, organic farming, renewable energy, e-learning, and flexible, frugal, smart, and democratic practices, possess the capacity to tackle worldwide issues like inequality and climate change (Pociovălişteanu et al., 2016; Grosclaude et al., 2014). However, it is important to design technology that balances economic, environmental, and social considerations, benefiting all stakeholders while minimizing negative impacts (Majerník et al., 2023). The development of eco-innovation in the business sector and industrial enterprises, with government incentives, is crucial for a greener future (Islam, 2023).

Sustainable Finance

One facet of the financial domain that is crucial to sustainable finance is the development and application of tailored strategies that are carefully tailored to the unique needs and inclinations of individual investors, all with the ultimate goal of utilizing the infinite possibilities that come with sustainable development (Weber, 2023). Investments in businesses and projects promoting ecological regeneration and preservation are crucial for a harmonious, sustainable coexistence between humans and the environment, ensuring a brighter future for everyone. Through funding eco-friendly initiatives and businesses, sustainable finance seeks to attain a careful balance between environmental stewardship and economic growth—two seemingly irreconcilable objectives (Stojanović, 2020).

A range of studies have explored the potential of sustainable finance to unlock green development. Nassiry (2018) and Kochhar (2022) both emphasize the role of financial technologies and products in driving sustainable investment, with a focus on blockchain and the need for greater awareness and analytical capabilities among investors. Clark et al. (2018) and Zorlu (2018) highlight the challenges and opportunities in scaling up private investment for climate action and sustainable development, calling for coordinated efforts, fiscal and policy reform, and international action.

Collaboration and Partnerships

The achievement of sustainable and green development's complete potential requires the collaboration of diverse organizations, governments, businesses, civil society organizations, and communities (Eckerberg & Bjärstig, 2022). Collaborative initiatives and joint ventures enable stakeholders to share essential information, resources, and specialized talents, promoting a positive transition and resulting in beneficial advancements in society and the environment. Sustainable performance has been shown to be significantly influenced by collaboration, especially when it comes to environmental governance and management (Niesten et al., 2017; Feist et al., 2020). It can enhance sustainable benefits, reduce waste, and improve environmental and social performance (Niesten et al., 2017). Trust building, social learning, and active involvement are crucial qualities for successful collaboration, leading to outcomes such as social learning and social capital (Feist et al., 2020). Still understudied, nevertheless, is the efficacy of cooperation as a substitute for conventional methods of sustainability and environmental preservation (Hartman et al., 2002). In spite of this, it has been shown that cooperation is a paradigm and leading practice in environmental governance, allowing for the integration of various viewpoints and expertise (Margerum et al., 2016).

Collaboration and partnerships are necessary to realize the full potential of sustainable and green development (Gilbert, 2007). These approaches can be particularly effective in local projects, where they can facilitate the incorporation of green infrastructure elements (Peat, 2005). However, to address global sustainability challenges, stakeholders and businesses must work together in novel ways, treating ecosystems as a whole and creating shared value (Nidumolu et al., 2014). A thorough assessment methodology, like the Global Sustainability Partnership Database, may help discover critical success criteria and further improve the efficacy of these collaborations (Pattberg et al., 2007).

Education and Awareness

Promoting education and raising awareness about sustainable development empowers individuals and communities to make informed decisions, fosters a sustainable mindset, and ensures the planet's future well-being. Fostering a sustainable attitude and empowering people and communities to make wise choices and take action that will benefit future generations are two things that education can greatly contribute to (Fulwari, 2017; Chalkley, 2006; Segovia, 2010; Fairfield, 2018). It provides the knowledge, skills, and values necessary for sustainable development (Fulwari, 2017) and can transform mindsets towards an ethics of life-giving relationships and interconnectedness (Segovia, 2010). Higher education, in particular, has a noteworthy role in producing graduates with sustainability literacy (Chalkley, 2006). However, education for sustainability must also raise awareness of global issues and elicit a new worldview and mindset (Fairfield, 2018).

Furthermore, according to O'Riordan et al. (2020), education works as a catalyst, pushing and pressing the next generation to actively engage in sustainable practices in order for them to become environmental stewards and advocates for a better future. Diverse approaches can achieve sustainable development by balancing social welfare, economic prosperity, and ecological balance, paving the way for a better future.

Education and awareness are crucial in unlocking the potential of sustainable and green development for a better tomorrow. Green education is crucial to raising awareness, changing behavior, and inspiring action, according to Aggarwal (2023). In their 2022 essay, Kaur & Mehndroo highlight the need for education and training for the transition to sustainable societies, while Zwolińska et al. (2022) stress the significance of incorporating sustainable development objectives into the curriculum. Middleton (2018) suggests promoting sustainable living through communication, values, and success stories, emphasizing the transformative power of education and awareness in driving green development.

CHALLENGES AND OBSTACLES IN SUSTAINABLE AND GREEN DEVELOPMENT

Innovation and economic development may be impacted by environmental rules in both good and bad ways. Although they may initially hinder development by placing limitations on output (Ricci, 2007), they can also promote growth by enhancing productivity, promoting innovation, and enhancing environmental quality (Moser et al., 2013; Jacobs, 2012). According to Papadimitriou & Hannsgen (2012), the coal industry opposed the Clean Power plan, which aimed to reduce greenhouse gas emissions by 32% by 2030, citing possible economic challenges (Peters & Hertel, 2017). Given that they may both help and impede economic growth, this emphasizes the nuanced link between environmental regulations and sustainable development.

Economic Challenges of Sustainable and Green Development

The economic challenges associated with the implementation of green development are indeed significant and can impact the feasibility of sustainable initiatives. Green development is crucial for long-term sustainability, but it often requires significant financial commitment and may face funding limitations, especially in low-income and developing nations (Zi, 2023). Integrating environmental protection with economic profit in green financing can create internal contradictions that require regulatory frameworks and market systems to address (Ilić et al., 2018).

Implementing green funding and taxes may hinder the achievement of the Sustainable Development Goals, potentially leading to increased inequality and energy poverty (Mpofu, 2022). The study emphasizes the importance of corporate innovation and environmental regulation adherence but suggests that enforcement can be ineffective if not properly aligned with institutional settings and governance characteristics (Xin & Senin, 2022). In summary, economic obstacles to green development, including financing constraints, potential social impacts, and environmental regulation complexity, significantly impact sustainability efforts' feasibility and long-term success.

Social Dimensions of Sustainable and Green Development

Sustainable development is a multifaceted endeavor that goes beyond economic goals, encompassing social dimensions as well (Husgafvel, 2021). In order to achieve a sustainable future for every member of society, the social implications of sustainable development include social justice, fair benefit distribution, and quality of life improvement (Doyle & Perez Alaniz, 2021). The significance of social capital and natural capital, which can support one another even in the absence of economic development, is being more acknowledged, which is interesting given that economic growth has historically been given priority (Chang, 2013). Moreover, the concept of social sustainability handprints highlights the role of various actors in promoting social sustainability through actions and changes that contribute to the well-being of society (Husgafvel, 2021).

REGULATORY IMPEDIMENTS AND SOLUTIONS TO SUSTAINABLE AND GREEN DEVELOPMENT

Encouraging sustainable development requires addressing regulatory barriers, as regulatory frameworks significantly impact the establishment of an environment conducive to sustainable practices and innovations. For instance, Farooq et al. (2024)

establish a negative association between environmental rules and investment choices but also acknowledge the favorable influence of such restrictions on green innovation, showing that well-designed policies may support both economic advancement and environmental sustainability.

Similarly, Muhammad et al. (2023) underscore the significance of clear legal frameworks in fostering sustainable finance in Asia and Africa, which may function as a stimulus for responsible investments. He argues that the legal structure may not fully support environmental protection and sustainable development objectives, needing legislative adjustments to effectively incorporate sustainability into corporate governance. While legislative frameworks may promote sustainable behaviors, they can also function as hurdles. Greenland (2019) explains how inadequate government and regulatory policies might limit the adoption of sustainable technologies. Sourani & Sohail (2011, December) highlight weak and inconsistent rules as impediments to sustainable building procurement in the UK. Hwang et al. (2017) also mention a lack of government backing as a fundamental hurdle to the development of green business parks. This suggests that while laws are crucial, they must be carefully crafted to prevent obstacles to sustainability, as regulatory frameworks can be a double-edged sword. They are vital for setting the scene for sustainable behaviors', as indicated by the favorable benefits of well-designed rules on green innovation (Farooq et al., 2024) and sustainable financing (Muhammad et al., 2023).

However, regulatory barriers, including poor regulations and a lack of assistance, might significantly impede the adoption of sustainable practices (Greenland, 2019; Hwang et al., 2017; Sourani & Sohail, 2011, December). Therefore, it's critical to modify and align regulatory policies with sustainable development goals to ensure that they function as facilitators rather than impediments (Muhammad et al., 2023; Farooq et al., 2024).

Economic Advantages of Sustainable Development

Examining the economic advantages of sustainable development gives a parallel viewpoint to overcoming regulatory constraints. Sustainable development provides both environmental and economic advantages. Literature consistently underscores the dual benefits of sustainable development, highlighting that it not only preserves natural resources and environmental quality but also fosters economic prosperity (Hecht & Fiksel, 2020). The concept of the green economy, as discussed in several studies, is illustrative of this dual advantage, where economic growth is achieved alongside the promotion of environmental sustainability (Qin & Li, 2023; Wen, 2022).

Interestingly, the study demonstrates a range of viewpoints on the economic-environmental connection. For instance, the study on young people's views in Sweden indicates differing opinions on how sustainable development and economic growth are related (Berglund & Gericke, 2018).

The perception and ranking of sustainable development benefits by various stakeholders is complex, despite their generally accepted advantages. It is a goal and a process that aligns economic prosperity with the preservation of ecological systems, thereby ensuring long-term human well-being (Hecht & Fiksel, 2020; Qin & Li, 2023). Literature has vowed the importance of education and stakeholder engagement in fostering a nuanced understanding of sustainable development's dual benefits (Berglund & Gericke, 2018). However, addressing socioeconomic inequities is crucial for sustainability, as adopting sustainable practices may lead to job losses, disproportionately affecting disadvantaged individuals. For instance, environmental measures such as a revenue-neutral carbon tax have been shown to raise unemployment rates more considerably among less-educated individuals (Yip, 2018).

Similarly, the greening of economies, although vital for environmental sustainability, demands a re-evaluation of labor market regulations to achieve an equitable transition that does not worsen existing disparities (Bohnenberger, 2022). Sustainable practices, like IT skill development, can boost employment opportunities, particularly for historically disadvantaged populations like women and the elderly, despite potential negative impacts. (Atasoy et al., 2021). Moreover, inclusive work redesign methods and active labor market policies may offer job possibilities for disadvantaged populations, leading to sustainable employment for all staff (Mulders et al., 2022).

To recap, although the transition to sustainable practices involves risks of employment losses in specific sectors, with disadvantaged populations possibly taking the brunt of these losses (Yip, 2018; Bohnenberger, 2022), there are measures to offset these consequences. These include offering IT training to increase employability (Atasoy et al., 2021) and promoting inclusive work redesign and active labor market policies (Mulders et al., 2022). Policymakers must assess the social implications of environmental policy and implement measures to safeguard disadvantaged workers during this transition.

Balancing Environmental Protection and Economic Growth

Sustainable development requires a balance between environmental preservation and economic growth, ensuring the well-being of current and future generations without compromising natural resources or environmental quality (Hecht & Fiksel,

2020). However, the balance between economic growth and environmental preservation is challenging due to inherent contradictions and political factors driving sustainable development policies (Garner, 2013; James et al., 2013). Remarkably, although certain research stresses the potential of green innovation and financial development in fostering environmental sustainability (Xu, 2023), studies highlight the importance of renewable energy sources and the role of economic tools like environmental taxes and emissions trading in environmental preservation (Das et al., 2022).

The notion of the blue economy and ecotourism are both given as models that blend economic success with environmental protection (Sambou et al., 2019). Yet, the current focus is on sustainable, inclusive development that balances economic, social, and ecological factors, as economic and technical growth have historically functioned in isolation (Acquah-Sam, 2020). Generally, innovative techniques and multi-stakeholder collaboration in sustainable development needed to achieve economic success while protecting the environment.

Importance of Public-Private Partnerships (PPPs)

Public-private partnerships (PPPs) are key to promoting sustainable development, addressing environmental issues, and contributing to the Sustainable Development Goals by fostering collaboration between the commercial and public sectors (Vassileva, 2022). Nevertheless, the effectiveness of PPPs in achieving sustainability goals is debatable.

Current methods for measuring their impact have limitations, leading to the development of conceptual frameworks like EASIER to evaluate their holistic contribution to the SDGs (Berrone et al., 2019). Moreover, the significance and value of PPPs in global environmental governance remain debated, with some partnerships concentrating more on technical execution than innovation (Mert & Pattberg, 2018). PPs are crucial for sustainable growth, but their performance and impact must be thoroughly reviewed to ensure sustainable practices are integrated into PPP infrastructure projects (Akomea-Frimpong et al., 2022), and the engagement of foreign investment in PPPs may be substantial, as demonstrated in China's approach to sustainable development (Si, 2022). However, the possibility of corruption, as demonstrated in Albania, underscores the necessity for adequate risk assessment and monitoring measures (AS & TO, 2023 May).

The public value theory gives a framework for understanding the multilayered performance expectations of PPPs (Esposito & Dicorato, 2020), and the use of PPPs in forest management highlights both the possibilities and constraints of this approach (Chisika & Yeom, 2021). The Greek municipal urban administration has successfully implemented public-private partnerships (PPPs) to overcome restrictions and promote local sustainability, as demonstrated by Kyvelou et al. (2011).

Incorporating Traditional Knowledge and Practices

Indigenous knowledge is crucial for sustainable development, encompassing natural resource management, agriculture, healthcare, and education, as well as cultural acceptance and social inclusion (Sharma & Kumari, 2021). Indigenous knowledge, passed down through generations, safeguards biodiversity, promotes sustainable use, and fosters cultural identity. However, industrialization and a lack of documentation may degrade it (Bandyopadhyay & Bandyopadhyay, 2018).

The integration of indigenous knowledge with scientific methodologies is deemed advantageous. For instance, indigenous soil knowledge has been recognized for its significance in increasing agricultural sustainability, particularly when paired with scientific soil knowledge (Handayani & Prawito, 2010).

Furthermore, policymakers' reluctance to include disadvantaged groups like sexual minorities in Sustainable Development Goals (SDG) policies is influenced by local politics and cultural values (Izugbara et al., 2022). In summary, political and financial support are crucial for achieving the SDGs, but inconsistent policies, coalition dynamics, and social norms can significantly hinder progress. Governments must promote inclusive policies and sustainable development to address global issues, aligning with the global pledge to leave no one behind. The information shows that, despite the obstacles, policies and initiatives may be implemented at all governmental levels to support the achievement of the SDGs.

Measuring Success in Sustainable Development

Sustainable development success necessitates clear objectives, continuous progress review, understanding of individual contexts, and a comprehensive strategy addressing socioeconomic inequities and political obstacles at organizational and national levels (Ramos & Caeiro, 2010; Ramos & Caeiro, 2009). However, a major gap in these tools is the absence of assessment of the performance measuring instruments themselves, which is necessary for analyzing the appropriateness and effectiveness of sustainability indicators (Ramos & Caeiro, 2009; Ramos & Caeiro, 2010). Despite the need for meta-evaluation, practical implementations like the Green Management Assessment Tool (GMAT) focus on analyzing progress towards sustainability principles at the facility level without evaluating the tools themselves (Eagan & Joeres, 1997).

Moreover, the emphasis on sustainability objectives, particularly in higher education, emphasizes the necessity of indicators that assess performance, encourage participation, and inform policy (Hands & Anderson, 2018). In summary, sustainable development projects' success relies on effective monitoring, critical analysis of assessment techniques, performance evaluation, impartiality, transparency, and openness (Ramos & Caeiro, 2010; Ramos & Caeiro, 2009). Stakeholder engagement is emphasized as a crucial aspect of sustainability assessments, facilitating cross-validation and enhancing their credibility (Hands & Anderson, 2018; Ramos & Caeiro, 2010; Ramos & Caeiro, 2009).

ACTIONABLE STRATEGIES FOR FOSTERING SUSTAINABLE AND GREEN DEVELOPMENT

This section emphasizes the importance of translating theoretical knowledge into practical action. Having established a foundational framework for understanding sustainable and green development, the authors advocate a shift towards actionable strategies. The following suggestions are designed to bridge the gap between theoretical ideas and the practical execution of sustainable and environmentally friendly practices.

Cultivating Environmental Literacy and Action

Education initiatives can foster environmental consciousness and empower individuals to adopt sustainable practices. Advocacy efforts can target local education departments to integrate sustainability education into curriculums. Supporting relevant organizations and hosting community events can further disseminate knowledge and inspire action towards a more sustainable future.

Driving Innovation for a Sustainable Future

To achieve a sustainable future, promoting clean technologies and green business practices is crucial. This involves increased public and private investment in renewable energy, sustainable materials, and clean production technologies. Policymakers can incentivize green businesses through financial instruments and promote eco-innovation within the private sector. This strategy will drive technological advancements and sustainable development.

Mobilizing Financial Resources for Sustainability

Achieving sustainable and green development requires a paradigm shift within the financial sector. This can be facilitated through the development and promotion of specialized investment products that channel capital towards environmentally friendly businesses and green projects. Furthermore, supporting the issuance of green bonds—debt instruments specifically earmarked for environmentally sustainable initiatives—presents a viable financing mechanism. Financial institutions should include ESG concerns when making investment decisions about where to allocate funds for sustainability programs.

Building Collaboration for Collective Action

This sub-topic proposes a three-part strategy. First, by forming partnerships that involve a variety of stakeholders. These collaborations would combine the resources and expertise of governments, industry, NGOs, and civil society groups. Second, by promoting models of governance that encourage shared decision-making with participation from diverse stakeholders on sustainability issues. Finally, by pushing for the building of venues for knowledge sharing and collaboration, these platforms would encourage cooperation and information exchange across different stakeholders, resulting in a more cohesive approach to sustainable development.

Strengthening the Policy Framework for Sustainability

This section underscores the importance of advocating for policy and regulatory reforms to achieve sustainable development. It provides a three-pronged approach: first, by enacting environmental legislation that incentivizes cleaner manufacturing, resource efficiency, and pollution reduction. Second, by promoting sustainable urban planning policies that prioritize green infrastructure, energy efficiency, and walkable communities. Finally, by strengthening international cooperation on environmental treaties, resource management agreements, and technology transfer specific to sustainable development initiatives.

To sum up, note that the adoption of these multidimensional strategies represents a significant opportunity to unlock the full potential of sustainable and green development. By working together across multiple sectors and adopting these ideas, it is possible to pave the road for a more prosperous and sustainable future for everybody.

CONCLUSION

The 21st century demands a shift in perspective. Sustainability is no longer an option but an imperative element for achieving a future that aligns social progress, environmental well-being, and economic prosperity for all. The European Green Deal, which emphasizes biodiversity, renewable energy, and innovation, demonstrates this approach. Similar strides are being made by countries like Rwanda and Morocco in ecotourism, sustainable agriculture, and renewable energy. Yet, significant challenges like climate change, population growth, and unemployment persist.

To address these challenges, a multi-faceted approach is needed. Building on existing strategies like green growth and the nexus approach, this chapter advocates a "symphony of solutions"—a m multi-pronged approach that tackles sustainability from various angles. This symphony includes elements like gamification, a wellbeing-centered paradigm, participatory development, a localized bioregional approach, and a transformational social learning platform. These approaches, working in harmony, can accelerate progress towards a sustainable future.

The true power lies not in the individual solutions but in their combined effect, amplified by active stakeholder engagement. Traditional models often fall short. This chapter proposes a novel solution: participatory governance. Participatory governance goes beyond merely bringing diverse stakeholders—businesses, governments, NGOs, and local communities—to the table. It promotes active involvement and collaborative problem-solving, generating a sense of ownership and responsibility among all participants.

Empowering local communities is crucial. Citizen science initiatives and multi-stakeholder governance boards further strengthen collaboration and knowledge sharing. Facilitating the open sharing of knowledge and best practices through different platforms and knowledge repositories is critical. This fosters cross-pollination of ideas and accelerates the diffusion of successful strategies, ultimately contributing to more rapid progress. The participatory governance model presents challenges, such as building trust and ensuring equitable representation. However, the potential benefits—more engaged citizens, more effective solutions, and a stronger sense of shared responsibility—make it a compelling approach worth pursuing.

The journey towards sustainability is continuous, demanding innovative ideas, collaborative efforts, and resolute commitment. By adopting new approaches such as participatory governance, we can close the knowledge-action gap, resulting in a more sustainable future for all. This presents not just a problem but a chance to establish a society in which mankind flourishes in symbiosis with the environment, resulting in a lasting legacy of a sustainable planet for everyone. Together, let's take on the role of change agents and pave the route towards a future that is both sustainable and wealthy for future generations. Let us rise to this challenge and unlock the potential for a truly sustainable and green tomorrow.

REFERENCES

Acquah-Sam, E. (2020). *The State as an Engine of Inclusive Sustainable Economic Growth and Development.* European Scientific Journal ESJ. 10.19044/esj.2020.v16n22p177

Adams, B. (2008). *Green Development: Environment and Sustainability in a Developing World* (3rd ed.). Routledge. 10.4324/9780203929711

Aggarwal, D. (2023). Green education for a sustainable future. *Journal of Environmental Impact and Management Policy (JEIMP)*, 27-30.

Agyeman, J., Bullard, R. D., & Evans, B. (2002). Exploring the nexus: Bringing together sustainability, environmental justice, and equity. *Space and Polity*, 6(1), 77–90. 10.1080/13562570220137907

Ahenkan, A., & Osei-Kojo, A. (2014). Achieving sustainable development in Africa: Progress, challenges, and prospects. *International Journal of Development and Sustainability*, 3(1), 162–176.

Akomea-Frimpong, I., Jin, X., & Osei-Kyei, R. (2022). Mapping studies on sustainability in the performance measurement of public-private partnership projects: A systematic review. *Sustainability (Basel)*, 14(12), 7174. 10.3390/su14127174

Ale Ebrahim, N., Ahmed, S., & Taha, Z. (2009). Innovation and R&D activities in virtual team. *European Journal of Scientific Research*, 34(3), 297–307.

Anderson, R. (2007). Thematic content analysis (TCA). *Descriptive presentation of qualitative data, 3*, 1-4.

Arntzen, J. (2000). *Environmental Protection in the Context of Sustainable Development.* Research Gate.

AS. P., & TO, B. (2023, May). Corruption In Public Private. On *7th FEB International Scientific Conference* (p. 257). Research Gate.

Atasoy, H., Banker, R. D., & Pavlou, P. A. (2021). Information technology skills and labor market outcomes for workers. *Information Systems Research*, 32(2), 437–461. 10.1287/isre.2020.0975

Attfield, R. (2023). *Sustainability. The International Encyclopedia of Ethics.* Portico., 10.1002/9781444367072.wbiee033.pub2

Ayres, R. U., Turton, H., & Casten, T. (2007). Energy efficiency, sustainability, and economic growth. *Energy*, 32(5), 634–648. 10.1016/j.energy.2006.06.005

Bandyopadhyay, D., & Bandyopadhyay, D. (2018). Protection of traditional knowledge and indigenous knowledge. *Securing Our Natural Wealth: A Policy Agenda for Sustainable Development in India and for Its Neighboring Countries*, 59-70.

Bansode, S. (2022). Sustainable Development and Environment. *RESEARCH REVIEW International Journal of Multidisciplinary*, 7(6), 65–67. 10.31305/rrijm.2022.v07.i06.010

Bartniczak, B., & Raszkowski, A. (2018). Sustainable development in African countries: An indicator-based approach and recommendations for the future. *Sustainability (Basel)*, 11(1), 22. 10.3390/su11010022

Beder, S. (2000). Costing the earth: Equity, sustainable development, and environmental economics. *NZJ Envtl. L.*, 4, 227.

Been, V., Cunningham, M. K., Ellen, I. G., Parilla, J., Turner, M. A., Whitney, S. V., & Yowell, A. (2016). *Building environmentally sustainable communities: A framework for inclusivity*. Research Gate.

Behera, D. K. (2023). Promoting Sustainable Development Through Environmental Policy, Green Technologies, and Effective Waste Management: A Comprehensive Review. *Journal of Multidisciplinary Science: MIKAILALSYS*, 1(2), 179–198. 10.58578/mikailalsys.v1i2.1675

Beretta, I. (2014). *Becoming a European Green Capital: a way towards sustainability?* Emerald. .10.1108/S1047-004220140000014014

Berglund, T., & Gericke, N. (2018). Exploring the role of the economy in young adults' understanding of sustainable development. *Sustainability (Basel)*, 10(8), 2738. 10.3390/su10082738

Berrone, P., Ricart, J. E., Duch, A. I., Bernardo, V., Salvador, J., Piedra Peña, J., & Rodríguez Planas, M. (2019). EASIER: An evaluation model for public–private partnerships contributing to the sustainable development goals. *Sustainability (Basel)*, 11(8), 2339. 10.3390/su11082339

Bohnenberger, K. (2022). Greening work: Labor market policies for the environment. *Empirica*, 49(2), 347–368. 10.1007/s10663-021-09530-9

Brouwer, F. (2023, May). A Resource Nexus Concept-Definition, design, and practice. In *EGU General Assembly Conference Abstracts (pp. EGU-3963)*.10.5194/egusphere-egu23-3963

Caldwell, L.K. (2007). *Principles of Sustainable Development.*

Chalkley, B. (2006). Education for sustainable development: Continuation. *Journal of Geography in Higher Education*, 30(2), 235–236. 10.1080/03098260600717307

Chang, C. T. (2013). The disappearing sustainability triangle: Community level considerations. *Sustainability Science*, 8(2), 227–240. 10.1007/s11625-013-0199-3

Chatjuthamard, P., Sarajoti, P., & Papangkorn, S. (2023). *Perspective Chapter: Sustainability and Corporate Innovation*. Chapters.

Chisika, S. N., & Yeom, C. (2021). Enhancing sustainable management of public natural forests through public private partnerships in Kenya. *SAGE Open*, 11(4), 21582440211054490. 10.1177/21582440211054490

Clark, R., Reed, J., & Sunderland, T. (2018). Bridging funding gaps for climate and sustainable development: Pitfalls, progress and potential of private finance. *Land Use Policy*, 71, 335–346. 10.1016/j.landusepol.2017.12.013

Cross, K. W. (2023). A critical evaluation of inter-generational equity and its application in the climate change context. In *Feminist Frontiers in Climate Justice* (pp. 40–67). Edward Elgar Publishing. 10.4337/9781803923796.00007

Darvishi, Y., Karami, H., & Goodarzian, F. (2023). Sustainable development in oxygenated fuels. In *Advancement in Oxygenated Fuels for Sustainable Development* (pp. 315–330). Elsevier. 10.1016/B978-0-323-90875-7.00013-7

Das, N., Bera, P., & Panda, D. (2022). Can economic development & environmental sustainability promote renewable energy consumption in India?? Findings from novel dynamic ARDL simulations approach. *Renewable Energy*, 189, 221–230. 10.1016/j.renene.2022.02.116

Dong, K. (2002). Intergenerational Equity and Sustainable Development. *Journal of Yanan University*.

Doyle, E., & Perez Alaniz, M. (2021). Dichotomous impacts on social and environmental sustainability: Competitiveness and development levels matter. *Competitiveness Review*, 31(4), 771–791. 10.1108/CR-05-2019-0055

Dumitriu, M. L. I. (2021). The Principles of Environmental Protection. *Perspective Politice*, 14(1-2), 125. 10.25019/perspol/21.14.10

Eagan, P. D., & Joeres, E. (1997). Development of a facility-based environmental performance indicator related to sustainable development. *Journal of Cleaner Production*, 5(4), 269–278. 10.1016/S0959-6526(97)00044-9

Eckerberg, K., & Bjärstig, T. (2022). Collaborative approaches for sustainable development governance. In *Handbook on the governance of sustainable development* (pp. 175–189). Edward Elgar Publishing.

Erdős, L. (2019). Al Gore – The Climate Crusader. *Green Heroes*, 207–211, 207–211. 10.1007/978-3-030-31806-2_41

Esposito, P., & Dicorato, S. L. (2020). Sustainable development, governance and performance measurement in public private partnerships (PPPs): A methodological proposal. *Sustainability (Basel)*, 12(14), 5696. 10.3390/su12145696

Fairfield, K. D. (2018). Educating for a sustainability mindset. *Journal of Management for Global Sustainability*, 6(1), 4. 10.13185/JM2018.06102

Farooq, U., Wen, J., Tabash, M. I., & Fadoul, M. (2024). Environmental regulations and capital investment: Does green innovation allow to grow. *International Review of Economics & Finance*, 89, 878–893. 10.1016/j.iref.2023.08.010

Fedotova, G., Kapustina, Y., Romadikova, V., Dzhancharova, G., Churaev, A., & Novikov, M. (2023). Green strategies for the sustainable growth of food security. In *E3S Web of Conferences* (Vol. 390, p. 04014). EDP Sciences. 10.1051/e3sconf/202339004014

Feist, A., Plummer, R., & Baird, J. (2020). The inner workings of collaboration in environmental management and governance: A systematic mapping review. *Environmental Management*, 66(5), 801–815. 10.1007/s00267-020-01337-x32734324

Fischer, M. (2023). The Concept of Sustainable Development. *SpringerBriefs in business.* Springer. 10.1007/978-3-031-25397-3_2

Fulwari, A. (2017). Role of education for sustainable development. *International Education and Research Journal*, 3(5), 546–549.

Gakh, D. (2023). Societal Patterns Evolution Model in Development of Economy,Society, and Environment. https://doi.org/10.20944/preprints202305.0632.v1

Garner, R. (2013). Politics and sustainable development. In *The Sustainability Curriculum* (pp. 208–217). Routledge.

Gilbert, B. C. (2007). *Collaborative synergy in resource and environmental management.*

Gorkina, T. И. (2023). Features of the energy transition in Asian countries. Journal of the Moscow University. Series 5. *Geography (Sheffield, England)*, (3), 18–29.

Greenland, S. J. (2019). Future sustainability, innovation, and marketing: A framework for understanding impediments to sustainable innovation adoption and corporate social responsibility. In *The Components of Sustainable Development: Engagement and Partnership* (pp. 63-80). Springer Singapore. 10.1007/978-981-13-9209-2_5

Grosclaude, J. Y., Pachauri, R. K., & Tubiana, L. (Eds.). (2014). *Innovation for sustainable development. The Energy and Resources Institute.* TERI.

Haase, D., Kabisch, S., Haase, A., Andersson, E., Banzhaf, E., Baró, F., Brenck, M., Fischer, L. K., Frantzeskaki, N., Kabisch, N., Krellenberg, K., Kremer, P., Kronenberg, J., Larondelle, N., Mathey, J., Pauleit, S., Ring, I., Rink, D., Schwarz, N., & Wolff, M. (2017). Greening cities–To be socially inclusive? About the alleged paradox of society and ecology in cities. *Habitat International*, 64, 41–48. 10.1016/j.habitatint.2017.04.005

Hallegatte, S., Heal, G., Fay, M., & Treguer, D. (2012). *From growth to green growth-a framework (No. w17841)*. National Bureau of Economic Research. 10.3386/w17841

Handayani, I. P., & Prawito, P. (2010). Indigenous soil knowledge for sustainable agriculture. *Sociology, organic farming, climate change and soil science*, 303-317.

Hands, V., & Anderson, R. (2018). *Local sustainability indicators and their role in the implementation of the sustainable development goals in the HE sector. Handbook of Sustainability Science and Research.* Springer. 10.1007/978-3-319-63007-6_16

Hartman, C. L., Hofman, P. S., & Stafford, E. R. (2002). Environmental collaboration: potential and limits. In *Partnership and leadership: Building alliances for a sustainable future* (pp. 21–40). Springer Netherlands. 10.1007/978-94-017-2545-3_2

Hasewend, B., & Jokic, T. (2020). How the European green deal promotes sustainable energy research and innovation. In *Solar Energy Conversion in Communities: Proceedings of the Conference for Sustainable Energy (CSE) 2020* (pp. 455-456). Springer International Publishing. 10.1007/978-3-030-55757-7_32

Hecht, A. D., & Fiksel, J. (2020). Sustainability and Sustainable Development. In *Landscape and Land Capacity* (pp. 411-417). CRC Press. 10.1201/9780429445552-52

Hidayati, S. N., Suyono, J., & Hartomo, D. D. (2022, December). The role of budgeting in realizing a green economy and economic growth. []. IOP Publishing.]. *IOP Conference Series. Earth and Environmental Science*, 1114(1), 012077. 10.1088/1755-1315/1114/1/012077

Hordofa, T. T., Vu, H. M., Maneengam, A., Mughal, N., & Liying, S. (2023). Does eco-innovation and green investment limit the CO2 emissions in China? Economic research-. *Ekonomska Istrazivanja*, 36(1), 634–649. 10.1080/1331677X.2022.2116067

Hülsmann, S., & Jampani, M. (2020). The nexus approach as a tool for resources management in resilient cities and multifunctional land-use systems. In *A Nexus Approach for Sustainable Development: Integrated Resources Management in Resilient Cities and Multifunctional Land-Use Systems* (pp. 1–13). Springer International Publishing.

Husgafvel, R. (2021). Exploring social sustainability handprint—part 2: Sustainable development and sustainability. *Sustainability (Basel)*, 13(19), 11051. 10.3390/su131911051

Hwang, B. G., Zhu, L., & Tan, J. S. H. (2017). Green business park project management: Barriers and solutions for sustainable development. *Journal of Cleaner Production*, 153, 209–219. 10.1016/j.jclepro.2017.03.210

Ilić, B., Stojanovic, D., & Pavicevic, N. (2018). Green financing for environmental protection and sustainable economic growth–a comparison of Indonesia and Serbia. *Progress in Economic Sciences*, (5).

Ilic, S., Petrovic, T., & Djukic, G. (2022). Eco-innovation and sustainable development. *Problemy Ekorozwoju, 17*(2).

Imperatives, S. (1987). Report of the World Commission on Environment and Development: Our common future. *Accessed Feb, 10*(42,427).

Ioannou, A. E., & Laspidou, C. S. (2023). Cross-mapping important interactions between water-energy-food nexus indices and the SDGs. *Sustainability (Basel)*, 15(10), 8045. 10.3390/su15108045

Islam, M. T. (2023). Newly developed green technology innovations in business: Paving the way toward sustainability. *Technological Sustainability*, 2(3), 295–319. 10.1108/TECHS-02-2023-0008

Isopescu, D. N. (2018, August). The impact of green building principles in the sustainable development of the built environment. [). IOP Publishing.]. *IOP Conference Series. Materials Science and Engineering*, 399(1), 012026. 10.1088/1757-899X/399/1/012026

Izugbara, C., Sebany, M., Wekesah, F., & Ushie, B. (2022). "The SDGs are not God": Policymakers and the queering of the Sustainable Development Goals in Africa. *Development Policy Review*, 40(2), e12558. 10.1111/dpr.12558

Jacobs, M. (2012). *Far from being a drag on growth, environmental policy can actually help drive it.* British Politics and Policy at LSE.

James, K., Murry, A., & Pacheco, D. (2013). Strong communities: Integrating environmental, economic, and social sustainability. In *Social Sustainability* (pp. 54–78). Routledge.

Jordan, A. (1994). Managing. *Sustainable Development.*

Kamakia, A. (2015). A Discussion on Sustainable Development. *SSRN* 2653722.

Kaur, G., & Mehndroo, M. (2022). Education and enlightenment for sustainable development. *International Journal of Health Sciences*, (II), 7525–7530. 10.53730/ijhs.v6nS2.6810

Kochhar, K. (2022). Green Finance: An approach towards Sustainable Development Goals (SDGs). *Asian Journal of Management*, 13(1), 17–20. 10.52711/2321-5763.2022.00004

Krefeld-Schwalb, A., & Gabel, S. (2023). Empowering a Sustainable Future: Fostering Sustainable Behavior with Targeted Interventions. 10.31234/osf.io/nc2bh

Kumar, S., & Rathore, K. (2023). Renewable Energy for Sustainable Development Goal of Clean and Affordable Energy. *International Journal of Materials Manufacturing and Sustainable Technologies, 2*(1), 1–15. , 1.10.56896/ijmmst

Kyvelou, S., Marava, N., & Kokkoni, G. (2011). Perspectives of local public-private partnerships towards urban sustainability in Greece. *International Journal of Sustainable Development*, 14(1-2), 95–111. 10.1504/IJSD.2011.039640

Lafferty, W. M., & Meadowcroft, J. (2000). *Implementing sustainable development: Strategies and initiatives in high consumption societies.* OUP Oxford. 10.1093/0199242011.001.0001

Liu, J., Hull, V., Godfray, H. C. J., Tilman, D., Gleick, P., Hoff, H., Pahl-Wostl, C., Xu, Z., Chung, M. G., Sun, J., & Li, S. (2018). Nexus approaches to global sustainable development. *Nature Sustainability*, 1(9), 466–476. 10.1038/s41893-018-0135-8

Majerník, M., Chovancová, J., Drábik, P., & Štofková, Z. (2023). Environmental technological innovations and the sustainability of their development. *Ecological Engineering & Environmental Technology, 24.*

Malik, P., Malik, P. K., Singh, R., & Gehlot, A. (2023). Sustainable Development, Renewable Energy and Environment. In *Micro-Electronics and Telecommunication Engineering: Proceedings of 6th ICMETE 2022* (pp. 455–463). Springer Nature Singapore. 10.1007/978-981-19-9512-5_42

Margerum, R. D., & Robinson, C. J. (Eds.). (2016). *The challenges of collaboration in environmental governance: Barriers and responses*. Edward Elgar Publishing. 10.4337/9781785360411

Martins, F., Cezarino, L., Liboni, L., Hunter, T., Batalhao, A., & Paschoalotto, M. A. C. (2023). Unlocking the potential of responsible management education through interdisciplinary approaches. *Sustainable Development*.

Mathews, J. A. (2013). Greening of development strategies. *Seoul Journal of Economics*, 26(2), 147–172.

Mert, A., & Pattberg, P. H. (2018). How Do Climate Change and Energy-related Partnerships Impact Innovation and Technology Transfer?: Some Lessons for the Implementation of the UN Sustainable Development Goals. In *The Cambridge Handbook of Public-Private Partnerships, Intellectual Property Governance and Sustainable Development* (pp. 289-307). Cambridge University Press.

Messina, G. (2021). The role of the committee of the regions (CoR) to implement the Green Deal at the local level: An overview of Italy. *AIMS Geosciences*, 7(4), 613–622. 10.3934/geosci.2021037

Middleton, P. (2018). Sustainable living education: Techniques to help advance the renewable energy transformation. *Solar Energy*, 174, 1016–1018. 10.1016/j.solener.2018.08.009

Midilli, A., Dincer, I., & Ay, M. (2006). Green energy strategies for sustainable development. *Energy Policy*, 34(18), 3623–3633. 10.1016/j.enpol.2005.08.003

Mikhno, I., Koval, V., Shvets, G., Garmatiuk, O., & Tamošiūnienė, R. (2021). *Green economy in sustainable development and improvement of resource efficiency*.

Mohsin, M., Iqbal, N., & Iram, R. (2023). *The Nexus Between Green Finance and Sustainable Green Economic Growth. Energy RESEARCH LETTERS, 4*. Early View.

Moore, N. (2018, July 5). *Analysing desk research*. Facet eBooks. 10.29085/9781856049825.012

Morssy, A. (2012). Green growth, innovation and sustainable development. *International Journal of Environment and Sustainability*, 1(3). 10.24102/ijes.v1i3.94

Moser, E., Prskawetz, A., & Tragler, G. (2013). Environmental regulations, abatement and economic growth. In *Green growth and sustainable development* (pp. 87–111). Springer Berlin Heidelberg. 10.1007/978-3-642-34354-4_5

Mpofu, F. Y. (2022). Green Taxes in Africa: Opportunities and challenges for environmental protection, sustainability, and the attainment of sustainable development goals. *Sustainability (Basel)*, 14(16), 10239. 10.3390/su141610239

Mubera, S., & Jules, N. (2018). Nestor Uwitonze (2018) Energy Sector Development in Sub Saharan Africa: Case Study of Rwanda. *J Fundam Renewable Energy Appl*, 8(250), 2.

Muhammad, A., Ibitomi, T., Amos, D., Idris, M., & Ahmad Ishaq, A. (2023). Comparative Analysis of sustainable finance initiatives in Asia and Africa: A Path towards Global Sustainability. *Glob. Sustain. Res*, 2(3), 33–51. 10.56556/gssr.v2i3.559

Mulders, H., van Ruitenbeek, G., Wagener, B., & Zijlstra, F. (2022). Toward more inclusive work organizations by redesigning work. *Frontiers in Rehabilitation Sciences*, 3, 861561. 10.3389/fresc.2022.86156136189072

Mutangadura, G. B. (2005). Sustainable development in Southern Africa: Progress in addressing the challenges. *Journal of Sustainable Development in Africa.*

Nassiry, D. (2018). *The role of fintech in unlocking green finance: Policy insights for developing countries* (No. 883, ADBI working paper).

Nidumolu, R., Ellison, J., Whalen, J., & Billman, E. (2014). The collaboration imperative. *Harvard Business Review*, 92(4), 76–84.24830283

Niesten, E., Jolink, A., de Sousa Jabbour, A. B. L., Chappin, M., & Lozano, R. (2017). Sustainable collaboration: The impact of governance and institutions on sustainable performance. *Journal of Cleaner Production*, 155, 1–6. 10.1016/j.jclepro.2016.12.085

O'Riordan, T., Jacobs, G., Ramanathan, J., & Bina, O. (2020). Investigating the future role of higher education in creating sustainability transitions. *Environment*, 62(4), 4–15. 10.1080/00139157.2020.1764278

Omer, A. M. (2021). Sustainable development in low carbon, cleaner and greener energies, and the environment. *Sinergi*, 25(3), 329–342. 10.22441/sinergi.2021.3.010

Osipov, V. I. (2019). Sustainable Development: Environmental Aspects. *Herald of the Russian Academy of Sciences*, 89(4), 396–404. 10.1134/S1019331619040087

Padilla, E. (2002). Intergenerational equity and sustainability. *Ecological Economics*, 41(1), 69–83. 10.1016/S0921-8009(02)00026-5

Pandey, D. J., & Ghasiya, P. R. (2023). Sustainable economic development and environment. *International Journal of Applied Research*, 9(5), 32–35. 10.22271/allresearch.2023.v9.i5a.10785

Papadimitriou, D. B., & Hannsgen, G. (2012). *Far from being a drag on growth, environmental policy can actually help drive it.* European Politics and Policy at LSE.

Pattberg, P., Biermann, F., Chan, M., & Mert, A. (2007). Partnerships for Sustainable Development: An Appraisal Framework. In *International Studies Association 48th Annual Convention.*

Peat, D. (2005). On building local partnerships. *The Health Service Journal*, 115(5941), 27.15795982

Peters, J. C., & Hertel, T. W. (2017). Achieving the Clean Power Plan 2030 CO2 target with the new normal in natural gas prices. *The Energy Journal (Cambridge, Mass.)*, 38(5), 39–66. 10.5547/01956574.38.5.jpet

Pinho, M., & Gomes, S. (2023). What Role Does Sustainable Behavior and Environmental Awareness from Civil Society Play in the Planet's SustainableTransition. *Resources*, 12(3), 42. 10.3390/resources12030042

Pociovălişteanu, D. M., Silvestre, B., Novo-Corti, I., & Răbonţu, C. I. (2016). Innovation for sustainable development. *Journal of Cleaner Production*, 100(133), 389–390. 10.1016/j.jclepro.2016.05.152

Qin, Y., & Li, J. (2023). Research on sustainable development of China's Green Enterprise Economy. *American Journal of Economics and Business Innovation*, 2(2), 86–92. 10.54536/ajebi.v2i2.1891

Ramos, T. B., & Caeiro, S. (2009). Meta-performance evaluation of sustainability indicators. *Ecological Indicators*, 10(2), 157–166. 10.1016/j.ecolind.2009.04.008

Ricci, F. (2007). Channels of transmission of environmental policy to economic growth: A survey of the theory. *Ecological Economics*, 60(4), 688–699. 10.1016/j.ecolecon.2006.11.014

Ronald, K., Callixte, K., & Tushabe, E. (2019, April). Environmental Conservation and its Influence on Tourism Development in Rwanda: Case Study of Rwanda Environment Management Authority (REMA). In *International Conference on the Future of Tourism (ICFT)* (pp. 1-23). The Open University of Tanzania.

Rosol, M., Béal, V., & Mössner, S. (2017). Greenest cities? The (post-)politics of new urban environmental regimes. *Environment & Planning A*, 49(8), 1710–1718. 10.1177/0308518X17714843

Sambou, O., Riniwati, H., & Fanani, Z. (2019). Socio-economic and Environmental Sustainability of Ecotourism Implementation: A Study in Ubud Monkey Forest-Bali, Indonesia. *Journal of Indonesian Tourism and Development Studies*, 7(3), 200–204. 10.21776/ub.jitode.2019.007.03.09

Segovia, V. M. (2010). *Transforming mindsets through education for sustainable development.*

Setiawan, H. H., & Wismayanti, Y. F. (2023). The green economy to support women's empowerment: social work approach for climate change adaptation toward sustainability development. In *Climate Change, Community Response and Resilience* (pp. 225-240). Elsevier. 10.1016/B978-0-443-18707-0.00012-6

Shaikh, Z. A. (2017). Towards sustainable development: A review of green technologies. *Trends in Renewable Energy*, 4(1), 1–14. 10.17737/tre.2018.4.1.0044

Sharma, S., & Ruud, A. (2003). On the path to sustainability: Integrating social dimensions into the research and practice of environmental management. *Business Strategy and the Environment*, 12(4), 205–214. 10.1002/bse.366

Si, T. (2022). Opportunities and Challenges for Foreign Undertakings in China's PPPs Market. *Eur. Procurement & Pub. Private Partnership L. Rev.*, 17(1), 33–43. 10.21552/epppl/2022/1/7

Simon, D. (1987). Our Common Future: Report of the World Commission onEnvironment and Development (Book Review). *Third World Planning Review*, 9(3), 285. 10.3828/twpr.9.3.x4k73r2p72w22402

Sourani, A., & Sohail, M. (2011, December). Barriers to addressing sustainable construction in public procurement strategies. [). Thomas Telford Ltd.]. *Proceedings of the Institution of Civil Engineers. Engineering Sustainability*, 164(4), 229–237. 10.1680/ensu.2011.164.4.229

Spijkers, O. (2018). Intergenerational equity and the sustainable development goals. *Sustainability (Basel)*, 10(11), 3836. 10.3390/su10113836

Stojanović, D. (2020). Sustainable economic development through green innovative banking and financing. *Economics of Sustainable Development*, 4(1), 35–44. 10.5937/ESD2001035S

Terrapon-Pfaff, J., Fink, T., Viebahn, P., & Jamea, E. M. (2019). Social impacts of large-scale solar thermal power plants: Assessment results for the NOORO I power plant in Morocco. *Renewable & Sustainable Energy Reviews*, 113, 109259. 10.1016/j.rser.2019.109259

Trotter, D. (2012). *Towards a green economy.*

Tubridy, F. (2021). The green adaptation-regeneration nexus: Innovation or business-as-usual. *European Planning Studies*, 29(2), 369–388. 10.1080/09654313.2020.1757625

Turok, I. (2013). Green Cities of Europe. *European Planning Studies*, 21(2), 281–283. 10.1080/09654313.2012.745261

United Nations General Assembly. (1987). *Report of the World commission on environment and development: Our common future. Oslo, Norway:* United Nations General Assembly, Development and International Co-operation. *Environment.*

Vassileva, A. G. (2022). Green Public-Private Partnerships (PPPs) as an Instrument for Sustainable Development. *Journal of World Economy: Transformations & Transitions*, 2(5).

Venkatesh, G. (2014). A critique of the European Green City Index. *Journal of Environmental Planning and Management*, 57(3), 317–328. 10.1080/09640568.2012.741520

Weber, O. (2023). Financial sector sustainability regulations and guidelines. In *Encyclopedia of Business and Professional Ethics* (pp. 902–907). Springer International Publishing. 10.1007/978-3-030-22767-8_40

Wen, W. (2022). Communication channels for the rule of law and environmental sustainability: Reflections from a green economy perspective. *Journal of Environmental and Public Health*, 2022, 2022. 10.1155/2022/1811896361055l7

Wolf, S., Teitge, J., Mielke, J., Schütze, F., & Jaeger, C. (2021). The European Green Deal—More than climate neutrality. *Inter Economics*, 56(2), 99–107. 10.1007/s10272-021-0963-z33840826

Xiaoyi, W. (2013). Building a Fair and Conservation-Oriented Society. *Social Sciences in China*, 34(4), 171–179. 10.1080/02529203.2013.849097

Xin, Y., & Senin, A. B. A. (2022). Features of environmental sustainability concerning environmental regulations, green innovation, and social distribution in China. *Higher Education and Oriental Studies, 2*(1).

Xing-ling, W. (2005). Construction and Realization of Green Values. *Journal of Southern Yangtze University.*

Xu, Y. (2023). Financial development, financial inclusion and natural resource management for sustainable development: Empirical evidence from Asia. *Geological Journal*, 58(9), 3288–3300. 10.1002/gj.4825

Yıldırım, S., & Yıldırım, D. Ç. (2020). Achieving sustainable development through a green economy approach. In *Advanced integrated approaches to environmental economics and policy: Emerging research and opportunities* (pp. 1–22). IGI Global. 10.4018/978-1-5225-9562-5.ch001

Yip, C. M. (2018). On the labor market consequences of environmental taxes. *Journal of Environmental Economics and Management*, 89, 136–152. 10.1016/j.jeem.2018.03.004

Yusif Asgarov, M. (2022). *"Avropa yaşıl sövdələşmə"nin əhəmiyyəti və əsas elementləri*. Scientific Work.

Zi, H. (2023). Role of green financing in developing sustainable business of e-commerce and green entrepreneurship: Implications for green recovery. *Environmental Science and Pollution Research International*, 30(42), 95525–95536. 10.1007/s11356-023-28970-337550481

Ziaul, I. M., & Shuwei, W. (2023). Environmental Sustainability: A Major Component of Sustainable Development. *International Journal of Environmental, Sustainability, and Social Science*, 4(3), 900–907. 10.38142/ijesss.v4i2.296

Zilincikova, M., & Stofkova, J. (2022). Integration Of Sustainable Development Measures in The Field of Eco-Schools. In *INTED2022 Proceedings* (pp. 7380- 7387). IATED. 10.21125/inted.2022.1863

Zorlu, P. (2018). *Transforming the financial system for delivering sustainable development: A high-level overview*. Institute for Global Environmental Strategies.

Zwolińska, K., Lorenc, S., & Pomykała, R. (2022). Sustainable development in education from students' perspective—Implementation of sustainable development in curricula. *Sustainability (Basel)*, 14(6), 3398. 10.3390/su14063398

Chapter 3
Green Transformational Leadership:
A Systematic Literature Review and Future Research Suggestion

Zeinab Afsharbakeshlo
https://orcid.org/0009-0005-7813-103X
Kharazmi University, Iran

Mohammadsadegh Omidvar
https://orcid.org/0000-0003-3304-2656
Kharazmi University, Iran

Iza Gigauri
https://orcid.org/0000-0001-6394-6416
St. Andrew the First-Called Georgian University, Georgia

ABSTRACT

Along with environmental concerns and sustainability trends, green transformational leadership (GTL) has gained the attention of scholars and practitioners. In response to the increasing environmental challenges, the need for companies to adopt responsibility strategies and management systems is growing. Therefore, this chapter presents a comprehensive and integrated review of research on GTL. A systematic literature review explores various definitions and theories of GTL, explains its behavioral, attitudinal, and performance outcomes, and illuminates the future of green transformational leadership. The conducted analysis covers all the relevant works indexed in the Scopus and Google Scholar databases throughout the period from 2013 to 2023. The research results demonstrate an emergent interest in GTL. The research contributes to leadership and sustainability literature by completing

DOI: 10.4018/979-8-3693-3439-3.ch003

the theory of green transformational leadership. It provides a practical implication to introduce green transformational leadership in organizations to respond to environmental challenges effectively.

INTRODUCTION

In the last decade, research related to environmental policy has indeed become an interesting subject. Environmental deliberation has become a commonly used concept for global environmental change, thereby challenging more organizations to pay greater attention to avail green services such as green transformational leadership (GTL) (Chen & Chang, 2013). In response to the increasing pressures coming from national and international regulations, and from society in general, corporations are gradually pushed towards the adoption of principles of both social and environmental responsibility within their strategies, structures and management systems (Giovannoni & Fabietti, 2013; Apostu & Gigauri, 2023). The value of leaders shapes the value of organizations when they are paired with policies and actions. The way in which leaders influence the values of the company is by setting out their mission, however, their actions display the organizational values (Ciulla, 2020). Besides, leaders play a critical role in enhancing environmental performance (Mittal & Dhar, 2016; Akkaya, 2020). Although the leadership literature has paid exhaustive attention to various leadership styles, there has not been a comprehensive review on green transformational leadership to delineate its aspects in detail.

Green transformational leadership is the product of transformational leadership in the field of environmental protection (Zhou et al., 2018). Based on previous theories, different degrees of cultural endorsement can lead to different kinds of transformational leadership (Muralidharan & Pathak, 2018). Since the idea of green transformational leadership is consistent with the need for social green development, it can also be seen as a kind of culturally endorsed transformational leadership (Zhou et al., 2018). If a transformational leader happens to have green values, we have reason to expect that he/she will exert an influence on his/her subordinates' green behaviors (Robertson & Barling, 2013). A green transformational leader can raise subordinates' concerns about environmental issues by establishing good relations with them and then convey them his/her own green values (Wang et al., 2018). Moreover, green transformational leadership plays a significant role in the social, economic and environmental traits, which consist of sustainability (Afzal et al., 2017).

There is a need for a comprehensive and integrated review of research on GTL for two main reasons. First, despite the increasing academic interest in green transformational leadership, there is still a lack of coherence and clarity in this field. While it has been more than a decade for GTL, this research field is fragmented across disciplines. Second, with a large body of empirical studies consistently demonstrating significant relationships between GTL and outcomes, it is essential to conduct a systematic literature review on green transformational leadership. Based on the given reasons, this paper answers the following research questions through the review process.

1- How is green transformational leadership understood and defined within the leadership literature?
2- How is green transformational leadership measured?
3- What are the outcomes of green transformational leadership and how it can be influenced?
4- What is the future of GTL?

To achieve its aims, this research presents a comprehensive and integrated review of GTL. A systematic literature review explores various definitions and theories of GTL, explains its behavioral, attitudinal, and performance outcomes, and illuminates the future of GTL. The research results demonstrate an increasing attention towards GTL. Moreover, an exhaustive theoretical background of the concept is established. Facilitators to implement green transformational leadership are classified and moderators of GTL are categorized. The research contributes to the field of leadership and sustainability by completing the theory of green transformational leadership and providing practical implications of introducing GTL in organizations as a response to environmental challenges.

MATERIALS AND METHODS

In order to answer the research questions, we conducted a systematic literature review. Systematic reviews aim to identify all research addressing a specific question so that they give a balanced and unbiased summary of the literature (Nightingale, 2009). In the beginning, the researchers individually extracted information from articles for cross-checking. After reviewing a few articles together, we reached an agreement on what to extract from the articles. Then, the researchers split up the work and maintained frequent communication during the data extraction process. Articles that were hard to decide on were discussed among the researchers (Xiao & Watson, 2019). We searched Google Scholar and Scopus, two frequently used databases by researchers in various fields. The Scopus database was selected as a principal search system because it is considered to be the largest database of peer-reviewed literature. Moreover, Scopus includes more journals covering the areas of business and management than Google Scholar thus decreasing the risk of missing documents for this study (Piwowar-Sulej & Iqbal, 2023). Besides, it has been suggested that Google Scholar should be considered as supplementary to the principle systems since it might still provide great benefits (Gusenbauer & Haddaway, 2020). The search strategy for this literature review was aiming to answer four research questions (Figure 1).

Figure 1. Article selection process

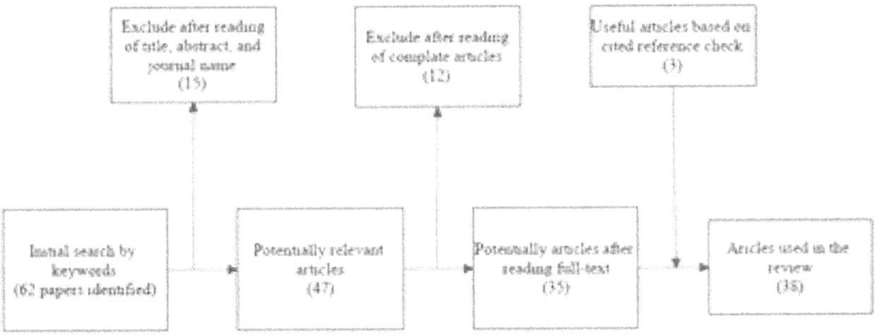

Source: Authors

The review process starts with the identification of articles. To increase inclusivity, we did not specify a fixed period. The inclusion and exclusion criteria were established before undertaking the literature search. For inclusion criteria, we only considered articles that have the word "green transformational leadership" in the title. Since it is a review on this topic, the title has to have the word. Therefore, we started the process by including studies that contained the keyword 'green transformational leadership'. As can be seen in Figure 1, 62 articles were identified in this step. Second, we followed a systematic process to clean these articles. Consequently, we limited our database by assessing a title, abstract and journal name to ensure that only rigorous and high-quality studies were incorporated into our review. We realized that 15 articles were irrelevant to this review and therefore they were excluded from the database and 47 articles were sent for the next revision. Then, we performed the content analysis and compared results, making a final list of documents. We included only those papers that claimed or provided evidence on green transformational leadership to establish whether a paper was in line with the aims of the current study. After this step, 35 articles constituted the final sample. Since we tried to ensure that relevant literature had not been overlooked in the previous search, we examined references associated with each of these articles. Accordingly, 3 new articles were found to be related to this review and therefore we include them in the database. As a result, our database consisted of 38 articles.

The conducted analysis covers the period from 2013 to 2023 since that year featured the publication of the first peer-reviewed green transformational leadership scale by Chen and Chan (2013) was published. Because of the interdisciplinary character of leadership, a variety of publications have embraced green transformational leadership research (Table 1). From the beginning, GTL articles have been published in high-impact journals including Sustainability, Business Ethics and Journal of Cleaner Production.

Table 1. Journals publishing GTL research

Publication	Count of No
Academic Journal of Interdisciplinary Studies	1
Acta Psychologica Sinica	1
Agriculture	1
Bulletin of Business and Economics	1
Business Ethic	1
Business Strategy and the Environment	2
conference	1
Consumer Behavior in Tourism and Hospitality	1
corporate social responsibility and environmental management	1
Economic Research	1
European Journal of Business and Management Research	1
Frontiers in Psychology	5
International journal of environmental research and public health	1
International Journal of Hospitality Management	1
International Journal of Management Excellence	1
IOER International Multidisciplinary Research Journal	1
Journal of Cleaner Production	1
Journal of Hospitality and Tourism Insights	1
Journal of Innovation & Knowledge	1
Journal on Innovation and Sustainability	1
Management	1
PalArch's Journal of Archaeology of Egypt/Egyptology	1
Research in Business & Social Science	1
Sustainability	6
Technological Forecasting & Social Change	2
Technology Analysis & Strategic Management	1

continued on following page

Table 1. Continued

Publication	Count of No
Tourism Management	1
Grand Total	38

Source: Authors

FINDINGS

As can be seen in Figure 2, the number of articles on GTL has increased annually, therefore it is expected that this trend will continue for the next few years because of an increased interest in sustainability subjects. However, for 2023, the number of articles is decreasing. This data illustrates that the interest in GTL has been growing every year until 2023 suggesting the need of exploring new research themes, research directions and research gaps.

Figure 2. Green transformational leadership publications per year

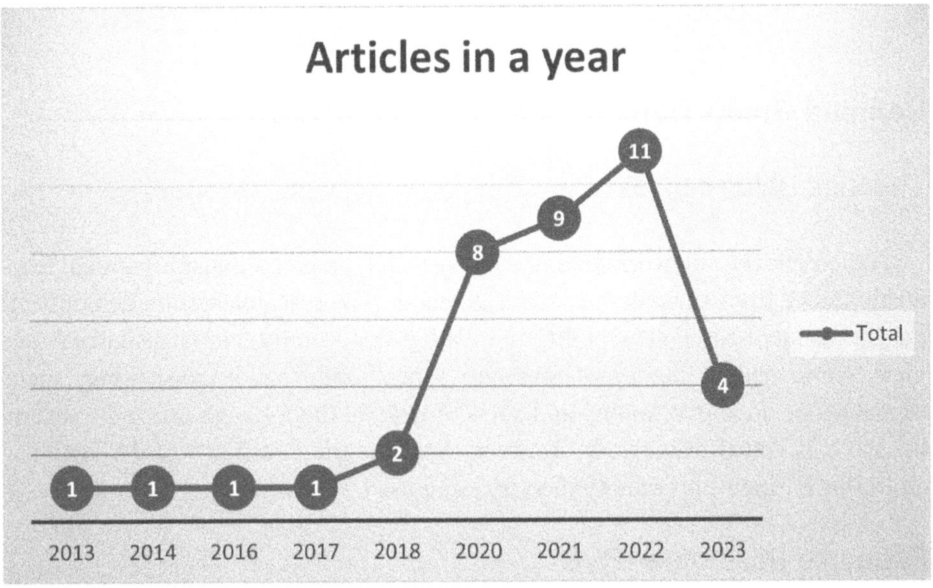

Source: Authors own research results

To find out the most interested country in GTL, a chart was prepared that displays countries (Figure 3). China and Pakistan have the greatest number of published articles on GTL.

Figure 3. Countries represented in the studies on GTL

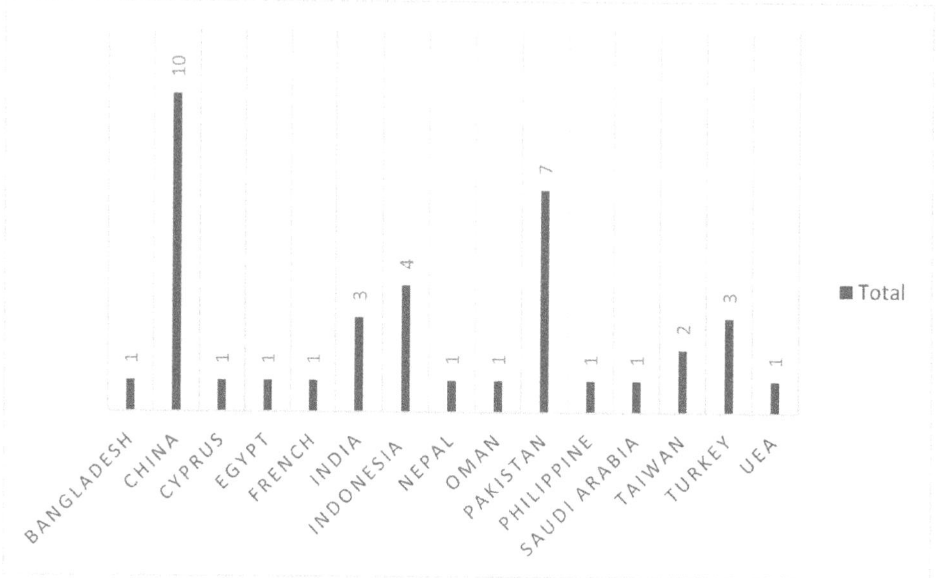

Source: Authors own research results

Defining Green Transformational Leadership

Theories Utilized in GTL

A theoretical framework for empirical research on green transformational leadership draws from various theoretical domains. The research results demonstrate that the resource-based view, ability-motivation-opportunity, natural resource-based view, componential theory of creativity, social information processing, social exchange, positive psychology and social cognitive theory were utilized to examine the conceptual framework. Between these theories, resource-based view and ability-motivation-opportunity theories were used predominantly.

Resource Base View (RVB)

Based on Barney, (1991) definition of RVB, a firm possesses a collection of resources that may lead the firm to enhance its competitive advantage, depending on the characteristics of resources (Barney, 1991). The central idea of RBV is that companies should develop integrated resources that are unique, valuable, rare, and imitable (Barney, 1991), to remain invincible in the violent competition (Chen &

Yan, 2022). Moreover, it was proposed that performance and competitive advantage are grounded upon how firms inspired their valuable strategic resources that are imperative, occasional, and problematic to replicate in the markets by the rivals (Sun et al., 2022). The implementation of green practices can be applied through RBV. RBV provides a critical analysis of resources to top management that aids in making strategies for the execution of green practices. Firms should use leadership and intellectual behavior as their competitive edge and make it beneficial for environment and economic performance through green transformational leadership for sustainable business practices (Al-Serhan, 2020).

Ability-Motivation-Opportunity Theory

Researchers are increasingly adopting what is known as the AMO framework. AMO theory is a combination of an employee's Ability (A), Motivation (M) and Opportunities (O) and it can provide a predictive measure of individual or aggregated performance (P) (Paauwe, 2009). According to AMO theory the abilities of employees access through recruitment or selection then training or development which is enriched by opportunities provided to employees by empowerment or teamwork which help in learning or improvement and motivation of employees boosted by rewards, compensations or incentives offered by organization on achieving the goals (Gerhart, 2005). AMO theory helped in the implication of green practices on employee behavior and job attitude for sustainable business practices. As AMO theory focuses on the link among human resources, innovation, and performance i.e. leaders motivate employees to seek opportunities and enhance their performance (Al-Serhan, 2020).

Natural Resource-Based View Theory (NRVB)

The natural resource-based view (NRBV) integrates the constraints imposed by the natural environment to conceptualize resources and it has three main focus groups: pollution prevention, product stewardship and sustainable development (Hart, 1995). Pollution prevention seeks to promote environmental sustainability whilst simultaneously cutting costs and maximizing efficiency throughout internal operations. Product stewardship extends environmental sustainability towards external operations, seeking conservation, avoidance of harmful substances and recyclability from a lifecycle perspective. Sustainable development promotes the consideration of economic, environmental and social issues on a global scale (McDougall et al., 2019). The NRBV framework aims to explain the connection between firms' resources, capabilities, and the natural environment. The NRBV is considered an important theory in the field of strategic management to examine technological and product innovation to combat environmental constraints (Begum et al., 2022).

Social Information Processing Theory

Social information processing theory, also known as SIP, is a psychological and sociological theory. This theory explores how individuals make decisions and form attitudes in a social context, often focusing on the workplace. It suggests that people rely heavily on the social information available to them in their environments, including input from colleagues and peers, to shape their attitudes, behaviors, and perceptions (Salancik & Pfeffer, 1978).

Social Exchange Theory

Social exchange theory studies the social behavior in the interaction of two parties that implement a cost-benefit analysis to determine risks and benefits. According to social exchange theory, relationships evolve over time into trusting, loyal, and mutual commitments (Cropanzano & Mitchell, 2005). Social exchange theory indicates that employees' positive job-related attitude depends on the company's trust, approval, and management toward them (Chen & Yan, 2022). It is imperative to note that the exchange timing plays a significant role in forming the relations between parties. Leaders and members start their relationship journey by testing one another in terms of obligations, and the quality of relations depends upon the reciprocity of commitments. Suffice it to say that positive psychological exchanges result in the exchange of positive psychological resources. Similarly, negative psychological exchanges result in the exchange of harmful psychological resources, which impact resulting relationships (Ahmad et al., 2023).

Positive Psychology

Positive psychology is the study of the conditions and processes that contribute to the flourishing or optimal functioning of people, groups, and institutions (Gable & Haidt, 2005). The major idea of positive psychology lay in the fact that positive personal characteristics, happiness, interest, and expectation were expected to improve the quality of individuals' lives (Sin & Lyubomirsky, 2009). Through positive psychology two new concepts related to green transformational leadership have been introduced: green organizational pride and green psychological capital (Chen & Yan, 2022).

Social Cognitive Theory

Social cognitive theory is a psychological perspective on human functioning that emphasizes the critical role played by the social environment on motivation, learning, and self-regulation (Schunk & DiBenedetto, 2020). The theory proposes that a variety of person, environmental, and behavioral variables can influence the pro-environmental behavior process (Sawitri et al., 2015) therefore, it is widely used to explain green concepts like GTL (Chen & Yan, 2022).

The preceding theories establish a critical foundation for the conceptualization and application of GTL. These primary sources not only delineate the underlying principles that inform GTL but also contextualize its development within the academic research. By utilizing these foundational theories, we can better comprehend the nuanced relationships and intersections that GTL shares with other established frameworks. Drawing upon these theories as guiding pillars, we are now poised to embark on a comprehensive exploration of GTL. In the next section, we will meticulously define GTL, intricately delineate its core principles, and systematically analyze its integrative role and profound impact within the wider field. Through this comprehensive investigation, we aim to provide a thorough understanding of GTL's definition.

Defining GTL

Global sustainability concerns demand a new kind of leadership that goes beyond self-interest to disperse leadership chances inside the company. Transformational leaders guide employees through motivation and inspiration in order to reach new perspectives (Avolio et al., 1999). Green transformational leadership was defined first in 2013 by Chen and Chang (2013). They have used transformational leadership aspects to delineate a new definition for GTL as they defined it as "behaviors of leaders who motivate followers to achieve environmental goals and inspire followers to perform beyond expected levels of environmental performance" (Chen & Chang, 2013). This type of green leadership encourages staff to prioritize corporate objectives over personal ones, it directs employees in all circumstances, offers assistance when needed, and instills a passion to come up with creative environmental ideas (Mittal & Dhar, 2016). Transformational leadership has four dimensions, "intellectual stimulation, individualized consideration, charisma, and inspirational motivation" (Bass, 1995). The charismatic ability of the transformational leader aids in the creation of inspirational ideas among the followers, which results in garnering their respect and subsequently their loyalty. The transformative leader may foster a sense of group accountability in their followers with the aid of his or her charismatic influence. Individualized consideration enables the transformational leader to develop a sense of community in their followers, which fosters the growth of concern for one another. Additionally, a transformational leader can develop a vision for the organization with the use of inspirational motivation. They can also assist their followers by illuminating the process by which the vision can be brought to life. Finally, the transformational leader can inspire followers' cognitive capacities through their capacity for intellectual stimulation, which in turn helps them become more creative (Gong et al., 2009).

Singh et al. (2020) described green transformational leadership (GTL) as a style of leadership in which the main objective is to inspire and motivate the workforce while also addressing their developmental needs in order to help the firm accomplish its environmental objectives. GTL motivates employees to acquire new knowledge and gets them involved and engaged in green processes and product innovation (Singh et al., 2020). Green transformational leaders are likely to lead their followers and make them self-motivated to achieve the organization's goal in a green way that improves their sustainability (Shah et al., 2020). Green transformational leadership includes four aspects: green idealized influence, green inspirational motivation, green intellectual stimulation, and green individualized consideration (Robertson, 2018). First, in showing idealized influence, leaders act as role models of environmental behavior and empower followers to adopt this kind of conduct. They also develop an environmental vision that inspires followers. Through their actions, green leaders demonstrate a vision that establishes high standards, presenting the company as a trustworthy institution. Second, leaders who demonstrate motivational leadership inspire followers by using their enthusiasm and idealistic drive to overcome emotional and physical obstacles (Robertson & Barling, 2017). By engaging in pro-environmental actions, they inspire them to go beyond what is advantageous for themselves (Robertson, 2018). Thirdly, intellectually stimulating leaders encourage followers to think about environmental issues, find innovative solutions, and challenge their company's environmental policies. Finally, leaders who exhibit individualized concern, establish strong bonds with workers to support environmental principles, and express sympathy and compassion for the well-being of followers. Additionally, they support people in developing their potential and skills (Robertson, 2018).

Measuring GTL

There is one green transformational leadership measurement in the body of existing literature. Chen and Chang (2013) proposed a green transformational leader based on previous literature on transformational leadership. They referred to Bass (1998) and Gardner and Avolio (1998) to explain the "behaviors of leaders who motivate followers to achieve environmental goals and inspire followers to perform beyond expected levels of environmental performance". In order to develop the measurement scale, they got help from the measurement of Podsakoff et al. (1996) for transformational leadership, and the final scale consists of six components:

1. The leader of the green product development project inspires the project members with environmental plans.
2. The leader of the green product development project provides a clear environmental vision for the project members to follow.
3. The leader of the green product development project gets the project members to work together for the same environmental goals.
4. The leader of the green product development project encourages the project members to achieve the environmental goals.
5. The leader of the green product development project acts by considering the environmental beliefs of the project members.
6. The leader of the green product development project stimulates the project members to think about green ideas.

The Theoretical Map of Green Transformational Leadership

Utilizing insights gleaned from a thorough literature analysis, the theoretical map of GTL has been meticulously crafted to categorize elements into antecedents, mediators, moderators, and outcomes (Figure 4). Each component was methodically assigned to its respective category, driven by its perceived significance and role within the GTL framework. This deliberate categorization aims to provide a structured and coherent representation of the intricate dynamics inherent to GTL processes. In the forthcoming sections, we will undertake a comprehensive exploration of each category, elucidating their respective roles and contributions within the GTL paradigm. Through this detailed examination, we will delve into the nuanced relationships and interactions between antecedents, mediators, moderators, and outcomes, drawing upon a rich body of literature and empirical research on GTL. By synthesizing these insights, we endeavor to offer a deeper understanding of the multifaceted complexities of GTL and its implications for various stakeholders and societal contexts.

Figure 4. Theoretical map of GTL

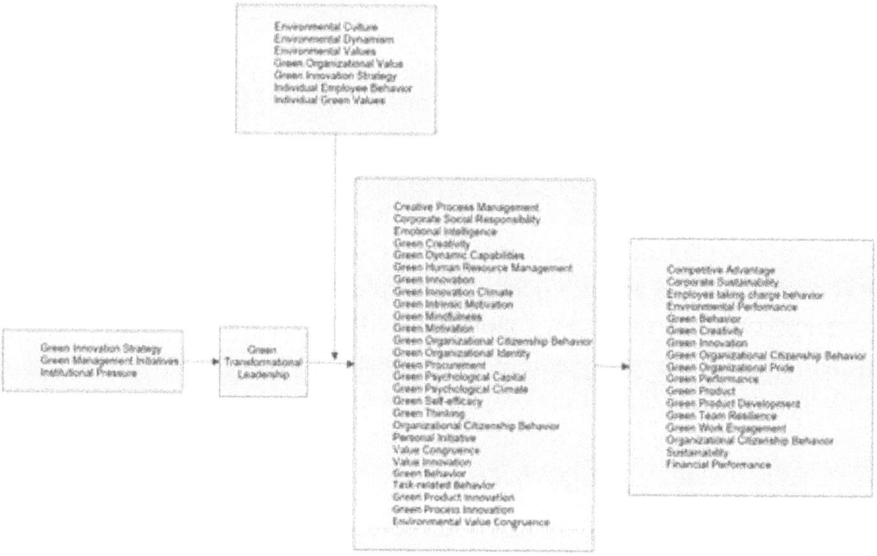

Source: Authors

Antecedent of GTL

Antecedents of leader behavior have been investigated comprehensively previously. Based on the leadership process model by Tuncdogan et al. (2017), an individual's character is the predictor of leader behavior as individual differences are split into physiological and psychological differences and each of them has its own sub-unit group (Tuncdogan et al., 2017). Another study classified the antecedent of transformational leadership into three groups: school leaders' internal qualities, organizational factors and leaders' colleagues 'characteristics. In the middle level, leaders' self-efficacy, values, emotional intelligence and cognitive capacities are the predictors of transformational leadership (Sun et al., 2017). Although there has been a notable number of articles that investigate green transformational leadership outcomes, there are only two articles that study antecedents of GTL.

Zhou et al. (2021) have introduced institutional pressure as an antecedent of GTL. Leaders are the ones who hold ultimate responsibility and not employees for the conduct of the company. Therefore, the response to institutional pressures will be mainly borne by leaders (Zhou et al., 2021). Previous studies indicated that institutional pressure enhances firms' seeking legitimacy (Qi et al., 2021). Because leaders are the first receivers of external pressure and are the main drivers to respond to these pressures. They are the ones who are mostly influenced by external pressures and are the members of a company to take actions to transform the company into a particular direction, such as inspiring greater green behaviors (Zhou et al., 2021).

Based on social information processing theory, leaders adopt a leadership style that is consistent with the strategies and environment of the company. Green HR policies lead managers to a suitable leadership style that can implement organizational strategies (Mansoor et al., 2021). Green management initiatives guide top managers to fulfill the green strategies of the organization. It provides direction, skills, knowledge, and necessary resources for attaining the objective of environmental care (Daily and Huang, 2001). Policies and strategies of the organization are implemented through their managers. Therefore, green HR practices, coupled with a green strategic focus, would become the motivating factor for managers to exhibit a green transformational leadership style (Mansoor et al., 2021).

Outcomes of GTL

Over the past decade, the majority of studies on GTL have focused on performance outcomes, while attitudinal and behavioral outcomes have seen little attention among scholars. Table. 2 displays GTL outcomes in three groups: Behavioral outcomes, attitudinal outcomes and Performance outcomes.

Table 2. GTL outcomes

Behavioral outcomes	**Attitudinal outcomes**	**Performance outcomes**
Green Behavior	Green creativity	Competitive advantage
Employee taking charge behavior	Green innovation	Corporate sustainability
Green organizational citizenship behavior	Green organizational pride	Environmental performance
Organizational Citizenship Behavior		Green performance
		Green product
		Green product development
		Green team resilience
		Green work engagement
		Sustainability
		Financial Performance

Source: Authors based on research results

Behavioral Outcomes

Research has been proven that green behavior (Agrawal & Pradhan, 2023; Farrukh et al., 2022; Jian et al., 2020; Wang et al., 2018), an employee taking charge behavior (Du & Yan, 2022), green OCB (Nurwahdah & Muafi, 2022) and OCB (Srour et al., 2020) are the behavioral outcomes for GTL. Research findings point out that GTL has a positive impact on given outcomes.

Attitudinal Outcomes

In this group, most of the studies focused on green creativity. The positive relationship between GTL and green creativity has been investigated multiple times (Al-Ghazali et al., 2022; Maitlo et al., 2022; Mansoor et al., 2021; Mittal & Dhar, 2016; Öğretmenoğlu et al., 2022; Sidney et al., 2022; Li et al., 2020; Zhang et al., 2020). Moreover, green innovation (Ahmad et al., 2022; Begum et al., 2022) and green organizational pride (Chen & Yan, 2022) were named as another outcome for GTL as their positive relationship has been proven.

Performance Outcomes

Environmental issues evoke customers to pressure businesses to adopt green policies, therefore performance outcomes have gained much attention among businesses and scholars. As for the performance level, competitive advantage (Suparna et al., 2021), corporate sustainability (Kurniasih & Nawangsari, 2020; Widisatria & Nawangsari, 2021), sustainability (Al-Serhan, 2020; Shah et al., 2020), environmental performance (Huelgas & Arellano, 2021; Singh et al., 2020; Perez et al., 2023; Rehman & Yaqub, 2021; Sobaih et al., 2022; Sun et al., 2022; Tian et al., 2023), financial performance (Özgül & Zehir, 2023) and green performance (Chen et al., 2014; Tosun et al., 2022; Zafar et al., 2017) were proved to be the outcomes for GTL. Previous studies also investigated the influence of GTL on product-related factors and identified that green products (Zhou et al., 2021) and green product development (Chen & Chang, 2013; Zhou et al., 2018) are positively influenced by GTL. In the team-level outcomes, it has been proved that GTL has a positive effect on green team resilience and green work engagement (Çop et al., 2020).

Mediator of GTL

Through previous studies, various parameters have been investigated as a mediator. According to Table 3, we split these factors into two groups: Climate and organizational-center mediator, Attitudinal and behavioral-center mediator. As can be seen in Table 3, scholars paid greater attention to behavioral and attitudinal factors.

Table 3. Mediator of GTL

Climate and organizational mediator	Behavioral and attitudinal mediator
Creative process engagement	Corporate Social Responsibility
Green Human Resource Manager	Emotional intelligence
Green innovation climate	Green creativity
Green process engagement	Green dynamic capabilities
Green procurement	Green intrinsic motivation
Green psychological capital	Green innovation
Green psychological climate	Green self-efficacy
Value congruence	Green mindfulness
Value innovation	Green motivation
Environmental Value Congruence	Green organizational citizenship behavior
	Green organizational identity
	Green thinking
	Organizational citizenship behavior
	Personal initiative
	Task-related Behavior
	Green Product Innovation
	Green Process Innovation

Source: Authors based on research results

Climate and Organizational-Center Mediator

In this group, green organizational identity (Mittal & Dhar, 2016), creative process engagement (Begum et al., 2022; Zhang et al., 2020), green dynamic capabilities (Ahmad et al., 2022), green human resource management (Farrukh et al., 2022; Huelgas & Arellano, 2021; Singh et al., 2020; Sidney et al., 2022; Sun et al., 2022), green process engagement (Sidney et al., 2022) and green procurement (Shah et al., 2020) were used as a mediator for GTL. Organizational climate represents the firm's characteristics such as attitudes, behaviors, and feelings that exist independently irrespective of the perceptions and understandings of the members of the organization (Ekvall, 1996), therefore green innovation climate (Maitlo et al., 2022) and green psychological climate (Zhou et al., 2018) have been investigated in previous researches. Since employees' values are affected by the environment around them (e.g., the leadership style), which in turn, affects their behavior (Stern et al., 1999), value congruence (Wang et al., 2018), environmental value congruence (Agrawal & Pradhan, 2023) and value innovation (Suparna et al., 2021) were studied as a mediator for GTL. Psychological capital refers to a vital and positive mental state associated with better performance or personal well-being. Chen and Yan (2022) introduced a new concept, green psychological climate, and studied it as a mediator for GTL (Chen & Yan, 2022).

Attitudinal and Behavioral-Center Mediator

As for individual and employee-center mediators, the number of studies is more than the previous group, therefore various parameters were investigated as a mediator of GTL. Behaviors like CSR (Tosun et al., 2022), personal initiative (Du & Yan, 2022), green intrinsic motivation (Li et al., 2020), green organizational citizenship behavior (Öğretmenoğlu et al., 2022) and organizational citizenship behavior (Widisatria & Nawangsari, 2021) were used as a mediator. As for attitudinal parameter, emotional intelligence (Nurwahdah & Muafi, 2022), green creativity (Chen & Chang, 2013), green innovation (Al-Serhan, 2020; Singh et al., 2020; Sun et al., 2022; Zhou et al., 2021), green self-efficacy and green mindfulness (Chen et al., 2014; Zafar et al., 2017), green motivation (Kurniasih & Nawangsari, 2020) and green thinking (Begum et al., 2022) were analyzed in previous studies.

Moderator of GTL

For moderators, we categorized them into three groups: individual level, organizational level and environmental level (Table 4). As can be seen in the Table, all groups have been paid the same attention. Due to the nature of sustainability and environmentally friendly green transformational leadership, the environmental level is at the center of more research.

Table 4. Moderator of GTL

Individual level	**Organizational level**	**Environmental level**
Individual green values	Green organizational identity	Environmental culture
Individual employee behavior	Green innovation strategy	Environmental dynamism
		Environmental values

Source: Authors based on research results

Individual Level

Contemporary literature has underscored the importance of individual values in explaining individual attitudes and behaviors (Zhou et al., 2018) and these values should be satisfied, trained and socially entitled to their responsibilities. Therefore, Rehman and Yaqub (2021) conducted a study that used individual employee behavior as a moderator (Rehman & Yaqub, 2021). Moreover, Zhou et al. (2018) considered individual green values as a moderator of their study (Zhou et al., 2018). At the organizational level, green innovation strategy (Zhang et al., 2020) and green organizational identity (Du & Yan, 2022) were used as a moderator. Self-determination theory suggests that individuals have an extrinsic motivation to assimilate and integrate external values, which can be progressive in accordance with the degree of employee autonomy (Ryan & Deci, 2000). Consequently, green organizational identity and green innovation strategy enhance the influence of green transformational leadership. According to social cognitive theory, the employees' environmental behavior can be gradually influenced by external factors (Bandura, 1986). Therefore, environmental culture (Chen & Yan, 2022), environmental dynamism (Ahmad et al., 2022) and environmental values (Sun et al., 2022) were used as moderators in the GTL research.

DISCUSSION AND FUTURE RESEARCH

This chapter aimed to advance the field of green transformational leadership research by doing a thorough analysis of the literature on the subject from 2013 to 2023. We designed a conceptual framework and assessed the research's methodological quality after reviewing the literature. Based on the conducted research the key conclusions are highlighted and future study directions are suggested for the field of green transformational leadership development.

First of all, through reviewing the literature, we found that there is ambiguity in the definition of GTL. Chen and Chang (2013) stated that GTL motivates employees to perform beyond their tasks at the environmental level. However, Singh et al. (2020) described it as a style of leadership that motivates followers in order to help a firm accomplish its environmental goals. From the first definition, it can be realized that pro-organizational behaviors are the result of GTL, whereas the second definition states that satisfying current environmental goals is the outcome. Therefore, it is crucial for researchers to investigate this concept more precisely to delineate its objectives. For a better explanation, it is suggested to utilize the sustainable leadership definition since they share similar aims. Sustainable leadership means having long-term decision-making ability, promoting systematic innovation, cultivating a loyal staff team, and providing high-quality products, services and solutions. Its purpose is to balance the relationship between people, profits and the earth, and promote the sustainability of the enterprise through corresponding management practices (Avery, 2005).

Another important observation from the review is that many studies were performed in China and Pakistan. Therefore, their result can be generalized to other parts of the world. Values, ethics and culture are significant determinants of sustainable behavior (Yin et al., 2018; Gigauri et al., 2023). It has been proved that national culture, tradition and value have a significant impact on the green behavior of people across different countries (Halder et al., 2020). In addition, previous studies proved that religiosity influences green behavior, namely green purchases (Alotaibi & Abbas, 2023; Wang et al., 2020). Hence, there is a need to conduct more research in other parts of the world with different cultures and religious to have more general results. It is suggested to conduct more research in piloted countries like Iran, Japan or the United States of America since these countries are considered as the most polluted areas in the world.

Furthermore, regarding theoretical venues, it could also be interesting to look at a potential 'dark sides' of GTL. Since leaders motivate followers to engage in pro-organizational behavior, its aims might be misunderstood wrongly. It is true that the intention of GTL is good but the comprehension might be different. Effelsberg et al. (2014) proved that transformational leadership can contribute to unethical pro-organizational behavior since followers are motivated to perform beyond their tasks to help their firm and supervisor. We propose that future studies should investigate the potential negative effect of GTL on follower's behavior through qualitative or quantitative research. Since business literature has focused only on positive aspects of GTL and scholars have never considered a negative outcome from this leadership style, a qualitative study will better capture a comprehensive insight.

Finally, through the theoretical framework that obtained from the systematic literature review in this paper, we realized that there is a shortage of research on the antecedent of GTL. The main concern of previous research was the outcome of GTL and only three parameters were introduced as influencers of GTL. Environmental and genetic factors have been explored as antecedents of leadership style. Previous studies investigated environmental factors that influence GTL (Mansoor et al., 2021; Sidney et al., 2022; Zhou et al., 2021), whereas there is not any investigation on genetic factors and individual characteristics. It has been stated that leader traits including physiological, psychological and background have a significant impact on leader behaviors and leadership styles (Tuncdogan et al., 2017). In another study, it was proved that the character of a leader is important according to leaders and their subordinates (Grahek et al., 2010). Therefore, there is a need to investigate the effect of individual characteristics on GTL to realize how different individuals behave towards GTL.

CONCLUSION

In order to provide answers to the research questions regarding green transformational leadership, the goal of this article was to conduct a thorough literature review. We identified 38 papers published in journals with different fields. A systematic literature review was applied to investigate possible shortages in the field of GTL. We started the review process by presenting different definitions of GTL. The measurement scale was brought and a theoretical map of GTL has been designed offering scholars an overview of what has been studied thus far. Finally, we discussed the limitations of previous studies and provided some suggestions for future research.

The research results have both theoretical and managerial implications. Theoretically, it completes the concept of GTL and suggests future study directions in this important field. In addition, companies can facilitate the development of leaders based on the findings of this research. Enhancing green transformational leadership can improve sustainability performance and influence green creativity. In pursuit of the green agenda, companies can meet stakeholders' demand and increase competitiveness while reducing negative environmental footprints or industrial waste. Green strategies through GTL expand the market capabilities of businesses. Furthermore, GTL promotes the green behavior among employees, and strengthens green innovation and green product development, leading to sustainable transformation of organizations.

REFERENCES

Afzal, F., Lim, B., & Prasad, D. (2017). An investigation of corporate approaches to sustainability in the construction industry. *Procedia Engineering*, 180, 202–210. 10.1016/j.proeng.2017.04.179

Agrawal, S., & Pradhan, S. (2023). Employee green behavior in hotels: The role of green human resource management, green transformational leadership and value congruence. *Consumer Behavior in Tourism and Hospitality*, 18(2), 241–255. 10.1108/CBTH-11-2022-0191

Ahmad, B., Shafique, I., Qammar, A., Ercek, M., & Kalyar, M. N. (2022). Prompting green product and process innovation: Examining the effects of green transformational leadership and dynamic capabilities. *Technology Analysis and Strategic Management*.

Ahmad, R., Nawaz, M. R., Ishaq, M. I., Khan, M. M., & Hafiz, A. A. (2023). Social exchange theory: Systematic review and future directions. *Frontiers in Psychology*, 13, 1015921. 10.3389/fpsyg.2022.101592136710813

Akkaya, B. (2020). Review of leadership styles in perspective of dynamic capabilities: An empirical research on managers in manufacturing firms. *Yönetim Bilimleri Dergisi*, 18(36), 389–407. 10.35408/comuybd.681427

Al-Ghazali, B. M., Gelaidan, H. M., Shah, S. H. A., & Amjad, R. (2022). Green transformational leadership and green creativity? The mediating role of green thinking and green organizational identity in SMEs. *Frontiers in Psychology*, 977998, 977998. 10.3389/fpsyg.2022.97799836211888

Al-Serhan, A.F. (2020). Role of Green Transformational Leadership in Sustainable Business Development: Mediating Effect of Green Technology Innovation. *PalArch's Journal of Archaeology of Egypt/Egyptology,* 15178–15194.

Alotaibi, A., & Abbas, A. (2023). Islamic religiosity and green purchase intention: A perspective of food selection in millennials. *Journal of Islamic Marketing*, 14(9), 2323–2342. 10.1108/JIMA-06-2021-0189

Apostu, S. A., & Gigauri, I. (2023). Mapping the Link Between Human Resource Management and Sustainability: The Pathway to Sustainable Competitiveness. In *Reshaping Performance Management for Sustainable Development*, 31-59. 10.1108/S2051-663020230000008003

Avery, G. (2005). *Leadership for Sustainable Futures*. Edward Elgar. 10.4337/9781845425494

Avolio, B. J., Bass, B. M., & Jung, D. I. (1999). Re-examining the components of transformational and transactional leadership using the Multifactor Leadership. *Journal of Occupational and Organizational Psychology*, 72(4), 441–462. 10.1348/096317999166789

Bandura, A. (1986). *Social foundations of thought and action*. APA.

Barney, J. (1991). Firm Resources and Sustained Competitive Advantage. *Journal of Management*, 17(1), 99–120. 10.1177/014920639101700108

Bass, B. M. (1995). *Leadership and Performance Beyond Expectations*. Free Press.

Bass, B. M. (1998). *Transformational leadership: Industrial, military, and educational impact*. Erlbaum.

Begum, S., Ashfaq, M., Xia, E., & Awan, U. (2022). Does green transformational leadership lead to green innovation? The role of green thinking and creative process engagement. *Business Strategy and the Environment*, 31(1), 580–597. 10.1002/bse.2911

Chen, Y.-S., & Chang, C.-H. (2013). The Determinants of Green Product Development Performance: Green Dynamic Capabilities, Green Transformational Leadership, and Green Creativity. *Business Ethics (Oxford, England)*, 107–119.

Chen, Y.-S., Chang, C.-H., & Lin, Y.-H. (2014). Green Transformational Leadership and Green Performance: The Mediation Effects of Green Mindfulness and Green Self-Efficacy. *Sustainability (Basel)*, 6(10), 6604–6621. 10.3390/su6106604

Chen, Y.-S., & Yan, X. (2022). The small and medium enterprises' green human resource management and green transformational leadership: A sustainable moderated-mediation practice. *Corporate Social Responsibility and Environmental Management*, 29(5), 1–16. 10.1002/csr.2273

Ciulla, J. B. (2020). The Importance of Leadership in Shaping Business Values. In *Corporate Ethics and Corporate Governance* (pp. 67–77). Springer Berlin Heidelberg New York.

Çop, S., Olorunsola, V. O., & Alola, U. V. (2020). Achieving environmental sustainability through green transformational leadership policy: Can green team resilience help? *Business Strategy and the Environment*, •••, 1–12.

Cropanzano, R., & Mitchell, M. S. (2005). Social Exchange Theory: An Interdisciplinary Review. *Journal of Management*, 31(6), 874–900. 10.1177/0149206305279602

Daily, B. F., & Huang, S. (2001). Achieving sustainability through attention to human resource factors in environmental management. *International Journal of Operations & Production Management*, 21(12), 1539–1552. 10.1108/01443570110410892

Du, Y., & Yan, M. (2022). Green Transformational Leadership and Employees' Taking Charge Behavior: The Mediating Role of Personal Initiative and the Moderating Role of Green Organizational Identity. *International Journal of Environmental Research and Public Health*, 19(7), 4172. 10.3390/ijerph1907417235409857

Effelsberg, D., Solga, M., & Gurt, J. (2014). Transformational Leadership and Follower's Unethical Behavior for the Benefit of the Company: A Two-Study Investigation. *Journal of Business Ethics*, 120(1), 81–93. 10.1007/s10551-013-1644-z

Ekvall, G. (1996). Organizational climate for creativity and innovation. *European Journal of Work and Organizational Psychology*, 5(1), 105–123. 10.1080/13594329608414845

Farrukh, M., Ansari, N., Raza, A., Wu, Y., & Wang, H. (2022). Fostering employee's pro-environmental behavior through green transformational leadership, green human resource management and environmental knowledge. *Technological Forecasting and Social Change*, 179, 121643. 10.1016/j.techfore.2022.121643

Gable, S. L., & Haidt, J. (2005). What (and Why) Is Positive Psychology? *Review of General Psychology*, 9(2), 103–110. 10.1037/1089-2680.9.2.103

Gardner, W. L., & Avolio, B. J. (1998). The charismatic relationship: A dramaturgical perspective. *Academy of Management Review*, 23(1), 32–58. 10.2307/259098

Gerhart, B. (2005). Human resources and business performance: Findings, unanswered questions, and an alternative approach. *Management Review*, 174–185.

Gigauri, I., Palazzo, M., & Ferri, M. A. (Eds.). (2023). *Handbook of Research on Achieving Sustainable Development Goals With Sustainable Marketing*. IGI Global. 10.4018/978-1-6684-8681-8

Giovannoni, E., & Fabietti, G. (2013). What is sustainability? A review of the concept and its applications. *Integrated reporting: Concepts and cases that redefine corporate accountability*, 21-40.

Gong, Y., Huang, J.-C., & Farh, J.-L. (2009). Employee learning orientation, transformational leadership, and employee creativity: The mediating role of employee creative self-efficacy. *Academy of Management Journal*, 52(4), 765–778. 10.5465/amj.2009.43670890

Grahek, M. S., Thompson, A. D., & Toliver, A. (2010). The character to lead: A closer look at character in leadership. *Consulting Psychology Journal*, 62(4), 270–290. 10.1037/a0022385

Gusenbauer, M., & Haddaway, N. R. (2020). Which academic search systems are suitable for systematic reviews or meta-analyses? Evaluating retrieval qualities of Google Scholar, PubMed, and 26 other resources. *Research Synthesis Methods*, 11(2), 181–217. 10.1002/jrsm.137831614060

Halder, P., Hansen, E. N., Kangas, J., & Laukkanen, T. (2020). How national culture and ethics matter in consumers' green consumption values. *Journal of Cleaner Production*, 265, 121754. 10.1016/j.jclepro.2020.121754

Hart, S. L. (1995). A natural-resource-based view of the firm. *Academy of Management Review*, 20(4), 986–1014. 10.2307/258963

Huelgas, S.M. & Arellano, V.A. (2021). Green Transformational Leadership, Green Human Resource Management and Green Innovation: Key to Environmental Performance of Selected Port Management Offices of Philippine Ports Authority. *IOER International Multidisciplinary Research Journal*, 48–58.

Mansoor, A., Farrukh, M., Lee, J. K., & Jahan, S. (2021). Stimulation of employees' green creativity through green transformational leadership and management initiatives. *Sustainability (Basel)*, 13(14), 7844. 10.3390/su13147844

McDougall, N., Wagner, B., & MacBryde, J. (2019). An empirical explanation of the natural-resource-based view of the firm. *Production Planning and Control*, 30(16), 1366–1382. 10.1080/09537287.2019.1620361

Mittal, S., & Dhar, R. L. (2016). Effect of green transformational leadership on green creativity: A study of tourist hotels. *Tourism Management*, 57, 118–127. 10.1016/j.tourman.2016.05.007

Muralidharan, E., & Pathak, S. (2018). Sustainability, transformational leadership, and social entrepreneurship. *Sustainability (Basel)*, 10(2), 567. 10.3390/su10020567

Nightingale, A. (2009). A guide to systematic literature reviews. [Oxford]. *Surgery*, 381–384.

Nurwahdah, A. & Muafi (2022). The influence of green transformational leadership and green attitude on green organisational citizenship behaviour mediated by emotional intelligence. *International Journal of Research in Business and Social Science*, 99–111.

Öğretmenoğlu, M., Akova, O. & Göktepe, S. (2022). The mediating effects of green organizational citizenship on the relationship between green transformational leadership and green creativity: evidence from hotels. *Journal of Hospitality and Tourism Insights*, 734–751.

Özgül, B., & Zehir, C. (2023). How Managers' Green Transformational Leadership Affects a Firm's Environmental Strategy, Green Innovation, and Performance: The Moderating Impact of Differentiation. *Sustainability (Basel)*, 15(4), 3597. 10.3390/su15043597

Paauwe, J. (2009). HRM and Performance: Achievements, Methodological Issues and Prospects. *Journal of Management Studies*, 46(1), 129–142. 10.1111/j.1467-6486.2008.00809.x

Peng, J., Yin, K., Hou, N., Zou, Y., & Nie, Q. (2020). How to facilitate employee green behavior: The joint role of green transformational leadership and green human resource management practice. *Acta Psychologica Sinica*, 52(9), 1105–1120. 10.3724/SP.J.1041.2020.01105

Perez, J. A. E., Ejaz, F., & Ejaz, S. (2023). Green Transformational Leadership, GHRM, and Proenvironmental Behavior: An Effectual Drive to Environmental Performances of Small- and Medium-Sized Enterprises. *Sustainability (Basel)*, 15(5), 4537. 10.3390/su15054537

Piwowar-Sulej, K., & Iqbal, Q. (2023). Leadership styles and sustainable performance: A systematic literature review. *Journal of Cleaner Production*, 382, 134600. 10.1016/j.jclepro.2022.134600

Podsakoff, P. M., MacKenzie, S. B., & Bommer, W. H. (1996). Transformational leader behaviors and substitutes for leadership as determinants of employee satisfaction, commitment, trust, and organizational citize. *Journal of Management*, 22(2), 259–298. 10.1016/S0149-2063(96)90049-5

Qi, G., Jia, Y., & Zou, H. (2021). Is institutional pressure the mother of green innovation? Examining the moderating effect of absorptive capacity. *Journal of Cleaner Production*, 278, 123957. 10.1016/j.jclepro.2020.123957

Rehman, A., & Yaqub, M. S. (2021). Determining the influence of green transformational leadership, green innovation and green hrm practices on environmental performance of hospitality industry of pakistan: A moderating role of individual employee behaviour under COVID-19. [BBE]. *Bulletin of Business and Economics*, 10(2), 100–114.

Robertson, J. L. (2018). The nature, measurement and nomological network of environmentally specific transformational leadership. *Journal of Business Ethics*, 151(4), 961–975. 10.1007/s10551-017-3569-4

Robertson, J. L., & Barling, J. (2013). Greening organizations through leaders' influence on employees' pro-environmental behaviors. *Journal of Organizational Behavior*, 34(2), 176–194. 10.1002/job.1820

Robertson, J. L., & Barling, J. (2017). Toward a new measure of organizational environmental citizenship behavior. *Journal of Business Research*, 75, 57–66. 10.1016/j.jbusres.2017.02.007

Ryan, R. M., & Deci, E. L. (2000). Self-determination theory and the facilitation of intrinsic motivation, social development, and well-being. *The American Psychologist*, 55(1), 68–78. 10.1037/0003-066X.55.1.6811392867

Salancik, G. R., & Pfeffer, J. (1978). A social information processing approach to job attitudes and task design. *Administrative Science Quarterly*, 23(2), 224–253. 10.2307/239256310307892

Sawitri, D. R., Hadiyanto, H., & Hadi, S. P. (2015). Pro-environmental behavior from a socialcognitive theory perspective. *Procedia Environmental Sciences*, 23, 27–33. 10.1016/j.proenv.2015.01.005

Schunk, D. H., & DiBenedetto, M. K. (2020). Motivation and social cognitive theory. *Contemporary Educational Psychology*, 60, 101832. 10.1016/j.cedpsych.2019.101832

Shah, A.K., Jintian, Y., Sukamani, D. & Kusi, M. (2020). How green transformational leadership influences sustainability? Mediating effects of green creativity and green procurement. *Journal on Innovation and Sustainability*, 69–87.

Sidney, M. T., Wang, N., Nazir, M., Ferasso, M., & Saeed, A. (2022). Continuous Effects of Green Transformational Leadership and Green Employee Creativity: A Moderating and Mediating Prospective. *Frontiers in Psychology*, 13, 840019. 10.3389/fpsyg.2022.84001935645899

Sin, N. L., & Lyubomirsky, S. (2009). Enhancing well-being and alleviating depressive symptoms with positive psychology interventions: A practice-friendly meta-analysis. *Journal of Clinical Psychology*, 65(5), 467–487. 10.1002/jclp.2059319301241

Sobaih, A. E. E., Hasanein, A., Gharbi, H., & Abu Elnasr, A. E. (2022). Going Green Together: Effects of Green Transformational Leadership on Employee Green Behaviour and Environmental Performance in the Saudi Food Industry. *Agriculture*, 12(8), 1100. 10.3390/agriculture12081100

Srour, C. K. G. E. K., Kheir-El-Din, A., & Samir, Y. M. (2020). The effect of green transformational leadership on organizational citizenship behavior in Egypt. *Academic Journal of Interdisciplinary Studies*, 9(5), 1–16. 10.36941/ajis-2020-0081

Stern, P. C., Dietz, T., Abel, T., Guagnano, G. A., & Kalof, L. (1999). A value-belief-norm theory of support for social movements: The case of environmentalism. *Human Ecology Review*, •••, 81–97.

Sun, J., Chen, X., & Zhang, S. (2017). A Review of Research Evidence on the Antecedents of Transformational Leadership. *Education Sciences*, 7(1), 15. 10.3390/educsci7010015

Sun, X., El Askary, A., Meo, M. S., & Hussain, B. (2022). Green transformational leadership and environmental performance in small and medium enterprises. *Ekonomska Istrazivanja*, 35(1), 5273–5291. 10.1080/1331677X.2021.2025127

Suparna, G., Yasa, N. N. K., Giantari, I. G. A. K., Sukaatmadja, I. P. G., & Setini, M. (2021). Green transformational leadership to build value, innovation and competitive advantage in era digital. *Webology*, 18(Special Issue 04), 102–115. 10.14704/WEB/V18SI04/WEB18117

Tian, H., Siddik, A. B., Pertheban, T. R., & Rahman, M. N. (2023). Does fintech innovation and green transformational leadership improve green innovation and corporate environmental performance? A hybrid SEM–ANN approach. *Journal of Innovation & Knowledge*, 8(3), 100396. 10.1016/j.jik.2023.100396

Tosun, C., Parvez, M. O., Bilim, Y., & Yu, L. (2022). Effects of green transformational leadership on green performance of employees via the mediating role of corporate social responsibility: Reflection from North Cyprus. *International Journal of Hospitality Management*, 103, 103218. 10.1016/j.ijhm.2022.103218

Tuncdogan, A., Acar, O. A., & Stam, D. (2017). Individual differences as antecedents of leader behavior: Towards an understanding of multi-level outcomes. *The Leadership Quarterly*, 28(1), 40–64. 10.1016/j.leaqua.2016.10.011

Wang, L., Weng Wong, P. P., & Elangkovan, N. A. (2020). The Influence of Religiosity on Consumer's Green Purchase Intention Towards Green Hotel Selection in China. *Journal of China Tourism Research*, 16(3), 319–345. 10.1080/19388160.2019.1637318

Wang, X., Zhou, K., & Liu, W. (2018). Value Congruence: A Study of Green Transformational Leadership and Employee Green Behavior. *Frontiers in Psychology*. Frontiers.

Widisatria, D., & Nawangsari, L. C. (2021). The influence of green transformational leadership and motivation to sustainable corporate performance with organizational citizenship behavior for the environment as a mediating: Case study at PT Karya Mandiri Sukses Sentosa. *European Journal of Business and Management Research*, 6(3), 118–123. 10.24018/ejbmr.2021.6.3.876

Xiao, Y., & Watson, M. (2019). Guidance on Conducting a Systematic Literature Review. *Journal of Planning Education and Research*, 39(1), 93–112. 10.1177/0739456X17723971

Yin, J., Qian, L., & Singhapakdi, A. (2018). Sharing Sustainability: How Values and Ethics Matter in Consumers' Adoption of Public Bicycle-Sharing Scheme. *Journal of Business Ethics*, 149(2), 313–332. 10.1007/s10551-016-3043-8

Zafar, A., Nisar, Q.A., Shoukat, M. & Ikram, M. (2017). Green Transformational Leadership and Green Performance: The mediating role of Green Mindfulness and Green Self-efficacy. *International Journal of Management Excellence,* 1059–1066.

Zhang, W., Xu, F., & Wang, X. (2020). How Green Transformational Leadership Affects Green Creativity: Creative Process Engagement as Intermediary Bond and Green Innovation Strategy as Boundary Spanner. *Sustainability (Basel)*, 12(9), 3841. 10.3390/su12093841

Zhou, J., Sawyer, L., & Safi, A. (2021). Institutional pressure and green product success: The role of green transformational leadership, green innovation, and green brand image. *Frontiers in Psychology*, 12, 704855. 10.3389/fpsyg.2021.70485534671290

Zhou, S., Zhang, D., Lyu, C., & Zhang, H. (2018). Does seeing "mind acts upon mind" affect green psychological climate and green product development performance? The role of matching between green transformational leadership and individual green values. *Sustainability (Basel)*, 10(9), 3206. 10.3390/su10093206

Chapter 4
Green Hotels Between Circular Economy Objectives and Sustainable Development Goals

Katica Radosavljevic
https://orcid.org/0000-0002-5609-8399
Institute of Agricultural Economics, Belgrade, Serbia

Branko Mihailovic
https://orcid.org/0000-0002-2398-6568
Institute of Agricultural Economics, Belgrade, Serbia

ABSTRACT

The goal to be achieved through the implementation of the concept of sustainable development is to limit pollution. In most European Union countries, sustainable development is one of the key strategies that will be implemented in the coming years in order to achieve satisfactory economic growth and aid the stabilization process. Achieving sustainability in the Republic of Serbia requires a strategic approach that is long-term and integrates and unifies various development processes, in order for them to be as sophisticated as the challenges of development are complex. The European Union has recognized the importance of the circular economy concept and has devoted considerable attention to it in recent years. The hotel industry has direct and indirect impacts on the environment. The pollution generated by this industry has attracted attention in recent years, and consumers are becoming more aware of the importance of environmental protection. As a result, green hotels have

DOI: 10.4018/979-8-3693-3439-3.ch004

become a new industry trend.

INTRODUCTION

The concept of sustainable development is particularly relevant in the era of technological advancement, multinational corporation development, and mass production. The contribution to the development of intellectual capital is a contribution to the adoption of proactive strategies for sustainable development. The development of intellectual capital and the use of technology influence people's awareness of the importance of a higher quality and healthier way of life, as well as freedom of expression, creativity, and ideas that support the concept of sustainable development.

The dimensions of sustainable development are economic, social, and environmental goals that have a certain interdependence. These goals complement each other but at the same time represent mutual competitors, so the concept of sustainable development implies establishing a balance between them. This further means that taking measures aimed at achieving one of these goals should consider and respect the minimal standards required by the other two goals.

According to the new concept of sustainable development, the focus is placed on humans and creating an environment in which they have freedom and opportunities for their development. This seemingly trivial idea contradicts the goals of materialism, namely the creation of financial wealth.

On the contrary, sustainable development focuses not only on the quantity but also on the quality of growth. This is what gives sustainable development its special value. The nature of economic growth and the distribution of its results are crucial for the concept of sustainable development. It is aimed at shaping new, sustainable models of economic expansion.

Zero growth would have negative consequences for the environment. Developing countries would be forced to excessively exploit available natural resources and degrade the natural environment, while wealthy countries would have fewer opportunities to develop environmentally safer technology and provide additional resources to assist the poor (Mitrović, 2015; Gligorić & Jovanović-Gavrilović, 2017).

Achieving sustainable development does not mean denying growth but establishing optimal growth, both quantitative and qualitative. Optimal growth is growth that will not lead to waste or excessive consumption of natural and economic resources, or marginalize and degrade underdeveloped countries, which can negatively impact the developed part of the world. Therefore, it can be concluded that sustainable development supports economically, socially, and environmentally quality and sustainable growth.

Many countries currently experience the impact of moderate to severe pollution, exerting significant pressure on the quality of water, soil, and air. Despite efforts to "clean up" in many countries and sectors, the widespread use of chemicals worldwide, exposure to pesticides, heavy metals, and other substances continues to affect human health and the environment.

Current patterns of production and consumption, as well as global climate change, raise questions about the capacity of a country's natural resources to sustain the food and growth needs of urbanized populations and provide space for waste. Research following the COVID-19 pandemic, particularly focusing on green food packaging, encompasses the sustainability issue that is lacking in scholarly literature (Kwok & Lin, 2023).

The necessity to find solutions for such a situation has led to the emergence of the concept of sustainable development as a way to establish coordinated development and protect the environment on a global level. The optimal solution is to develop a strategy for sustainable development of domestic agriculture that fully respects the projected dimensions of the EU agricultural market, while the development and exchange policy should be designed to maximize the benefits it offers and neutralize negative effects (Radosavljević, 2017).

The occurrence of natural disasters as a consequence of climate change in recent decades necessitates a revision of the principles of sustainability. The impact of crises and disasters on tourism can be complex, depending on their nature, magnitude, and scale (Backer & Ritchie, 2017). It is estimated that the contribution of tourism to global warming and gas emissions will increase significantly by 2035, mostly due to aviation (Vieira do Nascimento, 2016). The size of the impact that climate has on the visiting probability of a tourist destination is corroborated by the research conducted within ski resorts and seaside destinations (Scott, 2006).

The influence of globalization processes strongly affects the contemporary development of tourism. The increasing need for information, air and other forms of transportation, the emergence of numerous new destinations, the rise in education and cultural levels of the population, and changes in tourists' habits and desires have led to the need for business adaptation (Gradinac & Jegdić, 2016). This can aid in promoting a culture of responsible consumption that values quality over quantity and encourages people to make decisions about what they eat and how they dispose of it after consumption (Agarwal et al., 2024).

Tourism, more than other industries, relies on the quality of the environment, making its connection with the environment particularly significant. Studies on the crucial role of managers in procurement and spreading sustainability throughout the supply chain contribute to operations management and sustainability (Khan & Hinterhuber, 2024).

Hotels consume a large amount of energy, resulting in the burning of fossil fuels, increased emission of carbon dioxide (CO2) into the atmosphere, and intensification of the greenhouse effect and global warming.

The use of energy-efficient technologies in the planning and construction of green hotels enables energy and cost savings, enhances the internal comfort of the facility, and increases their market value. Moreover, the materials used in the construction of these buildings must to some extent be organic, natural, or obtained through the recycling of old materials.

As one of the major environmental polluters, the hotel industry has developed a new type of tourism called eco-tourism as a means to address this global issue. Eco-tourism focuses on the construction and outfitting of "green hotels" that aim to reduce the amount of physical, chemical, and biological waste.

In the early debates, the ecological aspect dominated, but over time, the concept expanded to include two other important components: economic and social. The contemporary approach to sustainable development represents a balanced progress in the economic, social, and environmental spheres. It is often misconstrued that sustainable development is against growth.

This study employs a qualitative analysis and literature review approach to examine the role of the circular economy in the context of sustainable development, using the example of green hotels.

Multiple data sources are analyzed, including articles from academic journals, policy reports, reports and statistics from public institutions, as well as official macroeconomic and environmental data.

Special attention is given to research that provides insights into the utilization of new technologies in production through the application of the circular economy in European countries.

Second, the implementation of the circular economy through the construction of green hotels is explored, considering its impact on the tourism sector.

Finally, the focus is directed towards the environmental challenges in Serbia, particularly the risks posed by climate change, and how green hotels can respond to these challenges through investment decisions and risk prevention strategies to avoid the creation of an unsustainable system.

Based on a thorough analysis of this data, conclusions and recommendations are drawn regarding the role of constructing green hotels in risk prevention and the development of the hospitality industry in the Serbian tourism market. Effective marketing strategies for green hotels assist hotel managers in devising and implementing profitable operations for green hotels (Waris et al., 2023). The sustainability models cited in the literature on the circular economy are not sufficiently comprehensive to prevent the shifting of issues, and it can be argued that they lack a solid theoretical and conceptual foundation (Borrero & Yousafzai, 2024). Systems thinking at all levels of implementation is the solution for achieving the goals of the circular economy (Renfors, 2024). Over time, environmental degradation has been contributed to by individual behaviors and combined actions of businesses and organizations (Patwary et al., 2024).

A novel approach to sustainability practices in the hospitality industry holds a key position, especially in Turkey. The implementation of these concepts can bring environmental and economic benefits, offering invaluable insights to hotel managers and policymakers on integrating smart technologies with sustainability (Akel & Noyan, 2024). While the hotel sector significantly contributes to employment and economic growth on a global scale, its activities harm the environment through pollution, excessive use of natural resources, and solid and liquid waste (Umoh, 2024).

BACKGROUND

Many countries around the world, including the United States, Japan, and China, have recognized the need to transition to a new, circular economic model. More recently, the European Union has also joined this movement and is undertaking numerous activities in line with the circular economy principles.

The sustainable development agenda, which envisions a world without hunger, highlights one of the greatest challenges facing the world: ensuring that the growing food needs driven by the global population growth are met (it is estimated that the population will increase by 2 billion by 2050). To feed an additional 2 billion people, food production needs to be increased by 50% (Goddek et al., 2019, p. 5).

The currently dominant economic model worldwide is the linear model of economy, also known as a linear economy. This model is based on the exploitation of natural resources and the increasing generation of waste, posing a threat to the prospects of future generations' well-being. In contrast to this model, the circular model of economy, also known as a circular economy, has emerged as its antithesis, significantly differing from its predecessor, particularly in the mentioned characteristics. The circular economy takes into account the slowly depleting natural resources and aims to achieve zero waste.

Additionally, there is another economic model that lies between these two models, representing a step closer to the circular model. This is referred to as a chain economy. In a chain production system, resources have two directions: a portion ends up as waste, while another portion of materials participates in the recycling process.

From a systemic perspective, resources in the linear production system are of an external nature, always extracted from nature at the beginning. In the chain production system, there is still a need for resources of an external nature, but it is reduced, along with the reduction in waste.

The linear economic model leads to unnecessary waste or loss of resources in several ways (Mitrović, 2015):

- Generation of waste in the production chain (during the production process itself);
- Generation of waste at the end of the product life cycle;
- Unutilized energy from reuse;
- Degradation of ecosystem services quality.

To avoid waste, the most important aspect is waste prevention, which is achieved through the aforementioned special product design that promotes longer product lifespan, incorporates environmentally friendly materials that are non-hazardous, and includes parts that can be repaired, replaced, and recycled.

In contrast to the linear economic model, which, considering its characteristics, can jeopardize the well-being of future generations and is environmentally unsustainable and economically inefficient due to resource exploitation and waste generation, the circular model aligns with the goal of achieving sustainable development on both national and global levels.

The basic principles underlying the circular economy are as follows (Mitrović, 2015):

- Creating products that do not become waste;
- Distinguishing between consumable and durable product components;
- Relying on renewable energy sources;
- Regarding waste as input (raw material);
- Embracing the principle of cascading use;
- Shifting from consumers to users (sharing economy).

The transition to a circular economy can lead to a 3% annual increase in resource productivity in Europe. This would create benefits from primary resources amounting to 0.6 billion euros. Additionally, there would be non-resource-related benefits and external benefits estimated at 1.2 billion euros, resulting in a total of 1.8 billion euros compared to the current state (McKinsey Quarterly, 2017). The introduction of a circular economy in Europe could lead to greater prosperity, GDP growth, and employment. It is estimated that household income could increase by 11%, and GDP by 7% (Eurostat, 2020).

It is expected to equally meet not only economic but also social and environmental sustainability goals:

(1) use natural resources effectively,

(2) be integrated into regional economy and society, and
(3) make a significant contribution to environmental protection (Mihailović et al., 2020).

Decent work and economic growth - new circular business models are the main potential sources of resource efficiency and effectiveness, waste valorization, and green jobs. Studies show that the global implementation of the circular economy can create trillions of opportunities, with annual net benefits of 1.8 trillion euros in the EU alone by 2030 (Schroeder, Anggraeni, & Weber, 2018).

For example, in the hotel industry, kitchen waste does not have to be just waste. Fats, oils, and similar products, although seemingly useless, can be easily monetized through recycling. Investing in systems that prevent the wastage and disposal of oils and fats in various ways requires significant financial resources.

However, knowing that operating in an environmentally friendly manner and recycling or disposing of almost all waste of this kind adequately justifies such investments. The implementation of systems containing filters that accept all types of waste generated in kitchens is recommended.

Through excessive and uncontrolled exploitation, we have created a continuous ecological debt to planet Earth. Every year, starting from 1970, the "Ecological Debt Day" is measured. It represents the date within a calendar year when humanity's needs for natural resources exceed what the planet's ecosystems can renew during that year.

On Image number 1, it depicts the movement of Ecological Debt Day since its inception. It is calculated by observing the water, forests, metals, and other resources present on the planet and the rate at which they are being consumed. We can see that every year this day occurs earlier, indicating that the global population starts using resources that the planet will be able to produce in the following year.

Circular economy is still largely a theoretical concept, and achieving sustainable development in the future will be closely linked to progress in its implementation. The contribution of circular economy to sustainability can be seen through its alignment with the Sustainable Development Goals (SDGs). The SDGs, consisting of 17 goals, provide a plan for achieving a better and more sustainable future for all by 2030.

Simultaneously, the concept of circular economy as an alternative economic framework has gained significant momentum in recent years, serving as an approach to achieving local, national, and global sustainability. The growing interest in circular economy can be seen through the involvement of numerous stakeholders such as governments, cities, and companies actively exploring ways to transition to a circular economy.

Although the goals of the circular economy and the goals of sustainable development broadly align, the connection between these two agendas is not immediately apparent. The concept of the circular economy does not appear in any part of the Agenda 2030 on Sustainable Development Goals, which includes both the goals themselves and their interconnected targets.

Figure 1. Ecological Debt Day, 1970-2019

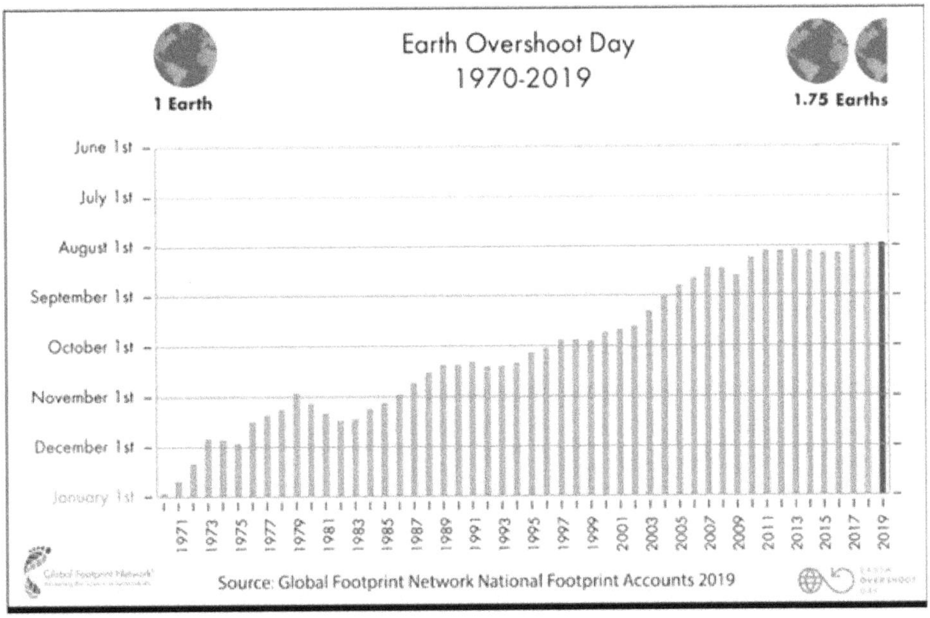

The next image 2, provides an overview of these goals. It illustrates that all 17 goals are connected to the circular economy and adopting circular economy practices is necessary to achieve many goals, not just Goal 12, which directly relates to responsible consumption and production. Furthermore, progress in some of the goals can contribute to the transition towards a circular economy (Einarsson, 2019).

We would highlight goals 6, 7, 8, 12, and 15, where the implementation of the circular economy directly contributes to achieving these goals.

Goal 6 - Clean Water and Sanitation: The practice of the circular economy, which involves water purification, sustainable sanitation, wastewater treatment, water reuse and recycling, nutrient replenishment, and biogas systems, can help increase access to safe drinking water, sanitation protection, reduce pollution, and improve water quality.

Goal 7 - Affordable and Clean Energy: Circular economy practices encompass renewable energy systems, which significantly contribute to this goal.

Goal 8 - Decent Work and Economic Growth: New circular business models are major potential sources of resource efficiency, waste valorization, and green jobs. Studies show that the global implementation of the circular economy could create trillion-dollar opportunities, with annual net benefits of 1.8 trillion euros in the EU alone by 2030 (Schroeder, Anggraeni, & Weber, 2018).

Goal 12 - Responsible Production and Consumption: The practice of the circular economy involves decoupling economic activity from resource use and addressing the associated environmental and social impacts, which is at the core of this goal. It is also crucial for achieving most of the other goals, deepening the indirect impact of the circular economy on sustainable development.

Goal 15 - Life on Land: The fundamental goal of the circular economy practice is the restoration of natural capital. This includes adopting sustainable and regenerative agricultural and agroforestry practices that protect biodiversity and return biological materials back to the soil as nutrients. This practice is crucial for the restoration of terrestrial systems.

In addition to direct contributions, the practice of the circular economy can indirectly contribute to several other goals. By directly influencing the aforementioned goals, it provides positive contributions to other goals. The strongest indirect relationships are related to goals 1, 2, 11, and 14.

Figure 2. Interconnection between the circular economy and sustainable development goals

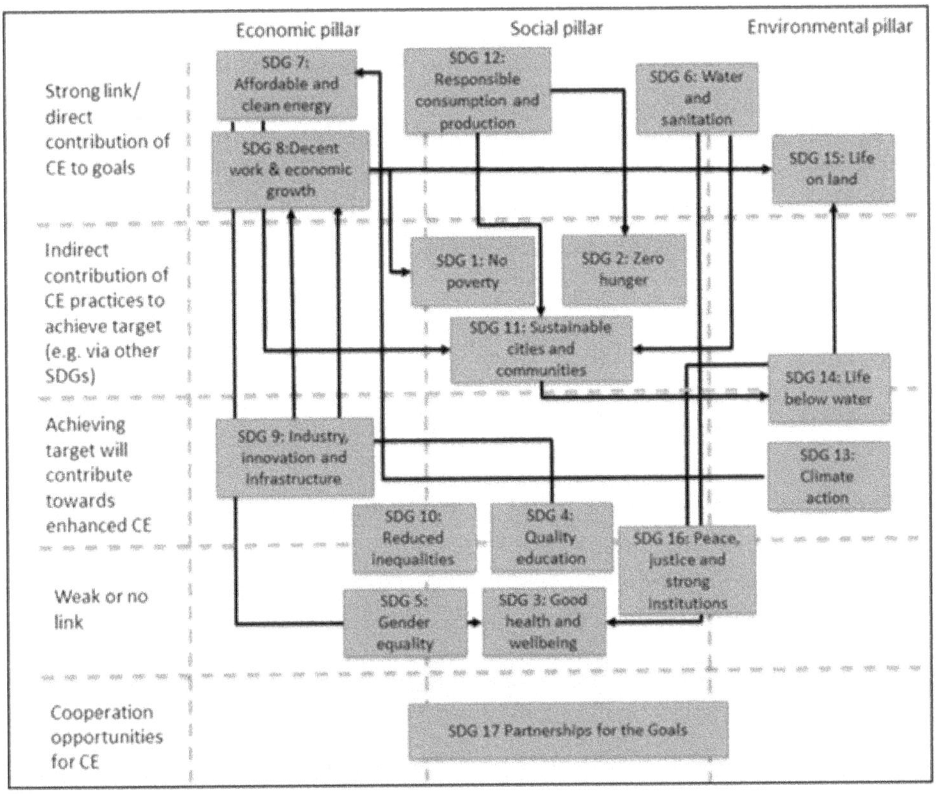

Goal 1 - No Poverty: Circular economy practices related to repair, refurbishment, and recycling can lead to job creation, indirectly contributing to poverty reduction. Additionally, practices related to water management and agriculture make significant contributions. There is a strong synergy with goals 8 and 9.

Goal 2 - Zero Hunger: Implementing circular economy principles in local agriculture, such as composting, improves soil quality, increasing agricultural productivity. When combined with initiatives related to a circular food system that reduces food waste and/or utilizes food waste for animal feed, it can free up agricultural land for human food consumption.

Goal 11 - Sustainable Cities and Communities: It is expected that by 2050, three-quarters of the world's population will live in cities (Schroeder, Anggraeni, & Weber, 2018). Considering this, the transition to a circular economy is necessary to reduce resource consumption in cities and mitigate environmental impacts.

Additionally, the principles of the circular economy, such as inclusive design, can enable affordable housing solutions for low-income groups.

Goal 14 - Life Below Water: By practicing circular economy principles, such as waste prevention on land, the amount of waste entering the oceans can be reduced. It also allows for the recovery of nutrients from wastewater streams before they reach the oceans. Furthermore, the contribution of the circular economy to combating climate change will indirectly reduce ocean acidification.

The cause-and-effect relationship between these goals and the circular economy can be observed in practice. The impact is mutual, and we can distinguish direct and indirect contributions of the circular economy to achieving the set goals.

DISCUSSION

Quantifying Sustainable Development

People and their well-being are at the center of the concept of sustainable development. The essence of sustainable development lies in shaping new models of growth, whose quality is assessed through the prism of economic, social, and environmental sustainability. Quality measurement of sustainable development implies the existence of an appropriate framework within which various collected data and information can be interconnected. Two frameworks have been developed:

- The P-S-R (Pressure-State-Response) model, which, as the name suggests, is based on three outcomes: environmental pressure, the state in which the environment is found, and the response or reaction of society to the existing state.
- The model based on national accounts, which involves linking various financial and accounting data. This model initially covered economic and social aspects, considering the state of the economy after World War II. However, over time, the situation has significantly changed, with the recognition of limited resources. Therefore, the model based on national accounts expanded to include the third aspect of sustainable development, the ecological aspect, also known as "green accounts."

Indicators of sustainable development include:

1. Sectoral indicators;
2. Resource indicators;
3. Outcome indicators;

4. Composite indicators.

These indicators form a pyramid-like structure, with sectoral indicators at the bottom. They reflect how movements within each sector define economic, social, and environmental goals. Resource indicators, as the name implies, focus on various types of resources, their availability, and utilization, occupying the second level of the pyramid. The third level consists of outcome indicators, providing information on the quality and direction of the observed development. Composite indicators encompass and summarize different data to obtain an overall assessment of progress achieved. They include indicators such as the Human Development Index (HDI), Gross Domestic Product (GDP), "genuine savings," and national wealth (Jovanović-Gavrilović, 2013).

Various reports have contributed to the analysis of constraints and negative aspects of the environment that hinder the achievement of sustainable development. These reports have encompassed broader aspects of society beyond economic, social, and environmental dimensions. Some of these reports include:

- Global Environment Outlook 2000; Global Environment Outlook 3(UNEP 1999, 2002)
- World Resources Report (WRI/UNDP/UNEP/World Bank 2000)
- DAC Development Report 2000 (OECD DAC 2001)
- Human Development Report 1999 (UNDP 1999, 2001).

Population growth is expected to exacerbate these pressures, although the level of localized concentration of people or their resource consumption has a greater impact than measuring population growth alone. Sustainable development strategies are measures aimed at achieving a sustainable combination of development integration and natural resource conservation. The systemic foundations of sustainable development encompass economic sustainability, social sustainability, and environmental sustainability. Economic sustainability involves maximizing income while maintaining or increasing natural capital. Social sustainability entails maintaining the stability of social and cultural systems, while environmental sustainability involves maintaining the resilience and equilibrium of biological and physical systems.

Green Hotels: An Example of Sustainable Development in Tourism

Sustainable tourism represents a development concept that balances the environmental, socio-cultural, and economic aspects of the environment with tourist satisfaction. Introducing norms in tourist behavior is one of the solutions (Wasaya,

Prentice, & Hsiao, 2023). Existing studies have primarily relied on consumers' pro-environmental attitudes, knowledge, and a selective list of green hotel attributes to predict intentions to visit a green hotel (Sharma & Chen, 2023). Other research indicates that owners act as both barriers and drivers of sustainability initiatives in the Australian hotel industry (Khatter et al., 2021).

This concept helps in finding an optimal form of tourism development that will not degrade resources, allowing future generations to meet their tourism needs. The development of the hospitality industry entails significant changes in the understanding and philosophy of hospitality. The ultimate goal is to create sustainable hospitality that prioritizes profit, people, and the planet (Radosavljević & Mihailović, 2023).

The trend of ecotourism has captured the attention of many hoteliers and tourists worldwide, and its significance and environmental benefits have encouraged existing entrepreneurs and new investors to invest in the construction of green hotels. The aim is to adopt a sustainable development concept in their hotel policies to address this global issue.

The specific green policies of each hotel are based on energy and water conservation, the use of environmentally friendly and non-toxic products, implementing green public procurement, and practicing eco-friendly waste management (recycling). The principles of green policies can be found in all aspects of green hotels, ranging from architecture to responsible hotel management. Green hotels incorporate ecological standards and employ elements of new eco-friendly technologies, making a significant contribution to environmental protection while achieving better business outcomes.

The trend of green or eco-friendly management emerged in the 1920s and spread worldwide during the first decade of the 21st century. The international program "Green Key" has certified over 3,200 environmentally friendly hospitality establishments in 65 countries worldwide. The countries with the highest number of certified establishments currently include the Netherlands (666), France (644), Greece (360), and others (Green Key, 2023).

Green hotels have multiple advantages, both for the environment and for hotel owners. One of the main advantages is the reduction in energy and water consumption. Green hotels use energy-efficient lighting, appliances, and HVAC systems, as well as low-flow showers, faucets, and toilets that minimize water usage. By reducing energy and water consumption, these hotels automatically decrease operational costs by utilizing renewable energy sources such as solar power and wind energy, employing geothermal energy, and reducing the amount of waste they generate. Waste reduction is achieved by minimizing the use of disposable products like plastic bottles and packaging, implementing recycling waste systems, and practicing composting.

Another advantage of green hotels is the improvement of indoor air quality. Traditional hotels often use cleaning products and materials that contain strong chemicals, which can be harmful to human health. In contrast, green hotels utilize environmentally friendly products and materials.

It is also important to emphasize that these hotels have a positive impact on the local community. By utilizing locally sourced materials and products, green hotels support the local economy and reduce their carbon footprint by minimizing emissions from transportation.

The International Organization for Environmental Education is responsible for awarding green hotel certificates in Serbia, but data on the number of green hotels in Serbia indicates that the development trend of green hotels is still low.

The criteria for obtaining the Green Key certification are demanding and cover a wide range of conditions, including the type of materials used in hotel construction, the land on which the hotel is built, and the equipment and appliances used in food production processes.

There are numerous examples of best practices in foreign markets, but one notable mention is the Radisson Blu Hotel in Berlin, which actively promotes eco-friendly tourism and informs the public about its environmental achievements. The hotel's commitment to informing consumers about its eco-content has increased its advantages and made it a preferred choice for a significant number of ecotourists (Radisson Hotels, 2023).

In 2019, Hotel Mona Zlatibor and Hilton Belgrade were listed as green hotels in Serbia. However, green hotels in Serbia do not operate in a manner that fully complies with the Green Key certification, which emphasizes the importance of informing consumers, staff, and the wider public about the company's operations and ways individuals can reduce their ecological impact on the world around them. Serbia still has a low level of initiatives for the development of green hotel industry, while this trend is more prevalent in Slovenia, Croatia, and other European Union countries (Djurić, 2019).

Long-standing societal ignorance or negligence regarding environmental issues is not accidental. Environmental protection requires investments and allocation of societal resources. In today's society, these investments can take the form of relevant measures developed and implemented in response to environmental protection demands. Given the pervasiveness and worsening of environmental pollution, the ability to take action is crucial. By adopting environmentally friendly practices and integrating environmental management into hotel operations, green hotels embody the concepts of environmental protection, resource conservation, health, and safety. They implement green management and resource conservation measures and promote green consumption in terms of responsible resource usage.

The Trend of Sustainable Development in the EU as a Challenge for Serbia

In order for the circular economy to fully thrive, it is necessary for policymakers to respond, in addition to changing people's awareness. Changes in policies related to product design, eco-design, greening public procurement, and similar areas are necessary. Some governments are already providing incentives for the development of the circular economy, and their practices should be followed by all.

The European Union (EU) is one of the best examples of commitment to the development of the circular economy. This international integration is fully dedicated to transitioning towards a circular economy. Numerous activities and projects are being implemented, strategic documents are being drafted, all with the aim of making the EU a leader in this field. Namely, the significance of EU pre-accession funds and their impact on the competitiveness of the country and the achievement of sustainable development goals are emphasized (Šestović, Radosavljević, & Chroneos-Krasavac, 2017).

Adopting the trend of the European Union is recommended for developed countries, but special emphasis is placed on countries in transition that are at the beginning of transitioning to a circular model. Embracing the technologies that the European Union has already developed would significantly accelerate the adoption of the circular concept in these countries, including ours. The circular economy represents an opportunity pursued by developed economies globally and could also contribute to the acceleration of Serbia's economy. It would enable improvements in competitiveness, market development, horizontal diversification, and the development of business models.

The economy of the Republic of Serbia, as a country in transition, is assessed as quite volatile with a shallow market. This is contributed to, among other things, by low economic growth, a lack of predictability and long-term market stability, as well as inconsistent policies for long-term economic and social development.

Like in most countries worldwide, a linear business model dominates in Serbia. This model assumes that products are disposed of as waste at the end of their life cycle, negatively impacting the environment.

The business models offered by the circular economy, such as the sharing economy and service provision, reuse of resources, extended product lifecycles, and products as services, bring numerous benefits. They enable the maximum utilization of products, increase economic efficiency by eliminating material leakage and waste, retain value, save resources and energy, generate additional income, and promote product durability.

Implementing the circular economy in Serbia would lead to significant progress in environmental protection by reducing waste, greenhouse gas emissions, preserving natural resources, achieving energy independence, and utilizing renewable energy sources.

Annually, around 12 million tons of waste are generated in Serbia, equivalent to 1.74 tons per capita. Of this amount, citizens and industries generate 2.3 million tons of municipal waste (300g per capita) and (1.5 kg per capita), respectively. While the quantity of waste is not alarming, it is not negligible either. However, the main problem in the waste sector in our country lies in the (mis)management of waste. In 2018, out of the total amount of waste, 2 million tons were treated (only 4% of the total waste, or 0.3% of municipal waste, was reused or recycled, while three-quarters were incinerated or disposed of adequately). The rest ended up in landfills, unsanitary dumps, and uncontrolled dumping sites without proper technical conditions (Goddek et al., 2019, p. 5).

The Republic of Serbia has taken a small step towards the development of this model, but greater activation and involvement of key individuals and institutions are necessary. There are potentials for development, and their utilization would enable progress towards European and global trends in various fields.

Out of 2.3 million tons of municipal waste, estimates suggest that nearly 900,000 tons consist of food waste generated "from farm to fork" by households, the hospitality sector, and the public sector (Environmental Protection Agency, 2023). In Serbia, hospitality establishments procure a total of 123,000 tons of food annually, of which 20% is immediately discarded due to inedible parts (such as peels, rinds, bones, etc.), while an additional 15% remains uneaten on plates and is subsequently discarded (UNDP, 2023). However, as much as 99% of the waste generated in hospitality establishments ends up in landfills, releasing methane and carbon dioxide into the air.

Research shows that only 13% of hospitality establishments currently utilize waste management services provided by operators for the proper collection and treatment of food waste. Moreover, the prevailing practice in most of these establishments in Serbia is to dispose of food waste primarily in containers, which is then transported to landfills (NALED, 2020).

The research highlights some of the activities of green hotels in Serbia. As a notable example, Hotel Mona Plaza is located in the popular mountain destination of Zlatibor in western Serbia. This hotel promotes itself as a green hotel with ecological standards and initiatives. The hotel utilizes natural materials and reduces the use of plastics and other disposable products. Additionally, the food served is primarily sourced from local farms. Environmental protection activities include organizing nature cleaning actions and other ecological initiatives to contribute to nature preservation. Hotel Mona Plaza features a spa center with a pool, sauna, and other wellness amenities, all designed to be in harmony with nature and incorporating natural materials such as wood and stone.

The Green Hotel Stara Planina is a modern hotel situated on the slopes of Stara Planina. It is renowned for its environmental awareness and sustainable operations. The hotel utilizes renewable energy sources and maintains low carbon dioxide emissions, making it an ideal destination for those seeking to contribute to nature conservation.

The Hyatt hotel chain is known for operating according to environmental standards, both in Serbia and worldwide. As an example, the Park Hyatt Sydney hotel showcases differences in operations primarily due to location and consequently, state standards. The Hyatt Regency in Belgrade was the first hotel to initiate green hotel actions in Serbia and has its green team. This initiative aims to enhance the capital's ecological and touristic profile, reducing consumption by 20% through the implementation of new technologies. This includes the introduction of a new HVAC thermal system, occupancy-based lighting controls, sensor installations in offices and other spaces, frequency regulators in the hotel kitchen and laundry room, enabling energy savings by automatically turning off lights when rooms are unoccupied or stopping water flow from taps after a period. Recycling has been introduced for all waste materials used in the hotel, along with the use of energy-efficient light bulbs.

In contrast to the Hyatt Regency in Belgrade, the Park Hyatt Sydney hotel is renowned for its environmental initiatives, distinguishing it as a green hotel. Rainwater harvesting is one such initiative, utilized for garden irrigation and toilet use, reducing the hotel's water consumption. Additionally, the hotel features green roofs, aiding in reducing the building's heat absorption and thereby lowering the need for air conditioning. Park Hyatt Sydney employs energy-efficient systems such as LED lighting, motion sensor-based lighting control, and energy-efficient climate control devices. Sustainable materials were utilized during construction and furnishing, including wood from renewable sources, low-emission glass, and natural materials like stone and wood. Waste management systems have been implemented to reduce the amount of waste sent to landfills, with initiatives such as waste recycling and the use of biodegradable products like paper straws. These are just some of the significant efforts that make Park Hyatt Sydney a green hotel. Like many others in the industry, they have recognized the importance of sustainable business practices and strive to minimize their environmental impact through innovative solutions and practices (Global Sustainable Tourism Council, 2013).

In the tourism sector, hotels are often significant contributors to environmental pollution. Therefore, it is extremely important for all hotels to establish an environmental management system to address sustainability issues through sustainable development. Hotel management must plan and consistently implement various measures and activities to preserve their ecological environment, as well as analyze the effects of all environmental measures and activities they undertake. Environmental issues and protection are becoming increasingly prevalent in the hotel industry today and are significant factors in their development. The growing popularity of ecology and environmental protection has led to the emergence of eco-hotels and "green" hotels as the latest trends. Well-known international hotel chains have recognized the importance and role of environmentally sustainable behavior and business by implementing numerous activities and measures in their operations. On the other hand, it should be noted that in Serbia, a very small number of hotels understand the importance of environmental sustainability and do not pay enough attention to environmental preservation, except for hotels belonging to large international hotel chains operating in Serbia.

The problem lies in the fact that there is still an insufficient number of people globally who show concern for their environment and accordingly change their behavior. Technological and scientific advancements have led to the emergence of mass production and subsequently mass consumption. The linear model in consumer society poses significant environmental issues related to climate, pollution, waste generation, and depletion of natural resources.

On the other hand, consumer society satisfies the needs imposed by the industry to facilitate the path of mass production – more work is done to generate higher income and buy more material goods. Transforming the working class into a consumer society, where happiness is equated with material possessions (consumerism), along with continuous technological progress leading to constant introduction of new products and models at lower prices, has created opportunities for increased consumption and resulted in significant negative consequences. One of these consequences, which the circular model primarily aims to address and from which other negative impacts stem, is the generation of substantial amounts of waste. This consequence is directly linked to the still dominant linear model, where products that are no longer in use end up being disposed of in various landfills.

The circular model solves the aforementioned problems. Each individual must be aware of their ecological footprint and change their habits and behavior. The circular economy would transform consumer society or give rise to a new society, with an emphasis on not assuming constant production and purchasing of new items but rather repair, reuse, and renting instead of new purchases. Besides the positive impact on the environment, this would also have a positive effect on the psychological state of today's individuals, whose lives are consumed by an endless race for more money and possessions, neglecting the non-material values that truly bring satisfaction and happiness.

SOLUTIONS AND RECOMMENDATIONS

In contemporary society, there has been a shift towards prioritizing technology over nature. This trend is driven by the increased convenience and connectivity technology brings to our daily lives. While technological advancements are essential for global development, it's important to recognize the fundamental role nature plays in maintaining our health and well-being (Mihailović, Radosavljević, & Popović, 2023).

The hotel industry plays a significant role in both contributing to environmental issues like climate change through high resource consumption, as well as advancing solutions within the framework of the circular economy. Transitioning to more sustainable operations can help green hotels reduce their impacts while supporting critical goals for responsible consumption, clean energy access, economic growth and terrestrial ecosystem protection (Quan, Koo, & Han, 2023).

Using the method of comparison, analysis, and synthesis, along with a broader spectrum of literature from the hospitality industry, including theoretical and empirical studies, knowledge of production methods in the EU aided by new technology in production through the application of circular economy principles, as well as reports on public policy, macroeconomic environmental data, we have arrived at key solutions and recommendations for green hotels in Serbia, employing circular economy principles and sustainable development.

- Prioritize renewable energy and energy efficiency. Hotels should undertake comprehensive audits to identify top areas for reduction and switch to renewable sources like solar, geothermal, wind or hydropower wherever feasible. Building automation and IoT (Internet of Things) solutions can optimize systems in real-time.
- Implement sustainable waste management practices. Develop standard operating procedures for waste segregation, tracking waste streams, and ensuring proper handling and disposal of hazardous materials. Engage staff and guests in conservation efforts through signage and training.
- Incorporate eco-friendly building materials and furnishings. Consider whole lifecycle impacts and embodied carbon when selecting supplies. Pursue green building certifications that require materials assessments and maintenance/disassembly plans.
- Establish green procurement guidelines. Vet suppliers through audits or third-party certifications to ensure compliance with social and environmental standards. Incentivize suppliers to take back end-of-life products.
- Offer immersive guest experiences. Curate interactive tours and activities centered on sustainability topics to foster stewardship values. Partner with local artisans, farmers and non-profits to promote community development.

- Adopt a full cost accounting approach. Quantify economic value of natural assets and costs associated with health, climate and biodiversity impacts to make more informed financial decisions.
- Advocate for circular economy policies and incentives. Collaborate cross-sectorally to drive systemic shifts through research collaborations, pilot projects and input on relevant legislation, regulations and investments.
- Waste in Serbia can be utilized in the production of biodiesel and bioethanol, animal feed, electric energy from biogas, composting, and more. This type of waste can be repurposed in the economy to create new value and, notably, to employ new workers in environmental preservation jobs. However, a major problem is the lack of infrastructure, from specific waste separation containers to adequate sanitary landfills. Serbia has only 10 sanitary landfills and over 120 municipal ones that do not meet even the minimum standards. Additionally, there are as many as 2,170 illegal dumps (though estimates suggest there are over 3,500), located near populated areas and watercourses (UNDP, 2023) In practice, public institutions, primarily healthcare facilities, followed by establishments in the hospitality sector, have been identified as the largest producers of food waste. A comparative study was conducted in the latter half of 2019, involving a sample of 250 respondents, including 50 from healthcare institutions and 200 from the hospitality sector. According to the results, 21.1% of respondents have knowledge about proper food waste management. (NALED, 2021).

Hotel management should engage in all relevant environmental actions concerning water conservation and protection, wastewater management, air quality preservation, promotion of waste reduction and segregation initiatives, encouragement of locally sourced products, utilization of public transportation, and more. The outcomes of these actions will bring added value to the destination, enhance the hotel's offerings, elevate its image, and attract new target guests, especially environmentally conscious ones.

Transitioning to truly sustainable operations requires hotels to adopt a holistic, systems-level approach encompassing strategies across their value chains. The recommendations discussed provide a starting point, but will necessitate ongoing innovation and stakeholder cooperation. By prioritizing circular solutions, the hospitality sector can make significant progress in addressing pressing global challenges while strengthening resilience and competitiveness over the long term.

FUTURE RESEARCH DIRECTIONS

With growing awareness of sustainable development, a greater number of hotels are adopting environmentally friendly practices (Yang, Jiang, & Wang, 2023). As the global emphasis on environmental sustainability grows, there is a pressing need to explore innovative strategies and solutions that can effectively integrate sustainability principles into hotel operations while enhancing overall guest experiences (Prakash et al., 2023). By delving into key areas such as consumer behavior analysis, policy evaluation, technological innovations, economic impact assessment, stakeholder engagement, and social impact assessment, researchers can contribute valuable insights to inform decision-making processes and support the transition towards a more sustainable and resilient tourism industry.

- Longitudinal study on green hotels: Conduct a longitudinal study to assess the long-term impact and effectiveness of green hotels in reducing environmental pollution and promoting sustainable development in the hospitality industry. This could involve tracking various environmental indicators, such as energy consumption, waste generation, and carbon footprint, over several years to measure the sustainability outcomes of green hotels.
- Consumer behavior analysis: Investigate consumer perceptions, preferences, and behavior towards green hotels. Understanding the factors influencing consumers' decisions to choose eco-friendly accommodation options can provide valuable insights for hoteliers and policymakers in promoting sustainability initiatives within the hospitality sector.
- Policy analysis and comparative studies: Conduct comparative analyses of policies and regulations related to sustainable tourism and circular economy practices in different countries or regions. This may entail examining the effectiveness of existing policies, identifying gaps and challenges, and proposing recommendations for improving regulatory frameworks to support the development of green hotels and sustainable tourism.
- Technological innovations and best practices: Explore emerging technologies, innovations, and best practices in green hotel design, construction, and operations. This could include advancements in energy-efficient building materials, renewable energy systems, water conservation technologies, waste management solutions, and smart building technologies aimed at reducing environmental impacts and enhancing the sustainability performance of hotels.
- Economic impact assessment: Evaluate the economic implications of transitioning towards a circular economy model in the hospitality industry, with a focus on the costs and benefits associated with implementing green initia-

tives in hotels. This may entail conducting cost-benefit analyses, assessing return on investment (ROI), and exploring financing mechanisms to support the adoption of sustainable practices by hotel owners and operators.

- Stakeholder engagement and collaboration: Investigate the role of stakeholder engagement and collaboration in promoting sustainable tourism and circular economy initiatives within the hospitality sector. This could include studying partnerships between hotels, government agencies, non-profit organizations, local communities, and other stakeholders to drive collective action towards sustainability goals and address shared challenges.
- Case studies and best practices sharing: Compile case studies and best practices from green hotels around the world to provide practical insights and inspiration for hoteliers interested in adopting sustainable practices. This may entail documenting successful sustainability initiatives, lessons learned, and challenges overcome by different hotels, with a focus on replicable strategies and scalable solutions.
- Social impact assessment: Assess the social impact of green hotels on local communities, including job creation, income generation, cultural preservation, and community engagement. This could involve conducting surveys, interviews, and focus group discussions with hotel employees, residents, and other stakeholders to understand the broader socio-economic implications of sustainable tourism development.

By exploring these future research directions, scholars and practitioners can further advance knowledge and understanding of the role of green hotels in promoting sustainable development, circular economy principles, and resilient tourism systems.

CONCLUSION

The transition to a circular economy would bring significant progress in the economic prosperity of Europe, considering the foundational principles of the concept, which involve optimizing resource yields, promoting system efficiency, minimizing negative externalities, and preserving and enhancing natural capital. The introduction of circular economy brings new technologies and business models that could maximize the value derived from assets and materials, enable internal growth (extracting value from existing product and material stocks), and thereby decouple value creation from the consumption of finite resources.

The European economy is highly wasteful in its value creation model but continues to operate within a take-produce-dispose system. Circular economy can help overcome this. In achieving sustainable development, the public sector serves as a regulatory body, working together with the private sector as the main actor in realizing economic, social, and environmental goals, and acting as a bridge to civil society.

The transition to a circular economy would entail significant costs, such as research and development expenses, investments in assets, expenditures on digital infrastructure, and promotion of new products in the market. However, if this transition is well managed, it can create significant opportunities for economic and industrial renewal, establishing an efficient system of reuse and recycling, renewable energy sources, and proper waste management.

The tourism sector, through the implementation of green hotels, is one of the few industries that applies circular economy principles in its business processes. Ecotourists can be defined as tourists who constitute a market segment with a clear awareness of environmental vulnerability. This segment includes ethical tourists, environmentally responsible tourists, good tourists, and ecotourists.

Interest in green hotels has been growing, and an increasing number of tourists choose to stay in establishments that support environmental protection and sustainable development principles. One of the most common challenges hoteliers face when building green hotels according to environmental standards is insufficient financial resources. Energy-efficient technology, procurement of smart and environmentally friendly materials for hotel construction and furnishing, and staff training require significant initial capital.

With globalization and standardization of the concept of sustainable development in the hotel industry, it is expected that the number of green hotels will increase both globally and in Serbia.

Green hotels in Serbia do not operate according to the requirements of the Green Key certification, which emphasizes in its criteria the importance of informing consumers, staff, and the general public about the company's operations and the possibilities for each individual to reduce their ecological impact on the world around them. Such information is of great importance for achieving environmental awareness and balance.

It is crucial to ensure an attractive range of local eco-products in Serbia's hotel offerings, which also dictates the broader community to implement potential measures at the tourist destination level to stimulate land cultivation while considering environmental perspectives. Constructing new and maintaining existing rainwater tanks and drains is beneficial, providing a useful water source for garden irrigation. Soil should be nourished naturally by composting organic waste and using it as eco-friendly fertilizer instead of chemical agents, which should be eliminated from plant protection areas. Consensus should be reached on maximizing the availability of such products at the destination level, which brings benefits. Earnings from the sale of local eco-products ensure funds for infrastructure investment, further encouraging sustainable development. A destination in Serbia capable of producing its own eco-hotels within its borders encourages the entire region to become wealthier and healthier.

One of the recommendations for further development in Serbia is to provide appropriate economic instruments for efficient waste management. Enacting adequate regulations in the hotel industry would have a significant impact on reducing the amount of food waste generated and significantly reducing the costs of establishing and managing this system.

It can be concluded that the strategies aimed at sustainable development adopted between 2000 and 2019 have had an impact on progress from economic, social, and environmental perspectives, with the economic goal being the dominant one. This is supported by indicators of poverty, economic growth, reduced inequality, productivity, etc. On the other hand, progress has also been made in the social and environmental aspects, while not neglecting the outcome of economic results that negatively affect the environment, such as industrialization and urbanization, which contribute to air pollution, waste production, ocean pollution, and global warming, despite the strategies requiring a balance among these goals.

ACKNOWLEDGMENT

Paper is a part of research financed by the MSTDI RS, agreed in decision no. 451-03-66/2024-03/200009 from 5.2.2024.

REFERENCES

Agarwal, A., Srivastava, S., Gupta, A., & Singh, G. (2024). Food wastage and consumerism in circular economy: A review and research directions. *British Food Journal*, 126(6), 2561–2587. 10.1108/BFJ-04-2023-0272

Akel, G., & Noyan, E. (2024). Exploring the criteria for a green and smart hotel: insights from hotel managers' perspectives. *Journal of Hospitality and Tourism Insights*.

Backer, E., & Ritchie, B. W. (2017). VFR travel: A viable market for tourism crisis and disaster recovery? *International Journal of Tourism Research*, 19(4), 400–411. 10.1002/jtr.2102

Borrero, J. D., & Yousafzai, S. (2024). Circular entrepreneurial ecosystems: A Quintuple Helix Model approach. *Management Decision*, 62(13), 188–224. 10.1108/MD-08-2023-1361

Djurić, Z. (2019). *Ekološka održivost poslovanja u hotelijerstvu*. Novi Sad: Biblioteka, Edukons univerzitet, Fakultet za sport i turizam.

Einarsson, S. F. (2019). *What is the link between Circular Economy (CE) and the Sustainable Development Goals (SDGs)?* LinkedIn. https://www.linkedin.com/pulse/what-link-between-circular-economy-ce-sustainable-goals-einarsson/

Environmental Protection Agency. (2023). *Ministry of Environmental Protection Republic of Serbia*. EPA. http://www.sepa.gov.rs/#

Eurostat. (2020). *Waste statistics*. Eurostat. https://ec.europa.eu/eurostat/web/waste/data/database

Gligorić, M., & Jovanović Gavrilović, B. (2017). Circular economy as the backbone of sustainable development of the economy of Serbia. *Economic perspectives. Society of Belgrade Economists, Belgrade*, 22(4), 119–132.

Global Sustainable Tourism Council. (2013). *Criteria for Hotels and Tour Operators. Washington*. Global Sustainable Tourism Council.

Goddek, S., Joyce, A., Kotzen, B., & Burnell, G. M. (2019). *Aquaponics Food Prodaction Systems*. Springer Nature Switzerland AG. 10.1007/978-3-030-15943-6

Gradinac, O., & Jegdić, V. (2016). Inter-destination cooperation as a factor in strengthening the competitiveness of a tourist destination. *Business Economics (Cleveland, Ohio)*, 10(2), 284–300.

Jovanović Gavrilović, B. (2013). Economic development with a human face. Center for publishing activities of the Faculty of Economics, Belgrade.

Key, G. (2023). *Unlocking sustainability in the hospitality industry.* Greenkey. https://www.greenkey.global

Khan, O., & Hinterhuber, A. (2024). Antecedents and consequences of procurement managers' willingness to pay for sustainability: A multi-level perspective. *International Journal of Operations & Production Management*, 44(13), 1–33. 10.1108/IJOPM-02-2023-0135

Khatter, A., White, L., Pyke, J., & McGrath, M. (2021). Barriers and drivers of environmental sustainability: Australian hotels. *International Journal of Contemporary Hospitality Management*, 33(5), 1830–1849. 10.1108/IJCHM-08-2020-0929

Kwok, L., & Lin, M. S. (2023). Green food packages' effects on consumers' pre-to post-consumption evaluations of restaurant curbside pickup service. *International Journal of Contemporary Hospitality Management.*

McKinsey, Q. (2017). *Mapping the benefits of a circular economy.* McKinsey. https://www.mckinsey.com/capabilities/sustainability/our-insights/mapping-the-benefits-of-a-circular-economy

Mihailović, B., Radić Jean, I., Popović, V., Radosavljević, K., Chroneos-Krasavac, B., Bradić-Martinović, A. (2020). Farm Differentiation Strategies and Sustainable Regional Development. *Sustainability, 12*(17), 1-18. 10.3390/su12177223

Mihailović, B., Radosavljević, K., & Popović, V. (2023). The role of indoor smart gardens in the development of smart agriculture in urban areas. *Ekonomika Poljoprivrede*, 70(2), 453–468. 10.59267/ekoPolj2302453M

Mitrović, Đ. (2015). Transition from linear to circular economy. *Thematic collection of papers Economic policy and development* (pp. 111-113). Belgrade: Center for publishing activities of the Faculty of Economics.

Patwary, A. K., Rasoolimanesh, S. M., Hanafiah, M. H., Aziz, R. C., Mohamed, A. E., Ashraf, M. U., & Azam, N. R. A. N. (2024). Empowering pro-environmental potential among hotel employees: insights from self-determination theory. *Journal of Hospitality and Tourism Insights*.

Prakash, S., Sharma, V. P., Singh, R., Vijayvargy, L., & Nilaish, . (2023). Adopting green and sustainable practices in the hotel industry operations-an analysis of critical performance indicators for improved environmental quality. *Management of Environmental Quality*, 34(4), 1057–1076. 10.1108/MEQ-03-2022-0090

Quan, L., Koo, B., & Han, H. (2023). Exploring the factors that influence customers' willingness to switch from traditional hotels to green hotels. *Journal of Travel & Tourism Marketing*, 40(3), 185–202. 10.1080/10548408.2023.2236649

Radosavljević, K. (2017). *Marketing channels of agricultural products*. Institute of Economic Sciences.

Radosavljević, K., & Mihailović, B. (2023). *Contemporary management problems in the hotel industry*. Belgrade Banking Academy. Faculty of Banking, Insurance and Finance.

Renfors, S. M. (2024). Education for the circular economy in higher education: An overview of the current state. *International Journal of Sustainability in Higher Education*, 25(9), 111–127. 10.1108/IJSHE-07-2023-0270

Schroeder, P., Anggraeni, K., & Weber, U. (2018). *The relevance of circular economy practices to the sustainable development goals*. Institute of Development Studies, University of Sussex.

Scott, D. (2006). Climate change and sustainable tourism in the 21st century, in: *Tourism Research: Policy, Planning, and Prospects* (J. Cukier, ed.) Waterloo, Department of Geography Publication Series, University of Waterloo.

Šestović, M., Radosavljević, K., & Chroneos-Krasavac, B. (2017). The importance of EU pre-accession funds for agriculture and their influence on country's competitiveness. *Economics of enterprise, 65*(7-8), 506-517.

Sharma, T., & Chen, J. S. (2023). Expected green hotel attributes: visit intentions in light of climate change and COVID-19 double whammy. In *Advances in Hospitality and Leisure* (pp. 155–176). Emerald Publishing Limited. 10.1108/S1745-354220220000018009

Umoh, S. U. (2024). Green Hotels and Green Practices in South Africa. In *Future Tourism Trends* (Vol. 1, pp. 91–98). Emerald Publishing Limited. 10.1108/978-1-83753-244-520241007

Vandermaesen, T., Humphries, R., Wackernagel, M., Murthy, A., & Mailhes, L. (2019). *Living beyond nature's limits*. World Wide Fund for Nature.

Vieira do Nascimento, D. (2016). Exploring climate finance for tourism adaptation development: An overview. *Worldwide Hospitality and Tourism Themes*, 8(5), 593–605. 10.1108/WHATT-06-2016-0036

Waris, I., Iqbal, A., Ahmed, R., Hashim, S., & Ahmed, A. (2023). Values and information publicity shape tourists' intentions to visit green hotels: An application of the extended value-belief norms theory. *Management of Environmental Quality*.

Wasaya, A., Prentice, C., & Hsiao, A. (2023). Norms and consumer behaviors in tourism: A systematic literature review. *Tourism Review*.

Yang, Y., Jiang, L., & Wang, Y. (2023). Why do hotels go green? Understanding TripAdvisor GreenLeaders participation. *International Journal of Contemporary Hospitality Management*, 35(5), 1670–1690. 10.1108/IJCHM-02-2022-0252

ADDITIONAL READING

Abdou, A. H., Hassan, T. H., & El Dief, M. M. (2020). A description of green hotel practices and their role in achieving sustainable development. *Sustainability (Basel)*, 12(22), 9624. 10.3390/su12229624

Acharya, M. P., & Mahapatra, S. S. (2022). Circular economy in enhancing brand sustainability of hotels. *Specialusis Ugdymas*, 2(43), 849–864.

Ahmed, M. F., Mokhtar, M. B., Lim, C. K., Hooi, A. W. K., & Lee, K. E. (2021). Leadership roles for sustainable development: The case of a Malaysian green hotel. *Sustainability (Basel)*, 13(18), 10260. 10.3390/su131810260

Cantó Calvo, V. M. (2022). *Development of a circular economy evaluation model for hotels* [Doctoral dissertation, Universitat Politècnica de València].

Fatimah, Y. A., Govindan, K., Murniningsih, R., & Setiawan, A. (2020). Industry 4.0 based sustainable circular economy approach for smart waste management system to achieve sustainable development goals: A case study of Indonesia. *Journal of Cleaner Production*, 269, 122263. 10.1016/j.jclepro.2020.122263

Li, K., Cipolletta, G., Andreola, C., Eusebi, A. L., Kulaga, B., Cardinali, S., & Fatone, F. (2023). Circular economy and sustainability in the tourism industry: Critical analysis of integrated solutions and good practices in European and Chinese case studies. *Environment, Development and Sustainability*, 26(7), 1–22. 10.1007/s10668-023-03395-7

Obeidat, S. M., Abdalla, S., & Al Bakri, A. A. K. (2023). Integrating green human resource management and circular economy to enhance sustainable performance: An empirical study from the Qatari service sector. *Employee Relations*, 45(2), 535–563. 10.1108/ER-01-2022-0041

Pamfilie, R., Firoiu, D., Croitoru, A. G., & Ionescu, G. H. I. (2018). Circular economy–A new direction for the sustainability of the hotel industry in Romania. *Amfiteatru Economic*, 20(48), 388–404. 10.24818/EA/2018/48/388

Pan, S. Y., Gao, M., Kim, H., Shah, K. J., Pei, S. L., & Chiang, P. C. (2018). Advances and challenges in sustainable tourism toward a green economy. *The Science of the Total Environment*, 635, 452–469. 10.1016/j.scitotenv.2018.04.13429677671

Prasad, M. N. V., Smol, M., & Freitas, H. (2023). Achieving sustainable development goals via green deal strategies. In *Sustainable and Circular Management of Resources and Waste Towards a Green Deal* (pp. 3–23). Elsevier. 10.1016/B978-0-323-95278-1.00002-4

Rodríguez, C., Florido, C., & Jacob, M. (2020). Circular economy contributions to the tourism sector: A critical literature review. *Sustainability (Basel)*, 12(11), 4338. 10.3390/su12114338

Yousaf, Z., Radulescu, M., Sinisi, C. I., Serbanescu, L., & Paunescu, L. M. (2021). Harmonization of green motives and green business strategies towards sustainable development of hospitality and tourism industry: Green environmental policies. *Sustainability (Basel)*, 13(12), 6592. 10.3390/su13126592

KEY TERMS AND DEFINITIONS

Bioeconomy: Bioeconomy refers to an economic system that utilizes renewable biological resources, such as plants, animals, and microorganisms, to produce goods, services, and energy in a sustainable and environmentally friendly manner. It encompasses various sectors, including agriculture, forestry, fisheries, and biotechnology, and seeks to promote the sustainable use of biological resources while minimizing negative impacts on ecosystems and biodiversity.

Circular Economy: The circular economy is an economic model that aims to minimize resource consumption and waste generation by maximizing the efficiency of resource use, promoting the reuse, recycling, and regeneration of materials and products throughout their lifecycle. It involves shifting from the traditional linear "take-make-dispose" model to a closed-loop system where resources are continuously cycled back into the economy, reducing the extraction of raw materials and the generation of waste.

Eco-Tourism: Eco-tourism is a form of tourism that emphasizes responsible travel to natural areas with a focus on conservation, environmental education, and cultural immersion. It involves visiting natural habitats, protected areas, and ecologically sensitive regions while minimizing negative impacts on the environment and supporting local communities. Eco-tourism aims to promote environmental awareness, biodiversity conservation, and sustainable development through tourism activities that contribute to the protection of natural resources and cultural heritage.

Green Hotels: Green hotels are accommodations that prioritize environmental sustainability and eco-friendly practices in their operations and management. These hotels implement measures to minimize their environmental impact, such as reducing energy and water consumption, minimizing waste generation, using renewable energy sources, promoting recycling and composting, and adopting green building design and construction practices. Green hotels aim to provide guests with a sustainable and environmentally responsible lodging experience.

Intellectual Capital: Intellectual capital refers to the intangible assets and resources owned or controlled by an organization that contribute to its value and competitive advantage. It includes knowledge, expertise, intellectual property, innovation capabilities, and organizational processes and systems. Intellectual capital plays a critical role in driving innovation, creativity, and sustainable growth within organizations by leveraging human capital, structural capital, and relational capital.

Pressure-State-Response (P-S-R) model: which, as the name suggests, is based on three outcomes: environmental pressure, the state in which the environment is found, and the response or reaction of society to the existing state.

Sustainable Development: Sustainable development refers to a holistic approach to societal progress that aims to meet the needs of the present generation without compromising the ability of future generations to meet their own needs. It involves balancing economic, social, and environmental considerations to promote long-term viability and resilience.

Chapter 5
Mapping Green Infrastructure Harnessing OSM Data for Sustainable Development

Munir Ahmad
https://orcid.org/0000-0003-4836-6151
Survey of Pakistan, Pakistan

ABSTRACT

The chapter provides a comprehensive analysis of global studies on urban green spaces (UGS), highlighting their diverse methodologies and findings. Spanning countries such as the USA, Kenya, Germany, Finland, Portugal, China, Brazil, Belgium, Ukraine, Norway, Spain, South Africa, and many more, these studies underscore the pivotal role of UGS in enhancing urban quality of life, addressing socio-economic disparities, and mitigating environmental challenges. Utilizing approaches such as citizen science mapping, spatial analysis, and socio-economic assessments, the research emphasizes the importance of equitable UGS access, efficient urban planning, and community engagement. Furthermore, the findings offer policy recommendations aimed at optimizing UGS provision, enhancing accessibility, and integrating green infrastructure into urban development strategies. This research highlights the worldwide importance of UGS and provides crucial insights for policymakers, planners, and communities aiming for healthier, more sustainable cities.

DOI: 10.4018/979-8-3693-3439-3.ch005

INTRODUCTION

Urban green spaces refer to any areas within urban environments that are predominantly covered by vegetation, such as parks, gardens, forests, and even roadside greenery. These spaces play crucial roles in enhancing the quality of urban life by providing recreational areas, promoting biodiversity, mitigating urban heat island effects, improving air quality, and offering opportunities for social interaction and physical activity. Urban green space (UGS) provides numerous environmental and social benefits and is increasingly prioritized in urban policies (Texier, Schiel, and Caruso 2018).

Spatial data, which includes geographic information system (GIS) data, remote sensing data, and other location-based information, can greatly aid in analyzing urban green spaces. Spatial data allows for the accurate mapping of urban green spaces, including their location, size, shape, and characteristics. This mapping can be done using satellite imagery, aerial photography, LiDAR data, and ground surveys. Spatial data can enable the quantification of various attributes of green spaces, such as vegetation cover, canopy density, species diversity, and habitat connectivity. This quantitative information helps in assessing the extent and quality of green spaces within urban areas.

GIS techniques can be used to perform spatial analysis on green space data. This includes proximity analysis to determine accessibility to green spaces, spatial interpolation to estimate vegetation density across urban areas, and hotspot analysis to identify areas with high or low levels of greenery. Spatial data can also be used to assess the environmental impact of urban development on green spaces. This includes analyzing land use changes, monitoring vegetation loss or fragmentation, and identifying areas at risk of habitat destruction.

OpenStreetMap (OSM) is a collaborative project that aims to create a free and editable map of the world. It allows users to contribute and edit geographic data to improve the accuracy and completeness of maps. OSM data can contribute to green space analytics in several ways. OSM provides a wealth of geospatial data, including information on parks, gardens, forests, and other green spaces within urban areas. This data can be accessed and used for various analytical purposes. OSM allows users to update and maintain information about green spaces in real time. This enables the continuous improvement of green space data, ensuring that it remains accurate and up-to-date.

Moreover, OSM data can be easily integrated with GIS platforms for spatial analysis and visualization. By combining OSM data with other spatial datasets, analysts can gain insights into the distribution and characteristics of urban green spaces. It can foster community engagement and collaboration, allowing users to contribute local knowledge about green spaces. This crowdsourced approach can help in identifying new green spaces, documenting their features, and advocating for their conservation and enhancement.

In light of this context, the primary aim of this chapter is to examine the applicability of OSM data for mapping green spaces. To accomplish this objective, the chapter is organized as follows: The second section elucidates an overview of green infrastructure. The third section elaborates on the methodology adopted to accomplish the objective of this chapter. The final section offers a concluding summary of the chapter with a window for future work.

BACKGROUND INFORMATION

Green Infrastructure

Green infrastructure is a holistic approach to land use planning and development that emphasizes the integration of natural and built environments to achieve multiple benefits for both people and the planet. It encompasses a wide range of elements, including parks, forests, wetlands, green roofs, permeable pavements, greenways, and urban agriculture, among others. These elements interact with one another and with surrounding landscapes to provide a host of ecosystem services and social amenities that are essential for sustainable living.

Environmental Quality

Green infrastructure plays a crucial role in improving environmental quality by mitigating various forms of pollution and enhancing ecological processes. For example, urban parks and green spaces act as natural filters, absorbing pollutants from the air and water and improving overall air and water quality. Wetlands and riparian buffers help to filter and purify water, reducing sedimentation, nutrient runoff, and pollutants before they enter rivers and streams. By preserving and restoring natural habitats, green infrastructure supports biodiversity and ecological resilience, ensuring the long-term health of ecosystems and the species that depend on them.

Public Health

Access to green spaces and nature has been linked to numerous physical and mental health benefits. Green infrastructure provides opportunities for physical activity, recreation, and relaxation, which are essential for maintaining healthy lifestyles and reducing the risk of chronic diseases such as obesity, diabetes, and cardiovascular disorders. Exposure to natural environments has also been shown to reduce stress, anxiety, and depression, contributing to overall well-being and quality of life. By providing accessible and attractive green spaces, communities can promote public health and social equity, ensuring that all residents have equal opportunities to enjoy the benefits of nature.

Community Well-Being

Green infrastructure enhances the livability and attractiveness of communities by creating vibrant, sustainable environments where people can live, work, and play. Parks and green spaces serve as gathering places for social interaction and cultural activities, fostering a sense of community and belonging among residents. Greenways and trails provide opportunities for walking, cycling, and commuting, promoting active transportation and reducing reliance on automobiles. Urban agriculture and community gardens contribute to food security, nutrition, and social cohesion, empowering residents to grow their own food and connect with their neighbors. By integrating green infrastructure into the fabric of cities and neighborhoods, communities can create inclusive, resilient, and vibrant places that enhance the quality of life for all.

Ecosystem Services

Green infrastructure provides a wide range of ecosystem services that are essential for human well-being and the functioning of natural systems. These services include carbon sequestration, which helps to mitigate climate change by absorbing and storing carbon dioxide from the atmosphere; air purification, which removes pollutants and improves air quality; and stormwater management, which reduces flooding and erosion by absorbing and infiltrating rainwater. Additionally, green infrastructure supports biodiversity by providing habitat for wildlife, supporting pollinators, and maintaining ecological balance. By enhancing ecosystem services, green infrastructure contributes to the resilience and sustainability of cities and regions, helping to mitigate the impacts of climate change and other environmental stressors.

OpenStreetMap (OSM)

OpenStreetMap (OSM) (https://www.openstreetmap.org/) is a collaborative, volunteer-driven project providing a free, editable, and user-generated global geographic information database, with applications in navigation and real-time updates. It is a user-generated street map project that follows the peer production model of Wikipedia, providing free, editable, and licensed under new copyright schemes (Weber and Haklay 2008). OpenStreetMap data is used for urban analysis, land cover mapping, routing and navigation, spatial analysis, visualizations, and various applications across software and hardware platforms. For example, OpenStreetMap data is used to analyze 27,000 US street networks at metropolitan, municipal, and neighborhood scales for urban form and street network characteristics (Boeing 2020a). Similarly, OpenStreetMap data is used to produce a global Open Land Cover (OLC) product, with complete coverage in Heidelberg, Germany, and an overall accuracy of 87% (Schultz et al. 2017). It is used to create land use and land cover maps for urban regions in London and Paris (Fonte et al. 2019). Moreover, OSM data can be employed to extract information about Local Climate Zones (LCZs), particularly for natural classes, in the region of Coimbra City, Portugal as noted by Lopes et al. (2017).

OSM data has been extensively used in navigation applications, providing instructions through textual and cartographic interfaces and augmented images showing way-finding objects (Amirian et al. 2015). Furthermore, OSM has been employed to analyze and visualize planning and design outcomes in the built environment, using visualization methods like figure-ground diagrams and polar histograms (Boeing 2020b). It has been used for real-time and exact shortest path computation on continental-sized networks with millions of street segments, and sophisticated features like draggable routes and round-trip planning (Luxen and Vetter 2011).

Additionally, OpenStreetMap data is widely used for global urban analyses, including tracking progress towards Sustainable Development Goals (SDGs). Herfort et al. (2023) analyzed the completeness of OpenStreetMap building data globally, considering various factors such as world region, human development index, and city size. OSM building completeness varies significantly across different urban centers, with some areas having over 80% completeness while others remain below 20%. The temporal evolution of inequality in urban OSM building mapping was examined using measures like the Gini coefficient and Moran's I, providing insights into the uneven distribution of building data over time. Over time, global spatial inequality in OSM building completeness has decreased, but local spatial autocorrelation has increased, especially in regions with higher human development indices.

METHODOLOGY

This chapter conducted an extensive literature review to get insights into the use of OSM for mapping urban green spaces. Google Scholar search engine has been employed to extract the literature. "Green Space" AND ("OSM" OR "OpenStreetMap") search string has been used to search relevant literature. The first 100 search results are examined and the most relevant studies are included in the results section.

RESULTS AND DISCUSSIONS

In cities worldwide, community-based mapping initiatives have leveraged OpenStreetMap (OSM) data to document and assess urban green spaces. For example, in New York City, USA, the organization NYC Parks launched the "TreesCount! 2015" campaign, which engaged volunteers in mapping the city's street trees using the OSM platform (NYC Parks 2015). By crowdsourcing tree data, including species, size, and condition, the project generated a comprehensive inventory of urban forests, which informed tree planting efforts, maintenance priorities, and canopy coverage assessments. Similarly, in Nairobi, Kenya, the group Map Kibera utilized OSM to map informal settlements and identify green spaces within densely populated urban areas (Map Kibera, n.d.). The project engaged local residents in mapping parks, gardens, and open spaces, which facilitated community-led initiatives for improving access to green infrastructure and enhancing environmental quality in informal settlements.

Researchers have utilized OSM data to analyze the distribution and accessibility of green infrastructure amenities and their impact on public health and well-being. For example, Liao, Zhou, and Jing (2021) analyzed five UK urban areas for diverse geographic and demographic representation and employed six open datasets including OSM. The analysis revealed that OSM datasets were top-performing datasets overall. The study also underpinned that careful selection of land-use/land-cover (LULC) classes is pivotal for effective green space mapping. Similarly, the study conducted by Almohamad, Knaack, and Habib (2018) contributes to understanding urban green space accessibility in Aleppo, Syria. Findings highlight disparities in park provision among different socioeconomic groups, emphasizing the importance of environmental justice principles in urban planning. The research underscores the need for equitable distribution of green spaces post-war, informing policymakers and decision-makers for balanced and sustainable reconstruction efforts.

The study (Yin et al. 2022) revealed that urban green spaces in Hangzhou, China have increased from 2017 to 2021. The increase is mainly concentrated in the urban core area, indicating significant achievements in green space planning. The increase in green spaces in the first ring belt was linked to the old town transformation program in residential land, while changes from residential parcels to business parcels drove growth in the second and third ring belts. Farmland transformation into impervious surfaces resulted in the conversion of open-space parcels to business parcels around the urban periphery. Similarly, the study (Trojanek, Gluszak, and Tanas 2018) found that proximity to urban green areas positively impacts apartment prices in Warsaw, Poland, with the presence of green areas within 100 meters increasing dwelling prices by 2.8% to 3.1% on average. This impact is more significant for newer apartments built after 1989, while close vicinity to urban green spaces boosts sales prices of apartments in new residential buildings by 8.0–8.6%.

The study conducted by L. Pinto, Ferreira, and Pereira (2021) found that activities in urban green spaces (UGS) in Coimbra, Portugal, vary based on factors such as age, gender, education level, income, transport type, and distance from residence to UGS. Moreover, accessibility to UGS is crucial for users, highlighting the importance of proximity and ease of access. The multifunctionality of UGS influences users' selection, indicating that users value spaces that offer a variety of activities. Furthermore, users generally do not perceive ecosystem disservices as a threat in the studied parks, although concerns such as mosquitoes and dangerous animals are noted in some areas. Users' motivations to visit UGS differ based on factors like accessibility, proximity to home or work, tranquility, landscape beauty, and the presence of water elements.

Unal Cilek and Uslu (2022) emphasized the standardization of appropriate urban green space characteristics to enhance thermal comfort across diverse urban landscapes in Adana, Tukey. Factors such as canopy cover ratio, local climate zone (LCZ), and UGS geometry play pivotal roles in influencing mean physiological equivalent temperature (PET). Additionally, shading and wind circulation are identified as positive contributors to UGS thermal comfort in hot-humid urban environments. Whereas, Ludwig et al. (2021) underscored the significance of urban green spaces for enhancing quality of life, highlighting the limitations of using Sentinel-2 imagery and OpenStreetMap data in mapping these spaces due to inherent uncertainties. Through the fusion of Sentinel-2 imagery and OSM data using Dempster–Shafer theory, the study demonstrated improved detection of green spaces, addressing uncertainties effectively. Utilizing a Bayesian hierarchical model alongside OSM data facilitated the distinction between public and private green spaces. Testing and validation in Dresden, Germany, achieved a 95% accuracy rate in mapping public urban green spaces, revealing that OSM data primarily comprises buildings with a small proportion designated as green spaces. Contextual indicators in OSM, such as footpaths and amenities, were crucial for distinguishing public green spaces, with further accuracy improvements achieved by incorporating additional indicators like benches and playgrounds.

Urban green infrastructure distribution in South Africa reflects socio-economic and racial disparities, with parks more prevalent in wealthier neighborhoods and white-dominated areas exhibiting higher tree cover. Inequities persist in both public and private spaces, exacerbated by historical spatial clustering and Apartheid-era influences (Venter, Shackleton, et al. 2020). Moreover, the study executed by Iraegui, Augusto, and Cabral (2020) assessed equity in accessibility to urban green spaces in Barcelona, Spain, considering spatial correlations with socioeconomic variables, such as income distribution, population density, and age demographics, highlighting the importance of fair access to UGS for all residents using OSM and ESRI datasets.

Korah, Akaateba, and Akanbang (2024) employed remote sensing, OSM, and cadastral datasets to examine the state of urban green spaces in Kumasi, Ghana, revealing a concerning trend of fragmentation and disconnection between 2013 and 2020, especially evident in the city's outskirts. Shockingly, around 58% of Kumasi's residents lack access to parks within a reasonable 30-minute walking distance. Whereas, Viinikka et al. (2023) investigated the associations between neighborhood-level socioeconomic status, accessibility, and quality of green spaces in Finnish urban regions using OSM, satellite images, and Google Earth data. The research explored the impact of urban green spaces on public health, physical activity, and well-being, emphasizing the importance of equitable access to these spaces. It revealed that residents in Finnish urban regions generally have good accessibility to green spaces, with 90% having very good access to any green area within 300 meters, but large green areas and forests are less accessible, with only 56% and 51% of residents living within 300 meters, respectively. Green spaces with additional quality factors like recreation routes and facilities have even lower accessibility, with only 20% of residents living within 300 meters.

The study (Sebestyén et al. 2024) presented the development of an objective well-being level (OWL) composite indicator for sustainable and resilient cities, employing multivariate methods encompassing physical, economic, social, environmental, and mental aspects in Hungary. It integrated various data sources like OpenStreetMap, Landsat, and NASA EarthExplorer, assessing urban well-being based on infrastructural elements, satellite images, and elevation data. The OWL methodology offered insights into sustainable city planning, revealing spatial patterns influenced by natural features, urban infrastructure, and accessibility to services. Street connectivity exhibits a stronger link to decreased PM2.5 emissions from transportation compared to density metrics as noted by (Rezaei and Millard-Ball 2023) in a global study of 462 cities using datasets like Global Human Settlement Layer and OpenStreetMap road network. The study revealed that generalizing urban form characteristics and impacts across income groups or geographic regions may not be appropriate due to context-specific correlations. Moreover, density alone is insufficient to represent urban form; multiple indicators like street connectivity are essential.

The study (Liu et al. 2020) utilized Weibo data and OpenStreetMap base map to analyze the behavior of millions of people in Shanghai's green spaces and employ spatial and temporal analysis methods to understand patterns and trends. Insights include peak visit times, gender-based differences, and seasonal variations, offering valuable recommendations for urban planners to enhance environmental sustainability and smart city architecture through improved access to quality green spaces. While, the study conducted by Venter, Barton, et al. (2020) showed that pedestrians and cyclists demonstrated intensified activity, especially in areas with higher green views and tree canopy cover, including city parks, peri-urban forests, and protected areas in Oslo, Norway using OpenStreetMap base layer and STRAVA data. Accessible large open green spaces, coupled with social distancing measures, helped alleviate the negative health impacts of physical mobility restrictions and reduce the risk of disease transmission. This underscored the crucial role of urban green spaces in promoting physical and mental well-being, emphasizing the necessity of conserving existing green areas and allocating urban land for new green spaces.

L. V. Pinto et al. (2022) compared the accessibility of urban green spaces in Vilnius, Lithuania, and Coimbra, Portugal, measuring factors such as proximity, size, and distribution using multiple datasets including Google Maps and OSM. Coimbra exhibits superior accessibility, attributed to historical urban development, topography, and city planning. Nonetheless, both cities encountered challenges in ensuring equitable green space access for all residents. Whereas, Chênes, Giuliani, and Ray (2021) estimated the accessibility to green spaces using OSM and SwissTopo datasets in Switzerland. The results showed that approximately 75% of the Swiss population can access the nearest urban green space within 5 min using motorized transport, with 72% able to reach the nearest forest patch within the same timeframe. Additionally, more than 55% of the Swiss urban population can access the nearest urban green space in less than 5 minutes of walking. Access to forests within 15 min travel time is high at the national level, with more than 92% of the population able to reach a forest. However, there is a disparity in access at sub-national levels, influenced by factors such as road density, green space density, and population distribution.

Novack, Wang, and Zipf (2018) generated customized pedestrian routes based on OpenStreetMap data, considering factors like green areas, sociability, and quietness. Greenness, sociability, and quietness factors are defined and extracted from OSM and then integrated into a routing cost function. Route lengths and factors are computed to ensure alternative routes are only slightly longer but significantly more social, greener, and quieter than the shortest routes. The system's usefulness, usability, and controllability/transparency were evaluated within the German context, with positive feedback indicating it's easy to use and provides users with control over route preferences. The results showed that users generally prefer walking routes influenced by green areas, social places, and less traffic noise, highlighting the importance of considering these factors in pedestrian route planning.

Shyshchenko, Havrylenko, and Tsyhanok (2021) assessed urban green space accessibility in compact cities like Kyiv, Ukraine through spatial and quantitative analysis using OpenStreetMap, Google Map geospatial data, and QGIS software. Pedestrian accessibility to greenery is determined based on walking distances from residential buildings, revealing an uneven distribution of UGS in different city districts. While Kyiv appears "green" with UGS accessible within 1,000m, there's a deficiency of UGS for daily recreation in some areas, with only 45.4% of residents having high pedestrian accessibility. Whereas, a study (Weigand et al. 2023) conducted using remote sensing, OpenStreetMap, and census data in Germany revealed that 19.2% of Germans lack the World Health Organization (WHO) defined target for PGS in their neighborhoods, with access varying based on housing types and demographic composition. Urban and rural areas showed distinct differences in green space availability, with implications for health and social equity.

Heikinheimo, Tiitu, and Viinikka (2023) investigated the value of different datasets related to green spaces in Finland. The results showed that data on green space quality and accessibility in Finland's seven largest urban regions are available, including information on different types of green spaces and their accessibility via walking and cycling, derived from Urban Atlas data and enhanced with national data on water bodies, conservation areas, and recreational facilities. In the study, network distances to green spaces are calculated using Python programming tools and the pedestrian street network from OpenStreetMap, aggregated into a 250m x 250m statistical grid interoperable with various statistical data from Finland. Various datasets from different sources, including those from the Finnish Environment Institute, National Land Survey of Finland, Metsähallitus, University of Jyväskylä, and OpenStreetMap contributors, contributed to the comprehensive analysis, enabling in-depth analyses and drawing meaningful conclusions about green space dynamics.

Texier, Schiel, and Caruso (2018) studied the impact of spatial data on urban green space provision and accessibility in Brussels, Belgium. The results revealed that variations in UGS indicators arise from different data sources like Landsat imagery, cadastre-based maps, and OpenStreetMap (OSM), especially in capturing private and public green space. Despite these differences, the interpretation of intra-urban spatial variations remains consistent, with centrality being a key determinant of UGS availability, fragmentation, and accessibility.

Ju, Dronova, and Delclòs-Alió (2022) created a 10 m resolution urban green space map for major Latin American cities using Sentinel-2 remote sensing images and OpenStreetMap (OSM) data to study urban green space using detailed information on area, spatial configuration, and human exposures. The overall accuracy of the UGS map in 11 randomly selected cities was 0.87, with better accuracies observed in cities with tropical climates compared to temperate and arid climates. Visual inspection and quality control were conducted to ensure mapping accuracy, involving two independent inspectors assessing all 371 cities and refining boundaries and labels for OSM polygons where necessary. Table 1 summarizes the key findings, methodologies recommendations, and dataset used in the above literature review.

Table 1. Role of OSM in mapping green infrastructure

Main Findings	Country	Analysis/ Methodology	Recommendations	Dataset Used	Reference
Engaged volunteers in mapping street trees using OSM, informing tree planting efforts.	USA	Citizen science mapping, data integration	Prioritize tree planting in areas with low canopy cover, engage communities	OSM	(NYC Parks 2015)
Used OSM to map informal settlements, facilitating community-led green infrastructure initiatives.	Kenya	Participatory mapping, community engagement	Develop green infrastructure projects in informal settlements, empower local communities	OSM	(Map Kibera, n.d.)
Analyzed OSM data for mapping green spaces, emphasizing the importance of land-use classification.	UK	Remote sensing, GIS analysis, land-use classification	Improve accuracy of green space mapping through refined land-use classification	OSM, Remote Sensing Data	(Liao, Zhou, and Jing 2021)
Highlighted disparities in park provision, stressing equitable distribution in urban planning.	Syria	Socioeconomic analysis, spatial equity assessment	Implement policies for equitable distribution of green spaces, prioritize underserved neighborhoods	Census Data, OSM	(Almohamad, Knaack, and Habib 2018)
Revealed an increase in urban green spaces from 2017 to 2021, driven by transformation programs.	China	Spatial-temporal analysis, land use change detection	Monitor urban green space changes regularly, integrate green space planning with urban development strategies	Satellite Imagery, OSM	(Yin et al. 2022)
Explored user preferences in urban green spaces, emphasizing accessibility and multifunctionality.	Portugal	User surveys, spatial analysis, activity mapping	Design green spaces for diverse user activities, improve accessibility for all demographic groups	User Surveys, OSM	(L. Pinto, Ferreira, and Pereira 2021)
Found proximity to green areas positively impacted apartment prices, influencing real estate dynamics.	Poland	Hedonic pricing model, spatial regression analysis	Consider green space proximity in real estate valuation, integrate green space planning with urban development	Real Estate Data, OSM	(Trojanek, Gluszak, and Tanas 2018)

continued on following page

Table 1. Continued

Main Findings	Country	Analysis/ Methodology	Recommendations	Dataset Used	Reference
Emphasized standardizing urban green space characteristics for enhancing thermal comfort.	Turkey	Thermal comfort modeling, GIS analysis	Design green spaces to optimize thermal comfort, incorporate green space standards into urban planning regulations	Thermal Comfort Models, OSM	(Unal Cilek and Uslu 2022)
Demonstrated urban green spaces' significance for quality of life, proposing improved mapping methodology.	Germany	Remote sensing, OSM data integration, quality of life assessment	Improve green space mapping for quality-of-life assessment, prioritize green space preservation	Remote Sensing, OSM	(Ludwig et al. 2021)
Highlighted socio-economic disparities in green infrastructure, advocating for equitable access.	South Africa	Socioeconomic analysis, spatial equity assessment	Implement policies to address historical inequities in green space provision, ensure equitable access for all	Census Data, OSM	(Venter, Shackleton, et al. 2020).
Assessed UGS accessibility, emphasizing fair access for all residents based on spatial correlations.	Spain	Accessibility modeling, spatial correlation analysis	Prioritize green space development in underserved areas, incorporate equity into the planning process	OSM, Socioeconomic Data, ESRI	(Iraegui, Augusto, and Cabral 2020)
Examined urban green space trends, highlighting fragmentation issues and park access disparities.	Ghana	Spatial analysis, fragmentation assessment	Address fragmentation through green space connectivity planning, allocate resources for park access improvement	OSM	(Korah, Akaateba, and Akanbang 2024)
Investigated associations between socioeconomics, accessibility, and green space quality.	Finland	Regression analysis, accessibility assessment, quality evaluation	Integrate socioeconomic factors into green space planning, prioritize equitable access and quality maintenance	OSM, satellite images, Google Earth data	(Viinikka et al. 2023)

continued on following page

Table 1. Continued

Main Findings	Country	Analysis/ Methodology	Recommendations	Dataset Used	Reference
Developed an objective well-being indicator for cities, integrating OSM data for comprehensive assessment.	Hungary	Well-being index development, data integration, spatial analysis	Utilize well-being indicators in urban planning, and integrate OSM data for comprehensive well-being assessment	Landsat, NASA EarthExplorer, OSM	(Sebestyén et al. 2024)
Linked street connectivity to decreased PM2.5 emissions, advocating for urban form considerations.	Global	Network analysis, air quality modeling	Design compacts urban forms to reduce emissions, integrate street connectivity into urban planning	OSM, Air Quality Data	(Rezaei and Millard-Ball 2023)
Analyzed user behavior in Shanghai's green spaces, offering recommendations for urban planners.	China	Social media data analysis, spatial-temporal clustering	Design green spaces for diverse user behaviors, leverage social media data for preference analysis	Weibo Data, OSM	(Liu et al. 2020)
Studied green views' impact on physical activity, suggesting accessible large green spaces promote well-being.	Norway	Physical activity assessment, green space proximity analysis	Design urban areas to maximize green space visibility, promote physical activity through accessibility	OSM, STRAVA	(Venter, Barton, et al. 2020)
Compare urban green space accessibility between cities, addressing disparities in access.	Portugal and Lithuania	Cross-city comparison, accessibility assessment	Learn from best practices in green space accessibility, address disparities through targeted interventions	Google Maps, OSM	(L. V. Pinto et al. 2022)
Estimated green space accessibility variations, proposing policies for improved access.	Switzerland	Accessibility modeling, sub-national analysis	Implement policies to improve green space accessibility in underserved regions, consider local population needs	OSM, SwissTopo	(Chênes, Giuliani, and Ray 2021)
Generated pedestrian routes considering green areas, sociability, and quietness for enhanced urban experiences.	Germany	Pedestrian route optimization, green space integration	Develop pedestrian routes prioritizing green areas, consider sociability and quietness in route planning	OSM	(Novack, Wang, and Zipf 2018)

continued on following page

Table 1. Continued

Main Findings	Country	Analysis/ Methodology	Recommendations	Dataset Used	Reference
Assessed UGS accessibility in compact cities, identifying distribution deficiencies for targeted improvements.	Ukraine	Accessibility assessment, compact city analysis	Improve green space accessibility in compact cities, address deficiencies through targeted development	OSM, Google Map	(Shyshchenko, Havrylenko, and Tsyhanok 2021)
Investigated green space availability disparities between urban and rural areas, recommending policy interventions.	Germany	Availability assessment, urban-rural disparity analysis	Prioritize urban green space development, address rural-urban disparities through policy interventions	OSM, census data	(Weigand et al. 2023)
Examined the value of different datasets for analyzing green spaces, informing comprehensive policy decisions.	Finland	Data comparison, policy analysis	Utilize multiple datasets for comprehensive green space analysis, inform policy decisions through integrated data	OSM, Urban Atlas, National Land Survey	(Heikinheimo, Tiitu, and Viinikka 2023)
Studied spatial data's impact on UGS provision and accessibility, recommending central areas for development.	Belgium	Spatial data analysis, UGS provision assessment	Integrate spatial data for accurate UGS provision assessment, prioritize central areas for development	OSM, Landsat imagery, cadastre-based maps	(Texier, Schiel, and Caruso 2018)
Investigated green spaces' role in mitigating urban heat island effects, proposing design interventions for cooling.	Latin American cities	Urban heat island analysis, green space design recommendations	Implement green space design strategies for urban cooling, prioritize vegetation in heat-sensitive areas	OSM, remote sensing images	(Ju, Dronova, and Delclòs-Alió 2022)

The table provides a comprehensive overview of diverse studies focusing on urban green spaces (UGS) worldwide, showcasing a range of methodologies and findings. These studies, spanning various countries including the USA, Kenya, China, and Brazil, highlight the significance of UGS in enhancing urban quality of life, addressing socio-economic disparities, and mitigating environmental challenges. Through approaches such as citizen science mapping, spatial analysis, and socio-economic assessments, the research underscores the importance of equitable access to green spaces, efficient urban planning, and community engagement. Moreover, findings suggest policy recommendations for optimizing UGS provision, improving accessibility, and integrating green infrastructure into urban development strategies. This breadth of research demonstrates the global relevance of UGS and provides valuable insights for policymakers, planners, and communities seeking to create healthier, more sustainable urban environments.

Benefits of OpenStreetMap in Mapping Green Infrastructure

OpenStreetMap stands as a pioneering platform in the realm of geospatial data, offering a collaborative environment where individuals and organizations worldwide can contribute to the creation, enhancement, and dissemination of geographic information. Based on the analysis of the literature following core benefits of OSM datasets for mapping green infrastructure have been identified.

Crowdsourced Mapping

One of the key strengths of OSM lies in its ability to harness the collective efforts of volunteers and enthusiasts in mapping green infrastructure. Through crowdsourcing, users can contribute their local knowledge and observations to document parks, green spaces, trails, wetlands, and other elements of green infrastructure with remarkable accuracy and detail. This decentralized approach enables the rapid collection of data across diverse landscapes and regions, providing a comprehensive and up-to-date inventory of green assets on a global scale.

Detailed Information

OSM's crowdsourced mapping methodology allows for the capture of nuanced information about green infrastructure features, including their spatial extent, connectivity, accessibility, and ecological characteristics. Contributors can add detailed attributes such as vegetation types, habitat quality, recreational amenities, and conservation status, enriching the dataset with valuable contextual information. As a result, OSM provides a rich and dynamic representation of green infrastructure that reflects the diverse needs and perspectives of local communities.

Interoperability and Integration

OSM's open data format facilitates interoperability and integration with a wide range of applications and analysis tools, making it an invaluable resource for researchers, planners, and policymakers interested in promoting sustainability and resilience. Data from OSM can be easily accessed, downloaded, and incorporated into Geographic Information Systems (GIS) software, web-based mapping platforms, and mobile applications, enabling users to visualize, analyze, and manipulate green infrastructure data in diverse contexts. Furthermore, OSM data can be combined with other datasets, such as satellite imagery, land cover maps, and environmental monitoring data, to create comprehensive spatial models and decision-support systems for green infrastructure planning and management.

Community Engagement and Empowerment

OSM's collaborative approach to mapping empowers local communities to actively participate in the documentation and stewardship of green infrastructure assets. By engaging citizens in data collection and validation processes, OSM fosters a sense of ownership and responsibility for green spaces, encouraging individuals to advocate for their preservation, enhancement, and equitable access. Community-based mapping initiatives can also serve as platforms for environmental education, capacity building, and civic engagement, fostering partnerships between diverse stakeholders and promoting collective action toward sustainable development goals.

CONCLUSION

The collective findings from the diverse array of studies presented in this chapter underscore the critical role of urban green spaces in enhancing urban quality of life, promoting social equity, and mitigating environmental challenges across various global contexts. Through methodologies ranging from citizen science mapping to spatial analysis and socio-economic assessments, these studies have contributed to a deeper understanding of the multifaceted benefits and challenges associated with UGS. Key conclusions drawn from this body of research emphasize the importance of equitable access to green spaces, the need for integrated urban planning approaches that prioritize UGS provision, and the significance of community engagement in UGS initiatives. Moreover, the insights garnered from these studies provide valuable guidance for policymakers, planners, and community stakeholders seeking to create more sustainable and livable cities.

Looking ahead, future research directions should focus on addressing existing gaps and advancing knowledge in several key areas. Firstly, there is a need for further exploration of the effectiveness of specific UGS interventions in addressing pressing urban challenges such as heat island effects, air pollution, and social inequalities. This could involve conducting longitudinal studies to assess the long-term impacts of UGS projects on urban environments and communities. Additionally, research efforts should aim to deepen our understanding of the mechanisms through which UGS influences public health, well-being, and social cohesion, with a particular emphasis on vulnerable and marginalized populations. Furthermore, there is a growing imperative to integrate emerging technologies such as remote sensing, artificial intelligence, and participatory mapping into UGS research and planning practices, enabling more accurate and inclusive decision-making processes. By pursuing these avenues of inquiry, future research has the potential to inform evidence-based policies and strategies that maximize the benefits of UGS for all urban residents while fostering more resilient and sustainable cities.

REFERENCES

Almohamad, H., Knaack, A. L., & Habib, B. M. (2018). Assessing Spatial Equity and Accessibility of Public Green Spaces in Aleppo City, Syria. *Forests*, 9(11), 706. Advance online publication. 10.3390/f9110706

Amirian, P., Basiri, A., Gales, G., Winstanley, A., & McDonald, J. (2015). The next Generation of Navigational Services Using OpenStreetMap Data: The Integration of Augmented Reality and Graph Databases. *Lecture Notes in Geoinformation and Cartography*, 0(9783319142791), 211–228. 10.1007/978-3-319-14280-7_11

Boeing, G. (2020a). A Multi-Scale Analysis of 27,000 Urban Street Networks: Every US City, Town, Urbanized Area, and Zillow Neighborhood. *Environment and Planning. B, Urban Analytics and City Science*, 47(4), 590–608. Advance online publication. 10.1177/2399808318784595

Chênes, C., Giuliani, G., & Ray, N. (2021). Modelling Physical Accessibility to Public Green Spaces in Switzerland to Support the SDG11. *Geomatics*, 1(4), 383–398. 10.3390/geomatics1040022

Fonte, C. C., Patriarca, J. A., Minghini, M., Antoniou, V., See, L., & Brovelli, M. A. (2019). Using OpenStreetMap to Create Land Use and Land Cover Maps: Development of an Application. In *Geospatial Intelligence* (Vol. 2). Concepts, Methodologies, Tools, and Applications. 10.4018/978-1-5225-8054-6.ch047

Heikinheimo, V., Tiitu, M., & Viinikka, A. (2023). Data on Different Types of Green Spaces and Their Accessibility in the Seven Largest Urban Regions in Finland. *Data in Brief*, 50, 109458. 10.1016/j.dib.2023.10945837600595

Herfort, B., Lautenbach, S., Porto de Albuquerque, J., Anderson, J., & Zipf, A. (2023). A Spatio-Temporal Analysis Investigating Completeness and Inequalities of Global Urban Building Data in OpenStreetMap. *Nature Communications*, 14(1), 3985. 10.1038/s41467-023-39698-637414776

Iraegui, E., Augusto, G., & Cabral, P. (2020). Assessing Equity in the Accessibility to Urban Green Spaces According to Different Functional Levels. *ISPRS International Journal of Geo-Information*, 9(5), 308. 10.3390/ijgi9050308

Ju, Y., Dronova, I., & Delclòs-Alió, X. (2022). A 10 m Resolution Urban Green Space Map for Major Latin American Cities from Sentinel-2 Remote Sensing Images and OpenStreetMap. *Scientific Data*, 9(1), 586. 10.1038/s41597-022-01701-y36153342

Kibera, M. (n.d.). *Mapping Nairobi's Informal Settlements*. Map Kibera. https://www.mapkibera.org/

Korah, P. I., Akaateba, M. A., & Bernard, A. A. A. (2024). Spatio-Temporal Patterns and Accessibility of Green Spaces in Kumasi, Ghana. *Habitat International*, 144, 103010. 10.1016/j.habitatint.2024.103010

Liao, Y., Zhou, Q., & Jing, X. (2021). A Comparison of Global and Regional Open Datasets for Urban Greenspace Mapping. *Urban Forestry & Urban Greening*, 62, 127132. 10.1016/j.ufug.2021.127132

Liu, Q., Ullah, H., Wan, W., Peng, Z., Hou, L., Rizvi, S. S., Haidery, S. A., Qu, T., & Muzahid, A. A. M. (2020). Categorization of Green Spaces for a Sustainable Environment and Smart City Architecture by Utilizing Big Data. *Electronics (Basel)*, 9(6), 1028. 10.3390/electronics9061028

Lopes, P., Fonte, C., See, L., & Bechtel, B. (2017). Using OpenStreetMap Data to Assist in the Creation of LCZ Maps. In *In 2017 Joint Urban Remote Sensing Event*. JURSE. 10.1109/JURSE.2017.7924630

Ludwig, C., Hecht, R., Lautenbach, S., Schorcht, M., & Zipf, A. (2021). Mapping Public Urban Green Spaces Based on OpenStreetMap and Sentinel-2 Imagery Using Belief Functions. *ISPRS International Journal of Geo-Information*, 10(4), 251. 10.3390/ijgi10040251

Luxen, D., & Vetter, C. (2011). Real-Time Routing with OpenStreetMap Data. In *GIS:Proceedings of the ACM International Symposium on Advances in Geographic Information Systems*. ACM. 10.1145/2093973.2094062

Novack, T., Wang, Z., & Zipf, A. (2018). A System for Generating Customized Pleasant Pedestrian Routes Based on Openstreetmap Data. *Sensors (Basel)*, 18(11), 3794. 10.3390/s1811379430404175

Pinto, L., Ferreira, C. S. S., & Pereira, P. (2021). Environmental and Socioeconomic Factors Influencing the Use of Urban Green Spaces in Coimbra (Portugal). *The Science of the Total Environment*, 792, 148293. 10.1016/j.scitotenv.2021.14829334147815

Pinto, L. V., Carla, S. S. F., Inácio, M., & Pereira, P. (2022). Urban Green Spaces Accessibility in Two European Cities: Vilnius (Lithuania) and Coimbra (Portugal). *Geography and Sustainability*, 3(1), 74–84. 10.1016/j.geosus.2022.03.001

Rezaei, N. & Millard-Ball, A. (2023). Urban Form and Its Impacts on Air Pollution and Access to Green Space: A Global Analysis of 462 Cities. *PLoS ONE18*. .10.1371/journal.pone.0278265

Schultz, M., Voss, J., Auer, M., Carter, S., & Zipf, A. (2017). Open Land Cover from OpenStreetMap and Remote Sensing. *International Journal of Applied Earth Observation and Geoinformation*, 63, 206–213. 10.1016/j.jag.2017.07.014

Sebestyén, V., Trájer, A. J., Domokos, E., Torma, A., & Abonyi, J. (2024). Objective Well-Being Level (OWL) Composite Indicator for Sustainable and Resilient Cities. *Ecological Indicators*, 158, 111460. 10.1016/j.ecolind.2023.111460

Shyshchenko, P., Havrylenko, O., & Tsyhanok, Y. (2021). "Accessibility of Green Spaces in the Conditions of a Compact City: Case Study of Kyiv." *Visnyk of V.N. Karazin Kharkiv National University, Series Geology. Geography.Ecology*, (55), 245–256. 10.26565/2410-7360-2021-55-18

Texier, M. L., Schiel, K., & Caruso, G. (2018). The Provision of Urban Green Space and Its Accessibility: Spatial Data Effects in Brussels. *PLoS One*, 13(10), e0204684. 10.1371/journal.pone.020468430332449

Trojanek, R., Gluszak, M., & Tanas, J. (2018). The Effect of Urban Green Spaces on House Prices in Warsaw. *International Journal of Strategic Property Management*, 22(5), 358–371. 10.3846/ijspm.2018.5220

Unal Cilek, M., & Uslu, C. (2022). Modeling the Relationship between the Geometric Characteristics of Urban Green Spaces and Thermal Comfort: The Case of Adana City. *Sustainable Cities and Society*, 79, 103748. 10.1016/j.scs.2022.103748

Venter, Z. S., Barton, D. N., Gundersen, V., Figari, H., & Nowell, M. (2020). Urban Nature in a Time of Crisis: Recreational Use of Green Space Increases during the COVID-19 Outbreak in Oslo, Norway. *Environmental Research Letters*, 15(10), 104075. 10.1088/1748-9326/abb396

Venter, Z. S., Shackleton, C. M., Van Staden, F., Selomane, O., & Masterson, V. A. (2020). Green Apartheid: Urban Green Infrastructure Remains Unequally Distributed across Income and Race Geographies in South Africa. *Landscape and Urban Planning*, 203, 103889. 10.1016/j.landurbplan.2020.103889

Viinikka, A., Tiitu, M., Heikinheimo, V., Halonen, J. I., Nyberg, E., & Vierikko, K. (2023). Associations of Neighborhood-Level Socioeconomic Status, Accessibility, and Quality of Green Spaces in Finnish Urban Regions. *Applied Geography (Sevenoaks, England)*, 157, 102973. 10.1016/j.apgeog.2023.102973

Weber, P., & Haklay, M. (2008). OpenStreetMap: User-Generated Street Maps. *IEEE Pervasive Computing*, 7(4).

Weigand, M., Wurm, M., Droin, A., Stark, T., Staab, J., Rauh, J., & Taubenböck, H. (2023). Are Public Green Spaces Distributed Fairly? A Nationwide Analysis Based on Remote Sensing, OpenStreetMap and Census Data. *Geocarto International*, 38(1), 2286305. Advance online publication. 10.1080/10106049.2023.2286305

Yin, J., Fu, P., Cheshmehzangi, A., Li, Z., & Dong, J. (2022). Investigating the Changes in Urban Green-Space Patterns with Urban Land-Use Changes: A Case Study in Hangzhou, China. *Remote Sensing (Basel)*, 14(21), 5410. 10.3390/rs14215410

Chapter 6
Navigating the Complexities of Green Human Resource Management Practices: Operational and Legal Hurdles

Gheorghe Dan Isbă oiu
Petroleum-Gas University of Ploiesti, Romania

Dana Volosevici
https://orcid.org/0009-0000-9109-4679
Petroleum-Gas University of Ploiesti, Romania

ABSTRACT

This chapter critically examines the alignment of green human resource management (Green HRM) practices—specifically in recruitment, training and development, and performance management—with legal standards, focusing on privacy protection, personal data security, and anti-discrimination laws. It also explores the potential to integrate sustainability features into established workplace systems and practices, such as near miss management systems, to enhance environmental responsibility within organizations. This method is advantageous as it utilizes existing tools and procedures familiar to employees, ensuring smoother implementation while leveraging prior legal evaluations.

DOI: 10.4018/979-8-3693-3439-3.ch006

INTRODUCTION

Green Human Resource Management (Green HRM) plays a pivotal role in steering organizations towards sustainable development and a green economy. Green HRM integrates environmental management into HR practices, aiming to encourage employees to adopt sustainable and eco-friendly practices both within and outside the workplace (Wielewska et al., 2023; Paillé et al., 2020). By embedding environmental concerns into HR policies and practices, organizations can nurture a workforce that is not only aware of environmental issues but also motivated to act in ways that reduce environmental footprints. This includes promoting energy-efficient practices, reducing waste, and encouraging the use of sustainable materials. Employees extrapolate these practices from the professional milieu to their daily existence, irrespective of whether it pertains to their personal conduct within society, their anticipations from governing bodies, or the upbringing of their progeny (Bombiak, 2019). Thus, the principles of sustainability are perpetuated beyond the confines of the workplace, engendering transformative effects at the societal level. Conversely, Green HRM enhances a company's societal reputation by elevating its employer brand (Wang et al., 2023; Guillot-Soulez et al., 2022). Or, a strong employment brand is crucial for attracting and retaining top talent in today's competitive job market, boosting the company's performance (Merlin & Chen, 2022; Wallace et al., 2014; Franca, 2012).

This chapter delves into the complexities of integrating Green HRM practices within companies, focusing particularly on the legal and operational challenges encountered. These objectives are important as most studies (Amrutha & Geetha, 2020, AlKetbi & Rice, 2024; Ren et al., 2018) have tended to focus on the management perspective of the subject and have not analysed the legal challenges of implementing green HRM practices. We contend that it is important to extend the research in this field with an approach that identifies and explains the potential legal risks arising from human resource practices aimed at integrating a green component. We argue this point because integrating green values into corporate goals necessitates that employees align with these values. This means that significant aspects of the employment relationship - such as recruitment, professional development, and performance evaluation - must incorporate green criteria in their assessment processes. As we will illustrate in this article, identifying and evaluating employees' green values and actions require careful consideration of elements protected by privacy and anti-discrimination laws. Therefore, HR professionals must be aware that broadening the criteria for employee evaluations should be done in a way that maintains a balance between the employer's desire to implement green policies and the employees' rights, including their basic human rights. This approach ensures that the integration of green objectives does not inadvertently lead to violations of employees' privacy or result in discriminatory practices. It is crucial to develop HR practices that not only support environmental goals but also respect and uphold legal protections for employees. By integrating legal validation into the initial stages of practice development, organizations can significantly reduce the risk of costly legal issues down the line, ensuring smoother, more effective operations and adherence to both the letter and the spirit of the law.

Additionally, leveraging existing and legally validated practices and systems to incorporate sustainability aspects into the employment relationship could be a prudent choice. Such an approach not only ensures compliance with legal standards but also enhances the efficiency and effectiveness of implementing green initiatives. One promising example is the near-miss management system, which has proven its value in various operational contexts by identifying and addressing potential risks before they result in actual incidents. Adapting this system for green training purposes could significantly benefit employees by fostering a proactive approach to sustainability. The near-miss management system can be tailored to monitor and report on environmental practices within the workplace, encouraging employees to identify and rectify behaviours that do not align with the company's green objectives. By integrating these established systems, companies can achieve a balanced approach that promotes sustainability while maintaining legal and operational integrity.

THE EVOLVONG NATURE OF GREEN HRM

The concept of Green HRM has transcended its initial boundaries, traditionally confined to the realm of human resource practices with minimal legal implications. Initially centred on enhancing environmental performance within the traditional scope of HRM, Green HRM has gradually embraced a wider spectrum of corporate social responsibility (Freitas et al., 2020; López-Concepción et al., 2022; Panait et al, 2023). This evolution marks a shift from merely managing human resources to addressing broader social and environmental obligations. The transition of Green HRM into a comprehensive framework for sustainability reflects its alignment with both public policy advancements and legislative changes. These influences have expanded the scope of Green HRM to encompass sustainable practices that not only benefit organizations but also contribute positively to societal welfare and environmental conservation. In the contemporary business environment, sustainability reporting has become increasingly mandated by law, underscoring the importance of integrating sustainable practices into core business strategies (Global Reporting Initiative, 2021). This legislative framework compels organizations to report on labour practices and their impact on the environment, thus placing workforce management at the heart of sustainability efforts. Thus, Non-Financial Reporting Directive (NFRD) 2014/95/EU has made non-financial reporting a legal requirement, thereby supporting the broader goals of the European Green Deal and aligning with global sustainability objectives (La Torre et al., 2020). the NFRD compelled large public-interest entities, with over 500 employees to disclose non-financial information, on various aspects, notably labor practices and environmental impact, as part of their annual public reporting. The importance of the NFRD lies in its role in enhancing transparency and accountability in corporate governance, particularly in the context of environmental, social, and governance (ESG) criteria. By requiring detailed reports on labor practices, companies must disclose their policies, outcomes, and risk management practices related to employee conditions, social dialogue, diversity, gender equality, and health and safety at work. This comprehensive disclosure helps stakeholders understand the company's approach to managing and mitigating risks related to labor practices and ensuring compliance with international labor standards (Evans & Nobes, 2021).

The Corporate Sustainability Report Directive (CSRD) 2022/2464/EU marks the biggest transformation in corporate reporting in nearly 20 years, with companies to be assessed not only from an economic-financial perspective, but also their ESG commitments, which are thus integrated into the business strategy and mission of an organization, to respond to regulatory frameworks and expectations from users of corporate information. Developed by the European Financial Reporting Advisory Group (EFRAG) under the mandate of the European Commission, the European Sustainability Reporting Standards (ESRS) are a set of guidelines designed to enhance the transparency and comparability of sustainability information disclosed by companies in the European Union. The standards cover a variety of specific topics, from climate change and resource use to social rights and the treatment of workers. By doing so, ESRS aims to promote a more sustainable economy, encourage responsible business practices, and contribute to the EU's goals under the European Green Deal.

One particular subject, ESRS S1 Own Workforce, encompasses the extensive field of employment conditions, such as secure employment, working time, adequate wages, social dialogue, freedom of association, the existence of works councils and the information, consultation and participation rights of workers, collective bargaining, work-life balance, health and safety, but also some sensitive issues regarding insuring equal treatment and opportunities for all. The aforementioned topic addresses issues including gender equality and fair compensation for equal work, as well as training and skill enhancement, employment and inclusion of individuals with disabilities, and strategies to prevent violence and harassment at work, alongside diversity. Additionally, ESRS S1 mandates reporting on a legal aspect concerning other work-related rights, which spans a broad range of concerns such as child labour, forced labour, adequate housing, and privacy.

The integration of environmental considerations into HR practices elevates the demands on companies' sustainability initiatives, extending beyond merely environmental concerns to encompass all aspects of human resources. This approach requires organizations to not only focus on reducing their ecological footprint but also to enhance their workforce policies in alignment with sustainable values. Companies are now expected to foster work environments that prioritize employee well-being, diversity, and inclusion, while also promoting eco-friendly practices and sustainability training. This holistic approach to sustainability underscores the interconnectedness of environmental health and employee welfare, pushing companies to innovate and implement comprehensive strategies that address both ecological and humanistic elements (Hronová & Špaček, 2021). Ultimately, these efforts contribute to a more sustainable and socially responsible corporate ethos.

The new sustainability reporting rules will begin to apply gradually between 2024 and 2028, being mandatory for public interest companies with over 500 employees, large companies (which exceed 2 of the size criteria: over 250 employees and/or 40 million euros in turnover and/or 20 million euros in total assets), and listed SMEs. Although the reporting obligation does not cover the entire spectrum of companies, the standards establish a new level of sustainability, which will also influence the sustainability policies of companies not covered by the reporting obligation.

HRM practices, previously guided by soft law and non-binding in nature, are now being converted into legally binding obligations for a significant number of companies. This shift underscores the urgent need to identify and analyze potential legal risks associated with implementing green HRM principles. In this context, we will explore several key Green HRM practices that significantly contribute to organizational sustainability (Yong et al., 2019), highlighting the hurdles companies might face in this endeavour. These practices include green recruitment and selection, where companies prioritize candidates who demonstrate a commitment to environmental values (Guerci et al., 2016), training and development, which focuses on equipping employees with the skills and knowledge necessary to engage in sustainable practices, and performance management, which integrates sustainability metrics into the evaluation of employee performance.

GREEN RECRUITMENT PRACTICES

Green recruitment practices focus on integrating environmental concerns into the hiring process to support sustainability and involves selecting candidates who demonstrate a commitment to environmental management and sustainability (Abiwu & Nunoo, 2021; Mwita & Kinemo, 2018). Profiling candidates in green recruitment involves identifying individuals who not only possess the necessary job skills but also align with the organization's commitment to environmental sustainability. A critical component of candidate profiling is assessing candidates' knowledge and skills in environmental issues, including their understanding of sustainable practices and previous experience with environmental projects (Adjei-Bamfo et al., 2019). It follows that, in this case, the scope of analysis in the selection process is much broader than in previous recruitment and selection processes. In addition to evaluating the knowledge, skills, and abilities related to the position, it will also be necessary to assess the candidates' knowledge and even their values and attitudes towards green issues. This new approach prioritizes the assessment of some pure subjective dimensions such as personal commitment to sustainability, which is crucial for organizations aiming to integrate environmental considerations into their core operations (Pham & Paillé, 2019; Mishra, 2017).

Green Recruitment and Privacy

During the selection process, companies can assess candidates' knowledge, values, and attitudes towards green issues through a variety of integrated approaches. Behavioral and situational interview questions are particularly effective for evaluating a candidate's past experiences and potential responses to environmental scenarios. This method allows interviewers to gauge how candidates have previously engaged with sustainability initiatives and how they might address green-related challenges in the future (Tirno et al., 2023). According to Ahmad (2015), these questions provide valuable insight into a candidate's commitment to sustainability and their problem-solving abilities in environmental contexts. Additionally, green knowledge tests measure a candidate's understanding of environmental issues, sustainability practices, and relevant regulations. By including questions on topics such as climate change, waste management, and energy efficiency, employers can ensure that candidates possess the technical knowledge necessary to support the company's green initiatives (Renwick et al., 2013). Personality and values assessments are useful in determining whether a candidate's values align with the organization's sustainability culture. Assessment centers offer a deeper insight into candidates' capabilities by engaging them in group discussions, role-playing, and case studies focused on environmental issues. These centers allow observers to evaluate candidates' teamwork, leadership, and attitudes towards sustainability in real-time scenarios, effectively mimicking workplace challenges (Lievens & Chapman, 2010). Furthermore, reference checks and background verifications can confirm candidates' past involvement in green projects or organizations. This step ensures that candidates have a proven track record in supporting sustainability initiatives, as noted by Chiang and Birtch (2012).

Therefore, it is evident from the above that the purpose of the evaluation is to establish the extent to which a candidate's values surpass traditional job requirements, ensuring that the workforce is not only skilled but also intrinsically motivated to engage in and advocate for sustainable practices. This method underscores a shift in recruitment paradigms, where the alignment of personal and organizational values towards sustainability becomes a critical factor in the hiring process. It becomes clear that the assessment process extends beyond merely evaluating competencies. This process involves a thorough examination that assesses not only a candidate’s knowledge, skills, and abilities but also delves into their personal values. This integration of values-based assessments introduces ethical and legal considerations, particularly regarding the protection of fundamental rights. The inclusion of personal values in the recruitment process must not infringe upon fundamental human rights, such as the right to privacy or freedom of thought. While public policies promoting sustainability are crucial, they cannot justify overriding or limiting candidates' rights.

Another significant legal risk in green recruitment concerns the protection of personal data. Throughout the employment relationship, including the recruitment and selection stage, the employer must comply with the set of principles laid down in Article 5 of the GDPR, namely lawfulness, fairness and transparency, purpose limitation, data minimization, accuracy, storage limitation, integrity and confidentiality. Data minimization requires that data collected during the recruitment process must be adequate, relevant, and limited to what is necessary for the purposes of processing. Employers should, therefore, clearly define the purpose of data collection and ensure that only the data needed to fulfil that purpose is collected. This means that any data gathering should be directly related to and justified by a legitimate goal, avoiding the collection of extraneous or irrelevant information (Keane, 2018).

The challenge, however, lies in determining to what extent collecting data on a candidate's sustainability and ecological values is “limited to what is necessary for the purposes of processing.” We consider that, for a position that might have a profoundly technical nature, the selection process would also analyze the candidate's personal aspects, including their values and attitudes towards sustainability and environmental protection. The question then arises: How deeply must sustainability values be embedded in a company's policy and activities for them to be considered “necessary” attributes in evaluating the competencies of any employee, regardless of the primary features of their role? If sustainability is a core aspect of a company’s strategy and operations, then it could be argued that alignment with these values is necessary for all roles within the organization. This would justify the collection of such data as being essential for the purpose of aligning employees with the company's overarching goals.

Another key consideration in the selection process is the sources used by recruiters to determine the candidate's values. For instance, assessing these values and attitudes often involves analyzing social media profiles, which can provide insights into a candidate's personality, lifestyle, and potential cultural fit within the company (Bohmova & Chudán, 2018; Saadaoui & Belmouffeq, 2023; Demir & Günaydın, 2023). However, this approach introduces various legal and ethical risks. These risks include potential violations of data protection regulations, privacy, the accuracy and relevance of the information gathered, and the possibility of biased judgments based on personal online activities (Landers & Schmidt, 2016).

Firstly, as highlighted by the Article 29 Data Protection Working Party (2017), employers must not assume they can use an individual's publicly accessible social media data for their own purposes without a legal basis, such as legitimate interest. Before examining a social media profile, it is crucial for employers to determine whether the profile is used for business or private purposes to establish the legality of accessing the data. Additionally, employers are permitted to collect and process personal data from job applicants only when it is necessary and relevant to the job for which the applicant is being considered.

Secondly, seeking characteristics and values in spaces not intended for work relationships and evaluating them in relation to the work environment can lead to a distortion of their meaning. Some organizations use innovative techniques like social media analytics to uncover a candidate's public endorsements of sustainability initiatives or participation in green projects, offering insights into their genuine interest and engagement with environmental issues (Kong & Ding, 2023). This screening method becomes increasingly invasive as AI-based tools penetrate the HRM sphere, allowing a comprehensive and exhaustive analysis of a candidate's public profile.

In the context of green recruitment practices, it must first be acknowledged that while profiling can be a highly effective strategy, it also introduces significant legal and ethical challenges, particularly concerning issues of privacy. Therefore, organizations must ensure that their profiling practices are transparent and comply with legal standards, taking in consideration the potential biases that could arise from subjective interpretations of 'green' behaviours or attitudes (Antignac et al., 2016). It follows that, although green recruitment practices by identifying the candidates' values could be effective for identifying those candidates who have values similar to the employer's values, pinpointing candidates who prioritize sustainability and have environmental expertise or abilities might entail legal liabilities derived from the data protection legislation.

Green Recruitment and Discrimination

Beyond the issue of privacy, attributing substantial weight to sustainability-related criteria in recruitment could engender challenges concerning discrimination against underprivileged groups or failing to provide equal opportunities to all individuals. For example, ESG factors often favor practices that may not be accessible to or feasible for underprivileged groups. As a result, giving preference to candidates who can afford to live sustainably, such as those owning electric vehicles or living in energy-efficient housing, may discriminate against economically disadvantaged candidates who lack the resources to meet such standards (Vetráková et al., 2018).

Furthermore, by emphasizing sustainability-related criteria, there is a risk of compromising the principle of equal opportunity. This principle asserts that all individuals should have a fair chance to succeed based on their merits, regardless of their background. However, if sustainability criteria do not account for the socioeconomic diversity of all applicants or stakeholders, they might skew opportunities towards those already in advantageous positions. This can lead to a cycle where underprivileged groups find it increasingly difficult to break into sectors or gain benefits that could actually help them advance economically and socially. Moreover, integrating AI tools in the recruitment process introduces additional challenges. AI systems, if not properly audited, can perpetuate biases present in the data they are trained on, leading to unfair hiring practices. Ensuring transparency and fairness in AI-driven recruitment is crucial to maintaining equal opportunities (Chamorro-Premuzic & Akhtar, 2019; Hilliard et al., 2022).

To mitigate these risks, organizations should develop inclusive sustainability criteria that recognize the diverse backgrounds of all candidates. This includes considering different ways candidates can demonstrate their commitment to sustainability, beyond just financial means, and ensuring that recruitment processes are transparent and free from bias (Barrena-Martínez et al., 2019; AlKetbi & Rice, 2024).

GREEN TRAINING AND DEVELOPMENT

Green Training and Development (T&D) practices encompass a broad spectrum of actions aimed at augmenting employees' comprehension of environmental matters, the organization's eco-friendly policies and procedures, and deepening their insight into the ways they can support sustainability objectives through their respective roles. The rationale for green T&D initiatives is twofold. Firstly, there is an increasing recognition that businesses play a crucial role in addressing global environmental challenges. Secondly, there is a growing demand from stakeholders, including consumers, employees, and investors, for businesses to demonstrate environmental responsibility. In response, organizations are not only modifying their operational processes and products but are also investing in training programs that can drive sustainable performance. Green T&D initiatives aim to equip employees with the knowledge and skills necessary to contribute to the organization's sustainability goals. These initiatives often include training on energy efficiency, waste reduction, sustainable procurement, and the implementation of eco-friendly technologies (Jamil et al., 2023; Saadaoui & Belmouffeq, 2023). The effectiveness of green T&D is highlighted in studies showing that such training can significantly impact environmental performance by enhancing employees' green competencies and motivations (Yafi et al., 2021). Additionally, green training fosters a culture of sustainability within the organization, encouraging employees to adopt environmentally friendly practices both at work and in their personal lives (Liu et al., 2020).

Effective green T&D programs often start with the assessment of existing knowledge gaps and the development of tailored training that aligns with the organization's environmental objectives. These programs might include awareness-raising sessions on global and local environmental issues, skill-building workshops on specific practices, such as energy-efficient operations or sustainable sourcing, leadership development programs focused on integrating sustainability into strategic decision-making, behavioral change campaigns, encouraging practices like recycling, sustainable commuting, and energy conservation.

However, their effectiveness is significantly increased when these initiatives are continuous and deeply embedded into the core values and everyday operational practices of a company, as opposed to being sporadic or singular events. Research (Molnar & Mulvihill, 2003) supports this view by emphasizing that continuous learning processes are crucial for embedding sustainability into a company's culture and operations. For example, ongoing green training programs are more likely to lead to lasting behavioral changes among employees, which is essential for achieving long-term sustainability goals. Moreover, integrating these training programs into core business values and practices ensures that sustainability becomes a part of the decision-making process at all levels of the organization, leading to more effective and sustainable outcomes.

Additionally, integrating sustainability values into the existing procedures, techniques, or tools used in the workplace can help embed these principles more deeply into the daily activities of employees. This approach ensures that sustainability becomes a natural element of job performance, enhancing environmental awareness without disrupting routine operations. Furthermore, by enriching standard operating procedures with sustainability practices, organizations can foster a culture of continuous environmental improvement. Research (Cherian & Jacob, 2012) suggests that when sustainability practices are seamlessly integrated into job roles, employees are more likely to adopt and champion these behaviors, leading to significant improvements in organizational sustainability performance.

Extending Near Miss Management Systems to Sustainability

Our analysis will explore the feasibility of applying industry-proven concepts, like Near Miss Management Systems (NMSs), to the realm of Green HRM as a means to enhance professional training in sustainability. By examining the potential for these established methodologies to be adapted for environmental objectives, we aim to understand how they can fortify green HR practices and contribute to the development of a workforce skilled in sustainable operations.

Over the years, NMSs have evolved and expanded across various sectors. Initially, these systems were implemented in industries known for significant accident risks, such as the chemical, nuclear, and airline sectors. The primary aim was to enhance safety by identifying and addressing incidents that could have led to severe accidents, even if no actual harm occurred. Recognizing the effectiveness of these systems in pre-empting disasters, other industries have since adopted similar approaches. Sectors like manufacturing, mining, and construction, where safety risks are also prevalent, have integrated NMSs into their safety protocols (Gnoni & Saleh, 2017). This adoption underscores a broader recognition of the value of proactive safety measures in preventing accidents and improving overall workplace safety across diverse industries. An analysis of the literature in the field from 1995 to 2021 reveals that articles on NMSs have also targeted other sectors, such as automotive, oil & gas, Seveso plants, and steel (Gnomi et al., 2022).

The near miss is defined by The American National Safety Council (2013) as "an unplanned event that did not result in injury, illness, or damage but had the potential to do so". In a wider prospective, Cavalieri and Ghislandi (2010) propose a definition which enlarge the contents of the notion of near miss: "a hazardous situation, event or unsafe act where the sequence of events could have caused an accident if it had not been interrupted. A learning experience for internal use by the company".

The primary advantage of NMSs is accident prevention, as these systems proactively identify potential hazards before they can escalate into actual accidents. However, the benefits of implementing an NMS extend beyond mere hazard identification. By promoting the systematic reporting and analysis of near-miss incidents, an NMS nurtures a safety-oriented culture within organizations. This, in turn, enhances workforce awareness and proactivity, fostering an environment where employees are more vigilant and engaged in safety practices (Phimister et al., 2003). Furthermore, NMSs are instrumental in facilitating continuous learning and improvement in safety protocols. Through the diligent analysis of near-misses, organizations can refine and adjust their policies and procedures to better mitigate risks. This iterative process of learning and adapting is crucial for the progressive enhancement of safety standards across the organization, ensuring that safety measures evolve in response to new insights and remain effective over time (Gnoni & Lettera, 2012). Moreover, NMSs may play a vital role not only in immediate safety improvements but also in supporting broader sustainability objectives within organizations. Their ability to prevent waste and accidents, coupled with fostering a proactive culture, aligns closely with sustainable development goals. The culture of continuous improvement developed through NMSs can extend to environmental performance, driving innovations that reduce the environmental footprint of operations (Schaaf, 1995).

The use of existing organizational systems for implementing green training and development practices offers several strategic advantages. By leveraging established systems, organizations can foster a more holistic approach to sustainability, embedding environmental and safety awareness deep within their corporate culture. This approach not only enhances the efficiency of training programs but also ensures that these practices are more aligned with the organization's long-term sustainability goals. The strategic use of existing systems in green training also addresses stakeholder demands for environmental responsibility, showcasing the organization's commitment to sustainability. It builds a cohesive strategy that supports not only the environmental goals but also enhances overall organizational performance by developing a workforce that is knowledgeable, motivated, and aligned with the company's sustainability vision (Gull & Idrees, 2022; Cheng et al., 2021).

Green Training for Green Employees

From another viewpoint, incorporating green practices into training and development necessitates active and direct participation from employees. This participatory approach can transform the traditional top-down imposition of policies into a more engaging process that empowers employees. As employees become more involved in the conception and implementation of these initiatives, they are more likely to take ownership of the sustainability goals. This shift not only boosts morale but also encourages a deeper commitment to the organization's environmental objectives.

The practical implementation of these training programs can be structured around existing Learning Management Systems (LMS) or through dedicated sustainability modules within existing training frameworks. Programs should focus not only on the 'why' of sustainability but also on the 'how', with practical steps and measures that employees can take in their daily operations. This might include training on resource conservation techniques, waste reduction practices, and proper handling and disposal of hazardous materials.

When companies integrate sustainability into the core functions of their employees' jobs - particularly those involving technical services - it transforms how employees perceive sustainability. Instead of viewing it as an imposed external value or a transient corporate trend, employees begin to see sustainability as a fundamental component of their daily responsibilities. This approach has significant advantages. First, it cultivates a genuine commitment to sustainability across the organization. Employees are more likely to adopt sustainable practices if they see them as part of their standard operating procedures rather than additional or optional tasks. This is crucial because sustainability initiatives can often falter if they are not perceived as relevant to the core business functions. Second, this integration ensures that sustainability becomes a consistent part of the decision-making process, rather than an afterthought. For technical roles, which often involve direct interaction with products, services, and customers, incorporating sustainability can lead to more innovative solutions that are both effective in fulfilling the service need and environmentally conscious. This could involve using less harmful materials, optimizing resource use, or improving waste management at various stages of the service lifecycle. Moreover, embedding sustainability into job roles helps prevent it from becoming just a slogan. When sustainability is only featured in company communications or as a peripheral policy, there is a risk that it won't translate into actual practice. It might be touted in mission statements or marketing materials without real substance behind it. By making it a part of the everyday tasks that employees engage in, companies ensure that their commitment to sustainability is tangible and impactful. This strategic integration not only meets stakeholder demands for environmental responsibility but also aligns with broader organizational strategies, enhancing overall performance and achieving long-term sustainability goals (Kang et al., 2022; Sun, 2018).

Furthermore, leveraging existing organizational systems for implementing green training and development practices optimizes resource use and ensures that sustainability initiatives are sustainable and scalable over time. This approach addresses stakeholder expectations and builds a cohesive strategy that supports both environmental goals and organizational performance (Cheng et al., 2021).

GREEN PERFORMANCE MANAGEMENT

As companies weave sustainability into the daily responsibilities of their employees, the need to incorporate environmental objectives and sustainability metrics into performance evaluation frameworks naturally emerges. This integration serves to align individual employee actions with broader organizational sustainability goals. By measuring sustainability performance, organizations can encourage employees to adopt and maintain practices that positively impact the environment. This approach also provides a clear structure for recognizing and rewarding employees who contribute significantly to sustainability efforts.

Incorporating these metrics into performance evaluations can lead to a deeper commitment to sustainability across all levels of the organization (Devi Kalpana, 2018). Employees become more aware of the environmental impact of their actions and more motivated to improve due to the direct link between their performance evaluations and sustainability outcomes. Additionally, this practice can stimulate innovation as employees seek more efficient ways to meet both their performance and sustainability targets. Ultimately, embedding sustainability into performance metrics not only reinforces the company's commitment to environmental stewardship but also fosters a culture where sustainable practices are valued and pursued consistently.

In the realm of performance management, the effective implementation of individual performance evaluations is critical and guided by legal frameworks. National legal systems typically recognize the employer's right to set individual performance objectives and evaluation criteria for employees. This legal framework supports the alignment of individual employee performance with the broader strategic goals of the organization, thus enhancing overall productivity and accountability. Employers can establish clear and measurable objectives that employees are expected to meet, facilitating a structured approach to performance management. This legal recognition is essential for effective human resource management, allowing employers to create transparent and fair performance evaluation systems. Such systems not only provide a basis for rewarding high performance but also help in identifying areas where employees may need additional training or support (Armstrong, 2017).

Job Performance and Sustainability

As highlighted in the recruitment context, evaluating aspects that are not directly related to the specific job function but rather aligned with the organization's values can introduce challenges in the evaluation process. Employees may perceive such evaluations as lacking objectivity, especially when "penalties" are imposed based on their personal values rather than their professional actions (DeNisi & Murphy, 2017; Armstrong, 2017). This perception can undermine the credibility of the performance evaluation system and potentially lead to disputes regarding the fairness and relevance of the criteria used (Pulakos, 2009). Therefore, to ensure the effectiveness and the fairness of the individual performance evaluation, employers must undertake a rigorous job analysis. This analysis serves as a foundational step in identifying the key responsibilities and expectations associated with a position. Citing Harvey (1991), it is noted that particularly for Task-Based Ratings, a method focused on specific job tasks, the precision in defining job functions is paramount.

Job analysis provides a detailed understanding of each role, which in turn informs the development of relevant and achievable performance objectives (Schneider & Konz, 1989).

This process not only aligns performance evaluations with organizational goals but also enhances the transparency and fairness of the evaluations, contributing to greater employee acceptance and motivation. By clearly defining what is expected of employees and how their performance will be measured, organizations can foster a more engaged and productive workforce. Moreover, well-defined performance objectives help in identifying training needs and planning further professional development, thereby strengthening the organization's overall competency and efficiency.

We wish to emphasize that, among the critical guidelines for ensuring the legal integrity of performance appraisals, the recommendations articulated by Malos in 1998 are particularly significant. Malos contends that performance appraisal criteria should be narrowly focused and directly related to specific job functions, rather than broad and generalized evaluations. He emphasizes the importance of objectivity in the appraisal process. The criteria must be job-related, derived from a thorough job analysis, and should aim to evaluate observable behaviors rather than subjective traits. These guidelines provide a foundational framework for developing and implementing performance evaluations that are both legally defensible and perceived as fair by employees. Job analysis involves examining the tasks, duties, and responsibilities that are essential to a job, as well as the skills, knowledge, and abilities required to perform it effectively. However, with the changing nature of work, traditional job analysis methods may become less applicable, prompting the need for more strategic and dynamic approaches. This includes adapting job analysis to the needs of emerging jobs and innovative organizational practices. Moreover, Green HR practices, such as green job design, green training, and green performance management, are increasingly integrated into job analysis to ensure that job roles contribute to sustainable organizational performance. These practices ensure that environmental considerations are embedded in the core functions and competencies required for various roles (Yong & Mohd-Yusoff, 2016) and influence employee satisfaction and motivation, which are critical for sustaining environmental goals (Abdelhamied et al., 2023).

While traditionally focused on optimizing employee performance and alignment with organizational goals, job analysis also has important legal implications. This is particularly relevant in performance evaluation, where the accuracy and fairness of job descriptions can influence legal compliance in areas such as employment equity and workplace discrimination.

Within the context of Green HRM, job analysis takes on an additional layer of complexity. As we pointed out above, Green HRM integrates environmental management goals with traditional HR practices, emphasizing sustainability in every aspect of human resource policies (Ali & Hassan, 2023). In this context, job analysis might identify environmental competencies as crucial job elements, contingent upon the role and the organization's sustainability objectives. Assigning appropriate weight to these green aspects in an employee's performance evaluation is imperative (Majid et al., 2023). It requires a careful balance between maintaining legal compliance- ensuring that job requirements are justifiable and non-discriminatory - and promoting the organization's commitment to environmental stewardship. Integrating environmental responsibilities into job descriptions poses legal risks, particularly when these additions are not universally acknowledged as essential for effective job performance in a specific role. These risks become pronounced when an employee meets all the specified tasks of a traditional job description but fails to fulfill the imposed sustainability values or behaviors. Penalizing an employee for not demonstrating certain sustainability behaviors can lead to contentious situations, potentially being perceived as legally precarious. The core issue lies in the tenuous link between non-role-specific sustainability values and the actual performance metrics directly tied to job responsibilities DeNisi & Murphy, 2017).

This challenge is especially significant in jurisdictions with stringent labor laws that protect employees from potentially unfair job requirements or where case law regarding performance evaluation is underdeveloped or inconsistent. Ensuring that performance evaluations are both legally defensible and aligned with the organization's sustainability goals requires a nuanced approach that balances these considerations carefully (Armstrong, 2017; Pulakos, 2009). The legal risks associated with such evaluations stem from the potential misalignment between the employee's understanding of job requirements and the employer's expectations of sustainability integration. This situation can result in disputes regarding what constitutes fair and equitable performance evaluations. Such disagreements not only pose legal risks but can also lead to employee demotivation and a decline in the organizational climate.

Intrusive Green Performance Evaluation

A potential legal risk emerges when performance evaluations encompass not only the actions of employees but also their sustainability values, reflected in behaviours both within and outside the organization. This approach entails assessing a sensitive dimension of an individual's personality - specifically, their beliefs and values - which are protected under legal frameworks that safeguard freedom of expression and the right to privacy. By incorporating such personal aspects into performance criteria, employers may inadvertently infringe upon these fundamental rights, leading to significant legal and ethical concerns.

Performance evaluations that probe into employees' values related to sustainability can be contentious because they blur the line between professional and personal domains. When values and beliefs are subjected to scrutiny, it raises issues of subjectivity and potential bias in the evaluation process. This can result in claims of discrimination or unfair treatment if employees feel that their personal beliefs are being penalized, especially when these beliefs are expressed outside the workplace. Legal protections for freedom of expression and privacy are designed to prevent such overreach, ensuring that individuals can hold and express personal beliefs without fear of retribution or unfair assessment in their professional roles (Malos, 1998; DeNisi & Murphy, 2017).

Moreover, national data protection authorities rigorously monitor the processing of personal data that pertains to the private lives of employees. H&M Nuremberg case is relevant for jurisprudence in this matter. In October 2020, H&M faced a significant data protection case resulting in a €35.3 million fine by the Hamburg Commissioner for Data Protection and Freedom of Information (HmbBfDI) in Germany. The case involved the extensive and unlawful monitoring of several hundred employees at H&M's service center in Nuremberg. The company was found to have recorded detailed information about employees' personal lives, including family issues, religious beliefs, and health data, without a legal basis. In accordance with the local practices, after holiday and sick leave - even short absences - the supervising team leaders conducted a so-called Welcome Back Talk, to collect information about employees' concrete holiday experiences or symptoms of illness and diagnoses. In addition, some supervisors acquired a broad knowledge of their employees' private lives through individual and corridor discussions, ranging from rather harmless details to family problems and religious beliefs. The findings were partly recorded, digitally stored and, in some cases, updated over time. The recordings were available for up to 50 other managers throughout the company. The data collected was utilized not only for evaluating individual work performance but also to create comprehensive profiles of employees for employment-related measures and decisions. The data protection authority found that H&M and the managers who collected and used the employee information violated Articles 5 and 6 of GDPR, Principles relating to processing of personal data and Lawfulness of processing. The Hamburg Commissioner (2020) highlighted that the integration of private life details with recorded activities constituted a "particularly intensive encroachment on employees' civil rights". The commissioner stated that the size of the fine was both proportional to the extent of the violation and useful as a deterrent for future company violations of employee data privacy, for both H&M and other corporations worldwide. H&M took full responsibility and implemented a number of measures, which included additional training for leaders in relation to data privacy and labour law and revised instructions for managers (H&M, 2020).

This example is significant as it illustrates that practices which may be deemed valid and effective from a human resource management perspective can be deemed invalid legally. This dissonance can expose organizations to legal challenges, emphasizing the importance of ensuring that all HR practices not only meet operational goals but also comply with legal requirements. It also illustrates the legal risks and potential penalties organizations face when they overstep boundaries in collecting and processing personal information that extends beyond what is necessary for legitimate HR purposes (Custers et. al, 2019).

DISCUSSIONS AND CONCLUSION

The critical role of Green HRM in fostering organizational and societal transitions towards sustainability cannot be overstated. As businesses increasingly recognize their part in addressing global environmental challenges, Green HRM emerges as a vital strategy, embedding sustainability into the core of human resource practices. This approach not only encourages eco-friendly workplace behaviors but also influences broader societal norms, demonstrating the profound impact organizations can have on promoting a sustainable future. Green HRM serves as a bridge between environmental responsibility and organizational performance, advocating for practices that reduce carbon footprints, enhance energy efficiency, and encourage the adoption of sustainable materials. By integrating these principles into employee recruitment, training, and evaluation processes, organizations cultivate a workforce deeply aligned with sustainability goals. This alignment not only boosts environmental performance but also enhances the company's reputation, making it more attractive to top talent and conscious consumers alike.

However, implementing Green HRM is not without its challenges. The identification and evaluation of an employee's green values and behaviors, both during recruitment and throughout the employment relationship, necessitate employers delving into aspects of the employee's life that extend beyond traditional work-related boundaries. This practice involves assessing the intrinsic beliefs and values of employees to determine their alignment with organizational values, which can potentially infringe on fundamental rights protecting privacy, freedom of conscience, and freedom of expression. The H&M case highlights the severe repercussions of processing private data, including personal beliefs and values, throughout the employment relationship. Such practices can lead to significant violations of civil rights and result in substantial legal liabilities for employers.

Furthermore, demonstrating the fairness and balance of incorporating green responsibility behaviors into job descriptions is challenging. These issues can arise during both recruitment and periodic performance evaluations. It is essential to determine an appropriate proportion for green components in job descriptions, alongside traditional knowledge, skills, and abilities. This balance ensures that sustainability values do not overshadow essential job functions.

Extending the evaluation scope to include sustainability behaviors and values poses a risk of violating the employee's right to an objective assessment, as it introduces the possibility of personal biases from evaluators. Without established and jurisprudentially validated practices and guidelines, there is a danger of abusive evaluation approaches based on subjective reinterpretations of employee behaviors.

Another significant legal risk involves potential violations of anti-discrimination laws. Demonstrating green values through actions that are inaccessible to underprivileged groups can lead to discriminatory practices. Efforts to promote sustainable behavior may inadvertently exclude or penalize individuals from lower socioeconomic backgrounds who cannot afford sustainable practices such as using electric vehicles, installing solar panels, or consuming local and organic food.

Organizations must navigate these complexities carefully, ensuring that their sustainability initiatives comply with legal standards while fostering an inclusive work environment. Operational challenges also abound, requiring companies to adapt their existing HR practices to incorporate sustainability goals effectively. As we have tried to demonstrate, an effective method for enhancing organizational practices involves integrating sustainability aspects into existing policies, practices, and tools. This approach not only streamlines the implementation process by building on established systems but also promotes a more sustainable operational framework. Our proposal regarding Near Miss Management Systems can undoubtedly be extended to other areas within the organization, such as resource management, waste reduction, and energy efficiency, thereby broadening the impact and fostering a culture of sustainability across all operational facets.

To successfully leverage Green HRM in driving sustainability, organizations must adopt a balanced approach. This means aligning environmental objectives with business strategies, ensuring legal compliance, and fostering an organizational culture that values and rewards sustainable practices. By doing so, companies can not only contribute to environmental conservation but also build a resilient, forward-thinking business model that thrives on innovation and inclusivity. In essence, the role of Green HRM in steering both organizational and societal change is pivotal. It exemplifies the power of integrating sustainability into everyday business operations, showcasing the potential for corporate practices to have a far-reaching impact on global environmental goals.

Our analysis in this chapter was confined to highlighting certain specific aspects that we deemed relevant to the theme of green HRM. We focused on particular elements within this field, considering their importance and implications for sustainable business practices. However, the scope of our study was limited, and there is significant potential for further research. Future studies could expand the analysis of green HRM practices to include a broader range of factors or delve more deeply into the aspects we have highlighted, examining their broader implications and effectiveness in promoting sustainability within organizations. Given the critical importance of sustainability and environmental protection in today's society, it is essential that research in this area continues. This ongoing research is necessary not only to enhance our theoretical understanding of green HRM but also to improve practical applications, helping organizations integrate these practices effectively and sustainably.

REFERENCES

Abdelhamied, H., Elbaz, A., Al-Romeedy, B., & Amer, T. (2023). Linking Green Human Resource Practices and Sustainable Performance: The Mediating Role of Job Satisfaction and Green Motivation. *Sustainability (Basel)*, 15(6), 4835. 10.3390/su15064835

Abiwu, L., & Nunoo, G. (2021). Green Recruitment Practices. In *Handbook of Research on Human Capital and People Management in the Tourism Industry* (pp. 73-93). https://doi.org/10.4018/978-1-7998-4522-5.ch005

Adjei-Bamfo, P., Maloreh-Nyamekye, T., & Ahenkan, A. (2019). The role of e-government in sustainable public procurement in developing countries: A systematic literature review. *Resources, Conservation and Recycling*, 142, 189–203. 10.1016/j.resconrec.2018.12.001

Ahmad, S. (2015). Green human resource management: Policies and practices. *Cogent Business & Management*, 2(1), 1030817. 10.1080/23311975.2015.1030817

Ali, M., & Hassan, M. (2023). Green management practices and trust for green behavioral intentions and mediation of ethical leadership: An attribution theory perspective in tourism. *International Journal of Contemporary Hospitality Management*, 35(9), 3193–3215. 10.1108/IJCHM-04-2022-0506

AlKetbi, A., & Rice, J. (2024). The impact of green human resource management practices on employees, clients, and organizational performance: A literature review. *Administrative Sciences*, 14(4), 78. 10.3390/admsci14040078

Amrutha, V., & Geetha, S. (2020). A systematic review on green human resource management: Implications for social sustainability. *Journal of Cleaner Production*, 247, 119131. 10.1016/j.jclepro.2019.119131

Antignac, T., Sands, D., & Schneider, G. (2016). Data Minimisation: A Language-Based Approach. *ArXiv*, abs/1611.05642. 10.1007/978-3-319-58469-0_30

Armstrong, M. (2017). *Armstrong's Handbook of Performance Management: An Evidence-Based Guide to Delivering High Performance*. Kogan Page Publishers.

Barrena-Martínez, J., López-Fernández, M., & Romero-Fernández, P. M. (2019). Towards a configuration of socially responsible human resource management policies and practices. *International Journal of Human Resource Management*, 30(17), 2544–2580. 10.1080/09585192.2017.1332669

Bohmova, L., & Chudán, D. (2018). Analyzing Social Media Data for Recruiting Purposes. *Acta Informatica Pragensia*, 7(1), 4–21. 10.18267/j.aip.111

Bombiak, E. (2019). *Green human resource management – the latest trend or strategic necessity?* Entrepreneurship and Sustainability Issues., 10.9770/jesi.2019.6.4(7)

Cavalieri, S., & Ghislandi, W. M. (2010). Understanding and using near misses' properties through a double-step conceptual structure. *Journal of Intelligent Manufacturing*, 21(2), 237–247. 10.1007/s10845-008-0193-2

Chamorro-Premuzic, T., & Akhtar, R. (2019). Should companies use AI to assess job candidates? *Harvard Business Review*. https://hbr.org/2019/05/should-companies-use-ai-to-assess-job-candidates

Cheng, T. C. E., Kamble, S. S., Belhadi, A., Ndubisi, N. O., Lai, K. H., & Kharat, M. G. (2021). Linkages between big data analytics, circular economy, sustainable supply chain flexibility, and sustainable performance in manufacturing firms. *International Journal of Production Research*. 10.1080/00207543.2021.1906971

Cherian, J. P., & Jacob, J. (2012). A Study of Green HR practices and its effective implementation in the organization: A review. *International Journal of Business and Management*, 7(21), 1–15. 10.5539/ijbm.v7n21p25

Chiang, F. F. T., & Birtch, T. A. (2012). The performance implications of financial and non-financial rewards: An Asian Nordic comparison. *Journal of Management Studies*, 49(3), 538–570. 10.1111/j.1467-6486.2011.01018.x

Custers, B., Ursic, H., & Schermer, B. (2019). *Discrimination and Privacy in the Information Society: Data Mining and Profiling in Large Databases*. Springer.

Demir, M., & Günaydın, Y. (2023). A digital job application reference: How do social media posts affect the recruitment process? *Employee Relations*, 45(2), 457–477. 10.1108/ER-05-2022-0232

DeNisi, A. S., & Murphy, K. R. (2017). Performance Appraisal and Performance Management: 100 Years of Progress? *The Journal of Applied Psychology*, 102(3), 421–433. 10.1037/apl000008528125265

Devi Kalpana, J. K. (2018). Influence of Green HRM practices on employees performance level – a study with reference to literature review. [IJRAR]. *International Journal of Research and Analytical Reviews*, 5(3), 329–333.

European Union. (2014). Directive 2014/95/EU of the European Parliament and of the Council of 22 October 2014 amending Directive 2013/34/EU as regards disclosure of non-financial and diversity information by certain large undertakings and groups. *Official Journal of the European Union, L 330*, 1-9. https://eur-lex.europa.eu/legal-content/EN/TXT/?uri=celex%3A32014L0095

European Union. (2022). Directive (EU) 2022/2464 of the European Parliament and of the Council of 14 December 2022 amending Directive 2013/34/EU, Directive 2004/109/EC, Directive 2006/43/EC and Regulation (EU) No 537/2014, as regards corporate sustainability reporting. *Official Journal of the European Union, L322*, 15-57. https://eur-lex.europa.eu/legal-content/EN/TXT/?uri=CELEX%3A32022L2464

Evans, L., & Nobes, C. (2021). Harmonization relating to auditor independence: The Eighth Directive, the UK and Germany. *European Accounting Review*, 7(3), 493–516. 10.1080/096381898336394

Franca, V. (2012). The Strength of the Employer Brand: Influences and Implications for Recruiting. *Journal of Marketing Management*, 3, 78.

Freitas, W. R. S., Caldeira-Oliveira, J. H., Teixeira, A. A., Stefanelli, N. O., & Teixeira, T. B. (2020). Green human resource management and corporate social responsibility: Evidence from Brazilian firms. *Benchmarking*, 27(4), 1551–1569. 10.1108/BIJ-12-2019-0543

Global Reporting Initiative. (2021). *Integrating the SDGs into corporate reporting: A practical guide*. Global Reporting. https://www.globalreporting.org/media/mlkjpn1i/gri-sasb-joint-publication-april-2021.pdf

Gnoni, M., & Lettera, G. (2012). Near-miss management systems: A methodological comparison. *Journal of Loss Prevention in the Process Industries*, 25(3), 609–616. 10.1016/j.jlp.2012.01.005

Gnoni, M. G., & Saleh, J. H. (2017). Near miss management systems and observability-indepth: Handling safety incidents and accident precursors in light of safety principles. *Safety Science*, 91, 154–167. 10.1016/j.ssci.2016.08.012

Gnoni, M. G., Tornese, F., Guglielmi, A., Pellicci, M., Campo, G., & De Merich, D. (2022). Near miss management systems in the industrial sector: A literature review. *Safety Science*, 150, 105704. 10.1016/j.ssci.2022.105704

Guerci, M., Montanari, F., Scapolan, A., & Epifanio, A. (2016). Green and non-green recruitment practices for attracting job applicants: Exploring independent and interactive effects. *International Journal of Human Resource Management*, 27(2), 129–150. 10.1080/09585192.2015.1062040

Guillot-Soulez, C., Saint-Onge, S., & Soulez, S. (2022). Green certification and organizational attractiveness: The moderating role of firm ownership. *Corporate Social Responsibility and Environmental Management*, 29(1), 189–199. 10.1002/csr.2194

Gull, S., & Idrees, H. (2022). Green training and organizational efficiency: Mediating role of green competencies. *European Journal of Training and Development, 46*(1/2), 105–119. 10.1108/EJTD-10-2020-0147

Harvey, R. J. (1991). Job analysis. In Dunnette, M. D., & Hough, L. M. (Eds.), *Handbook of industrial and organizational psychology* (2nd ed., pp. 71–163). Consulting Psychologists Press.

Hilliard, A., Kazim, E., Koshiyama, A., Zannone, S., Trengove, M., Kingsman, N., & Polle, R. (2022). Regulating the robots: NYC mandates bias audits for AI-driven employment decisions. *SSRN*. Retrieved from https://ssrn.com/abstract=408318910.2139/ssrn.4083189

H&M Group. (2020, October 1). *H&M has received a decision from the regional Data Protection Authority in Hamburg, Germany.* H&M Group. https://hmgroup.com/news/hm-has-received-a-decision-from-the-regional-data-protection-authority-in-hamburg-germany/?s=regional

Hronová, Š., & Špaček, M. (2021). Sustainable HRM practices in corporate reporting. *Economies, 9*(2), 75. 10.3390/economies9020075

Jamil, S., Zaman, S. I., Kayikci, Y., & Khan, S. A. (2023). The role of green recruitment on organizational sustainability performance. *Sustainability (Basel), 15*(21), 15567. 10.3390/su152115567

Kang, Y., Hsiao, H. S., & Ni, J. Y. (2022). The Role of Sustainable Training and Reward in Influencing Employee Accountability Perception and Behavior for Corporate Sustainability. *Sustainability (Basel), 14*(18), 11589. 10.3390/su141811589

Keane, E. (2018). The GDPR and Employee's Privacy: Much Ado but Nothing New. *King's Law Journal : KLJ, 29*(3), 354–363. 10.1080/09615768.2018.1555065

Kong, Y., & Ding, H. (2023). Tools, Potential, and Pitfalls of Social Media Screening: Social Profiling in the Era of AI-Assisted Recruiting. *Journal of Business and Technical Communication, 38*(1), 33–65. 10.1177/10506519231199478

La Torre, M., Sabelfeld, S., Blomkvist, M., & Dumay, J. (2020). Rebuilding trust: Sustainability and non-financial reporting and the European Union regulation. *Meditari Accountancy Research, 28*(4), 701–725. 10.1108/MEDAR-06-2020-0914

Landers, R. N., & Schmidt, G. B. (2016). *Social Media in Employee Selection and Recruitment: Theory, Practice, and Current Challenges.* Springer. 10.1007/978-3-319-29989-1

Lievens, F., & Chapman, D. (2010). Recruitment and selection. In S. Zedeck (Ed.), *APA handbook of industrial and organizational psychology, Vol 2: Selecting and developing members for the organization* (pp. 267-290). American Psychological Association. 10.4135/9780857021496.n9

Liu, Y., Qian, Y., & Lin, H. (2020). Green training and development for employees: A systematic literature review. *Journal of Cleaner Production*, 258, 120701.

López-Concepción, A., Gil-Lacruz, A. I., & Saz-Gil, I. (2022). Stakeholder engagement, CSR development, and SDGs compliance: A systematic review from 2015 to 2021. *Corporate Social Responsibility and Environmental Management*, 29(1), 19–31. 10.1002/csr.2170

Majid, F., Raziq, M. M., Memon, M. A., Tariq, A., & Rice, J. L. (2023). Transformational leadership, job engagement, and championing behavior: Assessing the mediating role of role clarity. *European Business Review*, 35(6), 941–963. 10.1108/EBR-01-2023-0028

Malos, S. B. (1998). Current legal issues in performance appraisal. In Smither, J. W. (Ed.), *Performance appraisal: State of the art in practice* (pp. 49–94). Jossey-Bass.

Merlin, M., & Chen, Y. (2022). Impact of green human resource management on organizational reputation and attractiveness: The mediated-moderated model. *Frontiers in Environmental Science*, 10, 1561. 10.3389/fenvs.2022.962531

Mishra, P. (2017). Green human resource management. *The International Journal of Organizational Analysis*, 25(5), 762–788. 10.1108/IJOA-11-2016-1079

Molnar, E., & Mulvihill, P. (2003). Sustainability-focused Organizational Learning: Recent Experiences and New Challenges. *Journal of Environmental Planning and Management*, 46(2), 167–176. 10.1080/0964056032000070990

Mwita, K., & Kinemo, S. (2018). The role of green recruitment and selection on performance of processing industries in Tanzania: A case of Tanzania Tobacco Processors Limited (TTPL). *International Journal of Human Resource Studies*, 8(4), 35. Advance online publication. 10.5296/ijhrs.v8i4.13356

Paillé, P., Valéau, P., & Renwick, D. W. (2020). Leveraging green human resource practices to achieve environmental sustainability. *Journal of Cleaner Production*, 260, 121137. 10.1016/j.jclepro.2020.121137

Panait, M., Gigauri, I., Hysa, E., & Raimi, L. (2023). Corporate Social Responsibility and Environmental Performance: Reporting Initiatives of Oil and Gas Companies in Central and Eastern Europe. In Machado, C., & Paulo Davim, J. (Eds.), *Corporate Governance for Climate Transition* (pp. 123–140). Springer. 10.1007/978-3-031-26277-7_6

Pham, D., & Paillé, P. (2019). Green recruitment and selection: An insight into green patterns. *International Journal of Manpower*, 41(3), 258–272. 10.1108/IJM-05-2018-0155

Phimister, J. R., Oktem, U., Kleindorfer, P. R., & Kunreuther, H. (2003). Near miss incident management in the chemical process industry. *Risk Analysis*, 23(3), 445–459. 10.1111/1539-6924.0032612836838

Pulakos, E. D. (2009). *Performance Management: A New Approach for Driving Business Results*. Wiley. 10.1002/9781444308747

Ren, S., Tang, G., & Jackson, S. (2018). Green human resource management research in emergence: A review and future directions. *Asia Pacific Journal of Management*, 35, 769–803. 10.1007/s10490-017-9532-1

Renwick, D. W. S., Redman, T., & Maguire, S. (2013). Green human resource management: A review and research agenda. *International Journal of Management Reviews*, 15(1), 1–14. 10.1111/j.1468-2370.2011.00328.x

Saadaoui, S., & Belmouffeq, B. (2023). Systematic Literature Review on social media in Employee Recruitment and Selection (2018-2022). *International Journal of Innovation and Scientific Research*, 67(2), 190–201.

Schaaf, T. (1995). Near miss reporting in the chemical process industry: An overview. *Microelectronics and Reliability*, 35(9-10), 1233–1243. 10.1016/0026-2714(95)99374-R

Schneider, B., & Konz, A. (1989). Strategic job analysis. *Human Resource Management*, 28(1), 51–63. 10.1002/hrm.3930280104

Sun, X. (2018). Integrating Sustainability into Construction Engineering Projects: Perspective of Sustainable Project Planning. *Sustainability (Basel)*, 10(3), 784. 10.3390/su10030784

The Hamburg Commissioner for Data Protection and Freedom of Information. (2020). *Hamburg Commissioner Fines H&M 35.3 Million Euro for Data Protection Violations in Service Centre*. Europea. https://www.edpb.europa.eu/news/national-news/2020/hamburg-commissioner-fines-hm-353-million-euro-data-protection-violations_en

Tirno, R. R., Islam, N., & Happy, K. (2023). Green HRM and eco-friendly behavior of employees: Relevance of proecological climate and environmental knowledge. *Heliyon*, 9(4), e14632. 10.1016/j.heliyon.2023.e1463237082624

Vetráková, M., Hitka, M., Potkány, M., Lorincová, S., & Smerek, L. (2018). Corporate sustainability in the process of employee recruitment through social networks in conditions of Slovak small and medium enterprises. *Sustainability (Basel)*, 10(5), 1670. 10.3390/su10051670

Wallace, M., Lings, I., Cameron, R., & Sheldon, N. (2014). Attracting and retaining staff: The role of branding and industry image. In Harris, R., & Short, T. (Eds.), *Workforce Development* (pp. 19–36). Springer. 10.1007/978-981-4560-58-0_2

Wang, Q., Gazi, M., Sobhani, F., Masud, A., Islam, M., & Akter, T. (2023). Green human resource management and job pursuit intention: Mediating role of corporate social responsibility and organizational reputation. *Environmental Research Communications*, 5(7), 075001. 10.1088/2515-7620/acda81

Wielewska, I., Kacprzak, M., Król, A., Czech, A., Zuzek, D., Gralak, K., & Marks-Bielska, R. (2023). Green human resource management. *Ekonomia i Środowisko - Economics and Environment*. https://doi.org/10.34659/eis.2022.83.4.496

Yafi, E., Tehseen, S., & Haider, S. A. (2021). Impact of green training on environmental performance through mediating role of competencies and motivation. *Sustainability (Basel)*, 13(10), 5624. 10.3390/su13105624

Yong, J., & Mohd-Yusoff, Y. (2016). Studying the influence of strategic human resource competencies on the adoption of green human resource management practices. *Industrial and Commercial Training*, 48(7), 416–422. 10.1108/ICT-03-2016-0017

Yong, J., Yusliza, M., & Fawehinmi, O. (2019). Green human resource management. *Benchmarking*, 26(3), 782–804. 10.1108/BIJ-12-2018-0438

ADDITIONAL READING

Afsar, B., & Umrani, W. A. (2020). Corporate social responsibility and pro-environmental behavior at workplace: The role of moral reflectiveness, coworker advocacy, and environmental commitment. *Corporate Social Responsibility and Environmental Management*, 27(1), 109–125. 10.1002/csr.1777

Bahuguna, P. C., Srivastava, R., & Tiwari, S. (2023). Two-decade journey of green human resource management research: A bibliometric analysis. *Benchmarking*, 30(2), 585–602. 10.1108/BIJ-10-2021-0619

Bazrkar, A., & Moshiripour, A. (2021). Corporate practices of green human resources management. *Foresight STI Governance*, 15(2), 97–105. 10.17323/2500-2597.2021.1.97.105

De Hert, P., & Papakonstantinou, V. (2021). The New General Data Protection Regulation: Still a Sound System for the Protection of Individuals? *Computer Law & Security Review*, 41, 105530. 10.1016/j.clsr.2021.105530

Dumont, J., Shen, J., & Deng, X. (2017). Effects of green HRM practices on employee workplace green behavior: The role of psychological green climate and employee green values. *Human Resource Management*, 56(4), 613–627. 10.1002/hrm.21792

Floridi, L., & Taddeo, M. (2020). The Ethics of Information: From Data Protection to Data Ethics. *Philosophy & Technology*, 33(3), 459–477. 10.1007/s13347-020-00417-335194548

Jerónimo, H. M., Henriques, P. L., de Lacerda, T. C., da Silva, F. P., & Vieira, P. R. (2020). Going green and sustainable: The influence of green HR practices on the organizational rationale for sustainability. *Journal of Business Research*, 112, 413–421. 10.1016/j.jbusres.2019.11.036

Johar, S., Ecer, F., & Altinay, L. (2021). Green HRM practices and employee outcomes: The role of employee green commitment. *Sustainability*, 13(8), 420. 10.3390/su13010420

Tang, G., Chen, Y., Jiang, Y., Paille, P., & Jia, J. (2018). Green human resource management practices: Scale development and validity. *Asia Pacific Journal of Human Resources*, 56(1), 31–55. 10.1111/1744-7941.12147

Xie, H., & Lau, T. C. (2023). Evidence-Based Green Human Resource Management: A Systematic Literature Review. *Sustainability (Basel)*, 15(14), 10941. 10.3390/su151410941

Chapter 7
Fostering Green Entrepreneurship Education and the Socioeconomic Inclusion of Women in the South Caucasus Region

Nargiz Hajiyeva
Azerbaijan State University of Economics, Azerbaijan

Zarina Burkadze
Ilia State University, Georgia

Saida Khalil
https://orcid.org/0000-0003-3695-7755
Azerbaijan State University of Economics, Azerbaijan

ABSTRACT

This research investigates the challenges and opportunities for fostering green entrepreneurship among women in Azerbaijan and Georgia, post-Soviet republics grappling with transitioning economies. Employing qualitative data from interviews with nine female entrepreneurs and green policy experts, alongside legislative analysis and descriptive statistics, the study illuminates a significant gap in understanding and utilization of green economy practices among these entrepreneurs. Despite their successes, participants faced hurdles in incorporating green principles, including regulatory complexities and resource limitations. Collaboration between govern-

DOI: 10.4018/979-8-3693-3439-3.ch007

ment, civil society, and the private sector emerges as crucial for supporting women entrepreneurs in embracing sustainability initiatives. The findings underscore the need for enhanced awareness and educational efforts to promote green practices and facilitate collaboration, thereby advancing sustainable development goals in the region.

INTRODUCTION

It is well-known that entrepreneurship contributes significantly to societal advancement (Schumpeter, 1934). Ironically, the same corporations have often been criticized for their detrimental effects on society due to their operations (Muo & Azeez, 2019). Green entrepreneurship integrates environmentally sustainable practices into business operations and management. This emerging field not only involves adopting green approaches in business activities but also emphasizes promoting and educating consumers about eco-friendly alternatives to conventional products.

Unlike traditional entrepreneurs, green entrepreneurs prioritize educating consumers on the benefits of eco-friendly products, which are often priced higher than conventional alternatives. This educational role is crucial because consumers are generally unaware of the long-term advantages of environmentally friendly products. Therefore, green entrepreneurs must convince consumers that the higher price of these products is justified by their environmental benefits.

Additionally, green entrepreneurs must stay informed about industry advancements and technological competition to maintain their competitive edge. Sustainable production and distribution methods are essential for these businesses, ensuring that their operations do not harm the environment (Sumathi et al., 2014). Scholars argue that eco-friendly entrepreneurial activities can yield significant ecological, socio-cultural, and economic benefits. These benefits include reducing carbon footprints, enhancing social cohesion, and fostering economic resilience. However, experiences in Western countries reveal that these activities can also contribute to the exclusion of disadvantaged groups and may increase social inequalities (Tubridy, 2020; Anguelovski et al., 2018). Such adverse outcomes often arise because both entrepreneurs and policymakers are strategically motivated, prioritizing growth and economic benefits over environmental considerations.

In developing countries, the situation is more complex. Regulatory environments are often weak, and entrepreneurial practices tend to favor powerful groups, making green policies less likely to be embraced. This is compounded by a low entrepreneurial culture and skewed deals that undermine sustainable practices. Understanding the decision-making processes in these contexts is crucial. Identifying who makes the decisions, what types of decisions are made, and the cost implications of these decisions for different groups can shed light on the challenges of promoting green entrepreneurship (Krueger & Gibbs, 2007).

State policies play a pivotal role in fostering green entrepreneurship. For instance, carbon pricing policies in the US at both federal and subnational levels serve as market-based instruments to promote environmentally safe practices (Narassimhan et al., 2022). Scholars argue that political legacy and regime path dependence significantly influence the extent to which states adopt regulatory policies (Narassimhan et al., 2022a; Anderson et al., 2020; Wettestad & Gulbrandsen, 2017). In developing countries, however, implementing green policies can entail high costs, necessitating financial aid from private sectors such as banks or from international financial institutions and donors. These financial mechanisms are often inconsistent due to various constraints, posing significant challenges for economies with small markets. Such economies may struggle to mitigate the conditions resulting from inconsistencies between private and international subsidies.

This study focuses on Azerbaijan and Georgia, post-Soviet republics striving to overcome Soviet legacies. Both countries face unique challenges in promoting green entrepreneurship due to their political, economic, and cultural contexts. Besides political structures, socially constructed and culturally defined perceptions about gender roles also impact entrepreneurship. Women entrepreneurs, in particular, may face additional challenges in promoting their business ideas and encounter veto actors when opting for green entrepreneurship. This research explores how female entrepreneurs in Azerbaijan and Georgia create the potential to reconcile sustainability, economic growth, and green policies.

Indeed, a notable limitation in the field of green entrepreneurship is its predominant focus on developed countries, often overlooking the potential impact and relevance in less wealthy regions, such as emerging economies. While green entrepreneurship is hailed as a source of long-term benefits for developed economies, its potential significance for less affluent regions, particularly in addressing environmental, social, and economic challenges, cannot be underestimated. (Hall et al., 2010) Cross-national evidence, especially from emerging economies, is crucial to understanding the socio-economic contexts shaping green entrepreneurship. Additionally, the lack of public perception and empirical studies in this newly emerging field, highlighted since the 2012 RIO+20 conference, presents a significant limitation that warrants further attention and research.

Current green policies emphasize climate change and reducing carbon emissions (Jonas et al., 2011). These factors are particularly relevant in the context of urbanization, where the construction of recreational, residential, and commercial facilities often neglects ecological concerns. Business and political elites typically view urbanization and modernization as sources of rapid economic growth and performance legitimacy. Consequently, underdeveloped or disregarded urban regimes and regulations can cause both direct and indirect harm to the environment and human health. Criticism is thus directed towards neoliberal financial instruments that incentivize entrepreneurs to sidestep green policies, especially in economically developing states.

This research employs three important criteria—political, economic, and cultural—to justify the case selection strategy. These criteria help understand whether structural factors affect the fostering of green entrepreneurship or if the shaping of eco-friendly entrepreneurial policies depends on decisions made by specific veto players and class interests. Additionally, this study investigates whether gender issues exacerbate these political, economic, and cultural challenges or derive from them. To answer these questions, the study first reviews the existing literature and suggests theoretical insights. It then discusses the methodological underpinnings, provides an empirical analysis of Azerbaijan and Georgia, and finally proposes tentative conclusions and policy recommendations.

LITERATURE REVIEW ON "GREEN ENTREPRENEURSHIP"

Economic globalization has led to critical green thinking in terms of consumption and production for long-term sustainability around the world, along with its environmental impacts. Renewed existing enterprises that are green or more environmentally friendly contribute to improved environmental quality and thus facilitate sustainable economic development (Isaak, 2017). Given our study focus is on women's role in green entrepreneurship, it is important to review the scholarly literature and how such a role is seen across the cases. Blanch, Tulla, and Vera analyzed the importance of environmental capital and the participation of women in local rural development and rural governance and drew conclusions that showed possible links between new women's entrepreneurship and the best use of local resources (Pallarès-Blanch, et al., 2015). The significant contribution of women entrepreneurs to global economic development, in low-and middle-income countries, is widely recognized. Investing in female entrepreneurship is a crucial approach for nations to significantly boost the influence of newly established businesses (Potluri & Phani, 2020). The countries stifle their chances to boost economic progress and place themselves at a disadvantage when they disregard the shown potential of women's entrepreneurship. Because of this, empowering women to participate in and succeed in entrepreneurship is essential for more successful and sustainable economic development across the board (Allen, et al., 2007). Although studies do not show significant difference in environmental attitudes between male and female entrepreneurs, women's motivations to make their environment better differ from that of male entrepreneurs; and women are more proactive in pursuing opportunities for building green networks where they can interact with like-minded, access more customers, access alternative resources, and expand their green business networks (Braun, 2010).

Another study found that many women's participation in green construction is hindered by the stressful nature of the job, low participation, limited career development and advancement opportunities, and inadequate investment in green jobs. Consequently, the research found three socioeconomic advantages of women's inclusion in green construction. These are family/woman benefits, environmental benefits and benefits related to the green energy market. The study suggested steps to increase women's involvement in green construction (Afolabi, et al., 2017). Sumathi (2014) and colleagues emphasize that as a green business, the owner can provide economically rewarding, socially responsible and environmentally beneficial, meaningful employment. It can also help women, who want to balance their family life with their professional goals. The green economy provides a win-win situation for women to remain committed to their values and financial success. Therefore, the current study focuses on identifying opportunities for women entrepreneurs in green, and the researcher is also trying to analyse women's perceptions of opportunities in the same field. A key strategy for reducing rural poverty and advancing sustainable rural development is the integration and empowerment of rural women through the encouragement of female entrepreneurship in green cooperatives. Encouraging women to start and run green cooperatives is a crucial way to help women take the lead in jobs and revenue-generating ventures while also enhancing their quality of life and contributing to sustainable development.

Along these lines, another important issue is green management, for which one of the critical points is the adoption of cleaner and more sustainable production (Mustapha, et al., 2017). The private sector is becoming more and more vital in providing answers to the world's sustainability problems by promoting economic growth and development. By contributing to the literature on quality management, green management, and sustainable practices (Yu & Huo, 2019), managers can influence green investment (Schaltenbrand et al, 2018). There is a belief that green management can help companies to do more than just increase their profits; it can also help companies to fulfill their social obligations towards the community and the environment The term 'green management' refers to an active strategy to reduce the environmental impact on the supply chain while improving its economic efficiency. Green management is a proactive strategy that aims to reduce the environmental impacts of a company's supply chain while increasing its economic efficiency. Green management is a proactive strategy that aims to reduce the environmental impacts of a company's supply chain while increasing its economic efficiency (Raut, et al, 2019). As well as reducing costs, green management can also help companies meet their social responsibilities through environmentally sustainable practices (Yu & Huo, 2019). Green management enriches the flow of information and expands research and development to promote innovation by encouraging companies to consider environmental issues and the of various partners (Zhou, et al, 2019). Previous research on green management tends to be limited to a single research theme, e.g.,), an industry (Bortolini et al., 2019), a sector (Gupta, 2018) and a country (Shu et al., 2016).

Farinelli et al. (2013) highlight that entrepreneurs can move away from the dirtier traditional business models, where the business organization is overly dependent on economic profit at the expense of sustainable development which was the primary thrust of green entrepreneurs. Since green economic growth connects the economy to its natural underpinnings, it's critical to identify alternative approaches to economic growth that address various facets of socioeconomic development (Lawson, 2006). In other words, it is a failure to recognize the opportunities of greening if entrepreneurs are unable to conduct their business within the scope of green entrepreneurship (Farinelli, 2011). Therefore, by filling these need gaps in emerging green markets, Dean and McMullen observe that green entrepreneurs exploit market failures of old business practices (Dean & McMullen, 2007). Furthermore, little research has not only investigated green entrepreneurship from the perspective of change management but has also identified outstanding issues within the area of green entrepreneurship, despite the relevance of the role of change management within any change process (Hörisch et al., 2017). For example, Pachecho et al. (2010) identify several cross-cutting conceptual issues from related fields, including business, entrepreneurial, financial, and accountancy. Several times, researchers have tried defining or describing green entrepreneurship in a way that makes it more comprehensible. The goal of green entrepreneurship is to adapt to the current social and economic landscape. Protecting the environment from any negative effects is one of the main goals of green entrepreneurship. The other principal objectives are waste product recycling, boosting the use of renewable energy sources, and establishing organic ranching and agriculture (Uslu et al., 2015). Green entrepreneurship success requires an enterprising individual, a suitable market niche, access to human resources, sufficient capital, and appropriate business support from the public or private sector (Schaper, 2016). The authors also define a green entrepreneur as someone who initiates and manages a business with environmentally friendly processes and outputs. Greater diversity is expected in developing nations, as they may vary in socio-cultural context, legal and constitutional frameworks, green entrepreneurial awareness and capacity, and other factors (Tien et al., 2020). New information technologies and global economic processes have significantly influenced traditional enterprise innovation methods, yet there remains a notable gap in sustainability (Audretsch et al., 2008). Similarly, Dale (2018) describes green entrepreneurship as a narrative process where a business owner gains stakeholder support for their goals. Green entrepreneurship is gaining prominence due to increased awareness of corporate responsibility towards the environment and the growing importance of ecological sustainability in strategic business development (Demirel et al., 2017). Furthermore, Malavisi posited that green entrepreneurship is the engagement with modern green business practices through creative and innovative capacities (Malavisi, 2018). Dale, on the other hand, argues for greener creativity as a means of mitigating global environmental problems, describing it from a greener entrepreneurial perspective as a revolutionary way of addressing current social, economic, and environmental issues (Dale, 2019). Both social and traditional entrepreneurship positively impact sustainable development by promoting societal progress and product differentiation. Sustainable entrepreneurship, which focuses on addressing social and environmental issues, is likely to have a more positive effect on sustainable development (Galindo-Martín et al., 2020).

We noted earlier that the effective implementation of green policies is a function of political and economic constraints. Regarding political constraints, the regulatory practices are important as well as how states design respective legislative frameworks to incentivize small and medium-range businesses to adopt green policies in their daily business routines. For instance, the Law of Georgia on Environmental Protection draws on relatively high standards and calls for all natural and legal entities or state authorities to perform their functions in line with key environmental principles. For the purpose of this Law, the environmental principles are viewed as *"risk reduction, sustainability, priority actions aimed at the environment and human health projection, the user and polluter pay principles, the biological diversity preservation principle, the waste reduction, the recycling, restitution, environmental impact assessment, the public participation, and the information accessibility principles (Article 5)."* (Georgian Environment Law, 1996) *The Constitution of Azerbaijan, adopted in 1995, includes provisions related to environmental protection. Article 52 of the Constitution stipulates that every person has the right to a favorable environment and the obligation to protect it. Azerbaijan adopted its Environmental Code in 1999, which serves as the primary legal framework for environmental protection in the country. The Environmental Code covers various aspects of environmental management, including pollution control, environmental impact assessment, waste management, biodiversity conservation, and natural resource management* (Azerbaijani Environmental Law, 1999). Even though there is a political willingness and appropriate legal framework, economic constraints that are manifested in smaller markets and consumptions can impose financial constraints on businesses and give them impetus to avert the application of green policies. In the empirical chapters, we attempt to provide an outlook of green politics in the cases of Azerbaijan and Georgia and test some of the above-mentioned theoretical assumptions.

Regarding the case selection strategies, we selected the two South Caucasian States – Georgia and Azerbaijan. They are interesting cases to compare because there is a stark difference in their economic performance. For instance, according to the World Bank data, Georgia's current gross domestic product (GDP) is 24.78, and GDP per capita equals to 6,675 USD. As for the human development index, it is 0.6 (scale from 0 to 1) (https://data.worldbank.org/country/georgia). As for Azerbaijan, the GDP is over 78,721,058.82, GDP per capita is 13,196 and the human development index equals to 0.6 (https://data.worldbank.org/country/azerbaijan). These parameters make Georgia and Azerbaijan economically different. In addition, selected cases also differ in terms of their political arrangements and cultural practices which helps us to understand the weights of such structural conditions as political, economic, and economic constraints.

For selecting these cases, a crucial factor was also the level of women's representation in small and medium businesses. The National Statistics Office of Georgia provides some descriptive statistics on women's engagement in entrepreneurship based on the parameters of newly registered enterprises, and small and medium businesses.

Figure 1. Newly registered enterprises in 2013-2022

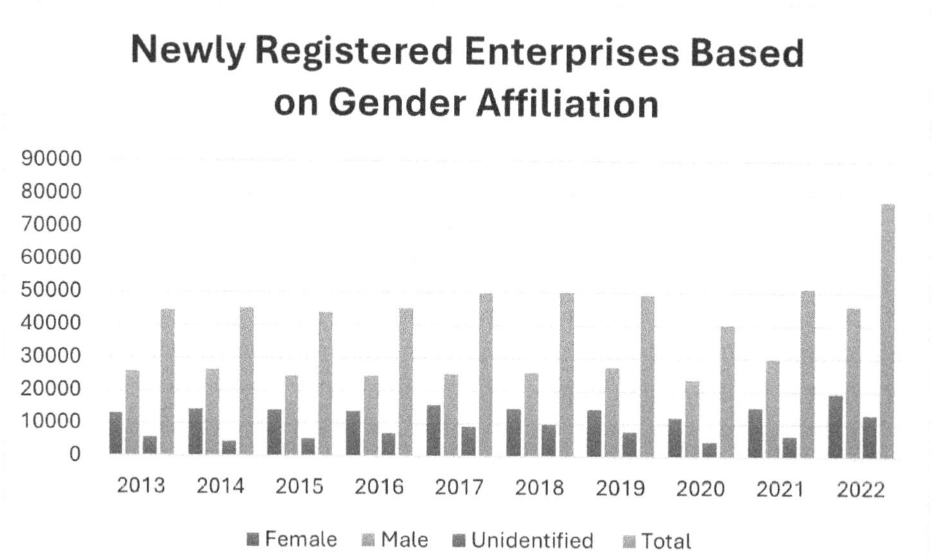

(The National Statistics Office of Georgia https://www.geostat.ge/en)

Figure 1 shows that over a period of eleven years, women's representation in newly registered enterprises increases slowly and remains stable. Regarding the gender distribution in small and medium businesses, we see that compared to males, female entrepreneurs are underrepresented, however, the increase and decrease in male and female engagement in small and medium businesses are linked to general economic conditions of the respective country, in this case, Georgia. For instance, the below given descriptive statistics from 2006 to 2022 indicate that when the economic conditions worsen, the engagement of both genders decreases, and vice versa (see the years of 2007 and 2008, before and after the Russia-Georgia War in August 2008). *We see that both females and males are more engaged in small businesses than in medium businesses, although in both businesses' women are underrepresented compared to men.* These descriptive data lend methodological support to our case selection criterion – *economic* and *political constraints, and the extent of women's engagement in entrepreneurship.*

Figure 2. Gender representation in small and medium businesses, 2006-2008

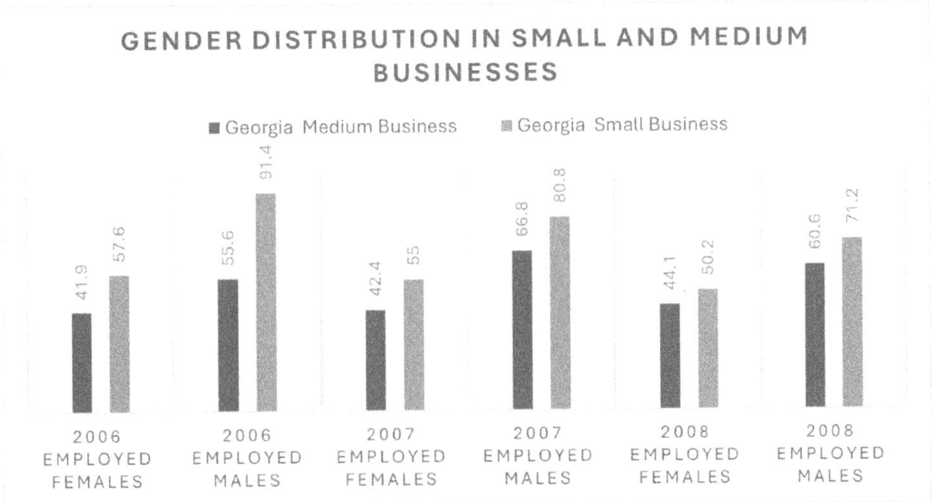

(The National Statistics Office of Georgia https://www.geostat.ge/en).

Figure 3. Gender representation in small and medium businesses, 2009-2011

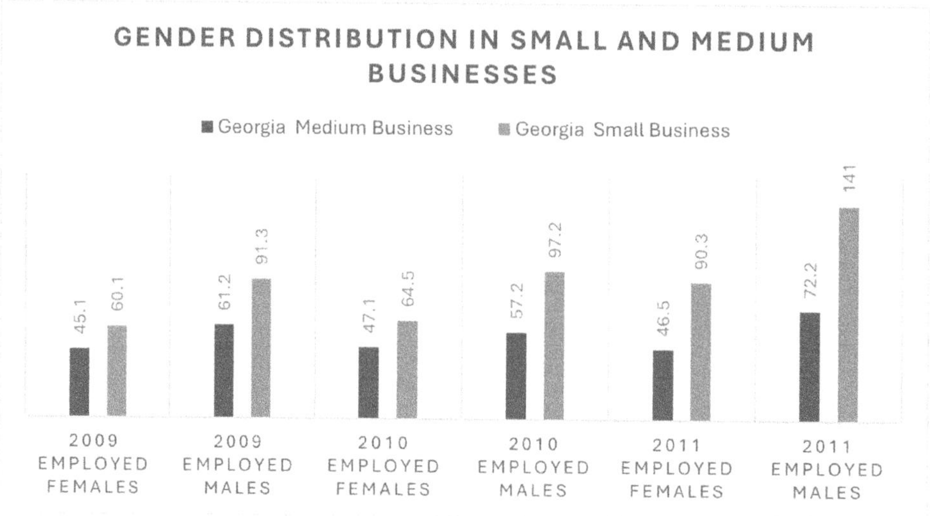

(The National Statistics Office of Georgia https://www.geostat.ge/en)

Figure 4. Gender representation in small and medium businesses, 2012-2014

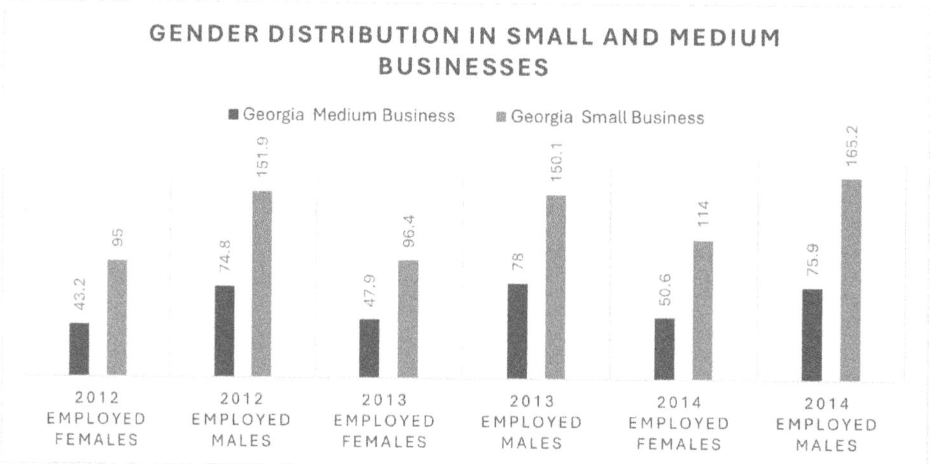

(The National Statistics Office of Georgia https://www.geostat.ge/en)

Figure 5. Gender representation in small and medium businesses, 2015-2018

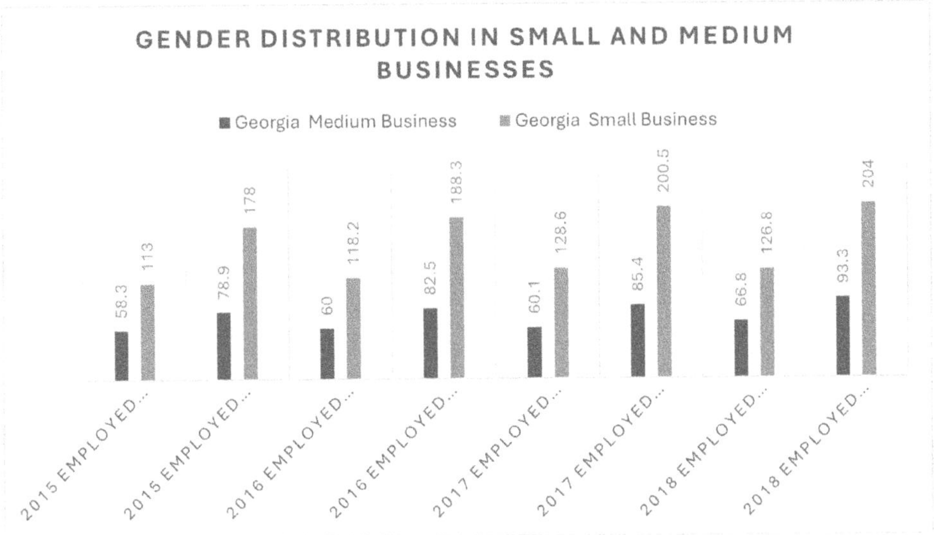

(The National Statistics Office of Georgia https://www.geostat.ge/en)

Figure 6. Gender representation in small and medium businesses, 2019-2022

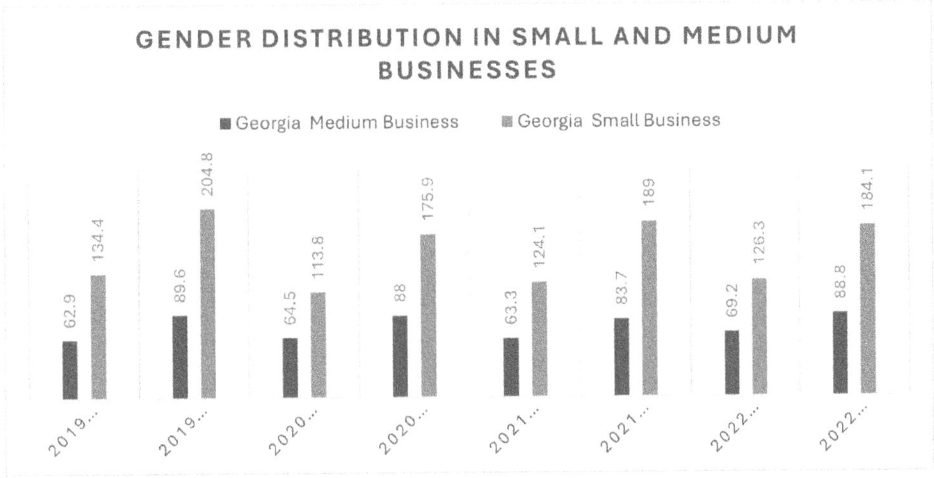

(The National Statistics Office of Georgia https://www.geostat.ge/en)

Figure 7. Distribution of individual entrepreneurs by gender by economic regions as January 2022

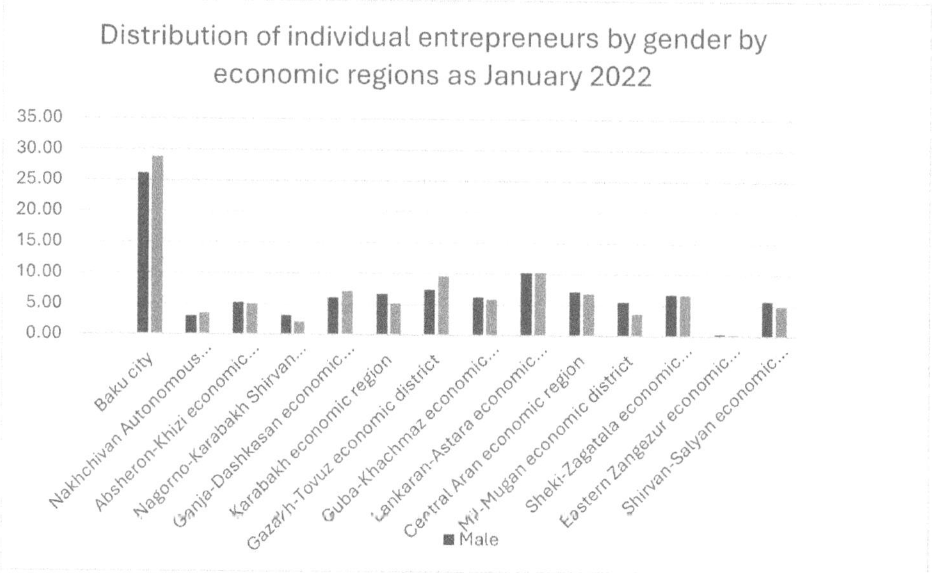

Source: State Statistical Committee of the Republic of Azerbaijan, 2023

Figure 8. Gender distribution of individual entrepreneurs by types of activity as of January 1, 2023 in Azerbaijan.

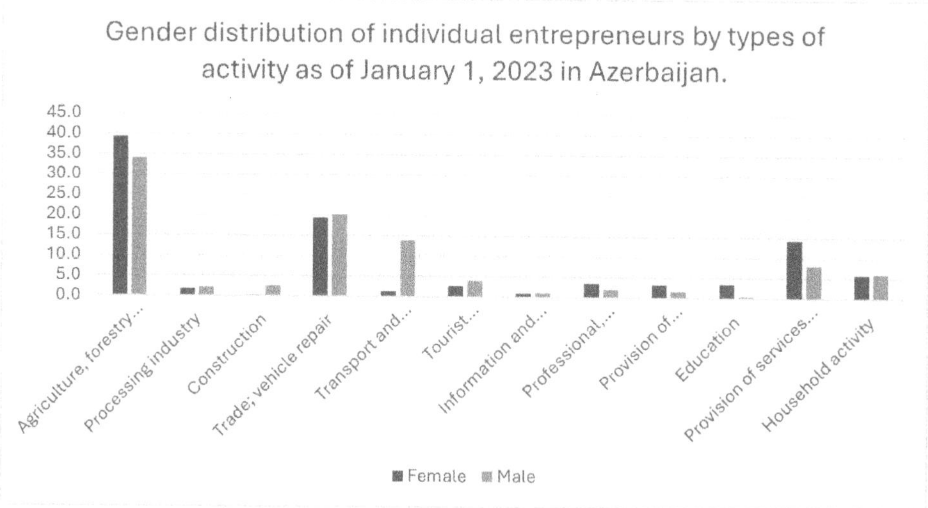

Source: *State Statistical Committee of the Republic of Azerbaijan, 2023*

Unfortunately, the State Statistical Committees in both countries do not provide specific statistical data related to the active involvement of women in entrepreneurial activities, particularly in the context of green growth policy and green entrepreneurship. This lack of data presents a significant challenge in assessing the extent of women's participation in these sectors in Azerbaijan. Additionally, on the Azerbaijani side, it is difficult to find comprehensive data regarding the active involvement of women in regional cities and the distribution of activities between men and women throughout the country. A key aspect of promoting sustainable development and fostering green entrepreneurship is ensuring gender equality and women's participation in economic activities. However, the absence of detailed statistical information hinders policymakers and researchers from accurately gauging the current situation and designing effective strategies to address any disparities that may exist. Therefore, there is a critical need for improved data collection mechanisms and efforts to gather gender-disaggregated data specifically focused on green growth and entrepreneurship initiatives. This approach would enable better monitoring of progress, identification of challenges, and formulation of targeted interventions to promote gender-inclusive sustainable development in Azerbaijan.

METHODOLOGY

To analyze the effects of poltical and econmic factors, and decisions of specific veto players and class interests, as well as the importance of gender varibale in fostering green entrepreneurship, we have collected qualitative data by interviewing nine female entrepreneurs and academics specialized on green polices (six in Azerbaijan and three in Georgia). Additionally, we studied the legislative frameworks of both states and collected descriptive statistics showing the degree of female engagement in green entrepreneurship.

In a recent engagement, we had the privilege of conversing with six accomplished women entrepreneurs from Azerbaijan, alongside three women from Georgia, including government officials and entrepreneurs. However, despite their successes, there was a surprising reticence towards interviews, with some citing scheduling conflicts and others hesitating due to time constraints. Upon reflection, it became evident that there exists a substantial gap in awareness and utilization of green economy practices among these entrepreneurs. Our interviews, spanning diverse sectors including logistics, sports, clothing, and food, revealed a lack of comprehension regarding the green economy concept. Despite efforts to elucidate its essence and potential impact on their ventures, many participants struggled to grasp its significance.

Our interview protocol, comprising 11-12 questions, aimed to gauge participants' familiarity with sustainable practices and their application within their businesses. A fundamental query at the outset, "What means green entreprenurship?" served as a litmus test to assess baseline knowledge. Unfortunately, responses varied widely, with some equating it to "nature" or "nature-friendly," while others admitted unfamiliarity, necessitating further explanation.

Analysis of the Georgian Case

Analyzing the green policies and conditions in Georgia involves reviewing environmental regulations, including the laws governing protection of natural resources and regulating the urban constructions, as well as managing wastes. Most challenging part with regard to this legal framework is the enforcement of regulatory mechanisms. While assessing key areas of green policies, we also take into account governmental efforts to promote renewable energy resources and expand the relevant infrastructure. Noteworthy is that Georgia prioritizes tourism as an important contributor to the development of its economy. Therefore, focusing on the effects of conservation policies to preserve biodiversity positively shapes Georgia's tourism potential. Regional and international partnerships can be used for raising public awareness and designing educational campaigns on green issues to inform the involved stakeholders and population at large. What we also lack in Georgia is the analysis of popular perceptions regarding green policies and conditions. Surveying public opinion can help to measure the extent to which the public supports green policies, and may provide insights into the effective enforcement of eco-friendly initiatives. Overall, we attempt to suggest a comprehensive analysis of the background conditions relating to green policies in Georgia and Azerbaijan. Among others, we regard women's participation in shaping green policies important to lead and advocate positive changes.

In the case of Georgia, the green policies are particularly neglected primarily due to economic and then political reasons. A notable example is the construction businesses, which carry out their businesses in violation of the key environmental principles. The business elites, who are responsible for or willing to participate in the urbanization projects of Georgia act to maximize their benefits. Such a mercantilist approach has its own structural and agency roots. Geologists, urban specialists, and academics identify three main problems in this regard. First are the outdated regulations that resemble the Soviet-era urban policies. Although the general framework of green policies seems in compliance with the EU standards and international practices, the challenging part remains their enactment into practice. This point directly relates to the second problem – the lack of professionals, who can credibly assess the validity and sustainability of urban projects and authorize them in due process. The final and perhaps critical issue is the absence of effective educational programs at universities to prepare and train geologists and urban specialists. City officials depend on either foreign or domestic outsourcing and by doing so state avoids responsibilities if the quality of any construction is questionable. Striking is the fact that there is a scarcity of domestic grassroot organizations that could lobby for green politics. The non-governmental mobilization mainly comes from the local activists, and it does not have lasting effects. One of such examples are the demonstrations against the Namakhvani Hydro Power Plant (The Namakhvani Project) to be built in Western Georgia on the Rioni River. The Namakhvani Project consisted of the Lower Namakhvani with 333 MW and Upper Namakhvani with 100 MW (ENKA, 2022). Since the local communities had environmental concerns that directly related to their physical and economic survival, the Namakhvani Project sparked massive protests across the West Georgia eventually diffusing in Tbilisi and forcing the ENKA Insaat to terminate the contract with the Georgian government.[1] The grassroot organizations demanded open dialogues to sustain forest management and safeguard biodiversity. While the law on environmental protection provides general provisions, other practical mechanisms, for example green audits on how to protect ecosystems, or replace fossil-based materials with low-carbon, renewable materials, are still underdeveloped.

Although, there are several interesting findings regarding the management of green polices in the case of Georgia. Because of the peculiarities of the Georgian market, specifically, its small-scale nature, there is a low demand for green products. Apart for this structural constraint, the women entrepreneurs face a wide array of challenges which disallow them implement green principles in their business activities. One of such difficulties are the lack of targeted investments to promote knowledge on green entrepreneurship and technology programs to support green politics and to create useful environment for women entrepreneurs for more inclusive green policies. In this regard, access to financial resources happens to be decisive instrumental factor for effective management of green politics. Another resource related issue is women's different roles in life, which forbids them to achieve balance in their personal and business lives. Women in conservative societies usually should undertake daily responsibilities at home in addition to their business activities. The combination of these resource-oriented factors prevents women entrepreneurs to implement modern technologies and adopt green policies. Nevertheless, women entrepreneurs in Georgia are focused on sustainable development and consider it necessary to base their economic activities on green principles. Non-governmental and non-profit regulatory agencies usually assist the entrepreneurs of harmless products to gain local quality assurances, which facilitates the management of waste. However, the same regulatory agencies emphasize the importance of promoting the acquisition of solar panel systems in agritourism and the need for the application of energy efficient measures. These agencies usually consider green economic principles as must criterion for the provision of products and services when applying for donor grants. Regulatory agencies also pay attention to raising awareness of eco-friendly production packaging. Women entrepreneurs and regulatory agencies name three main preconditions for the development of a green economy – *the availability of financial resources in energy efficient measures, packaging, and supply chain.* The significance of funding originates from the costly nature of green policies, which is a difficult requirement for the Georgian women entrepreneurs, particularly, for start-up businesses. This financial constrain deprives them from massive implementation of green principles.

In respect with the regulatory framework, Georgia has adopted respective legislation (The Law of Georgia on Environmental Protection, 1996) and regulatory documents to manage energy, water, waste, and land management. Some regulatory documents are not mandatory. The enforcement of environmental regulations may be voluntary that puts women entrepreneurs in unequal conditions and disincentivizes them to adopt green principles. However, global tendencies may be helpful to change local trends and facilitate the production of environmentally friendly products and services and Georgian women entrepreneurs undertake such initiatives. They easily adapt to the digital world and attempt to use their knowledge as much as possible. Women greatly contribute to reducing waste, saving energy and water, supporting local suppliers, and producers because they prioritize social and environmental responsibilities. Women entrepreneurs actively participate in different activities and events focused on sustainability and environmental protection, in cooperation with businesses, governmental and non-governmental organizations. Although, entrepreneurship differs in cities and villages depending on its substance. Nowadays, social networks have positive impact on rural women to bring their business closer to modern approaches. Existing conditions show that the collaboration among government, civil society and the private sector is critical to solve any challenge. Empowering women entrepreneurs should be one of the priorities, including the dissemination of information and increase access to financial resources to promote green entrepreneurship. In the case of large companies, the concern for environmental issues has shifted to the corporate social responsibility (CSR), which is an additional tool for women to gain data and knowledge on green entrepreneurship. For small and medium businesses, problematic issue is that either they need grants or loans from the banks to subsidize green principles in their entrepreneurial activities. In this case, gender does not play a role. Donors issue grants with special conditions and limited to certain locations, for instance, the Asian Development Bank grants funding in the distinct regions of Georgia, while other donors have different territorial preferences. Regarding the loans, banks have high interest rates that make businesses unprofitable if they apply green policies. The logical chain proceeds in this way – *if entrepreneurs want to follow green principles in their business activities, they need to produce quality products, which on its turn affects prices.* In Georgia, there are no able consumers to buy such quality products with such a high price, particularly, in the regions. Because of these regional inequalities, the entrepreneur who invokes green policies needs to realize such quality products in big cities as there is a high probability to reach out more financially stable consumers. Consequently, businesses are mainly concentrated in the capital city of Tbilisi. The implementation of green policies is directly related to the expanses, and this cost-benefit calculation constrains entrepreneurs. Nevertheless, they are willing to learn more about new green strategies and are receptive of specialized trainings or awareness raising campaigns. In addition to funding and knowledge factors, consulting is very much important for entrepreneurs. They need guidance to meet standards. For example, the Ministry of Education of Georgia had its sub agency – the Skills Agency – through which experts and consultants were helping the vocational and university establishments in quality management. Similar approach can assist entrepreneurs in Georgia to adopt green policies in their business activities. For any entrepreneur irrespective of gender, there is one strong motivation – *profit.* They strategically approach this issue and if the adoption of green principles is less costly, they will do it. Thus, joint efforts of governmental, and non-governmental agencies, businesses, and international actors may contribute to the effective implementation of green policies. In addition to this, the field-specific information campaigns will promote entrepreneurial engagement because instead of general information they receive knowledge tailored to their own needs and useful for making their entrepreneurial activities environmentally friendly.

The Case of Azerbaijan

Azerbaijan compared to Georgia has greater economic capacities given its oil resources. Thus, it is not surprising that the interest of the Azerbaijani government lies in green energy zones due to renewable energy sources (RES). Despite Azerbaijan's status as the primary oil and gas exporter in the region, the nation boasts considerable potential for renewable energy sources. The Ministry of Energy estimates the technical potential for solar energy at approximately 23,000 MW, with annual sunshine hours ranging from 2,400 to 3,200 and solar intensity between 1,500 to 2,000 kWh/m2, concentrated mainly in central river valleys and the northern and northwestern regions (Ministry of Energy, 2023).

Wind energy is also promising in Azerbaijan, particularly along the Caspian Sea coast, with an estimated technical potential of around 3,000 MW and an economic potential of 800 MW. This could generate approximately 2.4 TWh of energy and help reduce CO_2 emissions by conserving conventional fuel. Collaborative research indicates an average annual wind speed of 7.9 to 8.1 m/sec in Absheron, affirming the country's overall potential. Despite hydropower being a significant renewable energy source, Azerbaijan's small hydro potential remains largely untapped, with a technical capacity of 520 MW capable of generating up to 3.2 TWh annually. Geothermal energy is another viable option, with up to 800 MW of potential identified across 11 geothermal zones, each with water temperatures ranging from 30 to 100°C. The burgeoning industrial, agricultural, and social sectors present opportunities for biomass electricity generation, utilizing combustible waste. The Ministry of Energy estimates a potential of 380 MW in this area (IEA 2022, Ministry of Energy, 2023). Addressing energy efficiency is crucial, given Azerbaijan's commitment to reducing GHG emissions by 35% from 1990 to 2030 under the Paris Agreement. Legislation such as the Law on Efficient Use of Energy Resources and Energy Efficiency, enacted in June 2021, provides guidelines for energy audits, management, and services. Implementing minimum energy performance standards, inspired by IEA member countries' experiences, can enhance efficiency and reduce waste. Additionally, leveraging waste processing could help meet energy needs in urban centers like Baku, where over 2 Mt of solid waste is disposed of annually (Ministry of Economics, 2023, 2024).

Following the Second Karabakh War, the Azerbaijani government swiftly embarked on essential measures to reconstruct and revitalize the liberated territories. Notably, plans were set in motion to establish production and service areas dedicated to green technologies in these areas, as outlined in the "Action Plan for a Green Energy Zone Formation in the Recovered Areas for 2022-2026" ratified by the Cabinet of Ministers. The creation of a "green energy" zone in the liberated territories, particularly in Karabakh and its surroundings, holds immense significance for Azerbaijan. (Ministry of Economy of Azerbaijan, 2020)

In 2021, the Azerbaijani government decreed the establishment of such a zone post-liberation from Armenian occupation. Collaborating with the Japanese company TEPSCO, the Ministry of Energy of Azerbaijan inked an agreement to facilitate the formation of this green energy zone. The project aims to harness renewable energy potential, including wind, solar, hydro, geothermal, and bioenergy, through the development of energy-saving technologies and modern energy management approaches (SASME, 2023, World Bank, 2022).

In partnership with international entities like Switzerland, Azerbaijan seeks to leverage green economic models to optimize the utilization of renewable energy resources in the liberated territories. For instance, Swiss Urban Planning and Architecture Company, Sa_partners, won tenders to develop master urban design and green territorial planning for liberated districts such as Gubadli and Zangilan. Their expertise in sustainable urban development will contribute significantly to the region's green growth agenda.

Furthermore, Azerbaijan benefits from ongoing support from the EU through programs like the EU Environment Program, which aims to facilitate the country's transition towards a greener economy. By promoting ecological measures and enhancing environmental well-being, these initiatives align with Azerbaijan's goals of sustainable development and resource management (EU4Environment, 2021).

On December 17, 2022 Prime Minister Viktor Orbán signed a contract in Bucharest to facilitate the supply of electricity from Azerbaijan to Hungary via Georgia and Romania. This agreement involved the participation of key leaders, including Romanian President Klaus Iohannis, Georgian Prime Minister Irakli Garibashvili, Azeri President Ilham Aliyev, and European Commission President Ursula von der Leyen. This initiative stemmed from discussions held in August between Hungarian Foreign Minister Péter Szijjártó and the Azerbaijani Energy Minister, where Azerbaijan committed to producing green electricity for export. Hungary, in collaboration with Romania, secured EU funding for the project, which aims to establish a submarine pipeline route for transporting green electricity from Azerbaijan to Hungary via Georgia and Romania. The project, expected to take 3-4 years to complete, will contribute significantly to Hungary's efforts to achieve carbon neutrality. Furthermore, it builds upon the quadruple cooperation established between Hungary, Romania, Georgia, and Azerbaijan in December 2023, reinforcing regional efforts towards sustainable energy solutions (Euractiv, 2022).

In the context of Azerbaijan's green economy aspirations, engaging SMEs, including those led by women entrepreneurs, is pivotal for sustainable development. Despite significant challenges, such as limited resources and market access, SMEs play a crucial role in driving economic growth and job creation. However, their potential contribution to environmental sustainability remains largely untapped due to various barriers, including a lack of awareness, financial constraints, and limited access to green technologies (SASME, 2022; Ahmadov, et.al 2019).

The European Union actively supports women entrepreneurs in Azerbaijan through various initiatives aimed at fostering their business development and enhancing their skills. One such program is the Women in Business programme, facilitated by the European Bank for Reconstruction and Development (EBRD), which offers tailored support including business advice, training, and mentoring to women-led companies across the country. Moreover, the EU4Business initiative, funded by the EU, provides substantial support to small and medium-sized enterprises (SMEs) in Azerbaijan, with a notable focus on women-owned businesses. Through this initiative, women entrepreneurs receive assistance in accessing finance, training, and consultancy services. For instance, the European Fund for South East Europe (EFSE) collaborates with local partners to provide financial support to smaller businesses, including those owned by women, in various sectors such as agriculture, industry, trade, and services.

In 2022, the EU4Business initiative assisted almost 9,000 small and medium-sized enterprises (SMEs) in Azerbaijan, with 14% of them being women-owned. This assistance yielded notable results, including generating an additional €19 million in revenue, creating 3,639 new employment opportunities, achieving a 12% rise in turnover, and a 10% boost in exports. Several women entrepreneurs have reaped benefits from EU aid. For instance, Gulnara Hassanova, the Director of ESSE LLC, witnessed a remarkable improvement in her business performance post-sales training provided by the Advice for Small Businesses program. Similarly, Afet Akhmadova successfully launched a gourmet service with EU assistance, involving participation in global exhibitions and aid in website development and business planning. Additionally, Vusala Ahmadova expanded her education academy in Tovuz after engaging in tailored training offered by EU4Business for rural women. Similarly, Aytekin Sadiqova expanded her beekeeping enterprise with support from an EU-funded project, acquiring ten beehives. The EU-funded project 'VET for the future: development of VET providers' excellence in Azerbaijan' has significantly enhanced vocational training opportunities. During 2022-23, over 23,000 spots were available across 66 vocational educational institutions in Azerbaijan, covering 127 vocations. Furthermore, complimentary short-term inclusive courses in various fields, such as cooking, tailoring, and social media marketing, have been introduced. (EU Neighbours East, 2024)

An evaluation of the labor market has revealed persistent disparities between men and women that predate the pandemic. Similarly, gender-based income gaps persist. Particularly in rural regions, women encounter challenges in accessing financial support and acquiring the necessary skills to initiate their own ventures. The potential of women in remote areas is often underestimated, attributable to factors such as limited education, inadequate familial backing, and a dearth of gender-inclusive development strategies aimed at fostering women-led enterprises nationwide.(CESD, 2022) Women entrepreneurs in Azerbaijan face additional obstacles, including cultural norms and societal expectations, which can hinder their participation in green entrepreneurship. Despite these challenges, many women-led SMEs are pioneering innovative solutions to environmental issues and demonstrating the potential for inclusive and sustainable economic development. (Ahmadov, et.al, 2021) One such example is a small-scale agricultural enterprise run by a group of women entrepreneurs in rural Azerbaijan. Through the adoption of organic farming practices and the use of renewable energy technologies like solar-powered irrigation systems, they have not only reduced their environmental footprint but also improved their productivity and resilience to climate change. Their success story underscores the transformative potential of green entrepreneurship in empowering women and fostering sustainable development at the grassroots level (Ministry of Economics, 2023).

However, the challenges faced by SMEs, including women-led enterprises, in embracing green policies and practices are multifaceted. Apart from financial constraints, there is often a lack of technical expertise and knowledge about sustainable business practices. Moreover, the absence of supportive policies and incentives further discourages SMEs from investing in green technologies and initiatives. To address these challenges and promote green entrepreneurship among SMEs, targeted interventions are required. This could include capacity-building programs, access to finance and technology, mentorship and networking opportunities, and supportive policy frameworks. Additionally, raising awareness about the business case for sustainability and highlighting the potential economic benefits of adopting green practices is essential in changing mindsets and behaviors within the SMEs sector.

Collaborative efforts between government agencies, industry associations, academia, and civil society organizations are essential in fostering an enabling environment for green entrepreneurship. Initiatives such as business incubators, innovation hubs, and green investment funds can provide valuable support to SMEs, particularly those led by women entrepreneurs, in their transition towards sustainability.

Results

Findings unveiled challenges faced by women entrepreneurs in both Azerbaijan and Georgia in incorporating green entrepreneurship principles into their businesses. These challenges encompassed navigating regulatory frameworks, resource constraints, and a lack of support mechanisms. Despite expressed motivation to embrace green entrepreneurship, participants lacked clear strategies and sectoral insights. Furthermore, collaborative initiatives between government, civil society, and the private sector were highlighted as crucial for supporting women entrepreneurs in fostering green entrepreneurship. Participants also discussed initiatives to encourage greater adoption of green practices within society and industries.

Our findings underscore the pressing need for enhanced awareness and education initiatives to promote green economy practices among women entrepreneurs in both Azerbaijan and Georgia. Addressing identified challenges and fostering collaboration between stakeholders are vital steps towards advancing sustainability agendas within the entrepreneurial landscape. Further research and policy interventions are warranted to facilitate the integration of green entrepreneurship principles, thereby contributing to sustainable development goals in both countries.

Table 1. Summary of responses from interviews with women entrepreneurs on green entrepreneurship

Questions	Summary of Responses
Challenges faced in incorporating green entrepreneurship principles	Lack of awareness about green practices and their benefits, limited access to resources and information
Perception of importance of fostering green entrepreneurship	Recognize the importance of sustainability for long-term business success, desire to contribute to the environment
Strategies to integrate green policies and practices	Implementing energy-efficient technologies, sourcing eco-friendly materials, offering sustainable products and services
Support mechanisms/resources needed to implement green entrepreneurship initiatives	Access to training programs, financial incentives, networking opportunities, government subsidies
Navigation of regulatory frameworks and policies related to green entrepreneurship	Difficulty in understanding complex regulations need for simplified guidelines and assistance
Main motivations for embracing green entrepreneurship principles	Desire to make a positive impact on the environment, attract environmentally conscious customers
Role in promoting environmental awareness and sustainability within communities	Engage in community outreach, educate customers about eco-friendly practices, participate in local initiatives
Collaborative initiatives to support women entrepreneurs in fostering green entrepreneurship	Advocating for policy changes, forming partnerships with NGOs and businesses, participating in industry-wide sustainability initiatives

Source: General overview of interview results 2024/composed by authors.

Our findings suggest that while businesses may implement green policies, there is a considerable lack of knowledge sharing and awareness among entrepreneurs about the broader concepts and benefits of green entrepreneurship. This lack of deep background knowledge impedes the potential for sustainable practices to be fully integrated and maximized within businesses. Another important issue identified in our study is the lack of financial resources and support for marginalized women in remote areas of Azerbaijan and Georgia. These women face significant challenges in entering and sustaining businesses, particularly in the green entrepreneurship sector. The lack of financial resources is compounded by a deficiency in knowledge sharing and access to information, which further hinders their ability to adopt and implement green practices effectively.

Challenges Faced

In the course of conducting interviews with women entrepreneurs in remote areas of Azerbaijan, we encountered significant challenges rooted in deep-seated societal norms and cultural dynamics. These challenges manifested in various forms, including hesitation, fear, and unwillingness among the women to participate in the interview process. A notable impediment arose from the prevailing cultural expectation that women seek permission from their husbands or male family members before engaging in activities outside the home, including expressing their opinions or participating in professional endeavors. This phenomenon underscores a broader issue of gender inequality and the restriction of women's agency, particularly in patriarchal societies such as Azerbaijan. Despite possessing the legal status of entrepreneurs and being subject to tax codes and economic responsibilities, many women face barriers to exercising their physical and moral autonomy. This paradox highlights the complex interplay between legal frameworks and deeply ingrained cultural norms, wherein economic participation is permitted, yet social freedoms remain restricted. Moreover, the dearth of research addressing the social and cultural stereotypes surrounding women's entrepreneurship in the South Caucasus region, particularly in Azerbaijan and Georgia, is striking. Historically, data collection and analysis have predominantly focused on quantitative metrics and econometric models, overlooking the nuanced socio-cultural dimensions that shape women's experiences in the labor market.

The absence of ethnographic and anthropological studies further compounds this issue, as it precludes a comprehensive understanding of the lived realities of women entrepreneurs in the region. Without direct engagement with these communities through field research and observational studies, our comprehension of the socio-cultural barriers they face remains incomplete. Thus, to truly grasp the details of women's entrepreneurship in remote areas of Georgia and Azerbaijan and beyond, it is imperative to adopt a multidisciplinary approach that integrates econometric analysis with social research methodologies. By bridging the gap between quantitative data and qualitative insights, such an approach can offer a more complex understanding of the challenges and opportunities facing women entrepreneurs in the South Caucasus region. This holistic perspective is essential for devising effective policies and interventions aimed at promoting gender equality, empowering women economically, and dismantling entrenched cultural stereotypes.

In the bustling capitals of Tbilisi and Baku, examples of successful women entrepreneurs stand as beacons of progress. However, this narrative of success is not echoed in the remote areas and regional cities of these nations. Despite legal frameworks ostensibly supporting gender equality, societal norms persist as formidable barriers, impeding women's active participation in various spheres, including something as fundamental as attending interview processes. This dissonance begs critical questions: Who amplifies the voices of women in these marginalized areas? Who advocates for the dismantling of restrictive social norms? And why do these norms persistently obstruct women's agency and opportunities for advancement? In directing these inquiries, it becomes evident that entrenched societal norms, deeply rooted in patriarchal structures, play a pivotal role in shaping women's realities. These norms dictate societal expectations, prescribing roles, and behaviors that often limit women's autonomy and inhibit their full participation in economic and social spheres. Despite strides made in gender equality advocacy, these norms persist due to a complex interaction of historical precedent, cultural inertia, and systemic inequalities. The voices of women in remote regions are often drowned out or marginalized, exacerbating their exclusion from decision-making processes and economic opportunities.

CONCLUSION AND RECOMMENDATIONS

This comparative analysis suggests a significant gap in the financial resources to promote green policies in the case of Georgia, while such resources are more available for Azerbaijan due to its advantageous economic position in the region. In this respect, Azerbaijani can have more opportunities to design the mechanisms for subsidizing the promotion of green principles in practical terms. Given the size of the market, which is one of the economic constraints, the conjoint efforts of Azerbaijan and Georgia to ease trade barriers and enhance economic relations might encourage small and medium businesses to reduce costs, when implementing green policies in their entrepreneurial activities. The common characteristic for selected cases is the lack of knowledge on how to comply with their entrepreneurial activities with green principles and improve the quality of their production. In this sense, there is a need for a bottom-up approach and engagement of grassroot organizations to advocate eco-friendly business activities and bridge the collaborative gaps among government, non-governmental and business sectors, and international actors. We also find that economic constraints are more of structural nature, while political constraints are mainly related to the willingness of powerful veto-actors.

In the context of South Caucasus countries, particularly Azerbaijan and to some extent Georgia, there exists a substantial gap in gender studies. This gap encompasses various crucial areas including work-life balance analysis, empowerment of genders in the labor market, integration of women entrepreneurs, and the pervasive influence of moral and cultural stereotypes. Despite advancements in societal norms, these regions still lack comprehensive research in these domains. Moreover, the exploration of green entrepreneurship within the gender discourse remains largely unaddressed. Understanding the intricacies of work-life balance within these cultural contexts is essential for formulating effective policies that promote gender equality. Similarly, empowering women in the labor market requires targeted interventions such as training programs and policy reforms to mitigate existing disparities. Integration of women into entrepreneurship faces challenges including limited access to resources and prevailing stereotypes. Addressing these issues demands a deep dive into cultural and societal norms that shape perceptions of gender roles. Furthermore, exploring the intersection of gender dynamics with emerging sectors like green entrepreneurship holds promise for fostering sustainable development and gender inclusivity in the region. Closing this scientific gap through further research and awareness-raising efforts is crucial for advancing gender equality and inclusive growth in the South Caucasus. Considering these factors, both Georgia and Azerbaijan have the potential to foster green entrepreneurship among women. Georgia may have a more favorable environment in terms of cultural attitudes toward entrepreneurship and awareness of environmental issues. However, Azerbaijan's resource wealth and government support for economic diversification could provide opportunities for green entrepreneurship initiatives with the right policies and support mechanisms in place.

REFERENCES

Afolabi, A. O., Tunji-Olayeni, P. F., Oyeyipo, O. O., & Ojelabi, R. A. (2017). The socio-economics of women inclusion in green construction. *Construction Economics and Building*, 17(1), 70–89. 10.5130/AJCEB.v17i1.5344

Ahmadov, F., Zeynalova, R. A. U., Bayramova, R. A. U., & Quluzade, R. A. O. (2019). *Developmental Prospects of Women Entrepreneurs in Azerbaijan and an Analysis of the Problems They Face.*

Ahmadov, F., Zeynalova, U., Bayramova, U., & Mammadov, I. (2021). Analysis of educational impact on women entrepreneurs in sustainable social business: The case of Azerbaijan. [TURCOMAT]. *Turkish Journal of Computer and Mathematics Education*, 12(6), 1847–1856.

Allen, I. E., Langowitz, N., & Minniti, M. (2007). Global entrepreneurship monitor. *2006 report on women and entrepreneurship, 3*(1), 54-88.

Anderson, S. E., DeLeo, R. A., & Taylor, K. (2020). Policy entrepreneurs, legislators, and agenda setting: Information and influence. *Policy Studies Journal: the Journal of the Policy Studies Organization*, 48(3), 587–611. 10.1111/psj.12331

Anguelovski, I., Connolly, J. J., Garcia-Lamarca, M., Cole, H., & Pearsall, H. (2018). New scholarly pathways on green gentrification: What does the urban 'green turn' mean and where is it going? *Progress in Human Geography*, 43(6), 1064–1086. 10.1177/0309132518803799

Article 5 Main Environmental Principles, the Law of Georgia on Environmental Protection. Available at: https://matsne.gov.ge/en/document/view/33340?publication=21

Audretsch, D., Callejon, M., & Aranguren, M. J. (2008). Entrepreneurship, small firms and self-employment. In *High Technology, Productivity and Networks: A Systemic Approach to SME Development* (pp. 117–137). Palgrave Macmillan UK. 10.1057/9780230583726_6

Bortolini, M., Galizia, F. G., Gamberi, M., Mora, C., & Pilati, F. (2019). Enhancing stock efficiency and environmental sustainability goals in direct distribution logistic networks. *International Journal of Advanced Operations Management*, 11(1-2), 8–25. 10.1504/IJAOM.2019.098518

Braun, P. (2010). Going green: Women entrepreneurs and the environment. *International Journal of Gender and Entrepreneurship*, 2(3), 245–259. 10.1108/17566261011079233

CESD. (2022). *COVID-19 and female entrepreneurs in Azerbaijan: Challenges and outcomes. CESD PRESS. Center for Economic and Social Development*. CESD.

Dale, G. (2018). *The emergence of an ecological Karl Marx: 1818-2018.*

Dale, G. (2019). Climate, communism and the Age of Affluence. *Review of FALC.*

Dean, T. J., & McMullen, J. S. (2007). Toward a theory of sustainable entrepreneurship: Reducing environmental degradation through entrepreneurial action. *Journal of Business Venturing*, 22(1), 50–76. 10.1016/j.jbusvent.2005.09.003

Demirel, P., Li, Q. C., Rentocchini, F., & Tamvada, J. P. (2019). Born to be green: New insights into the economics and management of green entrepreneurship. *Small Business Economics*, 52(4), 759–771. 10.1007/s11187-017-9933-z

Environmental Protection Law of. 1999, No. 678–IQ, Azerbaijan (1999). https://www.fao.org/faolex/results/details/en/c/LEX-FAOC032661/

Farinelli, F., Bottini, M., Akkoyunlu, S., & Aerni, P. (2011). Green entrepreneurship: The missing link towards a greener economy. *Atdf Journal*, 8(3/4), 42–48.

Galindo-Martín, M. A., Castano-Martinez, M. S., & Méndez-Picazo, M. T. (2020). The relationship between green innovation, social entrepreneurship, and sustainable development. *Sustainability (Basel)*, 12(11), 4467. 10.3390/su12114467

Gomółka, K. (2021). The Self-employment of Women in Azerbaijan. *Studia Europejskie-Studies in European Affairs*, 25(2), 171–190. 10.33067/SE.2.2021.8

Government of Azerbaijan. (2020). *Energy potential of Karabakh and surrounding regions, Ministry of Energy of the Republic of Azerbaijan.* Government of Azerbaijan. https://minenergy.gov.az/en/xeberler-arxivi/dagliq-qarabag-ve-etraf-regionlarin-enerji-potensiali

Government of Azerbaijan. (2024). *Azərbaycanda bərpa olunan enerji mənbələrindən istifadə [Utilization of renewable energy sources in Azerbaijan].* Ministry of Energy of the Republic of Azerbaijan. Government of Azerbaijan. https://minenergy.gov.az/en/alternativ-ve-berpa-olunan-enerji/azerbaycanda-berpa-olunan-enerji-menbelerinden-istifade

Gupta, H. (2018). Assessing organizations performance on the basis of GHRM practices using BWM and Fuzzy TOPSIS. *Journal of Environmental Management*, 226, 201–216. 10.1016/j.jenvman.2018.08.00530119045

Hall, J. K., Daneke, G. A., & Lenox, M. J. (2010). Sustainable development and entrepreneurship: Past contributions and future directions. *Journal of Business Venturing*, 25(5), 439–448. 10.1016/j.jbusvent.2010.01.002

Heyat, F. (2020). Women and the culture of entrepreneurship in Soviet and post-Soviet Azerbaijan. In *Markets and Moralities* (pp. 19–31). Routledge. 10.4324/9781003085966-3

Hörisch, J., Kollat, J., & Brieger, S. A. (2017). What influences environmental entrepreneurship? A multilevel analysis of the determinants of entrepreneurs' environmental orientation. *Small Business Economics*, 48(1), 47–69. 10.1007/s11187-016-9765-2

Isaak, R. (2017). *Green logic: Ecopreneurship, theory and ethics.* Routledge. 10.4324/9781351283168

Jonas, A. E., Gibbs, D., & While, A. (2011). The new urban politics as a politics of carbon control. *Urban Studies (Edinburgh, Scotland)*, 48(12), 2537–2554. 10.1177/0042098011411951220818 34

Krueger, R., & Gibbs, D. (Eds.). (2007). *The sustainable development paradox: urban political economy in the United States and Europe.* Guilford Press.

Lawson, R. (2006). An overview of green economics. *International Journal of Green Economics*, 1(1-2), 23–36. 10.1504/IJGE.2006.009335

Malavisi, A. (2018). The urgency of the greening of ethics. *Australasian Journal of Logic*, 4(3), 593–609. 10.26686/ajl.v15i2.4872

Mustapha, M. A., Manan, Z. A., & Alwi, S. R. W. (2017). Sustainable Green Management System (SGMS)–An integrated approach towards organisational sustainability. *Journal of Cleaner Production*, 146, 158–172. 10.1016/j.jclepro.2016.06.033

Najafizadeh, M. (2016). Social entrepreneurship, social change, and gender roles in Azerbaijan. In *Routledge Handbook of Entrepreneurship in Developing Economies* (pp. 278–294). Routledge.

Narassimhan, E., Koester, S., & Gallagher, K. S. (2022). Carbon pricing in the US: Examining state-level policy support and federal resistance. *Politics and Governance*, 10(1), 275–289. 10.17645/pag.v10i1.4857

Narassimhan, E., Koester, S., & Gallagher, K. S. (2022). Carbon pricing in the US: Examining state-level policy support and federal resistance. *Politics and Governance*, 10(1), 275–289. 10.17645/pag.v10i1.4857

Neighbours East, E. U. (2024.). *You can too: How the EU supports women entrepreneurs in Azerbaijan.* EU Neighbours East. https://euneighbourseast.eu/news/explainers/you-can-too-how-the-eu-supports-women-entrepreneurs-in-azerbaijan/

Pacheco, D. F., Dean, T. J., & Payne, D. S. (2010). Escaping the green prison: Entrepreneurship and the creation of opportunities for sustainable development. *Journal of Business Venturing*, 25(5), 464–480. 10.1016/j.jbusvent.2009.07.006

Pallarès-Blanch, M., Tulla, A. F., & Vera, A. (2015). Environmental capital and women's entrepreneurship: A sustainable local development approach. *Carpathian Journal of Earth and Environmental Sciences*, 10(3), 133–146.

Potluri, S., & Phani, B. V. (2020). Women and green entrepreneurship: A literature based study of India. *International Journal of Indian Culture and Business Management*, 20(3), 409–428. 10.1504/IJICBM.2020.107675

Raharjo, K. (2019). The Role of Green Management in Creating Sustainability Performance on the Small and Medium Enterprises. *Management of Environmental Quality*, 30(3), 557–577. 10.1108/MEQ-03-2018-0053

Raut, R. D., Luthra, S., Narkhede, B. E., Mangla, S. K., Gardas, B. B., & Priyadarshinee, P. (2019). Examining the performance oriented indicators for implementing green management practices in the Indian agro sector. *Journal of Cleaner Production*, 215, 926–943. 10.1016/j.jclepro.2019.01.139

Schaltenbrand, B., Foerstl, K., Azadegan, A., & Lindeman, K. (2018). See what we want to see? The effects of managerial experience on corporate green investments. *Journal of Business Ethics*, 150(4), 1129–1150. 10.1007/s10551-016-3191-x

Schaper, M. (2016). Understanding the green entrepreneur. In *Making ecopreneurs* (pp. 7–20). Routledge. 10.4324/9781315593302

Schumpeter, J. (1934). *The theory of economic development*. Harvard University Press.

Shu, C., Zhou, K. Z., Xiao, Y., & Gao, S. (2016). How green management influences product innovation in China: The role of institutional benefits. *Journal of Business Ethics*, 133(3), 471–485. 10.1007/s10551-014-2401-7

Sumathi, K., Anuradha, T. S., & Akash, S. B. (2014). Green Business as a Sustainable Career for Women Entrepreneurs in IndiaAn Opinion Survey. *Advances in Management*, 7(5), 46.

Tien, N. H., Hiep, P. M., Dai, N. Q., Duc, N. M., & Hong, T. T. K. (2020). Green entrepreneurship understanding in Vietnam. *International Journal of Entrepreneurship*, 24(2), 1–14.

Tubridy, F. (2020). Green climate change adaptation and the politics of designing ecological infrastructures. *Geoforum*, 113, 133–145. 10.1016/j.geoforum.2020.04.020

Uslu, Y. D., Hancıoğlu, Y., & Demir, E. (2015). Applicability to green entrepreneurship in Turkey: A situation analysis. *Procedia: Social and Behavioral Sciences*, 195, 1238–1245. 10.1016/j.sbspro.2015.06.266

Wettestad, J., & Gulbrandsen, L. H. (Eds.). (2017). *The evolution of carbon markets: Design and diffusion*. Routledge. 10.4324/9781315228266

World Bank. (2022, December 8). *Azerbaijan Can Accelerate Its Green Economic Transformation, a World Bank Report Shows How* [Press release]. Woeld Bank. https://www.worldbank.org/en/news/press-release/2022/12/08/azerbaijan-can-accelerate-its-green-economic-transformation-a-world-bank-report-shows-how

Yu, Y., & Huo, B. (2019). The impact of environmental orientation on supplier green management and financial performance: The moderating role of relational capital. *Journal of Cleaner Production*, 211, 628–639. 10.1016/j.jclepro.2018.11.198

Zhou, Y., Shu, C., Jiang, W., & Gao, S. (2019). Green management, firm innovations, and environmental turbulence. *Business Strategy and the Environment*, 28(4), 567–581. 10.1002/bse.2265

ENDNOTE

1 ENKA 'Finally' Terminates Namakhvani HPP Contract, 24/03/2022, available at: https://civil.ge/archives/481355

Chapter 8
The Causality Between the Green Development and the Food Security Agendas in China

Anna Ivolga
Stavropol State Agrarian University, Russia

Alexander Arskiy
https://orcid.org/0000-0001-7417-6795
RUDN University, Russia

Elena Bogdanova
https://orcid.org/0000-0001-9610-4709
Financial University Under the Government of the Russian Federation, Russia

Denis Samygin
https://orcid.org/0000-0002-5715-1227
Penza State University, Russia

ABSTRACT

Despite China's impressive success in increasing domestic agricultural production in recent decades, the country has yet to ensure self-sufficiency in some food staples. Against the backdrop of the increasing volatility of climate conditions, the degradation of agricultural land, and the depletion of water resources endanger the sustainable development not only of agriculture, but also of rural communities. China's efforts in building a so-called ecological civilization involve curbing greenhouse gas emissions and prioritizing principles of green development. While converging in understanding the need to sustain development, the food security and

DOI: 10.4018/979-8-3693-3439-3.ch008

the green development doctrines differ in a way that increasing the agricultural output is hardly possible without aggravating anthropogenic pressure on ecosystems. In this chapter, the authors use the example of China trying to find common ground between ensuring food security for everyone and the important task of greening the agricultural sector.

INTRODUCTION

The modern era of post-industrial development in the world economy is characterized by a coexistence of several fundamental changes in the structure of the spatial distribution of productive forces (Zakaria & Buaben, 2021; Erokhin et al., 2023). In the XX century, the countries of the Global North acted as the drivers of world economic growth, while in recent decades, the geography of centers of economic and industrial development has increasingly shifted towards the countries of Global South and East (Liu et al., 2023). Due to large-scale industrialization, countries like China, Brazil, India, and the newly industrialized countries in Southeast Asia have turned from economies that are catching up to the developed world to new centers of the global economic order (Lopatnikov & Gorbanyov, 2020). However, every success comes at a cost. Along with the global shift in the balance of economic and productive power between the Global North and the Global South, the geography of environmental problems is changing (Bellamy, 2021). Industrialization is provided by the basic industries, such as metallurgy and energy, which are the major sources of emissions of various pollutants. The aggravation of environmental problems has been associated with an increasing accumulation of environmental damage and an increase in the negative impact of environmental degradation on the health and quality of life of people around the world (Shah et al., 2023). The extensive development of mineral resources and the irrational use of natural resources in the economic process exacerbate the problem of complex pollution in all ecosystems, including air, water, soil, plants, animals, and people (Sowah & Kirikkaleli, 2022). Taking into account the reduced cost of clean technologies and the benefits derived from a comprehensive model of development and exploitation of nature, the impact of dirty industries is gradually becoming less significant when compared to the costs that fall on health, social security, and insurance systems, as well as the quality of life for people (Constantin et al., 2021).

Environmental issues are interconnected. Some of these issues are linked by a common cause, such as the burning of fossil fuels, which can lead to both local air pollution and climate change (Jiang et al., 2022). Chlorofluorocarbons, for example, are both ozone-depleting and greenhouse gases that contribute to climate change (Luo & Lin, 2022). Sometimes, one environmental issue can lead to others. For instance, an increase in waste can not only cause difficulties in its disposal, but also contribute to water and air pollution (Xu et al., 2018; Alsaluli, 2023). Deforestation can have a negative impact on biodiversity, air quality, disaster resilience, local and global climate. Climate change can exacerbate water stress and negatively affect biodiversity and ecosystems (Fitzmaurice, 2021). Therefore, there are uncertainties related to the availability and quality of future drinking water sources, which are associated with the uncertainties of climate change predictions and industrial developments. The modern pollution of water sources, ineffective water treatment, and current climate change call for a reassessment of the provision of safe drinking water. Since the availability of high-quality drinking water is a fundamental pre-condition of the quality of life and sustainable development of the local communities worldwide (Bogdanova et al., 2023).

Environmental challenges, including deforestation, soil degradation, the depletion of aquifers, water and air pollution, poaching, and poor sanitation, stem from poverty and compound each other in developing countries. The decline in the fertility of agricultural land (Erokhin et al., 2020a, 2021b), the deterioration of water quality (Esaulko et al., 2023), the loss of biodiversity (Erokhin et al., 2020b), and the degradation of other agricultural resources all contribute to the problems of hunger and food insecurity worldwide, not just in the least developed countries (Erokhin et al., 2021a).

In light of the complexities of modern environmental challenges, so too is the complexity of the responses to those challenges. The environmental agenda has become increasingly intertwined with national development policies of individual countries, rather than being a separate issue. This implies a set of coordinated efforts by all states, companies, and society, aimed at achieving economic development goals while making rational and sustainable use of natural resources, and taking advantage of the potential of ecosystems (Balbi et al., 2022; Erokhin et al., 2021c). The UN Sustainable Development Goals (SDGs) clearly link the achievement of economic and social goals (such as eradicating extreme poverty and inequality, combating hunger, and ensuring food security) with solving the most pressing environmental challenges, such as climate change, greenhouse gas emissions, and water quality degradation. According to the United Nations [UN] (2024), poverty eradication measures should be implemented in parallel with efforts to promote economic growth (Sikandar et al., 2021, 2022) and address various issues in the areas of education (Raza et al., 2023a, 2023b), health (Gao et al., 2021), social protection (Panait et al., 2020), employment (Constantin et al., 2021), rural development (Gao et al., 2018), farmers' performance (Gao et al., 2019), as well as combat climate change and protect the environment.

The Sustainable Development Agenda is a shared commitment of all UN member states. They are committed to ensuring sustainable, inclusive, and progressive growth with the aim to integrate social issues and protect the environment (UN, 2024). The Green Agenda encompasses a range of measures designed to adapt to climate change and decarbonise the economy (Belmonte-Urena et al., 2021). Dozens of countries are committed to achieving carbon neutrality by the 2050s. While a full achievement of all goals by all countries is doubtful, it is certain that the pace of change will accelerate in the coming decade (Wang et al., 2022).

Despite the fact that achieving the SDGs is a universal challenge, success largely depends on the actions of the world's leading economies. Currently, China is one of the largest sources of environmental pollution in the world, accounting for 30% of the total carbon dioxide emissions. China, which has largely overcome the problem of poverty through several decades of rapid and extensive development, is now facing serious environmental challenges that are becoming one of the major obstacles to further economic growth and progress (Zhao et al., 2022). Rapid industrialization has led to significant environmental pollution. The amount of industrial waste has increased, and waste management practices are not well developed. Environmental problems have complicated the situation significantly in the field of food security (Erokhin et al., 2022). Frustratingly, the fertile soils and other agricultural resources in the country have been significantly degraded (Yu & Deng, 2022). Against the backdrop of significant population growth, this has aggravated the situation of providing the domestic market with enough food (Li et al., 2023; Erokhin et al., 2022).

For a long time, environmental development issues were not given the same level of importance as industrial development and the economic growth of the country (Dong et al., 2021). However, since the 1980s, China has begun to coordinate its economic development with green initiatives. Currently, China is transitioning to a new normal, characterized by slower, but higher quality economic growth (Hu et al., 2022). Since 2006, China has been implementing waste recycling, a rational use of land, reducing water consumption, and improving its quality. Despite significant efforts to improve the environmental situation in China, the country is still facing a number of significant structural challenges and inconsistencies between economic growth and sustainable development goals. One of the most pressing areas is agriculture, where compliance with sustainable development principles in the short term is clearly associated with a reduction in the intensity of using land and other agricultural resources, leading to a decline in agricultural production (Erokhin, 2020). Ensuring food security has become a major concern in recent decades for China (Erokhin et al., 2022). While converging in understanding the need to sustain development, the food security and the green development doctrines differ. Increasing the agricultural output to attain self-sufficiency is hardly possible without aggravating anthropogenic pressure on ecosystems, which contradicts the very idea of green development. In this chapter, the authors use the example of China trying to find common ground between ensuring food security for everyone and the important task of greening the agricultural sector.

BACKGROUND

In the last four decades, China's rise in economic power has been linked to an increasing need for energy (Erokhin & Gao, 2022a). This has been accompanied by a significant increase in energy imports from Middle East countries and Russia. The green agenda became a prominent part of the China's agenda almost immediately after the country began its reform and opening-up policy. However, it took some time for this movement to take shape and gain momentum. In the early stages of economic reform, two opposing views emerged in Chinese public and academic debate: the prioritization of economic development over environmental protection, and the impossibility of achieving economic growth without considering environmental consequences (Edmonds, 1999). According to Zhang et al. (2021) and Petushkova (2022), due its unique economic and social developments, China cannot accept a model of low economic growth. Even more unacceptable to China is a zero economic growth model. If both developed and developing countries adhered to the concept of zero growth in order to preserve the environment, it would serve to further increase inequality between them and maintain the poverty and backwardness of many countries (Fontana & Sawyer, 2023). None of the developing economies accepted the theory of global economic equilibrium based on the principle of zero economic growth (Petushkova, 2022). In 1992, the United Nations Conference on Environment and Development (UN, 1992) defined one of the conditions for the new model of global development as the rejection of the economic model, in which unrestricted economic growth is considered progress in order to increase the standard of living for the population. However, two years after adopting the principles of the Rio Conference, China's White Paper on Population, Environment, and Development in the 21st Century (Ministry of Ecology and Environment of the People's Republic of China, 1994) declared the commitment of the country to a model that maintains high rates of economic growth.

In the early years after the introduction of the White Paper, economic growth was primarily driven by the old, outdated industrial base, which had extremely high energy and resource use. This vision of development suggests that, on the early stages of industrialization, increasing the environmental impact is a necessary condition for building the foundation for future industrial growth and accumulating funds that can then be used to modernize industry facilities in line with environmental safety standards (Liao et al., 2023). The approach was clearly explained by China's

President Xi Jinping in 2016 on the case of the agricultural production and the food security issue: "In the past, due to low productivity, we had to reclaim land from forest, grassland, and sea to increase grain output, but since our people now have adequate food and clothing, eco-environmental protection should and must become an integral component of development" (Xi, 2017: 425).

In the 1990s and 2000s, China has experienced a number of environmental shocks (the drying up of the Yellow River due to overconsumption of water by industrial and agricultural enterprises, flooding on the Yangtze River due to deforestation for agricultural land in mountainous areas of the country (Kubota, 2016)), which accelerated the process of forming a legislative framework in the field of environmental protection, and also contributed to the gradual popularization of ideas about the need for a more careful attitude towards nature (Pyatachkova et al., 2022). Over three decades (1980-2010), a national legislative framework was established in the fields of environmental protection and sustainable development (the Law on Environmental Protection, the Law on Marine Protection, the Law on Prevention and Control of Water Pollution, the Law on Forestry, the Law on Atmospheric Pollution Prevention and Control, the Water Code, and the Law on Renewable Energy Sources, among others) (Mu et al., 2014; Petushkova, 2022).

Since 2006, China has been committed to the principles of green development, which are reflected in its five-year development plans (Organisation for Economic Co-operation and Development [OECD], 2024) (Table 1). In the 11th Five Year Plan (2006-2010), the country made a commitment to expand the use of renewable energy sources. The volume of investment in pollution control increased by 15% per year, reaching 1.33% of GDP in 2009. The 12th Five-Year Plan (2011-2015) prioritized reduction of emissions and improvement of quality of drinking water. Within the 13th Five-Year Plan (2016-2020), China continued its efforts towards green goals. Overall, China has achieved success in 13 out of 16 set goals (reducing the energy intensity of GDP and introducing new land for construction were not fully met). For the period from 2021 to 2025, China set indicators for reducing carbon emissions by 18% per unit of GDP and energy intensity by 13.5% (Pyatachkova et al., 2022).

Table 1. China's initiatives and targets in the sphere of environmental protection

Five-year period	Years	Priorities and results	Legislation
XI		The volume of investment in pollution control to be increased by 15% per year	Law on the Development of a Circular Economy (2008); Law on Coastal Island Protection (2009)
XII		The area covered by forests increased by 21.66%. Carbon emissions per unit of GDP reduced by 17%. Energy consumption per unit of GDP reduced by 16%	Regulation on Permit Administration for Pollutant Discharge (2011); Updating the Environmental Protection Law (2015)

continued on following page

Table 1. Continued

Five-year period	Years	Priorities and results	Legislation
XIII		Reduction of the energy intensity of GDP and introduction of new land for construction	Law on Soil Pollution Prevention and Control (2018); Introduction of an Emissions Permit Catalog for Fixed Sources of Pollution (2019)
XIV		Reduction of carbon emissions by 18% per unit of GDP and energy intensity by 13.5%	Yangtze River Protection Act (2021); Law on Noise Pollution Prevention and Control (2021); Wetland Protection Law (2021)

Source: authors' development based on OECD (2024), Pyatachkova et al. (2022), and Mu et al. (2014)

The special importance of the green agenda in China is confirmed by the attention given to relevant issues by the highest authorities in China. At the Fifth Plenary Session of 18th Central Committee in 2015, China's President Xi Jinping proclaimed that China "must take effective measures to promote ecological progress and address growing resource constraints, serious environmental pollution, and ecological degradation" (Xi, 2017: 421). The dual control approach to ensuring sustainable development encompassed putting a ceiling on both the total amount and the intensity of energy use, water consumption, and construction land utilization per unit of GDP. In 2016, ecological progress was declared to be an integral part of China's approach to building socialism with Chinese characteristics (Xi, 2017: 426). Since 2017, the green agenda has been actively pursued within the Belt and Road initiative (BRI). Guidelines have been developed that consolidate the promotion of green development and the establishment of a green platform for cooperation in several areas: political dialogue, infrastructure connectivity, unimpeded trade, financing, communication among peoples, and capacity building (Pyatachkova et al., 2022).

In 2024, President Xi Jinping emphasized the importance of jointly advancing ecological environmental protection and green and low-carbon development (State Council of the People's Republic of China [State Council], 2024b). In the sphere of agriculture, President Xi called for the advancement of agricultural operation by accelerating the cultivation and expansion of green practices and strengthening the conservation, intensive use, and recycling of resources. A significant step towards institutionalizing environmental protection was made by China's government in March 2024 by adopting the guidelines to strengthen region-specific environmental management (State Council, 2024a). The new guidelines break down the distinction between developmental and environmental functions for land use by dividing land into three categories (priority protection, critical control, and general control) and tailoring management strategies based on specific environmental conditions and risks.

Summarizing the review of the evolution of approaches to sustainable development in Chinese public and academic discourse over recent decades, it is essential to note the focus of government policy on coordinating economic growth with the sustainable utilization of natural resources and protection of the environment in a way that allows for current development to provide the foundation for future growth.

The sustainable management of natural resources and maintaining viable ecosystems are recognized as the two most significant pillars of sustainable development. Major features of China's environmental policy include a well-developed legislative framework, a system for monitoring the environment, scientific and technical support for environmental issues, state financing for environmental protection measures, and popularization of an environmentally friendly lifestyle among the general population.

MAIN FOCUS OF THE CHAPTER

China's Food Security Agenda

China has been one of the world's largest producers and consumers of different types of agricultural products for a long time. However, in recent decades, the economic and social development in the country has significantly changed both the role of agriculture in China's GDP and the specific features of the progress in agriculture and rural areas infrastructure. Over 50% of China's land area (approximately 5 thousand km^2) is being used for agricultural purposes, but due to the high degree of soil erosion, the lack of irrigation infrastructure, and the increasing frequency of extreme weather and climate events, the full utilization of the country's natural resources for agricultural production is not possible (Huang & Yang, 2017). In China, the basis of agriculture is crop production, with corn, rice, and wheat being the dominant crops. Together, they account for more than 75% of the total acreage in the country. Over the past years, the gross harvest of corn has increased by 6.3%, reaching 277 million tons (Table 2). The gross yields of rice and wheat vary, but are generally between 145 and 149 million tons for rice and 134 to 138 million tons for wheat. Among the products from the livestock sector, pork dominates. In 2022, its production increased by 34.8% compared to the previous year, reaching a maximum of 55 million tons. Since 2014, this is the highest production level in the last eight years. Further growth in pork production is expected in 2024, although not at the same level as in previous years.

Table 2. Output of basic agricultural products in China in 2020-2022, million tons

Products	2020	2021	2021 to 2020, %	2022	2022 to 2021, %	2022 to 2020, %
Corn	260.7	272.6	+4.56	277.2	+1.69	+6.33
Rice	148.3	149.0	+0.47	145.9	-2.08	-1.62
Wheat	134.3	136.9	+1.93	137.7	+0.58	+2.53
Soybeans	22.9	19.6	-14.41	23.5	+19.90	+2.62

continued on following page

Table 2. Continued

Products	2020	2021	2021 to 2020, %	2022	2022 to 2021, %	2022 to 2020, %
Pork	41.1	53.0	+28.95	55.4	+4.52	+34.79
Poultry	24.7	24.8	+0.40	24.4	+1.61	+1.21
Beef	6.7	7.0	+4.48	7.2	+2.86	+7.46
Mutton	4.9	5.1	+4.08	5.3	+3.92	+8.16
Aquaculture products	52.2	53.9	+3.26	54.6	+1.30	+4.60
Fish and seafood products	13.2	13.0	-1.51	12.9	-0.77	-2.27

Source: authors' development based on National Bureau of Statistics of China [National Bureau] (2024)

A crucial task for the government is to increase the overall harvest of major grain crops to reach the target of 650 million tons. This volume is necessary to maintain stable grain prices on the domestic market, which is one of the critical parameters of the accessibility pillar of food security (Andrei et al., 2022; Radulescu et al., 2022). However, this has not been achieved solely through domestic production so far. In 2023, the government announced plans to increase national grain production by an additional 50 million tons, and the area under cultivation has been increased by 30 million hectares. There has also been a systematic development of storage and processing capacities for agricultural raw materials as well as logistical facilities (Gao et al., 2018). Government subsidies encourage an increase in grain production, but many farmers have left for more lucrative sectors such as vegetable farming and fruit production. Over the past decade, the degree of mechanisation of crop farms has increased significantly, although it is still only about 70%.

The missing volumes of imported food are significant, as China is the world's largest net importer of cereals (Huang et al., 2017), including wheat and rice (Table 3). However, the most critical situation in terms of ensuring food self-sufficiency relates to soybeans and oilseeds (Erokhin et al., 2020c). The gross domestic harvest of soybeans barely exceeds 20 million tons, while China's annual demand exceeds 120 million tons. Production is concentrated in Heilongjiang Province, on chernozem soils. An increase in production has been strongly stimulated by various measures, including the adoption of a new standard for genetically modified soybean cultivation, which could significantly impact yield increases. Meanwhile, oilseed imports continue to be the main component of China's agriculture ($65.8 billion in 2022 or 29.8% of its total food imports). In total, China accounts for approximately 60% of the global soybean import market.

Table 3. Foreign trade in agricultural products in China in 2020-2022, balance, $ million

Products	2020	2021	2022
Live animals	-35.03	-384.66	-350.75
Meat of bovine animals	-10,177.64	-12,488.07	-17,757.44
Edible meat offal	-17,759.49	-16,335.43	-10,314.99
Milk, cream, and dairy products	-5,513.70	-7,562.00	-7,081.33
Butter and other fats	-541.99	-660.24	-919.79
Cheese and curd	-588.39	-811.61	-768.06
Eggs	+180.40	+214.71	+310.43
Fish, fresh, chilled or frozen	+1,572.19	+1,678.23	+459.79
Fish, dried, salted or smoked	+222.22	+235.44	+168.05
Crustaceans, mollusks, and aquatic invertebrates	+1,347.96	-2,181.08	-4,202.06
Fish and aquatic invertebrates, prepared and preserved	+5,224.20	+7,183.68	+6,519.63
Wheat and meslin, unmilled	-2,261.72	-3,036.69	-3,776.77
Rice	-542.69	-1,151.80	-1,588.99
Barley, unmilled	-1,880.19	-3,556.19	-2,052.24
Corn, unmilled	-2,476.82	-8,015.47	-7,099.91
Cereals, unmilled	-1,195.75	-3,119.03	-3,861.77
Meal and flour of wheat and flour of meslin	-13.53	+1.25	+10.30
Other cereal meals and flour	-36.00	-46.53	-39.98
Cereal preparations, flour of fruits or vegetables	-260.18	-302.33	-63.37
Vegetables	+5,939.54	+5,507.13	+4,738.99
Vegetables, roots, tubers, prepared and preserved	+6,130.94	+6,507.14	+7,520.36
Fruits and nuts	-4,819.46	-9,176.15	-10,427.61
Fruit, preserved and fruit preparations	+2,371.78	+2,205.01	+1,947.09
Fruit and vegetable juices, unferrmented	+238.73	+146.45	+363.68
Sugar, molasses, and honey	-1,371.10	-1,761.76	-1,924.96
Sugar confectionery	+840.43	+927.71	+1,262.41
Coffee and coffee substitutes	-351.29	-678.29	-807.05
Cocoa	-249.16	-336.05	-337.30
Chocolate	-210.94	-272.19	-172.79
Tea and mate	+1,969.72	+2,329.36	+2,114.36
Spices	+1,115.89	+818.92	+813.96
Feedstuff for animals	-2,487.11	-3,611.38	-4,542.84
Margarine and shortening	-442.74	-979.37	-1,455.34

continued on following page

Table 3. Continued

Products	2020	2021	2022
Edible products and preparations	-5,187.02	-3,524.35	-3,523.50
Oil seed and oleaginous fruits	-42,098.80	-56,935.77	-64,535.54
Total all food items and agricultural products	-90,242.63	-128,474.86	-138,184.99

Source: authors' development based on United Nations Conference on Trade and Development [UNCTAD] (2024)

The extent to which the country depends on imports of soybeans, cereal, and other products determines the specific nature of the modern food security policy of China's government (Erokhin et al., 2022). Adopted in 2019, the National Food Security Strategy outlines priorities in this area, such as increasing yields and overall grain harvests through improvements to soil characteristics and the development of irrigation systems. Additionally, the strategy aims to support Chinese agricultural producers by introducing innovations along the entire food production and distribution chain (Erokhin et al., 2022).

The increase in China's self-sufficiency in basic food types corresponds to the country's strategic orientation towards food security, which aims to ensure the availability of food on the domestic market for as many people as possible. This approach is closely linked to policies aimed at sustainable rural development and the maintenance of rural lifestyles, rather than simply increasing agricultural output (Huang & Yang, 2017). Elements of this policy include combating rural poverty, creating stable sources of income for rural residents, preventing labor outflow from rural areas by developing social and institutional infrastructure there, and encouraging participation of rural residents and smaller farmers in the agricultural supply chain.

The agenda for sustainable rural development also includes efforts to strengthen the resilience of all sectors of the agricultural and industrial complex against climate change and extreme natural events (typhoons, floods, or droughts for crops, epizootic diseases for livestock). To respond to climate change, programs have been implemented to develop a green economy (reducing the use of chemical fertilisers, reducing emissions, organic agriculture, and the use of alternative and renewable energy sources in agriculture) and a blue economy (aquaculture based on renewable energy, controlling the use of marine and water resources, and conserving biodiversity) (Kennedy et al., 2016). Consequently, it is clear that China's agricultural policies fully comply with the SDGs and make a tangible contribution towards achieving these goals.

The Green Development Pathway

In 2017, China's President Xi Jinping declared the green development model as an essential element of China's new development concepts (Xi, 2017: 428), including giving top priority to ecological progress in the overall development strategy of China, following the basic state policy of resource conservation and environmental protection, and developing a resource-saving and eco-friendly land-utilization planning system (Xi, 2017: 428). In regard to promoting a green way of life, President Xi Jinping outlined six key tasks of the strategic development of China (Xi, 2017: 429-431):

- abandoning the model of extensive economic growth based on over-consumption of resources and energy and promoting an innovation-driven development;
- intensifying environmental management practices by carrying out the action plan on air pollution prevention, strengthening water pollution prevention and control, conducting soil pollution control and soil restoration projects, and reinforcing prevention and control of wide-spread pollution in agriculture;
- prioritizing conservation and promoting natural restoration, launching large-scale greening campaigns, and stepping up comprehensive control of soil erosion and desertification;
- promoting all-round resource conservation and efficient resource utilization and establishing a mindset of conserving, recycling, and efficiently using resources;
- enhancing publicity and education on the need to promote ecological progress and raising environmental consciousness among the people;
- improving the natural resource assets management system, strengthening natural resources and environmental regulation, implementing environmental inspections, and refining the system of public participation in the protection of the environment.

Despite the complexity and depth of its elaboration, the green agenda is a relatively new concept in China compared to other countries. As a separate field, the Environment-Society-Governance narrative (ESG) emerged in China later than in other countries (Ju et al., 2022). The first formal documents in this field date back to 2012. However, in recent years, this agenda has been growing rapidly. In 2016, the People's Bank of China, the Ministry of Finance, and several other regulatory bodies jointly published the Guidance on the Construction of a Green Financial System, which described the highest level of China's green finance system (Peng et al., 2018). In 2022, the Common Taxonomy of the EU and China (Common Ground Taxonomy) was published, which is a comparison between the taxonomies for green policies in the EU and China. It was expected that the publication of the Common Ground Taxonomy would improve transparency for investors and companies regarding requirements, as well as clarify the definition of environmentally sustainable investments in the jurisdictions of the International Platform for Sustainable Finance (IPSF). In 2021, the first green bonds that met the requirements of the Taxonomy were issued. In November 2022, OCBC Wing Hang Bank became the first foreign bank to successfully issue a green financial bond with a total volume of CNY 500 million. However, foreign participation in China's bond market (including green bonds) remains limited, with only 3.2% of total market transactions due to market barriers.

In addition to production requirements, ESG regulation in the financial sector has strengthened in recent years. For example, bond issuers must comply with disclosure rules about the impact of their operations on the environment. However, China's ESG-related guidelines primarily focus on loans from commercial banks. These banks must take into account environmental, social, and governmental requirements when drafting their independent risk management systems. To stimulate interest in ESG investments, these factors have also been included in the assessment of the effectiveness of financial institutions. Preferential mandatory reserve ratios and tax incentives for qualified banks have also appeared. Some provinces are developing their own green financing programs.

In general, the modern approach to sustainable development in China has some features that differ from commonly used international approaches (Shi & Yin, 2023). It combines the principles of environmental protection with the continuous development of a growing manufacturing sector. First, slowing down industrialization is not part of the Chinese interpretation of sustainable development. On the contrary, its continuation is seen as a way to solve environmental problems (Zhao et al., 2023). From this perspective, the increase and renovation of fixed assets in coal mining and other heavy industries stimulates the modernization of production. This increases the efficiency of resource utilization, allows for the discovery of more resource-conserving methods, and reduces energy intensity. Secondly, the government is developing the country's continental regions by implementing infrastructure projects, such as transferring water from the south to the north, expanding the transport network and stimulating the transfer of manufacturing businesses to new industrial zones by increasing the costs of land in other areas and enforcing national environmental standards (Zhao et al., 2023). Thirdly, sustainable development in China also has a social aspect, such as fighting poverty and promoting urbanization (Shi & Yin, 2023). To this end, reforms have been introduced, including restrictions on fertility and the migration of people to cities, as well as the modernization of villages, the implementation of public environmental initiatives (such as massive forest plantations), and public education programs.

The most significant feature of the China's contemporary economic development strategy is its attempt to combine sustainable development, innovation, and technological advancement (Lee & Wang, 2022). To simultaneously maintain production growth and implement initiatives relating to the green economy, the government has focused its efforts on supporting research and development and introducing new technologies into industry. This has led to a shift from low-value, labor-intensive products and services to knowledge-driven, high-value goods and services that are also more environmentally friendly.

Controversies: Reaching Food Self-Sufficiency vs. Ensuring Green Development

China's transition towards sustainable development path in the late 1990s was in no small part due to the emergency in the ecological status of the agricultural sector and, therefore, a threat to food security (Erokhin et al., 2022). By the mid-1990s, the combined effects of inefficient and unsustainable farming methods and overuse of natural resources led to widespread land degradation, causing droughts and floods, as well as numerous losses and rural poverty. The adverse effects of environmental pollution on the quality of agricultural lands and other agricultural resources have been acknowledged by China's President Xi Jinping. Thus, in 2015, President Xi Jinping emphasized a serious decline in land fertility, water and soil erosion, over-exploitation of ground water, soil degradation, and non-point source pollution that have become prominent problems that constrain the sustainable development of the agricultural sector (Xi, 2017: 422). Areas affected by natural disasters have substantially decreased over the past decade (Figure 1), but the environmental damage to agricultural lands and other agricultural resources still remains substantial.

Figure 1. Land areas affected by natural disasters in China in 2011-2021, million hectares

Source: authors' development based on National Bureau (2024)

Since 1998, China has significantly increased investments in sustainable rural development. By 2015, over $350 billion had been invested in more than 16 rehabilitation programs covering more than 620 million hectares – that is 65% of China's cultivated land. The results of the agricultural programs have generally been assessed as positive (Chen et al., 2021; Shi & Yang, 2022; Zhang et al., 2023). Deforestation has decreased and forest covers 22% of the country's territory now. Meadows have expanded and recovered. Desertification in many areas has been reversed. Although the expansion of deserts is largely attributed to climate change, efforts to restore land have proven effective (Ren et al., 2023).

However, despite significant progress in ensuring food security and, in general, improving the environmental conditions of agriculture in China, the country still cannot abandon its traditionally high dependence on dirty industries. One of the major problems is the high reliance on coal as a source of energy. Overall, China has achieved a remarkable success in reducing emissions of pollutants, but the amounts of emitted sulphur dioxide, nitrogen oxides, and particulate matter still account for millions tons (Figure 2).

Figure 2. Main pollutant emission in waste gas in China in 2011-2021, million tons

Source: authors' development based on National Bureau (2024)

The government has adopted a main guideline in terms of carbon emissions and decarbonization, which was approved back in 2020. During a meeting of the United Nations General Assembly, China's President Xi Jinping announced that by 2030, China plans to reach the emissions peak and then achieve carbon neutrality by 2060. The "30/60" policy sets the rules for the green agenda in all government agencies, including banks. After the signing of the Paris Agreement, China clarified its carbon intensity and designated it as 65% by 2030, compared to 2005. Exact carbon reduction targets for 2030 will also be set, and will be implemented in the 15th Five-year plan (2026-2030).

The share of coal in electricity production has decreased from 72.9% in 2000 to 68.6% in 2019. This is due to the gradual replacement of coal with new energy sources, which have seen special development over the last decade. These include nuclear energy (5%), wind power generators (5%), solar panels (3%), and biofuels (2%). Currently, China is a world leader in introducing renewable energy capacities, with the share of such energy from the total installed capacity reaching 47.3% in 2022. By 2025, the amount of energy produced from renewable sources is expected to exceed 30% of total energy generation in the country. China has already been a leader in investing in non-fossil fuel energy sources, such as electrified transportation and a closed-loop economic system. Investments in these areas have exceeded 35% of global figures. One of the key objectives is to implement a long-term plan to bring China to the top of the world in electricity production from nuclear power plants by 2030. This development in nuclear energy aligns with China's strategy for sustainable development and helps to address the country's resource scarcity, atmospheric pollution, and climate change.

Convergence: The Ecological Civilization Concept

The Chinese model of sustainable development is far more complex than just the environmental agenda (Shi & Yin, 2023; Hu et al., 2023). In 2012, a plan for "Five Interlinked Components of Building Beautiful China" (economic construction, political development, cultural growth, social development, and ecological civilization) was developed. In 2015, the government released a strategic document titled "The Position of the Central Committee of the Communist Party of China and the State Council on Accelerating the Construction of an Ecological Civilization". The main goal of the reform was to integrate environmental values and principles into all aspects of society, including education. The document proposed ten specific measures to establish a system of environmental accountability and new environmental standards. These measures included promoting energy efficiency, implementing resource-saving technologies, creating waste-free, circular production processes, establishing functional ecological zones for all territories, setting limits on acceptable levels of environmental impact, and incorporating environmental criteria into government certification systems at all levels. In total, the Position includes thirty specific tasks and can be considered a roadmap for further detailed state planning in all areas, aimed at transforming Chinese society into an ecological civilization.

In 2022, China outlined the parameters for a new model of development for China until 2050. This modern concept of ecological civilization in China is based on the commitment to environmental protection and the vision of President Xi Jinping of ecological civilization. It also emphasizes the principles of prioritizing human lives, green development methods, and cooperation with other countries to build an ecological civilization on a global scale. Building an ecological civilization requires balancing the interests of economic development with reducing carbon emissions. It means embracing green development and harmonizing human and natural interactions. The goal is to promote low-carbon growth and accelerate the modernization of environmental management systems (Xiu et al., 2023; Xu et al., 2023). The construction of an ecological civilization is a complex and challenging project that rejects the utilitarian notion of development and creates a new concept for the harmonious co-existence of humans and nature. It aims to develop and improve people's ecological awareness (Hanson, 2019). At the same time, the measures taken to reduce carbon footprints should not undermine the nation's energy and food security or the stability of its production and logistics systems (Voronovsky et al., 2022).

This statement fully characterizes the specific vision of China in transitioning to a sustainable form of development by comprehensively addressing environmental challenges, while maintaining the pace of economic growth (He et al., 2022). In contrast to the widely accepted concept of sustainable development, China's conceptualization of ecological civilization emphasizes political and cultural aspects, as well as defining new relationships between people and the environment (Hanson 2019). The construction of China's ecological civilization has enabled significant reductions in carbon emissions, increased levels of green innovation, and resource efficiency. It has also optimized industrial structures, promoting the distribution of economic development factors across regions and achieving green benefits. Additionally, it has improved the ecological environment and reduced environmental impact.

However, the concept of an ecological civilization as promoted by President Xi Jinping has both a global and national dimension. China aims to contribute to establishing a common global equilibrium between economic benefits and environmental sustainability (Xue et al., 2023). China's success in developing an ecological civilization is evident through increasing investments in environmental protection and the creation of global initiatives involving broad international participation (including the development of environmentally friendly supply chains with Chinese companies and the greening of the international connectivity initiatives) (Erokhin & Gao, 2022b). By making efforts to create a "Beautiful China" and promoting the development of the economy, politics, and culture, China creates the conditions for progressive and environmentally-friendly development throughout the world. This encourages the rejection of traditional energy sources and the search for and introduction of innovative environmental technologies. It also promotes sustainable development methods based on a deep understanding of the interconnectedness between humans and nature.

SOLUTIONS AND RECOMMENDATIONS

Achieving China's green development goals, including reaching a peak in carbon emissions by 2030 and achieving carbon neutrality by 2060, requires decisive and coordinated action in all sectors of the economy, not just the energy sector. To achieve these objectives, the following measures should be implemented:

- promoting integrated green transformation for economic and social development;

- deep restructuring and transformation of the industry, especially conventional industries and the energy sector;
- accelerating the development of a clean, low-carbon, safe, and efficient energy system;
- promoting the construction of a low-carbon transportation system;
- improving the quality and sustainability of green and low-carbon urban and rural development;
- conducting research on green and low-carbon technologies, and promoting their implementation;
- continued consolidation of existing carbon absorption capacity;
- promotion of environmentally friendly and low-carbon trade, as well as green investments;
- improvement of legislative norms, standards, and systems for monitoring carbon dioxide emissions;
- strengthening policy mechanisms for green finance, and providing benefits for green projects;
- coordinating the efforts of all government bodies at various levels to implement a green development agenda.

The authors identify a list of measures for certain areas of green development and individual sectors of China's economy within ten blocks of measures.

- The transition of the economy towards green and low-carbon energy sources (promotion of the substitution, transformation, and modernization of coal use; development of solar, wind, and hydro power; development of safe nuclear energy; regulation of oil and gas use; and development of a new energy supply system).
- Introduction of innovative environmental and low-carbon technologies as a priority pre-condition for re-evaluating industrial policy and transition to green energetic technologies.
- Reducing carbon dioxide emissions and increasing resource efficiency in improving energy conservation management capabilities; implementing key energy conservation and carbon emission reduction projects; promoting energy conservation and upgrading basic energy-consuming equipment; enhancing energy conservation and reducing carbon emissions in new infrastructure types.
- Promotion of environmentally friendly and low-carbon transportation (facilitation of the transition towards low-carbon vehicles and equipment; development of highly efficient and environmentally friendly transportation systems; acceleration of construction of green transportation infrastructure).

- Improving a closed-cycle economy (promoting the development of a closed-cycle economy in industrial parks to minimize waste and maximize resource utilization; expanding the integrated use of bulk solid waste; fostering the integration of bulk solid waste into industrial processes for more efficient use of resources and reduced environmental impact; enhancing the recycling infrastructure and systems in order to make it easier for businesses to reuse materials and reduce the amount of waste sent to landfills).
- Consolidating and enhancing carbon capture (strengthening the ability of ecosystems to sequester carbon; improving their ability to absorb carbon; supporting basic ecosystems carbon sinks, and contributing to the reduction of carbon emissions and storage in agriculture and rural areas; maintaining safe environment in the rural areas will have a positive impact on the fertility of agricultural land and will mitigate risks of food (in)security).
- Improving people's awareness of green development (strengthening environmental education; promotion of a green and low-carbon lifestyle; encouraging enterprises to fulfill their social obligations; strengthening training in environmental issues and the environmental agenda of the state).
- Achieving peak emission of carbon dioxide in China's provinces (setting emission targets; promoting green and low-carbon development based on local conditions; developing local carbon emission programs for higher and lower-level jurisdictions).

To address the problem of degradation of arable land, China should develop the crop rotation and land fallow systems by focusing on pilot projects in groundwater funnel areas and areas of heavy metal pollution and serious ecological degradation in accordance with the financial resources available and food supply and demand, arranging for certain areas of arable land to lie fallow, and giving the required food or cash subsidies to the farmers concerned (Xi, 2017: 422). In carrying out this program, the government should make sure that national food security and incomes of farmers are not affected. Also, the program should not reduce the arable land area, divert it to nonagricultural purposes, or weaken China's overall agricultural production capacity.

FUTURE RESEARCH DIRECTIONS

In a broad sense, the development paradigm, which involves the transition of society towards the principles of sustainable development, is based on the concept of rational environmental management. This approach aims to evaluate development by achieving economic gains while reducing environmental impacts. Obviously, this understanding of sustainable development will continue to be the main focus of research in the foreseeable future. At the same time, due to the increasing complexities of the interactions between economic, environmental, and social dimensions of development, it is essential to clarify the system for evaluating the progress of individual countries in the journey towards sustainable development. It seems that one of the promising areas of research will be the development of systems for assessing green development, based on the integration of economic, environmental, and aggregated indicators of progress and well-being (Erokhin et al., 2019; Bobryshev et al., 2023), as determined by national governments, depending on the level of development of the national economy and external conditions.

Another area of research is the internationalization of the green development agenda. The global restructuring of the world economy required to solve global environmental problems needs to be inclusive and build on the interests of both developed and developing countries (Erokhin et al., 2014; Erokhin, 2017a, 2017b). To this end, it is essential to move towards a cleaner development through collaborative efforts, introducing new rules and instruments for international economic relations, and global governance. These measures must emphasize the responsibility of both producers and consumers for environmental pollution, and provide real assistance for developed countries as they transition to a lower-carbon, greener economy for all countries. In particular, it is essential to elaborate the theoretical and practical foundations for creating a global financing system for green projects. This system will link the financial resources available to wealthy countries and those available for financing low-carbon developments with low-cost emission reduction projects mainly located in developing countries. The most significant area of research within the field of creating a joint green development plan is the establishment of effective international relations between China and its neighboring countries, including Russia. In recent years, China has become a significant trade, economic, and technological partner for Russia. It is particularly promising to explore the potential for the development of cross-border cooperation between the Russian Far East regions and the northeastern provinces of China, the largest producers of agricultural products in the country.

CONCLUSION

The interdependence between economic growth and its environmental consequences has become more and more complex, emerging into a global problem, rather than an issue of a few countries. In recent decades, the rapid industrialization in China has turned the country into the world's largest emitter of greenhouse gases and other pollutants, as well as it has significantly exacerbated the environmental problems within the country. Due to the extensive nature of resource usage, there have emerged serious problems across the sectors of the economy, including agriculture. The environmental degradation threatens not only the nation's food security but also the sustainability of its economic and social development. Due to the continuing efforts on resource conservation and environmental protection, which is part of the implementation of the country's national strategy for sustainable development, China has seen qualitative changes to its economy in recent years with the aim of achieving environmental goals. The land resources are being protected and used more productively, and the state of the water resources and atmosphere is under control. The level of major pollutants in the life-supporting components of the environment has been steadily decreasing. Regional plans for green development are being formulated more quickly, and the practice of creating eco-villages with improved transportation has become widespread. The low-carbon energy sector is growing, and electricity use is becoming more efficient. Over the past two decades, China has seen significant changes in its approach to environmental conservation. These efforts have laid the groundwork for a more sustainable future, with the goal of improving the environmental situation within the country and achieving its sustainable development and food security goals. In addition to pursuing national green development plans, China is actively involved in global environmental governance. As an active player in international cooperation, China is committed to the Paris Agreement and other international efforts on mitigating climate change, greening the economy, and improving global food security.

ACKNOWLEDGMENT

This research was funded by the Russian Science Foundation (RSF) and Penza Region, grant number 23-28-10277, https://rscf.ru/en/project/23-28-10277. Author 4, Denis Samygin from Penza State University, would like to express his gratitude to the above-mentioned organizations for their generous support during his studies in the sphere of exploring potential areas of cooperation between China and Russia in the development of green agenda and sustainable agriculture.

REFERENCES

Alsaluli, A. (2023). A Modern Waste Management Strategy for Reducing Urban Air Pollution in Taif, Saudi Arabia. *International Journal of Environment and Waste Management*, 31(4), 514–524. 10.1504/IJEWM.2023.131147

Andrei, J. V., Radulescu, I. D., Chivu, L., Erokhin, V., Nancu, D., Gao, T., & Vasic, M. (2022). A Short Descriptive Analysis of the European Evolutions of Input Price Indices of Agricultural Products between 2008-2017: Patterns, Trends, and Implications. *Strategic Management*, 27(3), 39–47. 10.5937/StraMan2200018A

Balbi, S., Bagstad, K. J., Magrach, A., Sanz, M. J., Aguilar-Amuchastegui, N., Giupponi, C., & Villa, F. (2022). The Global Environmental Agenda Urgently Needs a Semantic Web of Knowledge. *Environmental Evidence*, 11(1), 5. 10.1186/s13750-022-00258-y

Bellamy, A. S. (2021). Seeds of Change: Establishing Frameworks for Understanding Global Environmental Changes. *Ambio*, 50(7), 1281–1285. 10.1007/s13280-021-01509-x33713292

Belmonte-Urena, L. J., Plaza-Ubeda, J. A., Vazquez-Brust, D., & Yakovleva, N. (2021). Circular Economy, Degrowth and Green Growth as Pathways for Research on Sustainable Development Goals: A Global Analysis and Future Agenda. *Ecological Economics*, 185, 107050. 10.1016/j.ecolecon.2021.107050

Bobryshev, A., Chaykovskaya, L., Erokhin, V., & Ivolga, A. (2023). Sustaining Growth or Boosting Profit: Accounting Tools under Process-Based Management in a Transition Economy. *Journal of Risk and Financial Management*, 16(2), 92. 10.3390/jrfm16020092

Bogdanova, E., Lobanov, A., Andronov, S. V., Soromotin, A., Popov, A., Skalny, A. V., Shaduyko, O., & Callaghan, T. V. (2023). Challenges of Changing Water Sources for Human Wellbeing in the Arctic Zone of Western Siberia. *Water (Basel)*, 15(8), 1577. 10.3390/w15081577

Chen, Y., Han, Y., & Guo, L. (2021). Recent Development and Regional Disparity of the Rural Industries in China. *International Journal of Social Economics*, 48(5), 759–775. 10.1108/IJSE-07-2020-0481

Constantin, M., Radulescu, I. D., Andrei, J. V., Chivu, L., Erokhin, V., & Gao, T. (2021). A Perspective on Agricultural Labor Productivity and Greenhouse Gas Emissions in Context of the Common Agricultural Policy Exigencies. *Ekonomika Poljoprivrede*, 68(1), 53–67. 10.5937/ekoPolj2101053C

Dong, D., Xu, B., Shen, N., & He, Q. (2021). The Adverse Impact of Air Pollution on China's Economic Growth. *Sustainability (Basel)*, 13(16), 9056. 10.3390/su13169056

Edmonds, R. (1999). The Environment in the People's Republic of China 50 Years on. *The China Quarterly*, 159, 640–649. 10.1017/S0305741000003398201 01811

Erokhin, V. (2017a). Factors Influencing Food Markets in Developing Countries: An Approach to Assess Sustainability of the Food Supply in Russia. *Sustainability (Basel)*, 9(8), 1313. 10.3390/su9081313

Erokhin, V. (2017b). Self-Sufficiency versus Security: How Trade Protectionism Challenges the Sustainability of the Food Supply in Russia. *Sustainability (Basel)*, 9(11), 1939. 10.3390/su9111939

Erokhin, V. (2020). Produce Internationally, Consume Locally: Changing Paradigm of China's Food Security Policy. In Jean Vasile, A., Subic, J., Grubor, A., & Privitera, D. (Eds.), *Handbook of Research on Agricultural Policy, Rural Development, and Entrepreneurship in Contemporary Economies* (pp. 273–295). IGI Global. 10.4018/978-1-5225-9837-4.ch014

Erokhin, V., Diao, L., Gao, T., Andrei, J.-V., Ivolga, A., & Zong, Y. (2021a). The Supply of Calories, Proteins, and Fats in Low-Income Countries: A Four-Decade Retrospective Study. *International Journal of Environmental Research and Public Health*, 18(14), 7356. 10.3390/ijerph1814735634299805

Erokhin, V., Endovitsky, D., Bobryshev, A., Kulagina, N., & Ivolga, A. (2019). Management Accounting Change as a Sustainable Economic Development Strategy during Pre-Recession and Recession Periods: Evidence from Russia. *Sustainability (Basel)*, 11(11), 3139. 10.3390/su11113139

Erokhin, V., Esaulko, A., Pismennaya, E., Golosnoy, E., Vlasova, O., & Ivolga, A. (2021b). Combined Impact of Climate Change and Land Qualities on Winter Wheat Yield in Central Fore-Caucasus: The Long-Term Retrospective Study. *Land (Basel)*, 10(12), 1339. 10.3390/land10121339

Erokhin, V., & Gao, T. (2022a). Renewable Energy as a Promising Venue for China-Russia Collaboration. In Khan, S. A. R., Panait, M., Puime Guillen, F., & Raimi, L. (Eds.), *Energy Transition. Industrial Ecology* (pp. 73–101). Springer. 10.1007/978-981-19-3540-4_3

Erokhin, V., & Gao, T. (2022b). New Eurasian Land Bridge: The Connectivity-Inputs-Growth Triangle. *Rivista Internazionale di Economia dei Trasporti*, XLIX(2), 207–229. 10.19272/202206702004

Erokhin, V., Gao, T., Andrei, J. V., & Ivolga, A. (2020a). Transformation of Agricultural Land Distribution Patterns in Russia. *Ekonomika Poljoprivrede*, 67(3), 863–879. 10.5937/ekoPolj2003863E

Erokhin, V., Gao, T., Chivu, L., & Andrei, J.V. (2022). Food Security in a Food Self-Sufficient Economy: A Review of China's Ongoing Transition to a Zero Hunger State. *Agricultural Economics – Czech, 68*(12), 476-487. 10.17221/278/2022-AGRICECON

Erokhin, V., Gao, T., & Ivolga, A. (2020b). Structural Variations in the Composition of Land Funds at Regional Scales across Russia. *Land (Basel)*, 9(6), 201. 10.3390/land9060201

Erokhin, V., Gao, T., & Ivolga, A. (2021c). Cross-Country Potentials and Advantages in Trade in Fish and Seafood Products in the RCEP Member States. *Sustainability (Basel)*, 13(7), 3668. 10.3390/su13073668

Erokhin, V., Ivolga, A., & Heijman, W. (2014). Trade Liberalization and State Support of Agriculture: Effects for Developing Countries. *Agricultural Economics – Czech, 60*(11), 524-537. 10.17221/137/2013-AGRICECON

Erokhin, V., Li, D., & Du, P. (2020c). Sustainability-Related Implications of Competitive Advantages in Agricultural Value Chains: Evidence from Central Asia – China Trade and Investment. *Sustainability (Basel)*, 12(3), 1117. 10.3390/su12031117

Erokhin, V., Samygin, D., Tuskov, A., & Ivolga, A. (2023). Mitigating Spatial Disproportions in Agriculture through Revealing Competitive Advantages. *Ekonomika Poljoprivrede*, 70(4), 1157–1170. 10.59267/ekoPolj23041157E

Esaulko, A., Sitnikov, V., Pismennaya, E., Vlasova, O., Golosnoi, E., Ozheredova, A., Ivolga, A., & Erokhin, V. (2023). Productivity of Winter Wheat Cultivated by Direct Seeding: Measuring the Effect of Hydrothermal Coefficient in the Arid Zone of Central Fore-Caucasus. *Agriculture*, 13(1), 55. 10.3390/agriculture13010055

Fitzmaurice, M. (2021). Biodiversity and Climate Change. *International Community Law Review*, 23(2-3), 230–240. 10.1163/18719732-12341473

Fontana, G., & Sawyer, M. (2023). The Macroeconomics of Near Zero Growth of GDP in a World of Geopolitical Risks and Conflicts. *Journal of Environmental Management*, 351, 119717. 10.1016/j.jenvman.2023.11971738042081

Gao, T., Erokhin, V., & Arskiy, A. (2019). Dynamic Optimization of Fuel and Logistics Costs as a Tool in Pursuing Economic Sustainability of a Farm. *Sustainability (Basel)*, 11(19), 5463. 10.3390/su11195463

Gao, T., Erokhin, V., Arskiy, A., & Khudzhatov, M. (2021). Has the COVID-19 Pandemic Affected Maritime Connectivity? An Estimation for China and the Polar Silk Road Countries. *Sustainability (Basel)*, 13(6), 3521. 10.3390/su13063521

Gao, T., Ivolga, A., & Erokhin, V. (2018). Sustainable Rural Development in Northern China: Caught in a Vice between Poverty, Urban Attractions, and Migration. *Sustainability (Basel)*, 10(5), 1467. 10.3390/su10051467

Hanson, A. (2019). *Ecological Civilization in the People's Republic of China: Values, Action, and Future Needs*. Asian Development Bank., 10.22617/WPS190604-2

He, L., Wang, B., Xu, W., Cui, Q., & Chen, H. (2022). Could China's Long-Term Low-Carbon Energy Transformation Achieve the Double Dividend Effect for the Economy and Environment? *Environmental Science and Pollution Research International*, 29(14), 20128–20144. 10.1007/s11356-021-17202-134729713

Hu, P., Jeong, H., & Haque, P. S. (2022). An Empirical Study on Environmental Kuznets Curve in China. *Journal of China Area Studies*, 9(1), 227–256. 10.34243/JCAS.9.1.227

Hu, Z., Wu, Q., & Li, J. (2023). Thc Localization of SDGs in China: System Construction, Status Assessment and Development Reflection. *Ecological Indicators*, 154, 110514. 10.1016/j.ecolind.2023.110514

Huang, J., Wei, W., Cui, Q., & Xie, W. (2017). The Prospects for China's Food Security and Imports: Will China Starve the World via Imports? *Journal of Integrative Agriculture*, 16(12), 2933–2944. 10.1016/S2095-3119(17)61756-8

Huang, J., & Yang, G. (2017). Understanding Recent Challenges and New Food Policy in China. *Global Food Security*, 12, 119–126. 10.1016/j.gfs.2016.10.002

Jiang, K., Fu, B., Luo, Z., Xiong, R., Men, Y., Shen, H., Li, B., Shen, G., & Tao, S. (2022). Attributed Radiative Forcing of Air Pollutants from Biomass and Fossil Burning Emissions. *Environmental Pollution*, 306, 119378. 10.1016/j.envpol.2022.11937835500713

Ju, B., Shi, X., & Mei, Y. (2022). The Current State and Prospects of China's Environmental, Social, and Governance Policies. *Frontiers in Environmental Science*, 10, 999145. 10.3389/fenvs.2022.999145

Kennedy, C., Zhong, M., & Corfee-Morlot, J. (2016). Infrastructure for China's Ecologically Balanced Civilization. *Engineering (Beijing)*, 2(4), 414–425. 10.1016/J.ENG.2016.04.014

Kubota, J. (2016). China's Environmental Problems and Prospects for Japanese Cooperation. *Journal of Contemporary East Asia Studies*, 5(1), 3–10. 10.1080/24761028.2016.11869088

Lee, C., & Wang, C. (2022). Does Natural Resources Matter for Sustainable Energy Development in China: The Role of Technological Progress. *Resources Policy*, 79, 103077. 10.1016/j.resourpol.2022.103077

Li, F., Fang, L., & Wu, F. (2023). A Roadmap for Sustainable Agricultural Soil Remediation Under China's Carbon Neutrality Vision. *Engineering (Beijing)*, 25, 28–31. 10.1016/j.eng.2022.08.010

Liao, H., Wei, Y., Ali, S., Uktamov, K., & Ali, N. (2023). Natural Resources Extraction and Industrial Expansion: Natural Resources a Curse or blessing for the Industrial Sector of China? *Resources Policy*, 85, 103986. 10.1016/j.resourpol.2023.103986

Liu, Y., Li, X., Zhu, X., Lee, M., & Lai, P. (2023). The Theoretical Systems of OFDI Location Determinants in Global North and Global South Economies. *Humanities & Social Sciences Communications*, 10(1), 130. 10.1057/s41599-023-01597-y37007733

Lopatnikov, D., & Gorbanyov, V. (2020). China on the Way to "Green Civilization": First Results. *Regional Environmental Issues, 4*, 85-94. https://doi.org/10.24411/1728-323X-2020-14085

Luo, H., & Lin, X. (2022). Dynamic Analysis of Industrial Carbon Footprint and Carbon-Carrying Capacity of Zhejiang Province in China. *Sustainability (Basel)*, 14(24), 16824. 10.3390/su142416824

Ministry of Ecology and Environment of the People's Republic of China. (1994). *Report on China's Agenda 21.* MEE. https://english.mee.gov.cn/Events/Special_Topics/AGM_1/1994agm/meetingdoc94/201605/t20160524_345213.shtml

Mu, Z., Bu, S., & Xue, B. (2014). Environmental Legislation in China: Achievements, Challenges and Trends. *Sustainability (Basel)*, 6(12), 8967–8979. 10.3390/su6128967

National Bureau of Statistics of China. (2024). *National Data.* NBSC. https://data.stats.gov.cn/english/easyquery.htm?cn=C01

Organisation for Economic Co-operation and Development. (2024). *Green Growth in Action: China.* Organisation for Economic Co-operation and Development. https://www.oecd.org/fr/chine/greengrowthinactionchina.htm

Panait, M., Erokhin, V., Andrei, J. V., & Gao, T. (2020). Implication of TNCs in Agri-Food Sector – Challenges, Constraints and Limits – Profit or CSR? *Strategic Management*, 20(4), 33–43. 10.5937/StraMan2004033P

Peng, H., Luo, X., & Zhou, C. (2018). Introduction to China's Green Finance System. *Journal of Service Science and Management*, 11(1), 94–100. 10.4236/jssm.2018.111009

Petushkova, V. (2022). Experience and Perspectives of Sustainable Development in China. *Bulletin of the Russian Academy of Sciences. Physics*, 92(4), 384–393. 10.31857/S0869587322040065

Pyatachkova, A., Potashev, N., & Smirnova, V. (2022). *Green Agenda in China's Policy*. Russian Internartional Affairs Council.

Radulescu, I. D., Andrei, J. V., Chivu, L., Erokhin, V., Gao, T., & Nancu, D. (2022). A Short Review on European Developments in Agricultural Output Price Indices during 2008-2017: Are There Significant Changes? *Ekonomika Poljoprivrede*, 69(1), 107–117. 10.5937/ekoPolj2201107R

Raza, A., Tong, G., Erokhin, V., Bobryshev, A., Chaykovskaya, L., & Malinovskaya, N. (2023a). Sustaining Performance of Wheat-Rice Farms in Pakistan: The Effects of Financial Literacy and Financial Inclusion. *Sustainability (Basel)*, 15(9), 7045. 10.3390/su15097045

Raza, A., Tong, G., Sikandar, F., Erokhin, V., & Tong, Z. (2023b). Financial Literacy and Credit Accessibility of Rice Farmers in Pakistan: Analysis for Central Punjab and Khyber Pakhtunkhwa Regions. *Sustainability (Basel)*, 15(4), 2963. 10.3390/su15042963

Ren, Y., Zhang, B., Chen, X., & Liu, X. (2023). Analysis of Spatial-Temporal Patterns and Driving Mechanisms of Land Desertification in China. *The Science of the Total Environment*, 909, 168429. 10.1016/j.scitotenv.2023.16842937967628

Shah, M., Shuaibu, M. S., AbdulKareem, H. K. K., Khan, Z., & Abbas, S. (2023). Inequality Consequences of Natural Resources, Environmental Vulnerability, and Monetary-Fiscal Stability: A Global Evidence. *Environmental Science and Pollution Research International*, 30(8), 22139. 10.1007/s11356-023-25365-236650371

Shi, J., & Yang, X. (2022). Sustainable Development Levels and Influence Factors in Rural China Based on Rural Revitalization Strategy. *Sustainability (Basel)*, 14(14), 8908. 10.3390/su14148908

Shi, S., & Yin, J. (2023). Trends in the Evolution of Sustainable Development Research in China: A Scientometric Review. *Environmental Science and Pollution Research International*, 30(20), 57898–57914. 10.1007/s11356-023-26515-236973622

Sikandar, F., Erokhin, V., Shu, W. H., Rehman, S., & Ivolga, A. (2021). The Impact of Foreign Capital Inflows on Agriculture Development and Poverty Reduction: Panel Data Analysis for Developing Countries. *Sustainability (Basel)*, 13(6), 3242. 10.3390/su13063242

Sikandar, F., Erokhin, V., Xin, L., Sidorova, M., Ivolga, A., & Bobryshev, A. (2022). Sustainable Agriculture and Rural Poverty Eradication in Pakistan: The Role of Foreign Aid and Government Policies. *Sustainability (Basel)*, 14(22), 14751. 10.3390/su142214751

Sowah, J. K.Jr, & Kirikkaleli, D. (2022). Investigating Factors Affecting Global Environmental Sustainability: Evidence from Nonlinear ARDL Bounds Test. *Environmental Science and Pollution Research International*, 29(53), 80502–80519. 10.1007/s11356-022-21399-035725872

State Council of the People's Republic of China. (2024a). *Guidelines Promote Greener China.* State Council of the People's Republic of China. https://english.www.gov.cn/policies/policywatch/202403/21/content_WS65fb9595c6d0868f4e8e54e0.html

State Council of the People's Republic of China. (2024b). *Xi Calls for Solid Efforts to Further Development of Central Region.* State Council of the People's Republic of China. https://english.www.gov.cn/news/202403/22/content_WS65fd5482c6d0868f4e8e5585.html

United Nations. (1992). *United Nations Conference on Environment and Development, Rio de Janeiro, Brazil, 3-14 June 1992.* UN. https://www.un.org/en/conferences/environment/rio1992

United Nations. (2024). *Sustainable Development Goals.* UN. https://www.un.org/sustainabledevelopment/sustainable-development-goals/

United Nations Conference on Trade and Development. (2024). *Data Centre.* UN. https://unctadstat.unctad.org/datacentre/

Voronovsky, I., Ashmarina, T., Jiang, C., & Xiao, Y. (2022). Vector of Development of Ecological Civilization in China. *Law and Management, 10*, 219-225. 10.24412/2224-9125-2022-10-219-225

Wang, D., Huangfu, Y., Dong, Z., & Dong, Y. (2022). Research Hotspots and Evolution Trends of Carbon Neutrality - Visual Analysis of Bibliometrics Based on CiteSpace. *Sustainability (Basel)*, 14(3), 1078. 10.3390/su14031078

Xi, J. (2017). *The Governance of China II.* Foreign Languages Press.

Xiu, J., Zang, X., Piao, Z., Li, L., & Kim, K. (2023). China's Low-Carbon Economic Growth: An Empirical Analysis Based on the Combination of Parametric and Non-parametric Methods. *Environmental Science and Pollution Research International*, 30(13), 37219–37232. 10.1007/s11356-022-24775-y36567394

Xu, G., Zang, L., Schwarz, P., & Yang, H. (2023). Achieving China's Carbon Neutrality Goal by Economic Growth Rate Adjustment and Low-Carbon Energy Structure. *Energy Policy*, 183, 113817. 10.1016/j.enpol.2023.113817

Xu, Z., Assenova, A., & Erokhin, V. (2018). Renewable Energy and Sustainable Development in a Resource-Abundant Country: Challenges of Wind Power Generation in Kazakhstan. *Sustainability (Basel)*, 10(9), 3315. 10.3390/su10093315

Xue, B., Han, B., Li, H., Gou, X., Yang, H., Thomas, H., & Stückrad, S. (2023). Understanding Ecological Civilization in China: From Political Context to Science. *Ambio*, 52(12), 1895–1909. 10.1007/s13280-023-01897-237442892

Yu, Z., & Deng, X. (2022). Assessment of Land Degradation in the North China Plain Driven by Food Security Goals. *Ecological Engineering*, 183, 106766. 10.1016/j.ecoleng.2022.106766

Zakaria, W. F. A. W., & Buaben, J. M. (2021). The Theory of Post-Industrial Society. *Akademika*, 91(1), 139–149. 10.17576/akad-2021-9101-12

Zhang, S., Liu, Y., & Huang, D. (2021). Understanding the Mystery of Continued Rapid Economic Growth. *Journal of Business Research*, 124, 529–537. 10.1016/j.jbusres.2020.11.023

Zhang, X., Wu, H., Li, Z., & Li, X. (2023). Spatial-Temporal Evolution Characteristics and Driving Factors of Rural Development in Northeast China. *Land (Basel)*, 12(7), 1407. 10.3390/land12071407

Zhao, W., Zhou, A., & Yin, C. (2023). Unraveling the Research Trend of Ecological Civilization and Sustainable Development: A Bibliometric Analysis. *Ambio*, 52(12), 1928–1938. 10.1007/s13280-023-01947-937907802

Zhao, X., Jiang, M., & Zhang, W. (2022). The Impact of Environmental Pollution and Economic Growth on Public Health: Evidence From China. *Frontiers in Public Health*, 10, 861157. 10.3389/fpubh.2022.86115735419328

ADDITIONAL READING

Cao, Y., Xu, C., Kamaruzzaman, S. N., & Aziz, N. M. (2022). A Systematic Review of Green Building Development in China: Advantages, Challenges and Future Directions. *Sustainability (Basel)*, 14(19), 12293. 10.3390/su141912293

Chen, S., & Zhao, Y. (2022). Ecological Civilization: A Blindspot in Global Media Coverage of China's Environmental Governance. *Environmental Communication - A Journal of Nature and Culture, 16*(2), 195-208. 10.1080/17524032.2021.1981419

Cheshmehzangi, A., Xie, L., & Tan-Mullins, M. (2021). Pioneering a Green Belt and Road Initiative (BRI) Alignment between China and Other Members: Mapping BRI's Sustainability Plan. *Blue-Green Systems*, 3(1), 49–61. 10.2166/bgs.2021.020

Erokhin, V. (Ed.). (2018). *Establishing Food Security and Alternatives to International Trade in Emerging Economies*. IGI Global. 10.4018/978-1-5225-2733-6

Erokhin, V., & Gao, T. (Eds.). (2020). *Handbook of Research on Globalized Agricultural Trade and New Challenges for Food Security*. IGI Global. 10.4018/978-1-7998-1042-1

Erokhin, V., Gao, T., & Andrei, J. V. (Eds.). (2021). *Shifting Patterns of Agricultural Trade: The Protectionism Outbreak and Food Security*. Springer Nature. 10.1007/978-981-16-3260-0

Erokhin, V., Gao, T., & Andrei, J. V. (2023). *Contemporary Macroeconomics: New Global Disorder*. Springer Nature. 10.1007/978-981-19-9542-2

Feng, W., Bilivogui, P., Wu, J., & Mu, X. (2023). Green Finance: Current Status, Development, and Future Course of Actions in China. *Environmental Research Communications*, 5(3), 035005. 10.1088/2515-7620/acc1c7

Ji, Q., Li, C., & Jones, P. (2017). New Green Theories of Urban Development in China. *Sustainable Cities and Society*, 30, 257–262. 10.1016/j.scs.2017.02.002

Li, C., & Song, L. (2022). Regional Differences and Spatial Convergence of Green Development in China. *Sustainability (Basel)*, 14(14), 8511. 10.3390/su14148511

Liang, K., Li, Z., & Luo, L. (2023). Measurement, Dynamic Evolution and Influencing Factors of Green Development Efficiency in Western China: Based on Ecological-Economic-Social System. *PLoS One*, 18(12), e0290472. 10.1371/journal.pone.029047238117813

Liu, K., Shi, D., Xiang, W., & Zhang, W. (2022). How Has the Efficiency of China's Green Development Evolved? An Improved Non-radial Directional Distance Function Measurement. *The Science of the Total Environment*, 815, 152337. 10.1016/j.scitotenv.2021.15233734958840

Liu, Y., & Zhou, Y. (2021). Reflections on China's Food Security and Land Use Policy Under Rapid Urbanization. *Land Use Policy*, 109, 105699. 10.1016/j.landusepol.2021.105699

Mi, L., Jia, T., Yang, Y., Jiang, L., Wang, B., Lv, T., Li, L., & Cao, J. (2022). Evaluating the Effectiveness of Regional Ecological Civilization Policy: Evidence from Jiangsu Province, China. *International Journal of Environmental Research and Public Health*, 19(1), 388. 10.3390/ijerph1901038835010650

Qiao, J., Cao, Q., Zhang, Z., Cao, Z., & Liu, H. (2022). Spatiotemporal Changes in the State of Food Security Across Mainland China During 1990-2015: A Multi-scale Analysis. *Food and Energy Security*, 11(1), e318. 10.1002/fes3.318

Thou, Z. (2010). Achieving Food Security in China: Past Three Decades and Beyond. *China Agricultural Economic Review*, 2(3), 251–275. 10.1108/17561371011078417

Wang, Q., & Zhou, C. (2023). How Does Government Environmental Investment Promote Green Development: Evidence from China. *PLoS One*, 18(10), e0292223. 10.1371/journal.pone.029222337824472

Wang, X., Zhao, G., & Xiong, H. (2022). The Temporal-Spatial Evolution and Driving Mechanism of Rural Green Development in China. *Polish Journal of Environmental Studies*, 31(6), 5313–5327. 10.15244/pjoes/150642

Xiao, C., & Sun, J. (2022). Institutional Governance Influence Mechanism and Model of Regional Green Development in China. *Scientific Programming*, 2169684, 1–9. Advance online publication. 10.1155/2022/2169684

Xiao, R., Hao, H., Zhang, H., Liu, Y., & Liu, M. (2023). The Development of Ecological Civilization in China Based on the Economic-Social-Natural Complex System. *Ambio*, 52(12), 1910–1927. 10.1007/s13280-023-01937-x37889463

KEY TERMS AND DEFINITIONS

Climate Change: Fluctuations in the Earth's overall climate or in its different regions over time, as expressed by statistically significant deviations in weather parameters from their long-term average values.

Ecological Civilization: A comprehensive vision of sustainable development, based on the rejection of the utilitarian approach to development and involving the creation of a new concept of harmonious development, co-evolution between society and nature, and improvement in environmental awareness.

Food Security: A state in which a country has ensured its independence in terms of food, ensuring physical and economic access to all citizens for food products that comply with the country's technical regulation requirements and meet the necessary nutritional needs for an active and healthy lifestyle.

Green Agenda: Comprehensive measures to adapt to climate change and decarbonize the economy, including by reducing greenhouse gas emissions and achieving carbon neutrality.

Green Development: Development policy aimed at stimulating economic growth, while preserving natural resources and their continuous provision of resources and ecosystem services, on which the well-being of future generations depends.

Sustainable Development: A type of economic development that provides solutions to both economic and social issues without exacerbating environmental problems.

Chapter 9
Supply Chain and ESG Concerns in the Food Sector

Erdem Kilic
Turkish-German University, Turkey

Sıtkı Sönmezer
https://orcid.org/0009-0007-4903-7604
Istanbul Commerce University, Turkey

Serkan Cankaya
Istanbul Commerce University, Turkey

ABSTRACT

The scope of the study is the examination of impact of ESG scores on the top 800 ESG-scored listed companies globally that may reflect supply chain performance. This study aims to shed light on how corporate governance issues affect supply chain processes. To this end, 800 globally listed companies are leveraged and assessed based on their ESG performance by incorporating Thomson Reuters environmental, social, and governance (ESG) scores into these models. The main objective of this study is to assess the extent to which environmental, social, and governance practices influence supply chain performance. To measure supply chain performance, the authors consider various indicators, including supply chain management score, monitoring score, and partnership termination scores. These metrics allow us to evaluate the effectiveness of supply chain processes over our sample period of ten years. To analyze the relationships between ESG scores and supply chain performance, the authors use partial least square (PLS) regression modeling.

DOI: 10.4018/979-8-3693-3439-3.ch009

SUSTAINABLE SUPPLY CHAIN IN FOOD SECTOR

The relevance of corporate sustainability has increased among commercial corporations in recent years, as the effects of climate change have become one of the most urgent global challenges. Business executives were forced to reconsider the role of business in society and the need for sustainable transformation recently as a result of several crises such as the COVID-19 epidemic, societal instability, and economic depression. Businesses across all sectors have begun to prioritize their sustainability initiatives, such as environmental, social, and governance (ESG) initiatives, as they become more aware of the possible consequences of climate change and the integration of sustainability concerns into all facets of the company's operational framework.

A company's efforts to protect the needs and rights of all stakeholders—while also taking into account the interests of potential future stakeholders—are collectively referred to as corporate sustainability. The most widely accepted benchmark for evaluating corporate sustainability initiatives is the ESG strategies and operations. In recent times, there has been a noticeable and increasing influence of Environmental, Social, and Governance (ESG) factors on supply chain management. Companies are incorporating environmental, social, and governance (ESG) standards more frequently into their procurement strategies as they realize how crucial it is to create supply chains that are both legally compliant and environmentally sustainable (Stan et al., 2023). In particular, "green supply chain management" refers to a kind of supply chain management used by businesses that takes into account the negative environmental effects of supply chain operations while integrating resource efficiency, sustainability, and environmental concerns.

In recent years, ESG has emerged as a key metric for assessing corporate sustainability in both academic and business research. The ESG scores are commonly recognized and utilized as a symbol for the company's Corporate Social Responsibility (CSR) and sustainability-related accomplishments (Whitelock, 2019). The transition of the concept of CSR can be traced back to late 1800s. In a broader sense, corporate social responsibility (CSR) refers to businesses providing voluntary contributions to society in order to improve the community. Nonetheless, a wide range of academics and researchers have offered diverse interpretations and explanations of what is meant by CSR. Carroll (1999) explained the evolution of a definitional construct for CSR and defined corporate social responsibility as "The social responsibility of business that encompasses the economic, legal, ethical, and discretionary expectations that society has of organizations at a given point in time".

Recently, the dimensions of corporate social responsibility evolved into the combined performance of three distinct pillars known as ESG. The corporation's actions relating to pollution and environmental management are represented by the letter "E."

The firm's social work and community involvement initiatives, relationships with the company's employees, and interactions with internal and external stakeholders are all outlined in the "S" pillar. "G" refers to the company's internal management laws, strategies, and governing rules and regulations. The distinguished study "Who Cares Win" in 2006 presented and introduced the idea of ESG for the first time. The United Nations (UN) recognized and underlined the Principle of Responsible Investment (PRI) in 2006, taking into account the ethics and social responsibility of investments and corporate activities.

Eventually, supply chains adopted the concept of sustainability, which subsequently evolved into the theory and practice of sustainable supply chains (Dubey, et al., 2017). Sustainable supply chain management, or SSCM, is the set of measures used to increase and adopt sustainable ecological, environmental, and social effects while reducing the carbon pollution linked to the manufacturing process. Reducing supply chain emissions that are harmful and addressing other sustainability issues related to social and governance are important goals of Environmental, Social, and Governance (ESG) strategies and efforts. Businesses can improve their social standing, reduce their susceptibility to sustainability-related risks, and maintain more environmentally and socially responsible supply chains by integrating ESG considerations into their supply chain management procedures. The integration of various sustainability-related strategies and operations into the corporation's supply chain management is necessary due to the demand from stakeholders for both economically feasible and ecologically sustainable operations, as well as the implementation of environmentally conscious, socially responsible, and interconnected supply chains (Tundys & Wiśniewski, 2023). Benefits from these outcomes may include better connections with suppliers and customers, more operational efficacy, decreased costs, and other risk issues associated to sustainability.

One of the most crucial industries; the food industry showed a poor performance regarding sustainable supply chain activities. A Wall Street Journal survey on ESG metrics showed that out of 5500 publicly listed companies only one food company scored in the top 100. Despite its assertions of being consumer-focused, the food industry's risk aversion ensures that significant adjustments are only implemented when necessary, as the epidemic has demonstrated. According to Filho et al., (2022) agri-food industry supply chain consists several actors from agricultural production to manufacturing and wholesale and retail companies on a global scale. This makes sustainability-related themes and dimensions more complex and overlapping. As a result, agri-food restructuring is crucial to the required global shift towards sustainability. We believe it's critical to look into and comprehend the reasons why stakeholders in the agri-food supply chain haven't yet fully embraced sustainability management.

This research seeks to add to the body of knowledge in academia as well as have practical applications. First, this study will look at the relationship between ESG and supply chains to close the knowledge gap in the literature regarding the relationship between ESG performance and corporate sustainability in their supply chains. The scope of the study is the examination of impact of ESG scores on the top 800 ESG-scored listed companies globally that may reflect supply chain performance. This study aims to shed light on how corporate governance issues affect supply chain processes. To this end, 800 globally listed companies are leveraged and assessed based on their ESG performance by incorporating Thomson Reuters Environmental, Social, and Governance (ESG) scores into our models.

Second, the study's findings will also attempt to illustrate how, globally, the food industry's supply chain and ESG performance are related to one another and to various geographic locations. In order to help managers make decisions and incorporate sustainable efforts into daily operations, the study aims to demonstrate the importance of the interaction between the supply chain and environmental factors. Lastly, stakeholders and legislators can also get an understanding of how socially conscious and sustainable projects and practices can impact the management of food sector companies and their supply chains.

Global value chains are stressed and tested after COVID-19 period. Companies realize that they should not continue with their existing chains only. Lock-downs disabled suppliers to provide the necessary inputs. A closer look at global value chains can be found herebelow.

VALUE CHAINS

Global value chains are an opportunity for emerging countries as they enable them to develop new high value added components of products and services. Manufactured goods and food constitute 80% of world trade. Trade statistics neglect the value added at each link in the chain. They also do not fully reflect the developments in services like coding and logistics that are embedded in the value of the goods manufactured.

Employment levels are not much affected in United States; trades with China led to decreases in middle-skill manufacturing jobs but high-skill jobs have compensated for the loss. College education enjoyed higher salaries (Dollar, 2019). Countries shall develop their infrastructure, education and law system to take part in global value chains and Figure 1 shows how each country plays a role in the global value chain. It is important to notice the presence of China at the end of the majority of value chains.

Figure 1. China's domination in global value chain for electrical and optical exports

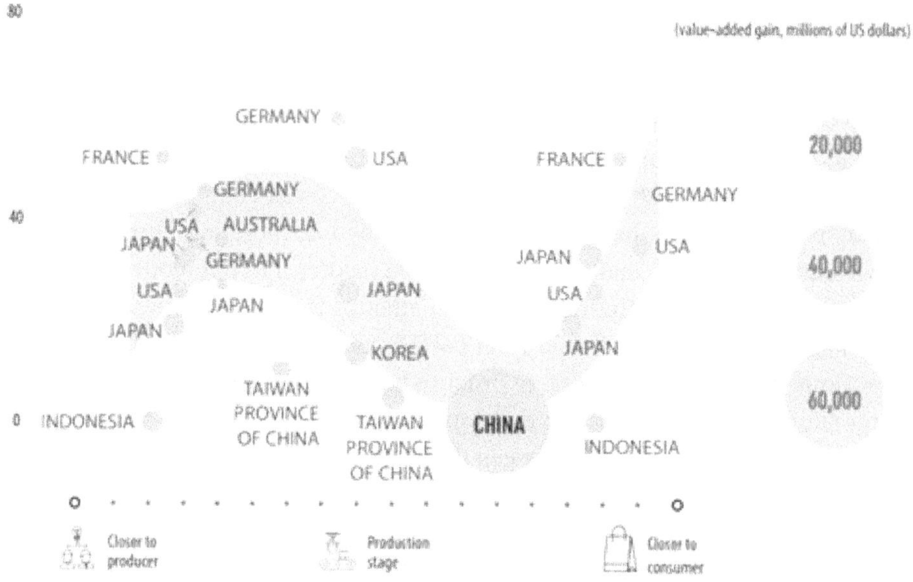

Source: World Trade Organization, *Global Value Chain Development Report 2019*.
Note: Figures are for 2009.

Impact of COVID-19 on Supply Chains

Trade of both goods and services declined significantly in the second quarter of 2020 but goods trade recovered by the end of the year. Trade partner lockdowns have led to a 60% decrease in imports that caused breaks in global value chains. Industries that depend on these value chains suffer from a lack of components such as chips (Malacrino et al, 2022).

Moreover, dependence on a global value chain made countries vulnerable to shocks and might have increased the importance of self-sufficiency after the COVID period. Feasibility of remote work, durability of goods and integration into global value chains are found to be effective on augmenting the trade of COVID-19 shocks for 28 exporting and some importing countries with monthly data (Espitia et al, 2021). When the economies halt in trade partners' economies, exporting countries suffer. Technology might have saved from remote work solutions, but heavy industry or food sector faced forgotten struggles during COVID-19.

World trade in goods and services fell 12.2% and 21.4% respectively with the onset of the COVID-19 pandemic. Trade in goods came to its pre-pandemic levels by October 2021. Transportation had obstacles during COVID-19 which resulted in a slower recovery. Lockdowns resulted in spillovers which are larger in downstream industries that are close to the final user. Global value chain-intensive industries such as electronics are affected more by spillovers. Global value chains adjusted themselves for supply shocks by diversifying away from domestic inputs.

To gain resilience against supply shocks there are two options. Diversification of supplier risk may help to reduce vulnerability, particularly for intermediate inputs. This risk can be diversified away across countries rather than products; instead of final goods, intermediate goods can be diversified or instead of producing intermediate inputs, use of intermediate inputs may be diversified.

The second option is regarding substitutability. When a producer is able to shift to another supplier from another country without facing detrimental obstacles, it means the producer can substitute the input easily (IMF, 2022). It can be inferred that locating and determining prospect suppliers seem to gain importance as various shocks may hit unexpectedly. To gain resilience, greater diversification and substitutability in inputs is required. To diversify, countries need 'friends' that can supply them the goods and services in a timely fashion (Malacrino et al., 2022).

Diversification and substitutability are also important features for the food sector as well. Russian and Ukrainian war hit the wheat production, importers in Europe and the neighboring countries had to find alternative suppliers. Trade from Australia and sluggish demand from China, EU and Turkiye had led to 1.2% decrease from 2022-2023 (AMIS, 2024).

Future of Supply Chains

Shocks and lockdowns have provided valuable feedback for countries that have concerns for the future. The countries may elect to repatriate their productions to their countries as some scholars call 'reshoring' (Hansen, 2022). Decisions to disintegrate themselves from global chains may affect the ones that are part of the chain. The countries that are going to stick to be a part of the value chain they are at, have to guess the moves of their counterparts.

Countries usually optimize their costs when they trade for goods. To maximize profits, they mitigate costs normally but with the adverse shocks and increasing frequency of shocks, countries may build trade relations with new partners to maintain a sustainable supply of goods in the future. Countries that can convince their counterpart with continuous supply in difficult times may increase their trade volumes despite their higher prices.

Some countries may try to benefit from supply shocks by holding excess inventory. If the goods are rare or hard to find, these countries may be paid handsomely for those goods at hand. In short, some countries may try to time the market by waiting for the upcoming supply shock.

Governors of countries may try to increase their countries' capabilities in critical sectors like food and agriculture so that they can be self-sufficient in harder times. At first, countries must be careful to determine their supply potential and future demand in the long term. When domestic demand exceeds the domestic supply, preemptively, investments in these vital sectors may be encouraged. Raising concerns may lead to boost investments in every country that aims to have resilience. In that case, there are two possible scenarios. First, when that happens, an oversupply of goods may float in international markets. Thus, producers will be hurt. The second one is when an exogenous shock hits again. The producers will enjoy higher profits as they can reap them from neighboring countries that lack the goods or they can trade with a global value chain with increasing negotiating powers.

The role of China in foreign trade will continue to be important in the near term. As discussed earlier, China currently dominates almost all of the global value chains. Countries may attempt for the edge that China has in the future. China will most probably try to maintain its strong position but as there are so many value chains. In the mid to long term, China may keep its strong position in value chains that they benefit the most and give up the less attractive ones. It is also reasonable to assume that countries may attempt to take part in value chains and even become key players in some of them.

Conditions and drivers of wheat are depicted in Figure 2. China, and India are crucial for wheat production. European Union countries, Russia, Ukraine, and Turkiye are also important for wheat production as well. A war broke out in recent years between Ukraine and Russia which resulted in an unexpected cut in the supply of the crop. Turkiye had intervened to open up a corridor between the two countries at war. As a result, countries came to terms to allow trade despite the ongoing disputes between countries. The main reason may be the fact that wheat is vital for the production of bread.

Figure 2. Conditions and drivers for wheat

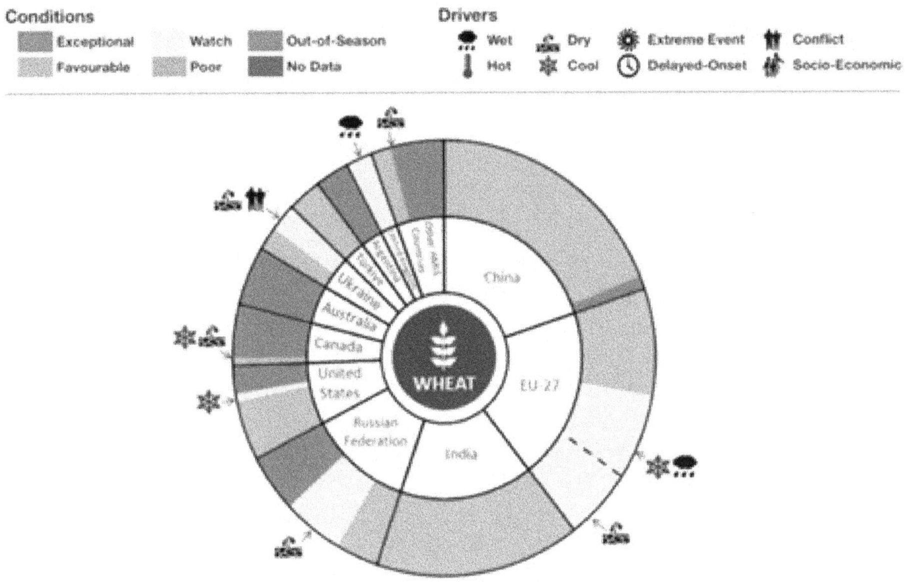

RESEARCH ON THE FOOD SECTOR

The food sector heavily depends on crops. Supply and demand for crops and the producing countries differ throughout the world. Climate change endangers the supply side and the increasing population of the world shifts the demand curve for crops. As can be seen in Figure 3, areas with exceptional conditions are almost extinct. Favorable areas for crops lie in central Europe, Turkiye, India, and the east coasts of China. The majority of lands of the world are out of season.

Figure 3. Crop conditions around the world

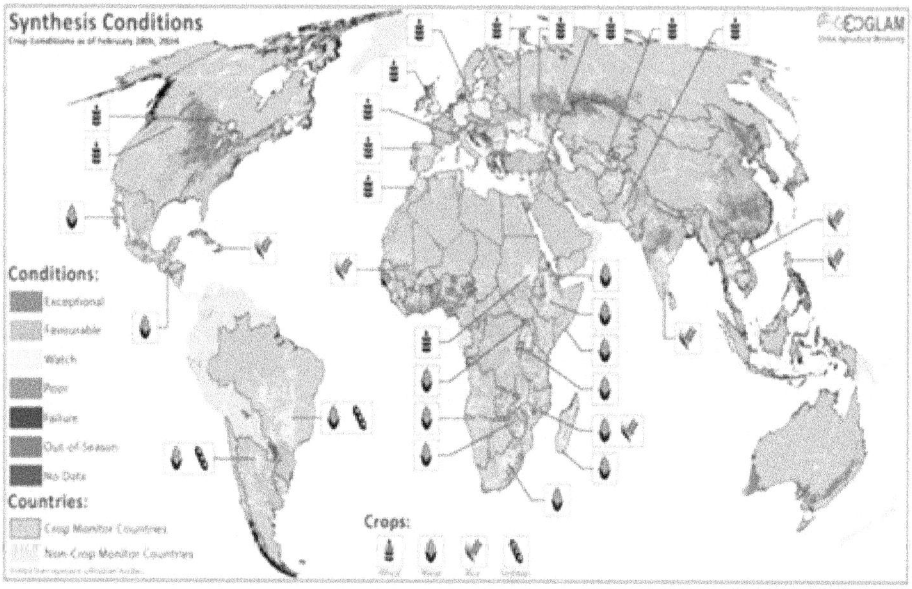

As Frenkel et al. (2016) point out the growing number of people involved in the industry, both as consumers and employees, the improvement of ESG practices in food supply chains is overdue. According to Matten and Moon (2008) these practices can be set explicitly or implicitly. By "explicit CSR," they refer to corporate policies that assume and articulate responsibility for some societal interests. Examples of these kinds of policies are voluntary programs and strategies by corporations that combine social and business values and address issues perceived as being part of the social responsibility of the company.

On the other hand, "implicit CSR," they refer to corporations' role within the wider formal and informal institutions for society's interests and concerns. Implicit CSR normally consists of values, norms, and rules that result in (mandatory and customary) requirements for corporations to address stakeholder issues and that define proper obligations of corporate actors in collective rather than individual terms.

Thus, a global standardization at a global scope is relatively burdensome to achieve, involved with national norms and rules and individual values and strategies.

Central importance should be given to global trade to understand the food supply chain. Since the driving force to supply and transfer food from one region to consumers to another region are opportunities of trade potentials.

However, international trade has a massive complexity, which may create both synergies and trade-offs. For example, carbon intensity of agricultural production is to be mentioned here, which requires governmental policy actions (OECD (2022)). According to the OECD's agricultural policy and monitoring evaluation report, countries should consider investing in transparency and trade facilitation, and should ensure that the policy environment is transparent, predictable, and rule based.

Although each food product has its own supply chain, the general supply in agri-business chain can be classification according to Figure 4.

Figure 4. Generalized stages of agribusiness chain

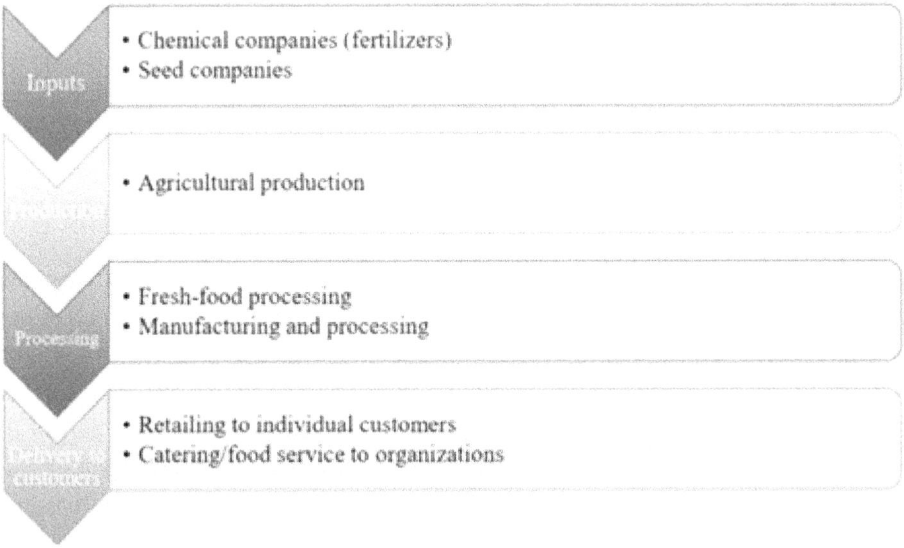

Adapted from Humphrey and Memedovic (2006:p.31).

At the beginning of the supply chain there are inputs produced by chemical and seed companies. In the next stage, agricultural production takes place. The following stage is the processing stage, where fresh food is manufactured and processed. The final stage is build up of delivery to the customers, which involves retailing to individual customers and food service to organizations.

The food supply chains are heterogeneous in terms of inputs and processing (Bukuevite et al., 2009). Since there is no global standardization in the food supply chain, each country has its own supply chain layout. To achieve higher efficiency in agricultural production, the OECD is advocating for a due diligence process in the agricultural sector.

Table 1. Five-step framework for due diligence in the agricultural sector

Step 1: Establish strong enterprise management systems for responsible supply chains.
Step 2: Identify, assess, and prioritize risks in the supply chain.
Step 3: Design and implement a strategy to respond to identified risks in the supply chain
Step 4: Verify supply chain due diligence.
Step 5: Report on supply chain due diligence.

Source: OECD (2013), OECD Due Diligence Guidance for Responsible Supply Chains of Minerals from Conflict-Affected and High-Risk Areas: Second Edition, OECD Publishing, Paris.

Despite competition, companies can leverage industry collaboration to enhance due diligence practices while optimizing costs.

Industry organizations can develop and manage initiatives that promote adherence to international due diligence standards. These frameworks should be designed to avoid sharing competitively sensitive information. Further applications in the agenda are cost-sharing within industry for specific due diligence tasks, co-ordination among industry members with same suppliers and cooperation among different segments of the supply chain, such as upstream and downstream enterprises.

The commission for OECD agricultural report 2023 states a strategy for a sustainable agricultural production and supply chain for the future.

The claim is that global agriculture is currently at a crossroad trying to balance emissions and adaptation. The ongoing climate change presents a major challenge for agriculture. Not only is agricultural production vulnerable to rising temperatures, erratic rainfall, and extreme weather events, but the sector itself contributes to greenhouse gas emissions. However, agriculture has the potential to be part of the solution. Practices that capture carbon in soil and plants can help mitigate climate change. The key to unlocking this potential lies in smart policy. Current agricultural subsidies often have unintended consequences, encouraging practices that harm the environment. To create a more sustainable future, there is the need for a new approach (OECD, 2023).

For a potential comprehensive policy agenda, the OECD Commission proposes the following six-point plan aiming to transform agriculture into a climate-friendly sector:

1. Eliminate subsidies that damage the environment and distort markets.
2. Redirect government support towards practices that improve overall agricultural performance, and thus investing in public goods.
3. Focus income assistance on those who need it most, freeing up resources for environmental initiatives.
4. Building Resilience by investing in data and tools to help farmers manage risks from climate change.

5. Application of Carbon Pricing and implementing systems that reward farmers for adopting low-emission practices.
6. Develop international strategies to significantly reduce emissions across the entire food system.

By implementing these reforms, the OECD expects a productive and sustainable agricultural sector that contributes to achieving global climate goals.

DATA AND METHODOLOGY

The sample period is given between 2010-2021. Data is annual for 800 top ESG score companies listed in Refinitive. Our dependent variables are Environmental Supply Chain Management Score, Environmental Supply Chain Monitoring Score, Environmental Supply Chain Partnership Termination Score, Health & Safety Policy Score, Policy-Environmental-Supply Chain Score. Partial Least Squares Regresyon (PLSR) provides a remedy to the difficulty faced by researchers when number of samples are low but there are numerous predicting variables that may be correlated among each other.

The main modeling steps are below. Equation (1) describes the main empirical regression model.

$$Y = XB + \varepsilon \tag{1}$$

is shown by

$$B = (X^T X)^{-1} X^T Y \tag{2}$$

Singularity is a major problem due to incomplete data sets and too many close to zero values in data set. Similarly, when the number of variables exceed the number of observation or negative impact of collinearity applies. To overcome this problem, X can be decomposed into orthogonal scores, T, and loadings, P.

$$X = TP \tag{3}$$

The objective to use PLRS model is to grasp the information both on X and Y when defining orthogonal scores and loadings. X and Y are selected so as the covariance of X and Y is prefunded.

Hypothesis Formation

ESG constituents of Environmental, Social and Governance their effect on ESG Score are tested as well as their effect on alternative ESG Scores, namely, ESG Combined and ESG Controversies Score. Finally, the relation between ESG Scores and Supply Chain are analyzed. The hypotheses tested are listed here below.

ESG Scores and ESG Constituents' Relations

$H_{0,1a}$: Social factors does not affect ESG scores.
$H_{0,1b}$: Environmental factors does not affect ESG scores
$H_{0,1c}$: Governance factors does not affect ESG scores

Alternative ESG Scores and ESG Constituents Relations

$H_{0,2a}$: Social factors does not affect ESG combined scores.
$H_{0,2b}$: Environmental factors does not affect ESG combined scores
$H_{0,2c}$: Governance factors does not affect ESG combined scores
$H_{0,3a}$: Social factors does not affect ESG controversies scores.
$H_{0,3b}$: Environmental factors does not affect ESG controversies scores
$H_{0,3c}$: Governance factors does not affect ESG controversies scores

ESG Scores and Supply Chain

$H_{0,4a}$: ESG scores does not affect Supply Chain.
$H_{0,4b}$: ESG combined scores does not affect Supply Chain.
$H_{0,4c}$: ESG controversies scores does not affect Supply Chain.
The related results are presented in Figure 5.

Figure 5. Impact of ESG scores on supply chain for food sector

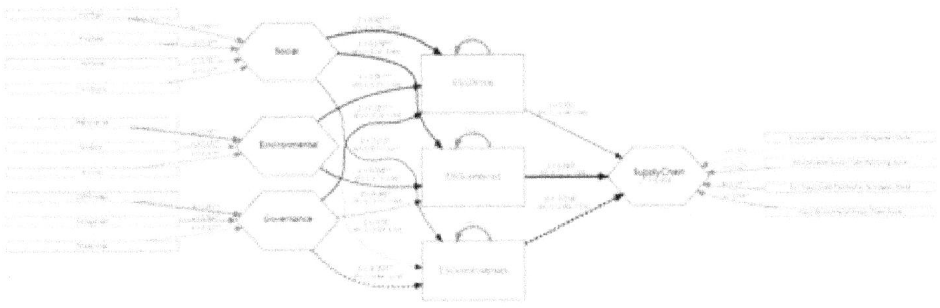

Notes: *The strength of the relations among nodes in our model is shown via boldness and dotted lines or straight lines.*

When we analyze the results in Figure 5, ESG Score is not statistically significant with a t-statistic of 0.72, but ESG Combined Score has a statistically significant effect (90%) on supply chain with a t-statistic of 1.73. Similarly, ESG Controversies score has a 95% significance and a negative impact on supply chain score with a t-statistic of 2. The results indicate that firms in food sector have to focus on their ESG Combined and ESG Controversies score rather than ESG score when they want to improve their overall supply chain scores.

Table 2. Measures of outer loadings, reliability, composite reliability and AVE for food sector

Latent Variables	*Indicators*	*Outer Loadings*	*Indicator Reliability*	*Composite Reliability*	*AVE*
Social	Community	0.2295	0.05271	0.7697	0.5431
	Human Rights	0.4218	0.1779		
	Product Responsibility	0.3801	0.1445		
	Workforce	0.2047	0.0419		
Environment	Emission	0.2149	0.04619	0.8775	0.6423
	Environmental Innovation	0.2473	0.06119		
	Resource	0.7663	0.5872		
Governance	CSR Strategy	0.5623	0.3162	0.4948	0.4655
	Management	0.5892	0.3472		
	Shareholders	-0.2326	0.05414		

For food sector in Table 2, Social and Environment composite reliabilities are above the critical threshold value. Governance composite reliability value is not acceptable as well as its AVE value. This makes inferences made from our models weak in terms of governance for food sector. This may be due to sample size and sample structure.

Table 3. Explanatory power of models for all sectors and food sector

Indicator	R^2	*Adjusted* R^2
Food Sector		
ESG Score	0.9485	0.9479
ESG Combined	0.4379	0.4316
ESG Controversies	0.05872	0.04817
Supply Chain	0.40409	0.3973

In Table 3, similar to Sachin and Rajesch (2022) adjusted R^2 for ESG Scores, our results are slightly lower than theirs (0.92). This is a very high R^2 value underlying the close relationship between ESG Score and Supply Chain score. As expected ESG controversies have limited explanatory power.

Table 4. Summary of hypothesis testing for supply chain in food sector

Hypothesis	*Relations*	*Beta*	*t-value*	*Decision*	*Conf. Int %5*	*%95*
$H_{0,4a}$	ESG Score ->Supply Chain	0,183	0,72	Do not reject	-0.26606465	0.69844379
$H_{0,4b}$	ESG Combined Score -> Supply Chain	0,543*	1,731	Reject	-0.1196608	1.06450797
$H_{0,4c}$	ESG Controversies Score -> Supply Chain	-0,538*	-2,003	Reject	-0.99606191	0.02760168

The following findings are estimated in Table 4. ESG score, ESG Combined (t-value 1.73) and ESG Controversies Score (t-value -2.00) both have a statistical significance and ESG combined Score has a positive effect on supply chain. Consequently, firms that are in the food sector has to focus on their alternate ESG scores.

Table 5. Summary of hypothesis testing for alternative ESG Scores for food sector

Hypothesis	*Relations*	*Beta*	*t-value*	*Decision*	*Conf. Int %5*	*%95*
$H_{0,1a}$	Social->ESG Score	0,427***	18,314	Reject	0.3776	0.4683
$H_{0,2a}$	Social->ESG Combined	0,378***	5,588	Reject	0.2408	0.5075

continued on following page

Table 5. Continued

Hypothesis	*Relations*	*Beta*	*t-value*	*Decision*	*Conf. Int %5*	*%95*
$H_{0,3a}$	Social-> ESG Controversies	0,212**	2.0623	Reject	0.01088	0.4171
$H_{0,1b}$	Environmental->ESG Score	0,361***	15,777	Reject	0.31936	0.4086
$H_{0,2b}$	Environmental ->ESG Combined	0,266***	3,831	Reject	0.13023	0.3988
$H_{0,3b}$	Environmental -> ESG Controversies	-0,054	-0,5318	Do not reject	-0.2339	0.1339
$H_{0,1c}$	Governance->ESG Score	0.321***	16,653	Reject	0.2840	0.3587
$H_{0,2c}$	Governance ->ESG Combined	0,0915*	1,668	Reject	-0.01065	0.2021
$H_{0,3c}$	Governance -> ESG Controversies	-0,303***	-3,838	Reject	-0.4443	-0.1479

Table 5 shows the results for alternative hypotheses in the food sector. Social variable has a positive and statistically significant impact on all three ESG scores. However, environmental variable can only explain the change in ESG score and ESG combined. The governance variable explain the change in all three ESG related scores in this study but significance is lower for ESG combined.

CONCLUSION

This research investigates how sustainable corporate governance and social responsibility practices influence supply chain performance. It focuses on the top 800 companies ranked by Environmental, Social, and Governance (ESG) scores. A Partial Least Square (PLS) model analysis is used to explore the complex connections between ESG factors and supply chain metrics. Interestingly, the research finds that while overall ESG scores are not statistically significant predictors of supply chain performance in the food sector, alternative ESG metrics, specifically ESG Combined and ESG Controversies Scores, do show a significant impact. This suggests that food companies would benefit from considering various aspects of ESG, particularly managing, and reducing controversies, to improve their supply chain performance.

The study also reveals that social and governance factors are strong drivers of ESG scores across all sectors. They significantly influence both overall ESG scores and ESG Combined scores, highlighting the importance of social responsibility and good governance practices in shaping a company's ESG profile. These findings offer valuable insights for both academics and practitioners. As companies increasingly embrace sustainability, understanding the connection between operational activities, firm characteristics, and responsible practices becomes crucial. This research underlines the economic advantages of environmental and sustainable practices, demonstrating that using ESG factors can not only enhance supply chain efficiency but also contribute to a more sustainable and resilient global economy.

The research concludes by emphasizing the dynamic and evolving nature of the interplay between corporate governance, sustainability, and supply chain processes. It suggests further research to empirically assess these connections at the individual firm level.

REFERENCES

Aiyar, S., Malacrino, D., Mohommad, A., & Presbitero, A. (2022). *International trade spillovers from domestic COVID-19 lockdowns*. International Monetary Fund.

AMIS. (2024). Market Monitor is a product of the Agricultural Market Information System. *Market Monitor, 116.*

Bukeviciute, L., Dierx, A., & Ilzkovitz, F. (2009). *The functioning of the food supply chain and its effect on food prices in the European Union*. European Commission.

Carroll, A. B. (2009). *A History of Corporate Social Responsibility (A. Crane, D. Matten, A. McWilliams* (Moon, J., & Siegel, D. S., Eds.). Vol. 1). Oxford University Press., 10.1093/oxfordhb/9780199211593.003.0002

Dubey, R., Gunasekaran, A., & Papadopoulos, T. (2017). Green supply chain management: Theoretical framework and further research directions. *Benchmarking*, 24(1), 184–218. 10.1108/BIJ-01-2016-0011

Espitia, A., Mattoo, A., Rocha, N., Ruta, M., & Winkler, D. (2021, February). Pandemic Trade: Covid-19. *World Bank Policy Research Working Paper*, PAPERS9. 10.1596/1813-9450-950833821085

Etim, N. N., & Djekic, I. (2022). An overview of the interactions between food production and climate change. *The Science of the Total Environment*, 838(Pt 3), 156438. 10.1016/j.scitotenv.2022.15643835660578

Filho, W.L., Ribeiro, P.C.C., Setti, A.F.F., Azam, F.M.S., Abubakar, I.R., Castillo-Apraiz, J., Tamayo, U., Özuyar, P.G., & Frizzo, K. (2023). *Toward food waste reduction at universities.*

Frenkel, S., Mamic, I., & Greene, L. (2016). *Global supply chains in the food industry: insights from the Asia-Pacific region.* International Labour Organization; ILO DWT for East and South-East Asia and the Pacific.

Humphrey, J., & Memedovic, O. (2006). *Global value chains in the agrifood sector, United Nations* [UN]. Industrial Development Organization.

IMF. (2022, April). World economic outlook, WEO, Occasional paper, World economic and financial surveys. *World Economic Outlook.*

Matten, D., & Moon, J. (2008). Implicit and explicit CSR: A conceptual framework for a comparative understanding of corporate social responsibility. *Academy of Management Review*, 33(2), 404–424. 10.5465/amr.2008.31193458

OECD. (2013). *OECD Due Diligence Guidance for Responsible Supply Chains of Minerals from Conflict-Affected and High-Risk Areas* (2nd ed.). OECD Publishing.

OECD. (2022). Agricultural Policy Monitoring and Evaluation 2022. *Reforming Agricultural Policies for Climate Change Mitigation.* OECD.10.1787/7f4542bf-en

OECD. (2023). Agricultural Policy Monitoring and Evaluation 2023. *Adapting Agriculture to Climate Change.* OECD. https://www.oecd.org/publications/agricultural-policy-monitoring-and-evaluation-22217371.htm

Stan, S. E. (2023). Measuring Supply Chain Performance from ESG Perspective. *International conference Knowledge-Based Organization.* Sciendo. 10.2478/kbo-2023-0026

Tundys, B., & Wiśniewski, T. (2023). Triple bottom line aspects and sustainable supply chain resilience: A structural equation modelling approach. *Frontiers in Environmental Science*, 11, 1161437. 10.3389/fenvs.2023.1161437

Whitelock, V. G. (2019). Multidimensional environmental social governance sustainability framework: Integration, using a purchasing, operations, and supply chain management context. *Sustainable Development (Bradford)*, 27(5), 923–931. 10.1002/sd.1951

Chapter 10
Airline Companies in Green Transformation:
A Comparison Through Websites

Fatma Selin Sak
Giresun University, Turkey

Güzide Karakuş
Necmettin Erbakan University, Turkey

ABSTRACT

Since the damage to the environment in the production of goods and services to meet human needs has emerged as a threat to global sustainability, it becomes critical to examine and reduce the environmental impacts of each activity undertaken. While this necessity forces all sectors to green transformation, it is of great importance that the aviation sector, which has a significant impact on all aspects of sustainability, is also addressed within this framework. In line with this necessity, the aim of this study is to identify the practices that reflect the green image of airline companies within the scope of green transformation. For this purpose, the information declared on the corporate websites of four selected airline companies were compared using content analysis methodology. It is aimed that the findings obtained will contribute to all businesses operating within the scope of green transformation together with the stakeholders in the sector.

DOI: 10.4018/979-8-3693-3439-3.ch010

INTRODUCTION

Aviation is recognized as one of the world's fastest-growing and innovative sectors, occupying a crucial role within the global economy. As the industry advances economically in tandem with escalating customer demand, it also endeavors to maintain equilibrium in matters of social development and environmental responsibility (Karakuş, 2023, 89). Given the substantial magnitude of the sector's contribution to global growth and environmental impact, it is not uncommon for the aviation industry to be positioned at the forefront of sustainability discussions (Hooper & Greenall, 2005, 156).

Aviation, despite its positive impact on global tourism and trade, is recognized as a priority sector that must be addressed within the framework of green transformation, given its environmentally unsustainable nature. It is crucial to define the activities implemented in the sector, identify areas requiring improvement, and contribute to the widespread adoption of best practices. Accordingly, the purpose of this study is to understand the green transformation activities that reflect the green image of airlines by using literature review and content analysis techniques and to seek answers to the following questions:

- *What kinds of initiatives are being undertaken by the largest airline companies globally as part of green transformation?*
- *Is there variation in the green transformation activities of airline companies based on the regions in which they operate?*

Following the introduction section of the study, the concepts of green marketing, green image, and green transformation in the aviation sector have been investigated. Subsequent to addressing similar studies in the literature, the methodology of the study has been presented. In the application section, information declared by Singapore Airlines, Qatar Airways, Air France, and Turkish Airlines regarding green transformation on their corporate websites has been scrutinized. The gathered data has been compiled allowing for comparisons to be made. Finally, in the conclusion section, the findings are assessed, and recommendations are developed based on the obtained results.

BACKGROUND

Green Marketing

Since the American Marketing Association (AMA) organized its inaugural workshop on "Ecological Marketing" in 1975, environmentally conscious marketing practices have begun to garner significance. Eventually, the term "green marketing" emerged in discussions by the late 1980s and early 1990s. (Choudhary & Gokarn, 2013). Green marketing refers to a variety of environmentally friendly marketing activities aimed at meeting consumers' desires and needs. Minimizing environmental impact is crucial while addressing consumer needs (Erbaşlar, 2012).

The concept of green marketing is centered on four distinct processes. The first process involves designing green products for environmentally conscious consumers, such as vehicles operating on alternative fuel technologies; this stage is termed green targeting. The second stage entails developing green strategies, such as reducing waste generation within the business. As the third stage is reached, it involves ceasing the production of non-green (environmentally unfriendly products), focusing solely on producing green products. In the final stage, it is not sufficient for the business to merely adopt green or environmentally conscious practices; it is imperative for the business to have embraced social responsibility comprehensively in all aspects. This development is contingent on the business culture and environmental factors (Alagöz, 2007).

The widespread adoption of green marketing strategies in businesses and the production of environmentally friendly products and services yield numerous benefits, such as gaining a competitive advantage, reducing costs, fostering creativity, recycling resources, and enhancing brand image (Özcan & Özgül, 2019). Despite the awareness of limited resources, the world, grappling with challenges like a continuously growing population, climate change, deforestation, greenhouse gas emissions, drought, and hunger problems, will gain a unique strength in addressing these issues through the application of green marketing practices and strategies by businesses in the context of globalization, where physical boundaries vanish in commercial activities. For enterprises aspiring to take a leading position in the fiercely competitive environment of price, product variety, and post-sales customer satisfaction, green marketing strategies play a crucial role (Gedik, 2020).

The primary advantages of green marketing are enumerated as follows (Priyadarshi & Prasad, 2023):

– Environmental issues are foregrounded in green consumption, contributing to sustainable growth.
– It contributes to the steady reduction of costs in the long term.

– Goods and services are marketed in parallel with consumers' environmental attitudes.
– Green businesses acquire a profitable and sustainable structure in the long term.
– Providing healthy goods and services gives businesses a competitive advantage.
– Working for an environmentally sensitive business enhances employees' morale and motivation.
– It enables the expansion of the business towards a new market niche consisting of ecologically and health-conscious consumers.

Preventing environmental pollution entails the elimination or reduction of waste before it is generated. To achieve this goal, all businesses implement green marketing programs such as designing and developing ecologically sound products, recyclable and biodegradable packaging, frequent pollution checks, and the creation of operations with high energy efficiency (Kotler & Armstrong, 2018). Accordingly, it is essential not only for the product itself to be environmentally friendly but also for environmentally conscious behavior to be adopted throughout all stages of its design, production, distribution, consumption, and post-consumption processes (Tekin & Zerenler, 2012). Environmentally conscious consumers evaluate all stages of a product when making decisions because these stages shape consumers' market behaviors and personal satisfactions. The eco-friendliness of the process of using, evaluating, and disposing of the product becomes crucial in decision-making as opportunities arise to reduce environmental impact at each stage (Nittala & Moturu, 2023).

With the advent of media tools that have become a powerful force in disseminating businesses' activities, consumers have started to behave more environmentally consciously while making their purchases. This awareness has led informed consumers to gravitate towards green products and services. Consequently, businesses have begun to develop environmentally friendly approaches, aiming both to increase profitability and to preserve nature, aligning with the preferences of consumers (Ceylan & Kıpırtı, 2021). The primary objective of green marketing, serving these purposes, is to design environmentally friendly products that are of high quality, high performance, affordable, and inflict minimal harm on nature. Additionally, a second significant aim of green marketing is to create a green image aimed at increasing awareness regarding the environmental impacts of the product and production process, thus fostering understanding of environmental achievements (Duru & Şua, 2013).

GREEN IMAGE

The green image is generally defined as a series of perceptions formed in consumers' minds regarding a business concerning environmental responsibilities and concerns (Wang vd. 2018). When airlines engage in environmental conservation activities, they can enhance their business performance not only by adhering to local and international standards and regulations but also by reducing costs. Additionally, they can emphasize corporate social responsibility to create a positive image, thereby garnering more consumer support (Rosskopf, Lehner, & Gollnick, 2014) and gaining the trust of existing passengers. However, for this to occur, airline management must establish a positive eco-friendly image among passengers to increase levels of satisfaction related to perceived green experiences (Wu, Cheng, & Ai, 2018).

When airlines offer products/services that meet the environmental needs of their passengers, the likelihood of creating an eco-friendly airline image is higher. Through successful environmental management, consumers exhibit a positive attitude towards eco-friendly airlines and have a strong desire to travel with them. At this point, to increase visibility, airlines need to reflect their environmental practices in their business policies (Hwang & Lyu, 2019). For instance, practices such as extending the meal selection option before flights to all classes (such as first, business, economy) can be announced to passengers through airline websites to garner their support and prevent food and material waste.

In creating a green image, environmental expenditures, practices, and corporate communication activities can be conducted through both traditional means and increasingly prevalent digital platforms. Among the digital tools most commonly utilized by businesses for this purpose are corporate websites. Through their corporate websites, businesses can convey their corporate information in line with their environmentally friendly attitudes, share their green products/services with customers, and conduct environmentally focused public relations activities. (Altuğ & Akyol, 2018).

Since websites are useful platforms for disseminating information, international airline companies publish the results of their environmental conservation activities on their own websites to create a favorable impression among passengers and gain their support (Niu, Liu, Chang, & Ye, 2016). Web siteleri sürdürülebilirlik raporları ile birlikte çevresel uygulamalara ilişkin önemli bilgileri vurgulayan infografikler aracılığıyla hedefler, emisyonlar ve haberler gibi ek bilgilere de yer vermektedirler. Havayolu işletmelerinin genel olarak kurumsal web sitelerinin ortak bir yönü, bu alandaki çabalarına ilişkin farkındalığı artırmak amacıyla grafik ve videoların yayınlanmasıdır (Bort, 2023). Especially, within the corporate websites of airline companies, alongside information pertaining to the organization such as its history, implemented policies, sponsorships, investor relations, and career opportunities, there are also details regarding their green activities conducted within the framework of sustainability initiatives.

MAIN FOCUS OF THE CHAPTER

Green Transformation in the Aviation Sector

Green transformation is defined as a combination of economic growth and environmental concern aimed at ensuring the improvement of the quality of life for current and future generations through the efficient and rational use of existing resources (Cheba, Bąk, Szopik-Depczynska, & Ioppolo, 2022). In today's world, multiple environmental stress factors such as climate change, air and water pollution, and decreasing biodiversity are increasingly on the rise (Scoones, Newell, & Leach, 2015). In an effort to address environmental issues, businesses are undergoing transformation in their mission, strategy, and policies by taking into account green tendencies, alongside promoting the Sustainable Development Goals and the widespread adoption of a green lifestyle (Pimonenko, Bilan, Horák, Starchenko, & Gajda, 2020). Given the high environmental impacts involved, environmental transformation is an important necessity for airline companies, just as it is in all sectors (Olk, 2021).

The expansion of commercial aviation activities has brought significant gains in mobility and economic prosperity to Europe. However, the concomitant rise in pollution and emissions has led to exacerbated environmental degradation. Between 2005 and 2020, prior to the pandemic, CO2 emissions from passenger and cargo transportation surged by 50%. Despite the pandemic disrupting commercial aviation in 2020 and resulting in a more than 50% reduction in CO2 emissions, by 2022, emissions had rebounded to an 86% increase compared to pre-pandemic levels. Furthermore, issues such as noise pollution, overconsumption, and the depletion of Earth's resources, including water, energy, and arable land, have hastened irreversible environmental harm (Fathi, Ansari & Ansari, 2023). The adoption of the Paris Agreement, aimed at combating climate change, with the participation of many countries worldwide, has prompted global efforts to reduce emissions. This has necessitated a reevaluation of the environmental footprints for many global airline companies (Amankwah-Amoah, 2020).

The use of modern aircraft (having a young fleet age), preference for turboprop aircraft over jet aircraft for their lower fuel consumption and consequently reduced greenhouse gas emissions, increasing aircraft capacity, utilization of biofuels, waste management, the use of recyclable products for in-flight catering, and consolidating multiple cabin classes into a single class to accommodate more passengers on board (increasing the number of passengers per kilometer while reducing the number of flights) are significant indicators for green transformation practices in airline operations (Mayer, Ryley, & Gillingwater, 2014).

From a commercial standpoint, airlines need to shape their corporate green images to attract the attention of customers. This can involve providing incentives to passengers and revitalizing their green transformation intentions (Chan, Wang, Zhang & Li, 2021). Indeed, acquiring new customers is approximately seven times more costly than retaining previous ones. Therefore, businesses need to leverage green strategies to increase sales, and to retain customers, they are required to produce customized and high-quality products (Gedik, 2020). Ultimately, airline companies should shift their focus towards fostering a green image rather than merely constructing a general brand perception, striving to differentiate themselves clearly from other airlines. This approach can provide a significant competitive advantage in the industry (Hagmann, Semeijn, & Vellenga, 2015).

In a business world where environmental concerns are gaining importance and commercial profits are decreasing, airline companies are striving to increase their revenues by preserving nature. Given that airline companies operate internationally, they can grasp global trends, preemptively identify passengers' views, and create an eco-friendly marketing strategy to garner their support. By doing so, they will not only achieve good business performance but also enhance sustainability (Niu, Liu, Chang, & Ye, 2016). The efforts of airline companies to adopt greener practices begin primarily with making a series of changes in their traditional marketing mixes. These changes may include selecting aircraft with lower emissions, increasing the number of passengers per flight, greening in-flight products (such as reducing waste by eliminating complimentary meal services), publicizing green activities through communication channels such as websites and advertisements, and including corporate social responsibility reports (Mayer, Ryley, & Gillingwater, 2014).

The inclusion of nature experiences in advertisements, which is a common communication tool, helps foster positive attitudes towards a brand. Therefore, if airline companies incorporate green advertisements featuring nature experiences such as forests, mountains, and rivers across various platforms (TV, websites, billboards, etc.), airline customers are likely to develop a positive attitude towards the airline portraying an eco-friendly image, thereby increasing their desire to travel with that airline (Hartmann & Apaolaza-Ibáñez, 2009). In addition, promoting eco-friendly travel options plays a significant role in shaping the image of airline companies and attracting environmentally conscious customers. Some airlines offer solutions such as encouraging direct flights with lower fuel consumption and developing incentives for customers to use public transportation at their destinations as eco-friendly travel options (Koç, 2023).

However, not all segments of society possess sufficient knowledge and awareness regarding the importance and necessity of environmental management. In this regard, airline companies should activate environmental learning by providing regular training to all employees to instill practices related to their environmental policies. Flight attendants, who have the most interaction with passengers, should convey the airline company's environmental practices to customers whenever appropriate, and the airline company should highlight these practices across all marketing channels (Hwang & Lyu, 2019). Increasing passengers' environmental awareness will influence their travel choices, directing them towards more environmentally conscious options and contributing to environmental sustainability.

METHOD

With the increasingly palpable negative impacts of climate change, the growing necessity for green transformation has become a central motivation globally, spanning across every region and industry. While the significance of the subject remains relevant for all sectors, considering the magnitude of its impact on sustainability, this study specifically focuses on airline companies, which are significant players in the aviation sector. The primary motivation behind this study is the escalating need for green transformation in response to the intensifying adverse effects of climate change. The scope of this study has been defined within the aviation sector, and the following research questions have been addressed:

- *What kinds of initiatives are being undertaken by the world's largest airline companies as part of the green transformation?*
- *Is there variation in the green transformation activities of airline companies based on the region in which they operate?*

The research utilized the purposive sampling method, and the selection of airline companies to be examined was based on two criteria.

1. Initially, the first ten airline companies featured in the "World's Best Airlines" list published annually by SKYTRAX for the year 2023 were identified.(https://www.worldairlineawards.com/worlds-top-10-airlines-2023/, Accessed: 14.01.2024):

Table 1. World's best airlines

S.N.	Airlines Company	Country	Region
1	Singapore Airlines	Singapore	Asia
2	Qatar Airways	Qatar	Middle East
3	ANA AII Nippon Airways	Japan	Asia
4	Emirates Airlines	United Arab Emirates	Middle East
5	Japan Airlines	United Arab Emirates	Middle East
6	Turkish Airlines	Turkey	Asia-Europe
7	Air France	France	Europe
8	Cathay Pacific Airways	Chinese	Asia
9	EVA Air	Taiwan	Asia
10	Korean Air	Korea	Asia

2. Subsequently, in order to understand whether regional differences make a difference in green transformation activities, Singapore Airlines from Asia, Qatar Airways from the Middle East, Air France from Europe and finally Turkish Airlines from Turkey, which is located between Asia and Europe, were selected as samples.

In the application part, multiple exploratory case studies, one of the qualitative research methods, were preferred. Although various approaches exist for analyzing qualitative data, this study opted for the method developed by Walcott (1994), which comprises description, analysis, and interpretation categories. Walcott's proposed method encourages researchers to narrate events in a specific order, emphasizing the direct transmission of the examined event to the reader (Walcott, 1994: 23-29; Özdemir, 2010: 331). The aim of descriptive analysis is to present the obtained findings to readers in a summarized and interpreted manner (Yıldırım & Şimşek, 2003).

RESULTS

The study initially aimed to evaluate and compare the green transformation activities of airline companies through sustainability reports. However, upon closer examination, it was found that Singapore Airlines had published sustainability reports starting from 2013, with the latest report containing data from April 1, 2022, to March 31, 2023. When examining Qatar Airways' sustainability reports, it was observed that the first report was issued in 2016, with the latest report covering data from April 1, 2019, to March 31, 2021. While corporate website pages of Air France provided declarations regarding environmental activities, no sustainability report for any year was found during the website review. Upon reviewing the corporate website of Turkish Airlines, statements regarding environmental activities were found, with some references made to sustainability reports in certain data. The sustainability reports page indicated that the first report was published in 2014, with the latest report containing data from January 1, 2022, to December 31, 2022. Due to the variability in the periods covered and the content of sustainability reports among airline companies, making comparisons was not feasible. Additionally, the absence of firm-specific reports from Air France further hindered comparative analysis. Therefore, to ensure traceability of environmental activities in the sector, the necessity of establishing a sectoral standard for reporting emerged once again.

As a result, the examination of websites became the most important method for comparing airline companies' green transformation activities in this study due to the lack of standardization in sustainability reports. Another important reason is the preference for examining green transformation from the perspective of customers. Sustainability reports are lengthy, detailed documents containing technical information, making it unlikely for customers to make purchase decisions based on them. In contrast, customers who consider environmental impact as a criterion for purchasing decisions can compare environmental activities declared on websites (due to their easily accessible information). Therefore, this study opted to compare environmental activities declared on websites to identify airline companies that create a green image for customers.

The numerical data regarding the examined airline companies are presented in Table 2 as part of the study.

Table 2. Numeric data for the examined airline companies

Airline Company	Year of Establishment	Country of Flights (2021)	Number of Aircrafts	Average Fleet Age (years)	Number of Employees	Number of Passengers (million)
Singapore Airlines + Scoot (Mart 2023)	1947	114	195	6,9	15,539	26,49
Qatar AirwayS (2019-2020)	1993	130	244	6	36,817	32,4
Air France (2023)	1933	120	255	13,7	39.000	83
Turkish Airlines (2022)	1933	129	394	8,7	29,520	71,8

The information presented in Table 2 has been compiled from corporate websites or sustainability reports of the respective airline companies. However, not all information may be up-to-date, and the dates covered by the reported information are provided alongside the names of the companies. As shown in Table 2, the oldest airline companies in terms of establishment year are THY and Air France, both founded in 1933. The youngest airline company is Qatar Airways, established in 1993. When examining the number of countries served by flights, it is observed that the numbers are close to each other across airlines. Regarding the number of aircraft, THY has the largest fleet with 394 aircraft. Examining the average fleet age, which is an important indicator for sustainability, Qatar Airways has the youngest fleet with 6 years, while Air France has the oldest fleet with 13.7 years. Regarding the number of employees, Air France has the highest number with 39,000 employees, and in terms of the number of passengers served, THY serves the highest number of passengers with 71.8 million.

In this section, the activities undertaken by the selected airline companies as part of their green transformation are presented based on declarations obtained from their corporate websites.

SINGAPORE AIRLINES

When examining the corporate website of Singapore Airlines (https://www.singaporeair.com/en_UK/tr/home#/book/bookflight, Accessed: Fabruary 2024), it is observed that it contains information about ticket sales along with the slogan "Welcome to the world class." There is no mention of environmental issues on the page. To understand the environmental activities of the company, one should navigate to the Sustainability tab under the Company section located at the bottom of the homepage. When reviewing the sustainability page (https://www.singaporeair.com/en_UK/tr/about-us/sustainability/, Accessed: Fabruary 2024), the slogan regarding sustainability is stated as "Every action is important for a sustainable sky." The company mentions its support for the United Nations 2030 Sustainable Development Goals in this section. Under the environmental heading in the table listing priority issues, the following items are included:

- Health and well-being,
- Clean water and sanitation,
- Affordable and clean energy,
- Industry, innovation, and infrastructure,
- Sustainable cities and communities,
- Responsible consumption and production,

- Climate action,
- Life on land,
- Partnerships for the goals.

The airline company mentioned its signature on the 10 principles of the United Nations Global Compact on its website, stating that information regarding these 10 principles can be found in the Sustainability Report. However, the link provided for reference leads to the company's 2019/2020 sustainability report. This discrepancy raises doubts about the currency of the page.

Additionally, the page mentions that projects are being carried out under the carbon offsetting program, and these projects are independently accredited. Carbon offsetting is defined on the page as follows (https://carbonoffset.singaporeair.com .sg, Accessed: 19.02.2024):

"Carbon offsetting allows individuals and businesses to reduce their environmental impacts. Travelers support environmental projects that either remove greenhouse gas emissions from the atmosphere (such as planting forests) or prevent future emissions (such as replacing a coal-fired power plant with a wind farm) by purchasing independently verified carbon offsets. One unit of carbon offsetting represents one metric ton of greenhouse gas emissions reduced or removed from the atmosphere."

When the links referenced under the heading are followed, a page is provided where individual travelers, cargo carriers, and corporate clients can calculate the carbon emissions related to their flights. On this page, when an example carbon offsetting calculation is conducted (https://carbonoffset.singaporeair.com.sg/, Accessed: 19.02.2024):

- Departure: Istanbul
- Arrival: Atlanta, USA
- Class: Economy – Round Trip
- CO2 Emissions: 684.06 kg
- Offset Cost: 8.89 SGD (Singapore Dollar) = 6.58 USD (United States Dollar) as calculated. The page also includes a payment screen.

The page provides three project examples for informational purposes on the impact of carbon offsetting:

1. **Conservation of Rainforests:** Following the information "Protect vital rainforests in Indonesia, conserve endangered species like orangutans, and support the development of local villages," successes achieved through the project are highlighted.
   - Over 7.5 million tons of greenhouse gas emissions are prevented annually,
   - More than 500 local individuals were directly employed to protect the forest from seasonal fires and manage the project,
   - Financial empowerment of over 850 local women was achieved through management workshops and microfinance distribution from forestry projects,
   - Learning resources were produced for local students and the community to educate them about ecosystem restoration and the health effects of forest fires.
2. **Solar Energy:** "Invest in solar energy projects that generate renewable electricity nationwide in India and support sustainable development of local economies," followed by the successes achieved through the project, is presented.
   - Over 815,000 tons of greenhouse gas emissions are prevented annually,
   - Engineering, commerce, and science graduates are employed in the projects, and a mentorship program is implemented to enhance their skills,
   - A portion of the revenue from these projects is allocated to support access to local health services, including check-up clinics and child health, and to provide families with healthy nutrition education.
3. **Clean Cooking:** "Assist in the distribution of efficient, clean-burning stoves to reduce smoke pollution and associated health risks for villagers in Nepal," followed by the successes achieved through the project are highlighted.
   - Each year, over 50,000 tons of greenhouse gas emissions are prevented.
   - More than 47,000 families in Nepal have been provided with stoves.
   - Exposure to health-damaging pollutants in the air is reduced thanks to the project.
   - Household fuelwood expenditures are reduced by up to 50% through the project.
   - The pressure on local forests for timber is alleviated through the project.
   - Community-led project management experience is developed through the project.

Additionally, the page includes a Frequently Asked Questions section, providing answers to questions such as "What is carbon offsetting?", "How does carbon offsetting work for flights?", and "How do you know offsetting has occurred?" Lastly, the company asserts its transparency by stating that it has provided a total of 11 sustainability reports on the page since the 2012/2013 reporting period.

QATAR AIRLINES

When accessing Qatar Airways' website (https://www.qatarairways.com/en-am/homepage.html, Accessed: 22.02.2024), it is noted that information regarding flight details, travel plans, promotions, and new route recommendations is provided, with no indication of any references to green transformation. Upon scrolling down the page, under the heading of **Qatar Airways**, a tab for **Environmental Sustainability** is visible (https://www.qatarairways.com/en/about-qatar-airways/environmental-awareness/climate-energy.html, Accessed: 22.02.2024). Upon visiting the ***environmental sustainability*** page under the Sustainability tab, a video addressing the company's environmental approach is presented alongside environmental initiatives. The slogan "Protecting Our Environment for a Sustainable Future" accompanies the company's environmental activities, which include:

1. **Climate and Energy:** The company has declared its adoption of the International Air Transport Association's (IATA) Four Pillars of Climate Strategy. Under the Technology heading, it is stated that the company supports goals of reduced noise and emissions with a modern fleet. Engineering efforts aimed at reducing friction and increasing efficiency for aircraft bodies and engines are highlighted. Under the Sustainable Aviation Fuel (SAF) heading, collaborative efforts with industry stakeholders are mentioned, with a commitment to achieving 100% SAF usage by 2030. Under the Compliance with Global Market-Based Measures heading, it is acknowledged that achieving climate goals requires technology, operational measures, and better infrastructure, with a commitment to measures aimed at emission reduction. Under the Zero Carbon Emissions by 2050 heading, Qatar Airways is stated to be committed to the ambitious goal of achieving net-zero carbon emissions by 2050.
2. **Waste and Water Management:** The initiatives implemented to reduce waste and promote recycling throughout all stages of operations in line with the principles of circular economy are listed:
   – ***Reduction of single-use plastics:*** It is noted that the use of recyclable and biodegradable products for in-flight meal services has increased by 80%.
   – ***Recycling materials:*** It is indicated that the catering department at Hamad Airport recycles over 1,000 tons of packaging materials, 52 tons of magazines, and 5,000 gallons of cooking oil annually, and green waste from landscaping is composted and used as fertilizer.
   – ***Reduction of food waste:*** Collaboration with local organizations is mentioned to distribute 200-300 kg of fruits and grains daily to those in need.

– ***Water conservation:*** The airline is recognized as the first to significantly reduce water usage during engine cleaning; smart water solutions such as sensor taps, utilizing condensation water from air conditioners for cleaning, and using recycled water for landscaping irrigation are adopted.

3. **Conservation of Wildlife:** The page first highlights Qatar Airways' leadership in preventing illegal wildlife trafficking through its partnership with United for Wildlife (UfW). It is then mentioned that the airline was the first to receive the International Air Transport Association's (IATA) certification for combating illegal wildlife trafficking in 2019. Finally, under the WeQare initiative, the "WeQare: Rewild the Planet" project launched in 2020 is highlighted, stating that endangered animals are transported to their natural habitats free of charge.

Upon accessing the information from https://www.qatarairways.com/en/about-qatar-airways/environmental-awareness/climate-energy.html, it was noticed that sustainability reports were not available, prompting a further search using search engines. Unlike the previous page, the website https://www.qatarairways.com/tr-tr/about-qatar-airways/environmental-awareness.html contains ***carbon offsetting programs*** and ***sustainability reports***. Clicking on the carbon offsetting program link leads to the "climate and energy" page; however, no information related to carbon offsetting is found on the page.

The website initially provides sustainability reports dating back to 2016, including those for the years 2017, 2018, 2019, and most recently, 2021.

The discrepancies between pages, the lack of consistency in sustainability reports, and the most recent report being for the year 2021 raise concerns about the traceability of Qatar Airways' green transformation efforts and call into question the seriousness of their commitment to the issue.

AIRFRANCE

When accessing the Air France website (https://wwws.airfrance.fr/), it is observed that it provides flight information, travel plans, news, promotions, and recommendations for new routes, without any indication of green transformation. Upon scrolling down and accessing the ***Air France Corporate*** link under the ***Air France and Partners*** section, the emphasis is on Current News. In the middle of the page, all key figures related to the company are provided, with a ***Sustainability*** subsection indicating the goal of "balancing CO2 emissions per passenger/kilometer with 2019 levels by 2030." Transitioning to the ***All Key Figures*** page (https://corporate.airfrance.com/en/about-air-france/key-figures, Accessed: 27.02.2024); various headings such as employees, fleet, sustainability, employer brand, employee diversity, passenger transportation, airport lounges, gastronomy, cargo, maintenance, IT and data technologies, ground services operation, social networks, Air France Foundation, and loyalty programs are listed. Upon accessing the ***Sustainability*** tab, the page displays the slogan "Taking action against the climate crisis" alongside the indication of the latest update being on April 26, 2023, and the presence of three goals:

- Reducing CO2 emissions per passenger/kilometer to 2019 levels by 2030,
- Achieving a 25% reduction in CO2 emissions for a new generation aircraft,
- Increasing the use of sustainable aviation fuel to 10% by 2030.

The page does not contain any other information regarding green transformation.

Upon returning to the Air France corporate tab, beyond the significant figures, information on **employment**, **sustainable development**, and **foundation** details is observed. Upon navigating to the sustainable development page (https://corporate.airfrance.com/en/sustainable-development, Accessed: 29.02.2024), alongside the slogan "The next generation is looking at us," on the left side of the page, there are sections titled "The next generation," "Our carbon footprint," "Other impacts," "Key figures," "Our commitments," and "Main actions."

When accessing the ***Our Carbon Footprint*** page, it is noted that nearly 90% of Air France's emissions stem from aircraft fuel consumption. It is emphasized that decarbonizing operations entails limiting fuel consumption and gradually replacing fossil fuels with alternative fuels emitting less CO2.

On the ***Other Impacts*** page, it is highlighted that besides CO2, aircraft also produce other emissions contributing to global warming, such as water vapor, particulate matter, and nitrogen oxides. It is mentioned that efforts are undertaken to address these emissions as well.

When you go to the ***Key Figures*** page https://corporate.airfrance.com/en/about-air-france/key-figures), you are directed to the information mentioned above.

When you click on the ***Our Commitments*** section, you will find information organized under three headings:

1. *To reduce CO2 emissions as soon as possible*: The target aims for a 30% reduction in emissions per passenger-kilometer **by 2030** compared to 2019. To achieve this, three main actions have been identified:
   - **Fleet renewal**: It is stated that transitioning to new-generation aircraft with 20-25% lower CO2 emissions is the most effective way to reduce the carbon footprint. These aircraft also reduce noise footprint by 40%. New-generation aircraft also reduce fuel consumption per passenger (currently, aircraft consume 3.3 liters of fuel per passenger per 100 km. The target is to consume less than 3 liters per passenger per 100 km by

2030. New-generation aircraft made with lightweight materials enable a 25% reduction in fuel consumption). It is aimed that 45% of the fleet will consist of new-generation aircraft by 2025 and 70% by 2030.
- **Gradual use of sustainable aviation fuel (SAF):** Air France states that it has been a pioneer in SAF usage since 2011. While noting that SAF production is limited, it is also mentioned that its price is 4 to 8 times that of regular fuels. Therefore, the company indicates its efforts to improve production in collaboration with academic and industrial partners. Targets for transitioning to SAF are declared as 10% by 2030 and 63% by 2050.
- **Eco-piloting:** Eco-piloting, which is environmentally sensitive piloting, aims to develop and implement piloting techniques to reduce fuel consumption and increase flight efficiency in the air and on the ground without compromising flight safety and punctuality. It is stated that eco-piloting practices lead to an average reduction of 4-5% in fuel consumption and CO2 emissions, although the target is 10%.

2. *Reducing our indirect CO2 emissions:* Efforts are being made to reduce indirect emissions through the development of alternative transportation and more responsible catering services activities in collaboration with the entire ecosystem (customers, suppliers, and partners). Under this heading, subcategories include **integrating different modes of transportation** and **responsible catering services**.
3. *Removing CO2 from the atmosphere:* Projects related to forests and mangroves that absorb and store carbon from the atmosphere are supported. Under this heading, it is stated that efforts are made to combat deforestation and that a research-action program aimed at preserving and restoring mangroves in Martinique under the French Low Carbon Label is supported.

Upon navigating to the ***Our main actions*** page, it is observed that there are four main headings, with the first three being identical to the items listed under the ***Our commitments*** heading, and they redirect to the same pages:

- Fleet renewal
- Sustainable aviation fuel
- Eco-piloting
- Integration of different modes of transportation: The page emphasizes opting for low-carbon alternatives for short journeys and more efficient flights for long journeys to reduce travel carbon footprint. The company has been offering a service for customers to combine train and air travel in the same

reservation with guaranteed connections for over 25 years. Efforts to expand the "Train + Air" offer are also mentioned.

- Under the "More responsible catering" heading, green transformation activities in catering services are highlighted.
- More responsible dining and fair consumption: Local and seasonal products are preferred on flights departing from Paris.
- Waste reduction: Stringent stock control policies are implemented to prevent waste. Passengers are encouraged to select their meals before flights, allowing only the consumed items to be loaded onto the aircraft, thereby reducing waste and contributing to fuel consumption reduction through weight reduction on the aircraft.
- Elimination of single-use plastics: Both onboard and on-ground plastic materials are being replaced with biodegradable alternatives. The commitment to replace single-use plastic items (cups, forks, knives, trays, etc.) on aircraft between 2018 and 2023 was stated on the page. However, as of February 2024, there is no information indicating the achievement of this goal.
- Recyclable packaging: Since 2019, all flights from Paris have separated packaging for recyclability. The aim is to expand this practice to all stations.

Upon a detailed examination of the corporate website, Air France presents its environmental activities and goals accompanied by successful visuals. However, there is no information indicating the publication of a sustainability report on the page. Subsequently, a search on search engines revealed that the airline partnership Air France-KLM, formed by the merger of French Air France and Dutch KLM in 2004, published a sustainability report for the year 2021 on June 28, 2022 (https://air-france-klm-2.foleon.com/sustainability-report-afklm/sustainability-report-2022/ , Accessed: 02.03.2024).

TURKISH AIRLINES

When accessing the website of Turkish Airlines (THY) (https://www.turkishairlines.com/tr-int/), flight information, campaigns, promotions, new route recommendations, and information about awards are visible, while no mention of green transformation is found. Upon scrolling down to the bottom of the page and entering the **Turkish Airlines** link under the **corporate** heading, a subheading for **sustainability** is observed. Upon visiting the page (https://www.turkishairlines.com/tr-int/turk-hava-yollarinda-surdurulebilirlik/, Accessed: 05.03.2024), at the top section:

- Sustainability at Turkish Airlines,

- Our Approach to Sustainability
- CO2mission
- Our Reports

the headings are seen to be present.

Under the title **sustainability** at Turkish Airlines, a sustainability strategy has been outlined. Underneath that, under the heading of ***sustainability policy***, the following items are listed:

- Embracing a corporate governance culture,
- Combatting climate change,
- Considering people and the environment while growing,
- Adding value to stakeholders,
- Enhancing gender balance among employees,
- Supporting innovation,
- Adding value to society,
- Compliance with ethical conduct principles,
- Sustainable growth and profitability,
- Continuous improvement.

On the page, there is no explanation provided for the items. As you scroll down the page, there are sections titled **High-Priority Issues** and **By the Numbers 2022**.

Under the **high-priority issues** section, climate change, waste management, fleet modernization and development are listed as very high-priority issues. Under the ***priority issues*** section, water management, single-use plastics, sustainable catering, noise management, responsible supply chain management are listed. Lastly, under the ***significant issues*** section, human-induced environmental disasters, animal welfare, and biodiversity loss are mentioned as green transformation-related issues.

When navigating to the page through the **CO2mission** *link on the sustainability page (https://www.turkishairlines.com/tr-int/co2mission/, Accessed: 05.03.2024), the first section encountered is titled "How Flight-related Carbon Footprint will be Balanced." Under this title, the following items are listed: "Identification of Flight Information," "Calculation of Carbon Footprint," "Equivalent of Calculated Emission Quantity," "Completion of the Process and Certification." However, none of these items appear to be active. Following the provided information, three headings are presented with accompanying visuals:*

- Explore renewable energy portfolio and renewable energy-related projects.

- Explore green world portfolio and review afforestation projects.
- Explore social benefit portfolio and obtain information about renewable energy sources and the cookstove project.

The above headings are not active, and no additional information can be accessed under the headings. Below the provided information, a website link is given under the title "CO2mission," where the carbon footprint calculation website initiated by THY can be accessed. When the link is clicked (https://turkishairlines.co2mission.com/ , Accessed: 06.03.2024), the website related to THY's carbon offsetting project is opened. By navigating to the calculation tab on the page, a calculation was performed using the example used in the carbon offsetting calculation of Singapore Airlines.

- Departure: Istanbul
- Arrival: Atlanta, USA
- Class: Economy - Round Trip
- CO2 Emissions: 383 kg

To offset the emissions, three different projects are presented, and the offsetting cost varies depending on the chosen project:

a. Renewable energy package: 80% wind energy, 15% hydroelectric, 5% solar energy - offsetting cost is calculated as 263.89 Turkish Lira = 8.25 US Dollars.
b. Social benefit package: 40% improved cooking stoves, 35% wind energy, 25% hydroelectric - offsetting cost is calculated as 369.45 Turkish Lira = 11.55 US Dollars.
c. Green world package: 45% afforestation, 40% wind energy, 15% solar energy - offsetting cost is calculated as 316.67 Turkish Lira = 9.90 US Dollars.

The carbon emission quantity for a flight from Istanbul to Atlanta (USA) in economy class is calculated as 684.06 kg by Singapore Airlines, whereas it is calculated as 383 kg by Turkish Airlines. While the difference in the proposed costs for carbon offsetting may be acceptable, the discrepancy in carbon emission values is not understandable. This situation once again highlights the necessity of established common standards within the industry.

Upon entering the flight details on the website and selecting the contribution to a specific project, the subsequent page provides information on how much offsetting is achieved under the headings of driving, meat consumption, lamp usage, glacier melting, along with the transition to payment details.

The project information, which is inaccessible despite being mentioned in the headings on the Turkish Airlines corporate website, is also available on the https://turkishairlines.co2mission.com/ page.

- **Renewable energy portfolio:**

1. ***Elazığ Turkey Gezin Solar Energy Project:*** Aims to generate electricity from solar energy to be transmitted to Turkey's national grid. (Offset: 76,524.25 kgCO2)
2. ***Gümüşhane Turkey - Büyükdüz Hydroelectric Power Plant:*** As a result of the project activities, no emissions will occur. Consequently, through a zero-emission project, reduction in greenhouse gas emissions will occur. (Offset: 3,139,572.75 kgCO2)
3. ***Balıkesir Turkey Bares II Wind Energy Plant:*** The objective of this project is to produce electricity from wind, a renewable source, and transmit it to Turkey's national grid. (Offset: 849,388 kgCO2)

- **Green World Portfolio:**

1. ***Belém Brazil Maisa REDD+ Project:*** The project aims to reduce emissions from unplanned deforestation, mitigate leakage risks, and address permanence risks related to forests. (Offset: 207,844.48 kgCO2)
2. ***Cerro Largo Uruguay Guanaré Forest Farming Project:*** This afforestation project targets wood production, land restoration, and carbon sequestration. (Offset: 199,894.72 kgCO2)
3. ***Elazığ Turkey Gezin Solar Energy Project:*** Aims to generate electricity from solar energy to be transmitted to Turkey's national grid. (Offset: 119,246.4 kgCO2)
4. ***Balıkesir Turkey Bares II Wind Energy Plant Project:*** The objective of this project is to produce electricity from wind, a renewable source, and transmit it to Turkey's national grid. (Offset: 317,990.4 kgCO2)

- **Social Benefit Portfolio:**

1. ***Anseba Eritrea Improved Kitchen Management Project:*** Involves the distribution of approximately 8,000 fuel-efficient cooking stoves to households in the Anseba region of Eritrea. (Offset: 39,246 kgCO2)

2. ***Gümüşhane Turkey - Büyükdüz Hydroelectric Power Plant Project:*** A river-type renewable energy plant located in Turkey. As a result of this project's activities, no emissions will occur, leading to a reduction in greenhouse gas emissions through a zero-emission project. (Offset: 8,903.75 kgCO2)
3. ***Balıkesir Turkey Bares II Wind Energy Plant Project:*** The project aims to generate electricity from wind, a renewable source, and transmit it to Turkey's national grid. (Offset: 12,465.25 kgCO2)

At the bottom of the page at https://www.turkishairlines.com/tr-int/co2mission/, frequently asked questions about carbon offsetting are provided to offer information on the subject. It remains unclear why details regarding carbon emissions, calculations, and related projects are not presented on this page, and instead, users are redirected to https://turkishairlines.co2mission.com/.

Finally, when the **Reports** section is accessed on the page https://www.turkishairlines.com/tr-int/turk-hava-yollarinda-surdurulebilirlik/,

- ***Sustainability reports:*** It is observed that Turkish Airlines has consistently prepared and published nine sustainability reports between 2014 and 2022.
- ***CDP reports:*** The Carbon Disclosure Project (CDP) reports for the years 2021, 2022, and 2023 are provided on the page.
- ***Environmental dimensions:*** The THY Environmental Dimensions and Impacts report is available. In this eight-page report, the environmental dimensions and impacts resulting from the company's activities, products, and services are identified, along with actions taken to reduce these impacts.
- ***Ethical values***
- ***Sustainability performance indicators:*** The 2022 sustainability performance indicators report is included. The report presents comparative data for all sustainability indicators for the years 2018, 2019, 2020, 2021, and 2022.
- ***Sustainability summaries and assessments:*** Sustainability reports for the years 2021 and 2022 are provided.
- ***SASB reports:*** The 2022 SASB report is included. (SASB - Sustainability Accounting Standards Board) which informs investors and the public about companies' sustainability-related activities through reporting (Öktem & Karabınar, 2022: 823)).
- ***Sustainable procurement policy:*** The document regarding the sustainable procurement policy is provided.

The examination revealed that Turkish Airlines (THY) has conducted more extensive work in sustainability reporting compared to other businesses.

CONCLUSION

This study was conducted within the scope of investigating green transformation activities carried out by airline companies in the current conditions where the effects of climate change are increasingly felt, aiming to reduce their environmental impacts. Four airline companies, operating in different regions and listed in the "World's Best Airlines" list, were selected using purposive sampling method for the research. In order to identify the green transformation activities of airline companies, a detailed examination of their corporate websites, which are crucial tools for portraying a green image, was conducted. Initially, the research sought answers to the question: "What kind of practices do the world's largest airline companies implement within the scope of green transformation?" The prominent green transformation activities identified through the examined websites are presented below:

- There is no mention of the environment on **Singapore Airlines'** corporate website. When the **Sustainability** tab under the **Company** section is accessed, the airline states that it is a signatory to the Ten Principles of the United Nations Global Compact and refers to the Sustainability Report for information on these ten principles. It is observed that the airline has published a total of 11 sustainability reports since the 2012/2013 period. On the page dedicated to carbon offsetting prepared by the airline, there is a carbon offsetting calculator, a payment screen for balancing the calculated value, and project examples related to the impacts that can be achieved with carbon offsetting. It is seen that the presented projects are implemented in Indonesia, India, and Nepal.
- On the website of **Qatar Airways**, under the Qatar Airways section, when the page for environmental sustainability is accessed, the company's environmental approach is expressed along with a video prepared about the environment. Under the climate and energy section of Qatar Airways, it is stated that ambitious goals are set to achieve 100% Sustainable Aviation Fuel (SAF) usage by 2030 and a net zero carbon emissions target by 2050, in collaboration with industry stakeholders. Additionally, the page presents the activities undertaken and achievements obtained in waste and water management.
- It is observed that Qatar Airways elaborates on its environmental activities and works on disseminating them to all personnel. Interestingly, Qatar Airways is noted for leading efforts to prevent illegal wildlife trade. The company has published sustainability reports for the years 2017, 2018, 2019, and 2021, with the first report being released in 2016. However, difficulties in accessing these reports, the lack of a consistent reporting period, and the most recent report being for 2021 limit the traceability of Qatar Airways' efforts in green transformation and raise questions about its seriousness regarding the matter.

– On the Air France website (https://wwws.airfrance.fr/), under the ***Air France and Partners*** section, when accessing the ***Air France Corporate*** link, it is evident that the "Latest News" section is highlighted. In the middle of the page, all important figures related to the company are provided, and under the ***Sustainability*** subheading, there is a goal stating that "By 2030, CO2 emissions per passenger/kilometer will be balanced with 2019 levels." Upon navigating to the ***Sustainability*** tab, the page indicates three defined goals alongside the slogan "Taking action against the climate crisis," with the latest update dated April 26, 2023. No other information related to green transformation is found on the page. **Under the Sustainable Development** section, which is located under the Air France corporate tab, subcategories such as "Our Carbon Footprint," "Other Impacts," "Key Points," "Commitments," and "Main Actions" are listed. Among the provided information, it is noteworthy that under the ***Other Impacts*** section, emissions other than CO2, such as water vapor, particulate matter, and nitrogen oxides, which contribute to global warming, are also acknowledged, indicating efforts are being made in this regard. *These activities should be considered as good practice examples for other businesses.*

– Air France stands out by featuring the **Eco-piloting** program, which is environmentally conscious pilotage, a practice not commonly found in other businesses, on its webpage. Additionally, under the title "Our Main Actions," the company introduces a unique practice of combining different modes of transportation. Through the "Train + Air" initiative, the company offers customers an alternative for low-carbon or more efficient travel. The environmentally friendly practices presented under the subheading of "More Responsible Catering" are significant for setting an example in the industry. However, it is noteworthy that the information on the page is not up-to-date. Although the sustainability report for 2021 of Air France-KLM, formed through a partnership with the Dutch airline KLM, is available, Air France itself has not published its own report.

– When accessing the Turkish Airlines corporate website and navigating to the **Turkish Airlines** section, under the **corporate** heading, there is a subheading for **sustainability**, followed by a ***sustainability policy*** and, beneath that, headings for ***priority areas***. In this section, priority areas related to green transformation are highlighted, including human-induced environmental disasters, animal welfare, and biodiversity loss, which differ from those of other businesses.

– When accessing the **CO2mission** link on the THY Sustainability page, information about carbon offsetting and related projects is provided, but the headings appear to be inactive. Users are redirected to a different page titled ***CO2mission***, where they can calculate the carbon footprint resulting from flights. However, upon visiting this page, it's noted that a sample calculation has been conducted, yielding different results compared to the carbon calculation option provided by Singapore Airlines. Additionally, three different project portfolios are presented on the page to offset the emissions, which is a practice not commonly found in other airline operators. The offsetting cost for flight-related emissions varies for each project portfolio, allowing customers the choice to select their preference.

– Under the THY corporate/sustainability heading, details of projects are provided, although their descriptions are inaccessible. Various projects are listed under three different project portfolios, but it's deemed inappropriate for the same project to appear under different headings. The implemented projects span across different regions, including Turkey (Elazığ, Gümüşhane, Balıkesir), Brazil (Belém), Uruguay (Cerro Largo), and Eritrea (Anseba), indicating THY's engagement in global environmental initiatives.

– Upon visiting the **Our Reports** section on THY's sustainability page, it is evident that the company has been regularly publishing numerous reports on sustainability and environmental matters since 2014. This indicates that the company is more successful in terms of reporting and monitoring environmental activities compared to other businesses.

As observed, all of the major airline operators selected as the sample implement both similar and different activities within the scope of green transformation. While Turkish Airlines stands out more prominently in terms of reporting, AirFrance appears to be more successful in innovative practices. In this context, it is recommended that airline operators ensure coherence in their core activities, follow good practice examples, and develop more innovative approaches within the scope of green transformation.

The investigations also addressed the question, *Do the green transformation activities of airline operators vary according to the regions where they operate?* Actions required to achieve net zero targets in sustainability in aviation include; - Increasing operational efficiency; - Using Sustainable Aviation Fuel (SAF), - Employing next-generation aircraft, and - Managing unavoidable emissions (source: https://www.semtrio.com, Accessed: 07.03.2024). It has been observed that all examined airline operators are conducting activities within the framework of these specified headings. The activities implemented by airline operators show parallelism with each other, and there is no regional difference apparent in their approaches.

Promoting eco-friendly travel options holds a significant place in shaping the green image of airline operators (Wu, Cheng, & Ai, 2018; Hwang & Lyu, 2019; Koç, 2023). However, the most notable commonality among all examined airline operators is the absence of any mention of green transformation on their corporate websites. Customers visiting the airline operator's webpage to purchase tickets do not encounter any information related to green transformation. This indicates the inadequacy of airline operators in creating awareness and their lack of enthusiasm in creating a green image.

Businesses disseminate their activities through their corporate websites to increase visibility and gain support from passengers (Niu, Liu, Chang, & Ye, 2016; Altuğ & Akyol, 2018). However, when looking at the airline operators included in the study, it is necessary to navigate between pages on corporate websites or even conduct new searches on search engines to identify their green transformation activities. This situation creates the perception that businesses undertake green transformation activities not for customers or society but rather to inform investors or industry stakeholders. It is recommended that green transformation activities be published on corporate websites and sales screens in the most accessible way possible to contribute to the development of passengers' environmental awareness. Additionally, this would ensure that relevant commitments are clearly articulated and their currency is monitored.

The most significant limitation of the study is that it was conducted within four airline operators. In future studies, it is recommended to expand the sample size and include sustainability reports in the research, or even conduct interviews with company officials to broaden the scope of research on green transformation.

REFERENCES

Alagöz, S. (2007). Yeşil pazarlama ve eko etiketleme. *Akademik Bakış*, (11), 1–13.

Altuğ, T., & Akyol, A. (2018). Kurumsal yeşil imajın kurumsal web sitelerinde aktarımı: arçelik ve bosch örneği. *İnif E-Dergi, 3*(1), 194-212.

Amankwah-Amoah, J. (2020). Stepping up and stepping out of COVID-19: New challenges for environmental sustainability policies in the global airline industry. *Journal of Cleaner Production*, 271, 1–8. 10.1016/j.jclepro.2020.12300032834564

Bort, S. (2023). *The Environmental Commitment Of European Commercial Aviation: The Case Of Low-Cost Airlines*. Universitat Jaume. https://repositori.uji.es/xmlui/bitstream/handle/10234/203491/TFG_2023_Beltran_Bort_Sergio.pdf?sequence=1

Ceylan, U., & Kıpırtı, F. (2021). Turizm işletmelerinde yeşil pazarlama faaliyetleri: literatür incelemesi. *Socrates Journal of Interdisciplinary Social Studies*, 23-37. .10.51293/socrates.22

Chan, G., Wang, B., Zhang, V., & Li, M. (2021). Predicting psychological benefit in green for airlines passengers affect organization corporate image to switching decision. [IJSSR]. *International Journal of Social Science Research*, 3(4), 183–200.

Cheba, K., Bąk, I., Szopik-Depczynska, K., & Ioppolo, G. (2022). Directions of green transformation of the European Union countries. *Ecological Indicators*, 136, 1–15. 10.1016/j.ecolind.2022.108601

Choudhary, A., & Gokarn, S. (2013). Green marketing: A means for sustainable development. *International Refereed Research Journal*, 4(3), 26–32.

Duru, M., & Şua, E. (2013). Yeşil pazarlama ve tüketicilerin çevre dostu ürünleri kullanma eğilimleri. *Ormancılık Dergisi*, 9(2), 126–136. 10.54452/jrb.993685

Erbaşlar, G. (2012). Yeşil pazarlama. *Mesleki Bilimler Dergisi*, 1(2), 94–101.

Fathi, B., Ansari, A., & Ansari, A. (2023). Green Commercial Aviation Supply Chain—A European Path to Environmental Sustainability. *Sustainability (Basel)*, 15(8), 1–14. 10.3390/su15086574

Gedik, Y. (2020). Yeşil pazarlama stratejileri ve işletmelerin amaçlarına etkisi. *Sosyal Bilimler Dergisi*, 6(2), 46–65.

Günaydın, D. (2018). Türkiye'de Dördüncü Sanayi Devrimini Beklerken: Çerkezköy Organize Sanayi Bölgesi'nde Bir Araştırma. *Istanbul Management Journal*, 73-106.

Hagmann, C., Semeijn, J., & Vellenga, D. (2015). Exploring the green image of airlines: Passenger perceptions and airline choice. *Journal of Air Transport Management*, 43(4), 37–45. 10.1016/j.jairtraman.2015.01.003

Hartmann, P., & Apaolaza-Ibáñez, V. (2009). Green advertising revisited. *International Journal of Advertising*, 28(4), 715–739. 10.2501/S0265048709200837

Hooper, P. D., & Greenall, A. (2005). Exploring the Potential for Environmental Performance Benchmarking in the Airline Sector. *Benchmarking*, 12(2), 151–165. 10.1108/14635770510593095

Hwang, J., & Lyu, S. (2019). Relationships among green image, consumer attitudes, desire, and customer citizenship behavior in the airline industry. *International Journal of Sustainable Transportation*, 1–11. 10.1080/15568318.2019.1573280

Karakuş, G. (2023). Türk Hava Yolları sürdürülebilirlik raporları üzerine bir araştırma. *Aerospace Research Letters (ASREL). Dergisi*, 2(2), 86–113. 10.56753/ASREL.2023.2.4

Koç, E. (2023). Green marketing strategies and climate change awareness in sustainable transportation: The case of airline companies. *Marine Science and Technology Bulletin*, 12(4), 459–472. 10.33714/masteb.1375842

Kotler, P., & Armstrong, G. (2018). *Pazarlama İlkeleri (Çeviri Editörü:A. Ercan Gegez)*. Beta.

Mayer, R., Ryley, T., & Gillingwater, D. (2014). The role of green marketing: Insights from three airline case studies. *The Journal of Sustainable Mobility*, 1(2), 46–72. 10.9774/GLEAF.2350.2014.no.00005

Nittala, R., & Moturu, V. (2023). Role of pro-environmental post-purchase behaviour in green consumer behaviour. *Vilakshan-XIMB Journal of Management*, 82-97.

Niu, S.-Y., Liu, C.-L., Chang, C.-C., & Ye, K.-D. (2016). What are passenger perspectives regarding airlines' environmental protection? An empirical investigation in Taiwan. *Journal of Air Transport Management*, 55, 84–91. 10.1016/j.jairtraman.2016.04.012

Öktem, B., & Karabınar, S. (2022). SASB Raporu Yayınlayan Şirketlerin Finansal Başarısızlıkları ile Sürdürülebilirlik Raporları Arasındaki İlişkinin Analizi. *Istanbul Journal of Economics/İstanbul Iktisat Dergisi, 72*(2).

Olk, S. (2021). The effect of self-congruence on perceived green claims' authenticity and perceived greenwashing: The case of EasyJet's CO2 promise. *Journal of Nonprofit & Public Sector Marketing*, 33(2), 114–131. 10.1080/10495142.2020.1798859

Özcan, H., & Özgül, B. (2019). Yeşil pazarlama ve tüketicilerin yeşil ürün tercihlerini etkileyen faktörler. *Türkiye Mesleki ve Sosyal Bilimler Dergisi*, 1(1), 1–18. 10.46236/jovosst.562230

Özdemir, M. (2010). Nitel veri analizi: Sosyal bilimlerde yöntembilim sorunsalı üzerine bir çalışma. *Eskişehir Osmangazi Üniversitesi Sosyal Bilimler Dergisi*, 11(1), 323–343.

Pimonenko, T., Bilan, Y., Horák, J., Starchenko, L., & Gajda, W. (2020). Green brand of companies and greenwashing under sustainable development goals. *Sustainability (Basel)*, 12(4), 1–15. 10.3390/su12041679

Priyadarshi, A., & Prasad, D. (2023). An evaluation of green marketing policies on millennial customers towards the environment. *SSRN*, 1-12. 10.2139/ssrn.4400380

Rosskopf, M., Lehner, S., & Gollnick, V. (2014). Economic-environmental trade-offs in long-term airline fleet planning. *Journal of Air Transport Management*, 34, 109–115. 10.1016/j.jairtraman.2013.08.004

Scoones, I., Newell, P., & Leach, M. (2015). The Politics of Green Transformations. I. (Editors) Scoones, P. Newell, & M. Leach içinde, *The Politics of Green Transformations* (s. 1-24). London and New York: Routledge.

Tekin, M., & Zerenler, M. (2012). *Pazarlama*. Günay Ofset.

Walcott, H. F. (1994). *Transforming qualitative data: Description, analysis and interpretation*. SAGE Publications.

Wang, J., Wang, S., Xue, H., Wang, Y., & Li, J. (2018). Green image and consumers' word-of-mouth intention in the green hotel industry: The moderating effect of Millennials. *Journal of Cleaner Production*, 181, 426–436. 10.1016/j.jclepro.2018.01.250

Wu, H.-C., Cheng, C.-C., & Ai, C.-H. (2018). An empirical analysis of green switching intentionsin the airline industry. *Journal of Environmental Planning and Management*, 61(8), 1438–1468. 10.1080/09640568.2017.1352495

Yıldırım, A., & Şimşek, H. (2003). *Sosyal Bilimlerde Nitel Araştırma Yöntemleri*. Seçkin Yayınları, Ankara. https://www.worldairlineawards.com/worlds-top-10-airlines-2023/,

KEY TERMS AND DEFINITIONS

Green Image: Consumers' perceptions of green activities related to a business.

Green Marketing: It is the realisation of marketing activities from an environmentalist point of view.

Sustainability: It is to act by considering environmental, economic and social parameters in all processes of businesses in order to be permanent.

Chapter 11
An Interdisciplinary Study on the Nexus of English Language, Social Psychology, and Emerging Global Economy

Sinan Özyurt
Gaziantep Islam Science and Technology University, Turkey

Mehmet Emin Kalgı
https://orcid.org/0000-0001-6999-5059
Ardahan University, Turkey

ABSTRACT

This study examines the interrelationship between English language, social psychology, and global economics. In this sense, through the present study, it is aimed to highlight their joint impact on behavior and societal norms. As the global lingua franca, the role of English in cultural adaptation and economic decision-making is investigated in order to reveal how linguistic proficiency and psychological factors influence economic behaviors and trends in a global context. The research delves into the effects of globalization and technology on language use and psychological well-being, suggesting that the synergy among these elements shapes economic resilience as well. By integrating insights across various disciplines, the findings propose a number of effective strategies for promoting economic growth and social cohesion by offering valuable implications for policymakers and business leaders

DOI: 10.4018/979-8-3693-3439-3.ch011

aiming at inclusive global development and economic resilience.

INTRODUCTION

In the contemporary era, characterized by an intricate web of global interconnections and the relentless pace of globalization, the imperative to navigate and comprehend the complex relationships among the English language, social psychology, and global economic movements has never been more critical. This complex interplay underscores the essence of adopting interdisciplinary perspectives that go beyond the confines of traditional academic disciplines, thereby providing a more nuanced and comprehensive understanding of the multifarious dynamics that govern our increasingly interconnected globe. In fact, the significance of interdisciplinary approaches cannot be overstated, as they offer a unique lens through which it gets likely to view and analyze phenomena that are inherently complex and multidimensional. These approaches allow for the integration of knowledge and methodologies from various fields—such as linguistics, psychology, and economics—to explore the intricate web of interactions and dependencies that lie at the heart of societal developments. Such a synthesis not only enriches the academic discourse by introducing diverse perspectives but also paves the way for innovative solutions to contemporary challenges, promoting a more integrated and holistic approach to problem-solving (Garcia et al., 2021).

The primary aims of this study are manifold. First, it is aimed to dissect and understand the collective influence exerted by the English language, social psychology, and global economic patterns on individual actions, societal norms, and economic structures. Second, it aspires to map out the complex web of interconnections among these spheres, illuminating the various pathways through which language, psychological processes, and economic activities reciprocally influence and mold each other. At the heart of our inquiry is the profound interconnectedness binding the English language, social psychology, and global economic trends in recent years. It is quite evident that English, as the global lingua franca, plays a pivotal role in facilitating international communication and exchange of knowledge, thereby acting as a bridge across cultural divides and enhancing cross-cultural comprehension (Smith & Johnson, 2020). Its influence, however, transcends communication; it also significantly influences social identities, cultural norms, and the dynamics of intergroup relations, which affects both individual and collective behaviors on a global scale (Brown & Lee, 2019).

Complementing the linguistic dimension, insights derived from social psychology are instrumental in decoding the psychological underpinnings of economic behavior. This discipline sheds light on how cognitive biases, social influences, and cultural contexts shape economic decisions, offering a refined understanding of the interplay between individual choices and the broader socio-economic environment (Jones & Garcia, 2018). Such insights are invaluable for comprehending the subtleties of economic phenomena and market dynamics in today's evolving global economy. Considering this, this interdisciplinary study aims to unveil new perspectives on the intricate dynamics that characterize our interconnected world. By undertaking a comprehensive examination of the intersections among the English language, social psychology, and global economic trends, this study seeks to contribute to a deeper appreciation of the forces that influence economic behavior, drive societal transformation, and underpin global prosperity in the 21st century. Through this holistic investigation, we endeavor to forge a path towards a more integrated understanding of the complexities that define our contemporary world, thereby informing policy, practice, and future research in these critical domains.

THE ROLE OF ENGLISH AS THE LINGUA FRANCA OF GLOBALIZATION

The ascendance of the English language as the lingua franca of globalization marks a pivotal shift in international communication, transcultural discourse, and the dissemination of knowledge over the last 30 years. This phenomenon has been extensively documented in the literature, which highlights the multifaceted roles English plays in facilitating global connections and exchanges. As Crystal (2012) suggests, the global dominance of English is not merely a linguistic occurrence but a catalyst for economic, cultural, and educational integration across borders. This unprecedented role of English underscores its significance in the contemporary world, acting as a bridge that connects diverse cultures and communities almost all over the world.

The role of English in transcultural discourse and the dissemination of knowledge is particularly significant. According to Jenkins (2014), English serves as a medium for international communication, enabling the exchange of ideas, information, and cultural values among people from different linguistic and cultural backgrounds. This transcultural discourse facilitated by English is crucial for global cooperation, understanding, and peace. Moreover, the role of English in knowledge dissemination is evident in its prevalence in scientific research, academia, and digital platforms, where it serves as the primary language for publishing research findings and educational materials. This dominance of English in academic and scientific communication not only accelerates the spread of knowledge but also ensures a wider audience and greater impact for research conducted around the world.

Furthermore, linguistic proficiency in English plays a critical role in shaping communal identities and intergroup dynamics. The mastery of English can significantly influence individuals' social mobility, access to education, and economic opportunities, thereby affecting communal identities and social stratification. As Graddol (2006) points out, English proficiency is often associated with modernity, progress, and a cosmopolitan identity, which can lead to shifts in social dynamics and intergroup relations. It is obvious that the ability to speak English can create divisions between those who have access to global networks and those who do not, thus influencing power dynamics within and between communities. Additionally, the spread of English and its adoption as a second language can lead to the erosion of linguistic diversity and the marginalization of indigenous languages, which further affects cultural identities and heritage.

Expanding on these insights, Kachru (1985) discusses the concept of the "three circles of English," which illustrates the global spread of English across inner, outer, and expanding circles, reflecting the varied nature of English use and proficiency worldwide. This model further emphasizes the complexity of English's global influence, highlighting its role not only as a tool for communication but also as a symbol of social status and opportunity. Moreover, Phillipson (1992) critiques the global dominance of English through the lens of linguistic imperialism. He further argues that the spread of English often comes at the expense of local languages and cultures by contributing to inequalities on a global scale. This perspective adds a critical dimension to the discussion of English as a lingua franca and invites a reassessment of how linguistic policies and practices can better support linguistic diversity and cultural preservation.

In essence, the role of the English language in globalization is multifaceted in that it serves as a tool for transcultural communication, knowledge dissemination, and the shaping of communal identities and intergroup dynamics. The linguistic dominance of English facilitates global interactions and exchanges but also raises important questions about linguistic equity, cultural preservation, and the implications for non-English speaking communities. Understanding the complexities in the global role of English, as argued by scholars like Crystal (2012), Jenkins (2014), Graddol (2006), Kachru (1985), and Phillipson (1992), is essential for examining the challenges and opportunities presented by globalization.

SOCIAL PSYCHOLOGY PERSPECTIVES ON ECONOMIC DECISION-MAKING

The intricate relationship between social psychology and economic decision-making forms a critical area of study within the broader interdisciplinary investigation of language, psychology, and economic dynamics. In this section it is examined how social psychology informs our understanding of economic behaviors, focusing on cognitive biases, socio-cultural imperatives, and the complex relationship between individual agency and broader economic conditions.

Examination of Cognitive Biases Influencing Economic Decision-Making

Cognitive biases, which are systematic deviations from typical or rational judgment patterns, have a notable impact on economic decision-making. These biases can cause individuals to make decisions that may not align with their optimal financial interests or go against the predictions of classical economic models. In this context, Tversky and Kahneman (1974) introduced the concept of heuristics and biases in decision-making, and they illustrated how individuals rely on mental shortcuts that can lead to predictable errors. For instance, the availability heuristic influences individuals to overestimate the probability of events by making them rely on their ability to recall examples. This can affect their financial decisions, such as making investment choices based on recent market trends rather than considering long-term data. Likewise, the overconfidence bias can cause individuals to overestimate their knowledge and prediction capabilities, which indeed influences their financial planning and risk assessment in the following years.

Building upon Tversky and Kahneman's foundational work, further studies have illuminated the extensive range of cognitive biases that affect economic decision-making. Confirmation bias, as investigated by Nickerson (1998), refers to the inclination to seek out, interpret, favor, and remember information in a manner that validates one's existing beliefs or hypotheses. This bias can lead investors to disproportionately weigh information that supports their initial investment choices, ignoring evidence that contradicts their decisions. The framing effect, another cognitive bias described by Tversky and Kahneman (1981), demonstrates how the way information is presented can significantly affect and alter decision-making. For instance, individuals might react differently to a 95% chance of success than to a 5% chance of failure, despite both probabilities being statistically equivalent. This effect has profound implications for marketing, advertising, and even the presentation of investment risks and benefits.

Gilovich, Griffin, and Kahneman (2002) further expanded the discussion on cognitive biases by examining how biases like the hindsight bias and the anchoring bias impact economic decisions. The hindsight bias, or the "I-knew-it-all-along" effect, can cause individuals to see past events as more predictable than they actually were, leading to overconfidence in their predictive abilities for economic trends.

Conversely, the anchoring bias pertains to the prevalent human inclination to place excessive reliance on the initial information provided (referred to as the "anchor") when making decisions. In financial contexts, this can lead to skewed asset valuations based on initial prices or estimates, regardless of subsequent information that might warrant a revision of those valuations.

Behavioral economists like Thaler and Sunstein (2008) have applied these concepts of cognitive biases to propose "nudges" as interventions designed to help individuals make better economic decisions without restricting their freedom of choice. They argue that by understanding how cognitive biases influence decision-making, policymakers and financial institutions can design environments that guide individuals towards more beneficial economic behaviors. Moreover, the research by Shiller (2015) on behavioral finance delves into how cognitive biases, combined with emotional reactions, influence the financial markets and lead to phenomena such as speculative bubbles and market crashes. Shiller's work indicates the importance of incorporating psychological insights into economic theories to better understand global market dynamics and investor behavior.

In this regard, the examination of cognitive biases influencing economic decision- making reveals a complex interplay between human psychology and economic activity. From the pioneering work of Tversky and Kahneman (1974) to the innovative approaches of Thaler and Sunstein (2008) and the insightful analyses of Shiller (2015), it is evident that a deep understanding of cognitive biases is crucial for both individuals and institutions aiming to investigate or evaluate the economic landscape effectively. These insights not only challenge the assumptions of classical economic models but also open new avenues for research and practice in behavioral economics, financial planning, and policy-making.

Examination of Socio-Cultural Imperatives and Motivational Determinants in Economic Conduct

It is well-known that socio-cultural imperatives and motivational determinants can significantly influence economic behavior as they highlight the importance of considering the cultural context in which economic decisions are made. Hofstede (1980) identified cultural dimensions such as individualism versus collectivism and uncertainty avoidance that affect economic conduct. He further suggests that, in cultures with high levels of uncertainty avoidance, for instance, individuals may be more risk-averse in their economic choices and tend to prefer stable investments and savings over speculative ventures. Similarly, the motivation behind economic behaviors can vary significantly across cultures, with some societies valuing communal wealth distribution and others emphasizing individual financial success.

Building upon Hofstede's foundational work, Triandis (1995) delved deeper into the nuances of individualism and collectivism, exploring how these cultural orientations shape people's attitudes towards money, wealth, and economic transactions. Triandis argued that collectivist cultures, which prioritize group goals over individual achievements, foster economic behaviors that are deeply intertwined with social relationships and communal responsibilities. This perspective adds a layer of complexity to understanding economic decision-making, as it underscores the role of social norms and values in shaping individuals' financial choices. Further investigation by Schwartz (1992) into the theory of basic human values has provided a broader framework for understanding how values influence behavior across various domains, including economics. Schwartz identified ten basic values, such as power, achievement, hedonism, and security, that drive human actions. His research suggests that the prioritization of these values not only differs across cultures but also has profound implications for economic behavior, including spending habits, investment strategies, and attitudes toward risk and uncertainty.

In addition to cultural values, motivational psychology offers insights into the individual determinants of economic conduct. Deci and Ryan's (1985) self-determination theory suggests that intrinsic and extrinsic motivations play critical roles in shaping behavior, including economic activities. Intrinsic motivation, which derives from taking pleasure in an activity itself, can lead to more sustainable and self-congruent economic decisions. In contrast, extrinsic motivation, driven by external rewards or pressures, may result in economic choices that align with societal expectations or immediate gains but do not necessarily reflect personal values or long-term interests.

The concept of social capital, as discussed by Putnam (2000), further illuminates the intersection between socio-cultural imperatives and economic behavior.

Social capital encompasses the intricate networks of relationships among individuals residing and working within a specific society, facilitating the efficient functioning of that society. Economic conduct, in this view, is not solely driven by individual rational choices but is deeply embedded in networks of social relations that facilitate or constrain economic opportunities. Moreover, the work of Akerlof and Kranton (2000) on identity economics introduces the idea that individuals' economic decisions are influenced by their social identities and the norms associated with those identities. This theoretical framework highlights how conformity to group norms can impact labor market behaviors, consumption choices, and investment decisions, further complicating the relationship between socio-cultural imperatives and economic conduct.

As can be clearly seen, the examination of socio-cultural imperatives and motivational determinants in economic conduct reveals a complex landscape where cultural values, social norms, and individual motivations intersect to shape economic behaviors. The contributions of scholars such as Hofstede (1980), Triandis (1995), Schwartz (1992), Deci and Ryan (1985), Putnam (2000), and Akerlof and Kranton (2000), provide a multifaceted understanding of how cultural context and motivational factors influence economic decisions. This expanded perspective not only challenges simplistic economic models based solely on rational choice but also opens new avenues for research and practice that take into account the rich tapestry of human culture and motivation.

Interplay Between Individual Volition and Broader Socio-Economic Factors

The relationship between individual volition and broader socio-economic factors is complex and multifaceted. On one hand, individuals exercise personal choice within the constraints of their economic environment. In this sense, they take into account their decisions about spending, saving, and investing based on their preferences, goals, and the information available to them. On the other hand, their economic behavior is influenced by larger socio-economic trends, such as inflation, employment rates, and fiscal policies. Regarding this, Bandura (1986) introduced the concept of reciprocal determinism, which indicates that personal factors, behaviors, and environmental influences interact in a dynamic cycle. In fact, this concept can be applied to economic decision-making, where individual choices are both shaped by and contribute to the economic climate. For instance, consumer confidence can drive spending patterns, which in turn influence economic growth or recession either directly or indirectly.

Delving deeper into the interplay between individual volition and socio-economic factors, Giddens (1984) articulated the theory of structuration, which proposes that while individuals are agents of their actions, these actions are deeply embedded within the constraints and opportunities provided by social structures. This duality of structure suggests that economic behaviors cannot be fully understood without considering the societal norms, regulations, and institutions that frame individual choices. For example, the cultural norm of saving in East Asian societies can be seen as both a personal choice and a reflection of broader societal values and economic strategies. Moreover, Sen (1999) introduced the capability approach, emphasizing the freedom of individuals to achieve well-being through economic activities that reflect their values and choices. This perspective shifts the focus from mere economic outcomes to the opportunities individuals have to pursue their goals, suggesting that broader socio-economic factors should enhance, not limit, individual agency. Sen's framework highlights how policies aimed at economic development must account for enhancing individual capabilities, suggesting a nuanced understanding of how socio-economic structures and individual choices interact.

The concept of economic resilience also plays a pivotal role in understanding this interplay. Martin and Sunley (2015) define economic resilience as the capacity of an economy to withstand or recover from market, financial, and demand shocks. This resilience is not only a property of economies at large but also of individual actors within these economies, who adapt, innovate, and make choices in response to changing economic circumstances. The resilience of individuals and businesses contributes to the overall resilience of the economy, showcasing the dynamic interaction between personal volition and socio-economic factors. In addition, Bourdieu's (1986) notion of habitus and economic capital further enriches this discussion by illustrating how individuals' economic behaviors are shaped by their social backgrounds and the resources available to them. Habitus, the deeply ingrained habits, skills, and dispositions that individuals develop from their cultural context, influences how they perceive and engage with the economic world. Economic capital, or the financial resources that individuals possess, interacts with habitus to enable or constrain economic choices. This interplay between habitus and economic capital highlights the importance of considering both the internal dispositions and external resources that guide economic behavior.

It is clear that the investigation of the relationship between individual volition and broader socio-economic factors reveals a dynamic and reciprocal relationship where personal choices and socio-economic structures continuously influence each other. Drawing upon the contributions of scholars such as Bandura (1986), Giddens (1984), Sen (1999), Martin and Sunley (2015), and Bourdieu (1986), it becomes evident that economic decision-making is a nuanced process shaped by a complex interplay of individual preferences, cultural norms, societal structures, and available resources. Understanding this interplay is crucial for developing policies and interventions that support individual agency, promote economic resilience, and foster well-being in an ever-changing economic context.

INTERCONNECTION OF LANGUAGE, SOCIAL PSYCHOLOGY, AND ECONOMIC FLUX

The close relationship between language, social psychology, and the dynamics of global economic flux is a multifaceted domain that merits comprehensive investigation. This section examines how globalization and technological innovation have reshaped linguistic practices and psychological well-being, the influence of economic changes on language use and psychological factors, and the role of these elements in fostering economic resilience amid global challenges in recent times.

Impact of Globalization and Technological Innovations on Linguistic Utilization and Psychological Well-Being

In recent times, technological advancements have played a significant role in driving globalization, resulting in substantial changes in how languages are utilized. Indeed, this has inevitably made English the lingua franca in many international contexts. This shift has profound implications for identity, communication, and cultural exchange. Steger (2017) argues that globalization facilitates a more interconnected world where linguistic proficiency, especially in English, becomes a crucial skill for global participation. However, this linguistic shift also poses challenges to psychological well-being as it may lead to cultural homogenization, loss of linguistic diversity, and identity crises among speakers of minority languages. In this regard, technological innovation, particularly in digital communication, has further transformed how language is used by enabling real-time interaction across different linguistic and cultural backgrounds. This democratization of communication has enhanced global collaboration but also introduced challenges such as digital divides and online echo chambers, which can impact psychological well-being by reinforcing cognitive biases and social isolation in diverse social groups or communities.

The expansion of digital communication platforms has significantly altered the landscape of linguistic utilization, enabling unprecedented levels of interaction across the globe. Prensky (2001) introduced the concept of "digital natives" and "digital immigrants" to describe the generational divide in the use of technology and its impact on language. Digital natives, who have grown up with the internet and social media, often adopt a hybrid linguistic identity, incorporating elements from multiple languages into their online and offline communications. This phenomenon, known as "translanguaging," has been examined by García and Wei (2014), who argue that it reflects the fluid and dynamic nature of language in the digital age. Translanguaging practices can enrich linguistic diversity but also raise questions about the preservation of linguistic heritage and the role of English as a dominant global language. Moreover, the psychological implications of linguistic changes due to globalization and technological innovations are significant. Norton (2013) explores the concept of "investment" in language learning, suggesting that learners' willingness to engage with a new language is tied to their identity and desires for future social interactions and community membership. This perspective highlights the emotional and psychological dimensions of language learning in a globalized world, where proficiency in English or other dominant languages can shape individuals' opportunities for personal and professional development.

The impact of technology on psychological well-being in the context of linguistic shifts is complex. Turkle (2015) discusses the paradox of connectivity offered by digital technologies, which, while facilitating global communication, can also lead to feelings of loneliness and isolation. The constant exposure to global languages and cultures through digital media may exacerbate these feelings, particularly among individuals who feel marginalized within their linguistic communities. Additionally, the rise of automated translation tools and artificial intelligence in language learning and communication poses new challenges and opportunities for linguistic interaction, as explored by Kohn (2020), who notes that these technologies can both bridge and reinforce language barriers. Furthermore, the effects of digital communication on cultural exchange and identity formation are profound. Jenkins (2006) examines how participatory cultures emerging from digital platforms allow for the creation and sharing of content that transcends linguistic and cultural boundaries, promoting a form of cultural hybridity. However, this process also involves complex negotiations of identity, as individuals navigate between global influences and local traditions.

In conclusion, the impact of globalization and technological innovations on linguistic utilization and psychological well-being encompasses a wide array of factors, from changes in language learning and use to the psychological effects of digital communication and cultural exchange. Scholars such as Steger (2017), Prensky (2001), García and Wei (2014), Norton (2013), Turkle (2015), Kohn (2020), and Jenkins (2006) provide valuable insights into these dynamics, highlighting the intricate relationships between language, technology, culture, and psychology. As the world becomes increasingly interconnected, understanding these relationships is crucial for investigating the challenges and opportunities of linguistic and psychological adaptation in the globalized digital age.

Examination of Economic Vicissitudes and Their Influence on Language and Psychological Determinants

Economic vicissitudes play a pivotal role in shaping the linguistic landscape and psychological well-being of societies. These fluctuations in economic conditions, ranging from periods of prosperity to times of recession, have profound impacts not only on the material conditions of life but also on the cultural and linguistic expressions and the psychological health of individuals and communities. Understanding the complex interplay between economic changes and their effects on language use and psychological states requires a multidisciplinary approach, drawing insights from economics, sociolinguistics, and psychology.

From an economic standpoint, downturns and upturns significantly affect employment rates, income levels, and social mobility, which in turn influence educational opportunities, access to cultural resources, and the vitality of linguistic communities.

Polanyi (1944) in his seminal work, "The Great Transformation," discussed how economic and societal changes are deeply interconnected, suggesting that shifts in economic structures inevitably lead to shifts in social and cultural configurations. This transformation can lead to changes in language use, as economic conditions affect migration patterns, urbanization, and the globalization of media, all of which contribute to the dynamism of linguistic ecologies.

Sociolinguistically, Bourdieu (1991) introduced the concept of linguistic capital, which refers to the social value attached to certain languages and forms of expression. Economic vicissitudes can alter the distribution and recognition of linguistic capital, privileging certain languages over others based on their perceived utility in accessing economic opportunities. During periods of economic globalization, for instance, languages with a wide international reach, such as English, may gain in prestige and utility, influencing language learning priorities and practices. Conversely, economic downturns may exacerbate the vulnerabilities of minority linguistic communities, whose languages may be further marginalized in the face of shrinking resources for language maintenance and education.

Psychologically, the stress and uncertainty associated with economic fluctuations can have significant impacts on individuals' mental health and well-being. The strain of economic hardship is known to exacerbate conditions such as depression and anxiety, which in turn can affect cognitive functions, including language processing and usage. Elder and Caspi (1988) in their study on the psychological effects of the Great Depression highlighted how prolonged economic hardship can lead to long-term psychological scars, affecting individuals' social interactions, communication patterns, and overall linguistic behaviors. Furthermore, the work of Diener, Oishi, and Lucas (2003) on subjective well-being and its relation to economic indicators underscores how perceptions of prosperity or hardship can influence individuals' happiness and life satisfaction, with consequent effects on social cohesion, communication practices, and cultural expressions. Economic pressures can also influence family dynamics, educational attainment, and community engagement, all of which play crucial roles in language transmission and psychological development. It is quite evident that the digital age introduces new dimensions to these dynamics, as technologies provide novel means of communication and information access, but also new sources of economic and psychological strain. The rise of the gig economy, digital divides, and the pervasive influence of social media on perceptions of success and failure all contribute to contemporary experiences of economic vicissitudes and their linguistic and psychological ramifications.

In summary, the examination of economic vicissitudes and their influence on language and psychological determinants reveals a complex web of causality and influence, necessitating interdisciplinary research to fully understand the phenomena. The foundational insights provided by scholars such as Polanyi (1944), Bourdieu

(1991), Elder and Caspi (1988), and Diener, Oishi, and Lucas (2003) offer valuable frameworks for exploring how economic changes shape linguistic practices and psychological states. As economies continue to evolve in the context of globalization and technological innovation, further research is needed to understand the implications for linguistic diversity, psychological health, and the fabric of societies.

Consideration of Linguistic and Psychological Factors in Economic Resilience Amidst Global Challenges

The resilience of economies in the face of global challenges is intricately linked to linguistic and psychological factors. Linguistic proficiency, particularly in a global lingua franca like English, enables individuals and communities to access international markets, information, and networks, fostering economic resilience. Moreover, psychological resilience—characterized by adaptability, optimism, and stress management—plays a critical role in overcoming economic uncertainties. Luthar, Cicchetti, and Becker (2000) highlight the importance of resilience as a psychological trait that enables individuals to thrive despite adverse conditions in social life. They further suggest that fostering psychological resilience can be a key strategy in promoting economic stability and growth.

This interplay between linguistic capability and psychological resilience underpins a broader framework where communication skills and mental fortitude become instrumental in navigating the complexities of the global economy. Masten (2001) expands on this by defining resilience as not just an individual trait but a process that encompasses interactions between individuals and their environments. This perspective is particularly relevant in a globalized world where economic pressures, cultural shifts, and technological advancements continuously reshape the landscape individuals and communities operate within. Additionally, the work of Youssef and Luthans (2007) on positive organizational behavior introduces the concept of psychological capital, which includes hope, efficacy, resilience, and optimism (HERO) as key components. They argue that these psychological resources can significantly enhance workforce performance and, by extension, economic resilience. This suggests that cultivating psychological resilience goes beyond individual well-being to become a strategic asset for organizations and economies at large.

Language plays a pivotal role in this dynamic, acting as a medium through which economic actors communicate, negotiate, and access knowledge. Grin (2003) discusses the economic value of multilingualism, arguing that linguistic diversity can enhance economic competitiveness and innovation by facilitating cross-cultural communication and understanding. In this context, linguistic proficiency becomes a form of social capital that individuals and societies can leverage to enhance economic resilience. In line with this, the advent of digital technology and the internet has further emphasized the importance of linguistic and psychological factors in economic resilience. Castells (1996) in his analysis of the network society points out how digital networks have transformed economic structures, making information and communication key drivers of economic growth. This digital economy not only prioritizes linguistic skills, particularly in widely spoken languages like English, but also places a premium on psychological attributes such as flexibility, creativity, and the ability to deal with information overload.

When tackling global challenges like climate change, political unrest, and public health emergencies, the significance of linguistic and psychological resilience becomes increasingly evident. Norris et al. (2008) note that community resilience, which encompasses both psychological resilience and collective efficacy, is crucial in responding to and recovering from such challenges. Language serves as a tool for mobilizing collective action, disseminating critical information, and fostering social cohesion, while psychological resilience equips individuals and communities with the mental strength to persevere through crises.

In conclusion, the interconnectedness of linguistic proficiency and psychological resilience with economic resilience offers a nuanced understanding of how societies can withstand and adapt to global challenges. The insights provided by scholars such as Luthar et al. (2000), Masten (2001), Youssef and Luthans (2007), Grin (2003), Castells (1996), and Norris et al. (2008) underscore the multifaceted nature of resilience in a globalized world. As economies continue to navigate the uncertainties of the 21st century, fostering linguistic proficiency and psychological resilience will be paramount in ensuring not just economic stability, but also the well-being and cohesion of societies.

SYNTHESIS OF PERSPECTIVES AND IMPLICATIONS

The comprehensive investigation of the interconnectedness among the English language, social psychology, and global economic trends underscores the critical importance of interdisciplinary approaches in addressing the complexities of globalization (Nisbett & Masuda, 2003; Huntington, 1996; Friedman, 2005). This synthesis of perspectives from linguistics, social psychology, and economics illuminates the multifaceted ways in which language acts as a conduit for global communication, psychological factors influence economic decision-making, and economic dynamics shape societal structures and individual lives (Chomsky, 2001; Kahneman, 2011; Piketty, 2014). The implications of this integrated understanding extend far beyond academic discourse and offer valuable insights for pedagogues, policymakers, and corporate leaders tasked with navigating the challenges and opportunities presented by an increasingly interconnected world.

Implications for Pedagogues

For educators and pedagogues, the findings of this study underscore the importance of integrating interdisciplinary content into educational curricula to equip students with the skills necessary to navigate the complexities of the global economy. As Gardner (1983) and Krashen (1982) have demonstrated, fostering multiple intelligences and understanding the nuances of language acquisition are foundational to developing well-rounded learners. Similarly, proficiency in English, given its status as the global lingua franca, is essential but should be augmented with comprehensive lessons on cultural awareness and the psychological factors influencing economic behaviors, as suggested by Hofstede (1980) and Vygotsky (1978).

Incorporating insights from cultural psychology can further enhance this educational approach by helping students understand how cultural contexts shape economic decisions and behaviors (Markus & Kitayama, 1991). This knowledge, coupled with an emphasis on critical thinking and cultural competence, prepares students to engage effectively in diverse international environments. Moreover, pedagogical strategies that promote empathy and resilience, drawing on the work of Seligman (1990) in positive psychology, can prepare students to face global challenges with optimism and resourcefulness.

Adopting this comprehensive educational framework not only fosters academic excellence but also cultivates global citizens capable of contributing to a more inclusive and empathetic world. By bridging linguistic mastery with cultural and psychological awareness, educators can play a pivotal role in shaping the leaders of tomorrow, ensuring they are prepared to navigate the complexities of international relations, global economics, and cross-cultural interactions with sensitivity and insight. Therefore, the implications for pedagogues extend beyond traditional educational outcomes to include the cultivation of global competencies that are increasingly vital in today's interconnected world. This holistic approach to education, underscored by interdisciplinary insights and a commitment to cultural and psychological understanding, promises to equip students with the necessary tools to thrive in a rapidly changing global landscape.

Implications for Policymakers

Policymakers are tasked with crafting policies that promote sustainable economic growth and social cohesion. The insights from this study suggest that policies should consider the psychological impacts of economic conditions, the importance of linguistic diversity alongside English language education, and the need for cultural sensitivity in an increasingly globalized society. Drawing on the work of Stiglitz (2002) and Nussbaum (2010), it becomes clear that integrating these dimensions into policy frameworks is essential for addressing the multifaceted challenges of the 21st century.

To mitigate the influence of cognitive biases on economic behaviors, policymakers could implement programs aimed at enhancing critical thinking and decision-making skills across the population. This could involve integrating behavioral economics principles into educational curricula and public information campaigns, thereby empowering individuals with the tools to navigate economic complexities more effectively. Furthermore, to support linguistic and cultural diversity, policies could encourage multilingual education and the preservation of minority languages, recognizing their intrinsic value for cultural identity and their potential to contribute to economic innovation and cross-cultural understanding. Investment in cultural exchange programs and initiatives that promote intercultural dialogue can also enhance global cooperation and foster a sense of shared humanity. Hence, by embracing a holistic approach that values psychological well-being, linguistic diversity, and cultural sensitivity, policymakers can create more resilient and inclusive societies. Such policies will not only facilitate economic growth but also enrich the social fabric, which can ultimately contribute to a more cohesive and understanding global community.

Implications for Corporate Leaders

Corporate leaders operating in the global market stand to gain significantly by integrating insights from the interplay between language, psychology, and economics into their strategic planning and organizational development. Knowledge of these interdisciplinary areas can drive international business expansion, foster innovation in global marketing strategies, and enhance human resource management, drawing on the foundational theories of Porter (1985) for competitive strategy and Goleman (1995) for emotional intelligence in leadership. Similarly, an appreciation for English as the dominant business lingua franca, coupled with a commitment to linguistic diversity, positions companies to navigate global markets more adeptly. It enables firms to tailor communication strategies that resonate across cultural boundaries, fostering inclusivity and enhancing brand reputation internationally. Moreover, by recognizing and valuing the diverse linguistic backgrounds of employees, companies can tap into a broader range of perspectives and ideas, driving innovation and creativity.

Understanding socio-cultural dynamics and psychological factors is equally critical in shaping consumer engagement and employee relations. Insights into consumer psychology can inform more targeted and culturally sensitive marketing campaigns, while an understanding of motivational psychology can improve employee satisfaction, engagement, and productivity. Corporate leaders who adeptly leverage these insights can cultivate a positive organizational culture, attract and retain top talent, and build strong, loyal customer bases. In other words, corporate leaders who embrace the complexities of language, psychology, and economics can forge more resilient, innovative, and globally competitive businesses. By prioritizing cultural sensitivity, psychological well-being, and strategic communication, they not only contribute to the success of their organizations but also to the broader goal of sustainable development and social cohesion in the global business landscape.

Recommendations for Evidence-Based Interventions

Based on the integrated insights from linguistics, social psychology, and economics, several recommendations emerge for promoting inclusive economic growth and social cohesion. First, initiatives aimed at improving access to quality education in English and other languages can help bridge communication gaps and foster global understanding (UNESCO, 2019). Second, programs designed to enhance financial literacy and awareness of cognitive biases could improve economic decision-making at both individual and organizational levels (Thaler & Sunstein, 2008). Finally, policies and practices that value cultural diversity and promote psychological well-being are essential for building resilient societies that are capable of facing the challenges of globalization (Seligman & Csikszentmihalyi, 2000).

As can be seen clearly, the synthesis of perspectives from linguistics, social psychology, and economics offers a holistic understanding of the forces shaping our globalized world. By integrating these insights, pedagogues, policymakers, and corporate leaders can develop strategies and interventions that can promote economic prosperity, cultural understanding, and social well-being in an interconnected and rapidly changing global landscape (Sachs, 2015; Pinker, 2018).

DISCUSSION

The analysis presented in this article underscores the profound interconnectedness among the English language, social psychology, and global economic advancement. These findings illuminate the intricate ways in which linguistic capabilities, psychological factors, and economic dynamics intersect and influence one another, shaping the fabric of globalized societies. Drawing upon the insights of scholars across disciplines (Crystal, 2012; Hofstede, 1980; Stiglitz, 2002), this discussion delves into the synergies and tensions that emerge from the interplay of language, psychology, and economics, and considers the practical applications of these interdisciplinary insights for addressing the complex challenges faced by contemporary globalized societies.

The ascendancy of English as a global lingua franca, as highlighted by Crystal (2012), has facilitated unprecedented levels of international communication and collaboration, driving economic globalization and cultural exchange. However, this linguistic dominance also raises concerns about cultural homogenization and the marginalization of minority languages (Skutnabb-Kangas, 2000), pointing to a tension between linguistic utility and cultural diversity. The role of psychological factors, particularly cognitive biases and socio-cultural imperatives in economic decision-making (Tversky & Kahneman, 1974; Hofstede, 1980), further complicates this picture, suggesting that economic behaviors are not merely rational choices but are deeply embedded in cultural contexts and psychological predispositions.

The synergies between linguistic proficiency, psychological resilience, and economic resilience are particularly evident in the context of global challenges such as the COVID-19 pandemic. The ability to communicate effectively in English has been crucial for the dissemination of scientific knowledge and public health information, while psychological resilience has emerged as a key factor in individuals' and communities' ability to navigate the economic uncertainties brought about by the pandemic (Southwick & Charney, 2012). These observations underscore the importance of interdisciplinary approaches that integrate linguistic, psychological, and economic perspectives in developing strategies to enhance resilience and well-being in the face of global crises.

Moreover, the practical applications of these interdisciplinary insights are vast and varied. In the realm of education, the integration of linguistic diversity and psychological insights into curricula can prepare students to thrive in a globalized economy, promoting cultural understanding and empathy (Gardner, 1983; Nussbaum, 2010). For policymakers, recognizing the interconnections among language, psychology, and economics can inform more holistic and inclusive policies that address the root causes of social and economic disparities (Stiglitz, 2002). In the corporate sector, leaders who understand these dynamics can foster more innovative, resilient, and culturally sensitive organizations (Porter, 1985; Goleman, 1995).

However, tensions between these perspectives also necessitate careful consideration. The drive for economic efficiency, for example, may conflict with the preservation of linguistic diversity and cultural heritage (Skutnabb-Kangas, 2000), while the push for global market expansion may overlook the psychological well-being of employees and consumers (Seligman & Csikszentmihalyi, 2000). Addressing these tensions requires a commitment to dialogue and collaboration across disciplines, and a recognition of the complex ways in which language, psychology, and economics are intertwined.

In conclusion, this discussion highlights the critical importance of interdisciplinary research and practice in understanding and addressing the challenges of globalized societies. By embracing the interconnectedness of language, psychology, and economics, scholars, policymakers, educators, and corporate leaders can work together to build more inclusive, resilient, and thriving global communities. As we move forward, the continued exploration of these synergies and tensions will be vital in navigating the complexities of the 21st century.

CONCLUSION AND SUGGESTIONS FOR FUTURE RESEARCH DIRECTIONS

This article has examined the extensive interrelationship among the English language, social psychology, and global economic trends. In this sense, it is aimed to shed light on the complex and nuanced interactions between these domains and their mutual impact on each other. Through an interdisciplinary lens, we have analyzed the pivotal role of English as the lingua franca of globalization, its implications for transcultural discourse, as well as its ability to influence communal identities and intergroup dynamics. Furthermore, we have investigated the profound impact of social psychology on economic decision-making, highlighting the significance of cognitive biases, socio-cultural imperatives, and the dynamic interplay between individual agency and broader socio-economic forces.

The analysis of the interconnection between language, social psychology, and economic flux has revealed how globalization and technological innovation can significantly affect linguistic utilization and psychological well-being. It has also examined the ways in which economic vicissitudes influence language use and psychological states, with emphasis on the importance of linguistic and psychological factors in fostering economic resilience amidst global challenges. The synthesis of perspectives from these diverse fields has underscored the multifaceted implications for pedagogues, policymakers, and corporate leaders, offering a blueprint for evidence-based interventions aimed at promoting inclusive economic growth and social cohesion.

Our investigation underscores the key finding that the English language, social psychology, and economic dynamics are profoundly interconnected, and each of them plays a crucial role in shaping the globalized world. In other words, English, as a global lingua franca, facilitates international communication and understanding, while social psychological insights into economic decision-making provide a deeper understanding of the forces driving economic behaviors and marketing trends. The economic context, in turn, influences linguistic and psychological dynamics, which indeed completes a complex web of interactions that define our global society. The interdisciplinary approach adopted in this study highlights the essential need for collaboration across different fields of study to fully comprehend the complexities of global phenomena. By integrating insights from linguistics, social psychology, and economics, we gain a more holistic understanding of the factors influencing global advancement, cultural exchange, and economic stability. This approach not only enriches our knowledge base but also enhances our ability to develop comprehensive strategies to address global challenges in today's world.

Looking forward, there is a vast potential for further research in interdisciplinary studies that build upon the foundations laid by this investigation. Future research endeavors may aim to examine into the nuances of how emerging technologies, such as artificial intelligence and machine learning, are reshaping linguistic practices, psychological well-being, and sustainability in the development of global economy. In addition, studies could investigate the impact of global environmental changes on economic decision-making processes and the role of language in mediating these effects. By continuing to examine these intersections, academics or scholars have the potential to enhance the creation of more impactful policies and interventions that cater to the requirements of a progressively intricate and interconnected world.

All in all, the investigation of the relationship between the English language, social psychology, and global economic trends offers invaluable insights into the mechanisms driving global interconnectedness. Such an interdisciplinary approach provides a comprehensive framework for understanding these dynamics, emphasizing the need for integrated solutions to foster a more inclusive, resilient, and prosperous global society. As we move forward, the continued pursuit of interdisciplinary research will be paramount in navigating the challenges and seizing the opportunities of our interconnected world.

REFERENCES

Akerlof, G. A., & Kranton, R. E. (2000). Economics and identity. *The Quarterly Journal of Economics*, 115(3), 715–753. 10.1162/003355300554881

Bandura, A. (1986). *Social foundations of thought and action: A social cognitive theory*. Prentice-Hall.

Bourdieu, P. (1986). The forms of capital. In J. Richardson (Ed.), *Handbook of Theory and Research for the Sociology of Education* (pp. 241-258). Greenwood.

Bourdieu, P. (1991). *Language and symbolic power*. Harvard University Press.

Brown, H., & Lee, J. (2019). The impact of linguistic proficiency on global intergroup relations. *International Journal of Intercultural Relations*, 45, 117–130.

Castells, M. (1996). *The rise of the network society*. Blackwell Publishers.

Chomsky, N. (2001). *9-11*. Seven Stories Press.

Conger, R. D., & Donnellan, M. B. (2007). An interactionist perspective on the socioeconomic context of human development. *Annual Review of Psychology*, 58(1), 175–199. 10.1146/annurev.psych.58.110405.08555116903807

Crystal, D. (2012). *English as a global language* (2nd ed.). Cambridge University Press. 10.1017/CBO9781139196970

Deci, E. L., & Ryan, R. M. (1985). *Intrinsic motivation and self-determination in human behavior*. Plenum. 10.1007/978-1-4899-2271-7

Diener, E., Oishi, S., & Lucas, R. E. (2003). Personality, culture, and subjective well-being: Emotional and cognitive evaluations of life. *Annual Review of Psychology*, 54(1), 403–425. 10.1146/annurev.psych.54.101601.14505612172000

Elder, G. H.Jr, & Caspi, A. (1988). Economic stress in lives: Developmental perspectives. *The Journal of Social Issues*, 44(4), 25–45. 10.1111/j.1540-4560.1988.tb02090.x

Friedman, T. L. (2005). *The world is flat: A brief history of the twenty-first century*. Farrar, Straus and Giroux.

Garcia, E., Liu, S., Mitchell, R., & Smith, Y. (2021). Interdisciplinary perspectives on globalization: Understanding the interconnectedness of economics, culture, and society. *The Global Studies Journal*, 13(4), 1–22.

García, O., & Wei, L. (2014). *Translanguaging: Language, bilingualism and education*. Palgrave Macmillan. 10.1057/9781137385765

Gardner, H. (1983). *Frames of mind: The theory of multiple intelligences*. Basic Books.

Giddens, A. (1984). *The constitution of society: Outline of the theory of structuration*. Polity Press.

Gilovich, T., Griffin, D., & Kahneman, D. (Eds.). (2002). *Heuristics and biases: The psychology of intuitive judgment*. Cambridge University Press. 10.1017/CBO9780511808098

Goleman, D. (1995). *Emotional intelligence: Why it can matter more than IQ*. Bantam Books.

Graddol, D. (2006). *English next: Why global English may mean the end of 'English as a Foreign Language*. British Council.

Grin, F. (2003). *Language policy evaluation and the European Charter for Regional or Minority Languages*. Palgrave Macmillan. 10.1057/9780230502666

Hofstede, G. (1980). *Culture's consequences: International differences in work-related values*. Sage Publications.

Huntington, S. P. (1996). *The clash of civilizations and the remaking of world order*. Simon & Schuster.

Jenkins, H. (2006). *Convergence culture: Where old and new media collide*. New York University Press.

Jenkins, J. (2014). *Global Englishes: A resource book for students* (3rd ed.). Routledge. 10.4324/9781315761596

Jones, A., & Garcia, S. (2018). Economic decision-making and the role of social psychology: Exploring cognitive biases and social influences. *Behavioral Economics Review*, 6(2), 54–67.

Kachru, B. B. (1985). Standards, codification and sociolinguistic realism: The English language in the outer circle. In Quirk, R., & Widdowson, H. G. (Eds.), *English in the world: Teaching and learning the language and literatures* (pp. 11–30). Cambridge University Press.

Kahneman, D. (2011). *Thinking, fast and slow*. Farrar, Straus and Giroux.

Kohn, M. (2020). *Digital transformation and public services: Societal impacts in Sweden and beyond*. Routledge.

Krashen, S. (1982). *Principles and practice in second language acquisition*. Pergamon Press.

Luthar, S. S., Cicchetti, D., & Becker, B. (2000). The construct of resilience: A critical evaluation and guidelines for future work. *Child Development*, 71(3), 543–562. 10.1111/1467-8624.0016410953923

Markus, H. R., & Kitayama, S. (1991). Culture and the self: Implications for cognition, emotion, and motivation. *Psychological Review*, 98(2), 224–253. 10.1037/0033-295X.98.2.224

Martin, R., & Sunley, P. (2015). On the notion of regional economic resilience: Conceptualization and explanation. *Journal of Economic Geography*, 15(1), 1–42. 10.1093/jeg/lbu015

Masten, A. S. (2001). Ordinary magic: Resilience processes in development. *The American Psychologist*, 56(3), 227–238. 10.1037/0003-066X.56.3.22711315249

Nickerson, R. S. (1998). Confirmation bias: A ubiquitous phenomenon in many guises. *Review of General Psychology*, 2(2), 175–220. 10.1037/1089-2680.2.2.175

Nisbett, R. E., & Masuda, T. (2003). Culture and point of view. *Proceedings of the National Academy of Sciences of the United States of America*, 100(19), 11163–11170. 10.1073/pnas.193452710012960375

Norris, F. H., Stevens, S. P., Pfefferbaum, B., Wyche, K. F., & Pfefferbaum, R. L. (2008). Community resilience as a metaphor, theory, set of capacities, and strategy for disaster readiness. *American Journal of Community Psychology*, 41(1-2), 127–150. 10.1007/s10464-007-9156-618157631

Norton, B. (2013). *Identity and language learning: Extending the conversation* (2nd ed.). Multilingual Matters. 10.21832/9781783090563

Nussbaum, M. C. (2010). *Not for profit: Why democracy needs the humanities.* Princeton University Press.

Phillipson, R. (1992). *Linguistic imperialism.* Oxford University Press.

Piketty, T. (2014). *Capital in the twenty-first century.* Harvard University Press. 10.4159/9780674369542

Polanyi, K. (1944). *The Great Transformation: The political and economic origins of our time.* Farrar & Rinehart.

Porter, M. E. (1985). *Competitive advantage: Creating and sustaining superior performance.* Free Press.

Prensky, M. (2001). Digital natives, digital immigrants. *On the Horizon*, 9(5), 1–6. 10.1108/10748120110424816

Putnam, R. D. (2000). *Bowling alone: The collapse and revival of American community*. Simon & Schuster.

Sachs, J. (2015). *The age of sustainable development*. Columbia University Press. 10.7312/sach17314

Schwartz, S. H. (1992). Universals in the content and structure of values: Theoretical advances and empirical tests in 20 countries. *Advances in Experimental Social Psychology*, 25, 1–65. 10.1016/S0065-2601(08)60281-6

Seligman, M. E. P. (1990). *Learned optimism: How to change your mind and your life*. Knopf.

Seligman, M. E. P., & Csikszentmihalyi, M. (2000). Positive psychology: An introduction. *The American Psychologist*, 55(1), 5–14. 10.1037/0003-066X.55.1.51392865

Sen, A. (1999). *Development as freedom*. Oxford University Press.

Shiller, R. J. (2015). *Irrational exuberance* (3rd ed.). Princeton University Press. 10.2307/j.ctt1287kz5

Skutnabb-Kangas, T. (2000). *Linguistic genocide in education or worldwide diversity and human rights?* Lawrence Erlbaum Associates.

Smith, L., & Johnson, M. (2020). English as a lingua franca in global communication: Bridging cultural divides. *Language and Intercultural Communication*, 20(3), 237–252.

Southwick, S. M., & Charney, D. S. (2012). *Resilience: The science of mastering life's greatest challenges*. Cambridge University Press. 10.1017/CBO9781139013857

Steger, M. B. (2017). *Globalization: A very short introduction* (4th ed.). Oxford University Press.

Stiglitz, J. E. (2002). *Globalization and its discontents*. W. W. Norton & Company.

Thaler, R. H., & Sunstein, C. R. (2008). *Nudge: Improving decisions about health, wealth, and happiness*. Yale University Press.

Triandis, H. C. (1995). *Individualism & collectivism*. Westview Press.

Turkle, S. (2015). *Reclaiming Conversation: The Power of Talk in a Digital Age*. Penguin Press.

Tversky, A., & Kahneman, D. (1974). Judgment under uncertainty: Heuristics and biases. *Science*, 185(4157), 1124–1131. 10.1126/science.185.4157.112417835457

Tversky, A., & Kahneman, D. (1981). The framing of decisions and the psychology of choice. *Science*, 211(4481), 453–458. 10.1126/science.74556837455683

UNESCO. (2019). *Global education monitoring report 2019: Migration, displacement and education: Building bridges, not walls*. UNESCO Publishing.

Vygotsky, L. (1978). *Mind in society: The development of higher psychological processes*. Harvard University Press.

Youssef, C. M., & Luthans, F. (2007). *Positive organizational behavior in the workplace: The impact of hope*. APA.

Chapter 12
Descriptive Analysis of Maize Characteristics

Biljana Grujić Vučkovski
https://orcid.org/0000-0003-2588-4888
Tamiš Research and Development Institute, Pančevo, Serbia

Irina Marina
https://orcid.org/0000-0002-5894-363X
Institute of Agricultural Economics, Belgrade, Serbia

ABSTRACT

In this chapter, the authors followed the trend of the movement of maize according to selected variables: harvested area (in ha), production (in t), and the value of maize exports (thousand USD). The movement of these variables was observed in the example of twenty-seven European countries that have available data in the period from 2010 to 2022. The aim of the research was to determine the changes that occurred in the analyzed countries during the observed time period and according to the variables in terms of growth and/or reduction of average indicator values. The basic source of data was the FAOSTAT database, but also other relevant scientific and professional literature. The results of applying descriptive statistics showed that the greatest deviation from the arithmetic mean was recorded in the value of maize exports (Cv = 209.3493), while the Pearson correlation coefficient showed that the strongest correlation was between production and area harvested of maize (.955). Finally, a conclusion was given according to the graphic presentation in the form of a trend line of maize production.

DOI: 10.4018/979-8-3693-3439-3.ch012

THE SCENARIO

Agriculture is a very complex activity that does not only include livestock production with livestock products, but also and plant production (Grujić Vučkovski et al., 2022; Marina et al., 2023). Considering rapid demographic, economic and lifestyle changes, the production of primary plant crops in the world increased by 50% in 2018 compared to 2000, i.e. by about 9.2 billion tons (FAO, 2020). There are forecasts that the demand for cereals at the global level could increase by approximately 10,094 million tons in 2030, i.e. 14,886 million tons by 2050, which is caused by increased pressures in the sphere of society, demography and economy. (Islam, Karim, 2020). Cereals are characterized by good nutritional values, primarily in terms of the content of minerals, vitamins and micronutrients. Also, the caloric values are very emphasized. A group of authors Farooq et al. (2023) have observed that developing countries consume more cereals than developed countries (per capita). The mentioned authors consider cereals to be a high-quality source of calories because they have a high caloric value, so they came to another conclusion, namely that in the population of developing countries, as much as 60% of the total calories consumed comes from cereals, while in developed countries this share is double less (about 30%). Although maize has a good caloric content, it is considered that it is not represented enough in human nutrition, taking only the third place. The explanation for this conclusion was found by the authors Gwirtz and Casal (2014), Okoruwa (1997), and Kaul et al. (2019). They consider that, on the one hand, the majority of the global population consumes food that is quickly prepared, while on the other hand, most countries grow corn that is for animal feed.

Along with wheat and rice, maize (*Zea mays*) is considered an important crop that contributes to global food security (Farooq et al., 2023, Dragomir et al., 2022). Maize is one of the most important cereals grown as an annual plant in different parts of the world, especially in the United States of America (abbr. USA) which accounts for 48% of world production. After the USA, among the leading countries in the world in maize production are China and Brazil (Kaushal et al., 2023).

As it is known there are several varieties of maize: sweet corn, popcorn maize, maize for cattle feed, etc. Maize can be used for different purposes: in its fresh state for human nutrition and making flour; for feeding cattle in the form of maize silage; in industrial production, maize is most often the raw material for biofuel production (Wallington et al. 2012; Courtois et al. 1991; Kaushal et al., 2023). Accordingly, the following is a brief overview of the significant economic, nutritional and biotechnical characteristics of maize, which make it considered one of the most important cereals at the global level:

- *Genetic diversity* - Maize has a high level of genetic diversity, which enables the selection and development of varieties that are adapted to different agro-ecological conditions (Bhadru et al., 2020). As the conditions of agricultural production change, it is necessary to adapt to those conditions. For this reason, the possibility of developing more resistant varieties is extremely important, primarily in terms of increasingly pronounced climate changes, the presence of diseases and pests.
- *High yields* - Maize is an extremely productive crop, precisely because of its genetic capabilities, and often achieves high yields per hectare (Iljkić et al., 2021). The biotechnical improvement of hybrids enables a combination of adequate characteristics when it is about high yields, but also in terms of previously mentioned problems such as resistance to pests and diseases, and better adaptation to different conditions during the production period. Maize is a plant that has high requirements in terms of additional water (Pejić et al., 2009) therefore, yield is dependent on drought and water availability during critical stages of development. This impact can be avoided by using hybrids that are more resistant to dry periods during the growing season (Anđelković et al., 2012).
- *Biodegradation*- Maize is often used for the production of fuel - biofuel (Sharma et al., 2016; Mohammadi Shad et al., 2021; Aghaei et al., 2022). This use of maize represents the potential for reducing the use of fossil fuels, which directly affects the emission of harmful gasses and the preservation of the environment.
- *Industrial use* - Maize is used in many industries, including the food, pharmaceutical and chemical industries (Jiao et al., 2022).
- *Diversification of agricultural production* - By including maize in the crop rotation (for example with wheat), it is possible to reduce the risk of diseases and weeds (Brankov et al., 2017) and pests. Applying this type of production directly affects the diversification of agricultural production, improving crop rotation
- *Animal food* - Maize is often used in cattle feed (Broocks et al., 2016; Ristić et al., 2023; Srećkov et al., 2023;). In some animal species, it is part of the nutrition during certain periods of development, while in others it is recognized as a basic component throughout life. The use of maize in cattle nutrition provides important nutrients for cattle, pigs, poultry and other animals.

Authors Farooq et al. (2023) had research on the impact of changes in climate indicators on the production and yield of maize. The general conclusion they reached is that maize yields are expected to be lower in countries that are close to the equator

(Mexico and Indonesia). In addition, in some countries, the increase in temperature and decrease in soil moisture will affect the decrease in maize yields.

A lot of literature that provides data on the production and harvested area under maize in the world, but in recent years Africa has taken a significant place. For sub-Saharan Africa, maize is a crop that provides them with food security (Wossen et al., 2023; Fisher et al., 2015; Foltz et al., 2012). In Nigeria, maize is grown by small agricultural holdings on an area of over 6.5 million hectares, where it is grown in several different microclimatic zones (Onumah et al., 2021; FAOSTAT, 2022). This data put Nigeria in the position of the second largest maize producing country in Africa and in West Africa (Wossen et al., 2023). This would mean that Nigeria could soon become the leading producer and exporter of maize in the world.

According to Trade Map data the export of maize globally was 204.4 million tons or USD 62.9 million during 2022. European countries exported maize worth about USD 16.7 million, which is slightly more than a quarter of the total world maize export (26.5%). If we observe the European countries individually by participation in their value of production, we notice Ukraine is dominated with 9.5%, followed by France with 3.8%, and in third place is Romania with 3.2%.

We could consider the USA as a world leading maize exporter since the beginning of the 21st century (2000-2009) when the export value was 526,670,541 metric tons (abbr. MT). The second place took Argentina with 123,527,253 MT (Brankov et al., 2014). Consequently, the USA is still the world's leading exporter of maize, 58.6 million tons was exported in 2022, while Brazil was in second place with 43.4 tons (Trade Map).

The authors noted that at the beginning of the COVID-19 pandemic, there were significant changes in the global trade of agricultural products, which may also refer to the production, trade and consumption of maize. The problems faced by the global markets at that time were reduction in transport, reduced consumption of the same, as well as uncertainty at the economic level. The transport of goods was almost suspended in order to implement social distancing measures and suppress the spread of the virus. Measures that included quarantine affected economic independence and changes in food consumption. Also, price changes affected the competitiveness of maize exports. These effects of the pandemic were specific to each country and region and depended on a number of factors. The situation has changed during the different phases of the pandemic, with changes in global trade still possible.

As a result of a crisis in Ukraine, it also appeared food shortages among the world's poorest people. Also, 30% and 20% of the total world export of maize and wheat comes from Ukraine and the Russian Federation (Farooq et al., 2023). The conclusion of these authors is aligned with the result of our research, which shows that Ukraine and the Russian Federation really occupy the first three places according to the average value of exports in the observed period (Figure 3).

Figure 1 shows spatial distribution of average share of arable land in agricultural land of the world from 2010 to 2021.

Figure 1. Average share of arable land in agricultural land of the world (in %), 2010-2021

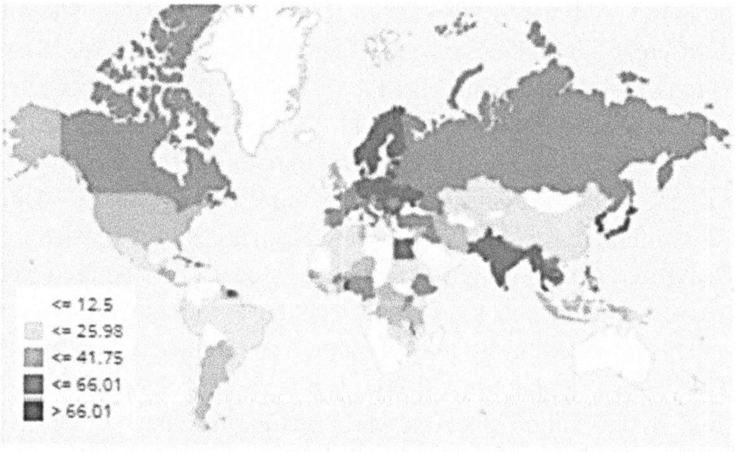

Source: FAOSTAT Database, Land Use, Visualize Data

Based on Figure 1. we notice that the countries of the world are evenly distributed according to the shown intervals of the average share of arable land in agricultural land in the period 2010-2021. Accordingly, the statistical database FAOSTAT showed that each value group contains about 45 countries of the world with about 20% participation.

Next overview (Figure 2.) gives the structure of average share of arable land in agricultural land by continents (in %) in analyzed time period.

Figure 2. Average share of arable land in agricultural land of the world (in %), 2010-2021

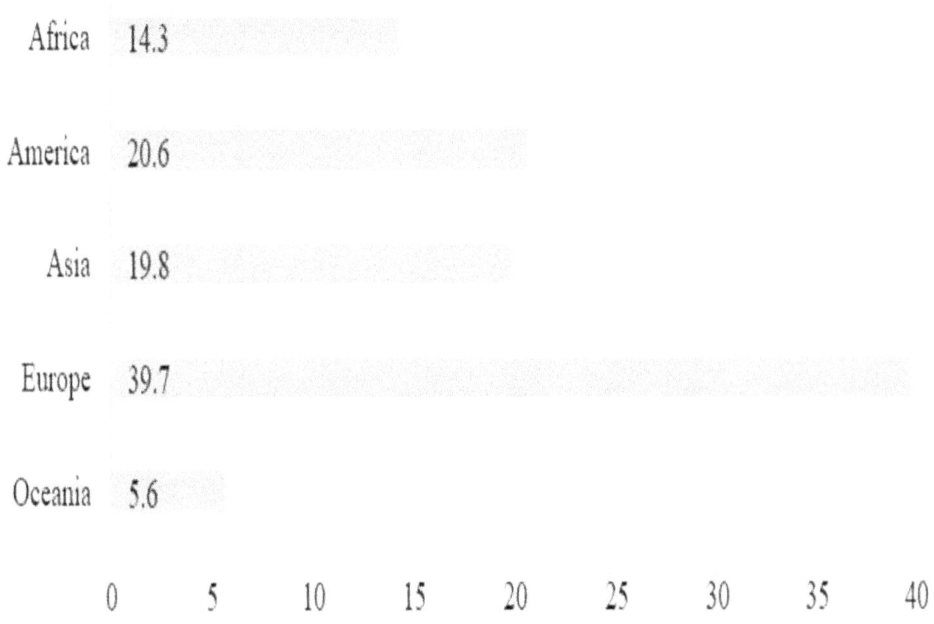

Source: Author's calculation based on FAOSTAT databases (Land Use)

In the graph above, we see that the highest average share of arable land in agricultural land was recorded in Europe with 39.7%, and the lowest in countries belonging to Oceania.

In the following figure (Figure 3) we have an overview of the top ten countries in the world with the highest average share of arable land in agricultural land in the analyzed period.

Figure 3. The first ten countries in the world with the highest achieved average share of arable land in agricultural land (in %), 2010-2021

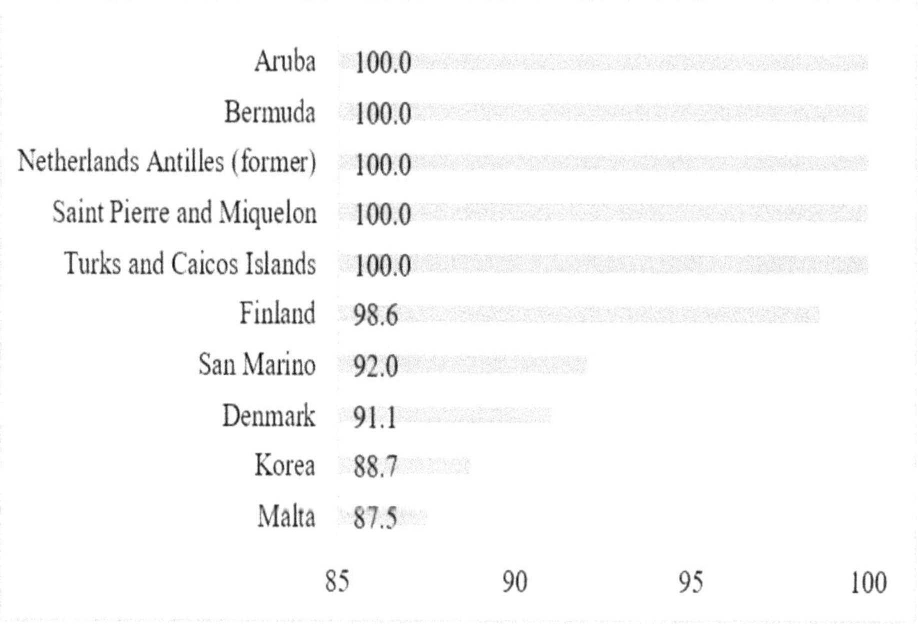

Source: Author's calculation based on FAOSTAT databases (Land Use)

From the display on Figure 3. we notice that out of ten countries in the world, three are European countries, half of the countries shown have complete coverage of agricultural land with arable land, and the high tenth place, occupied by Malta, implies as much as 87.5% average coverage of arable land in agricultural land in the observed period. In other words, we conclude that the first ten countries in the world achieved a very high average percentage of arable land in agricultural land.

Next figure (Figure 4.) shows the first five European countries with the highest achieved average annual values according to the observed variables.

Figure 4. The first five European countries with the highest average participation according to the observed variables, 2010-2022

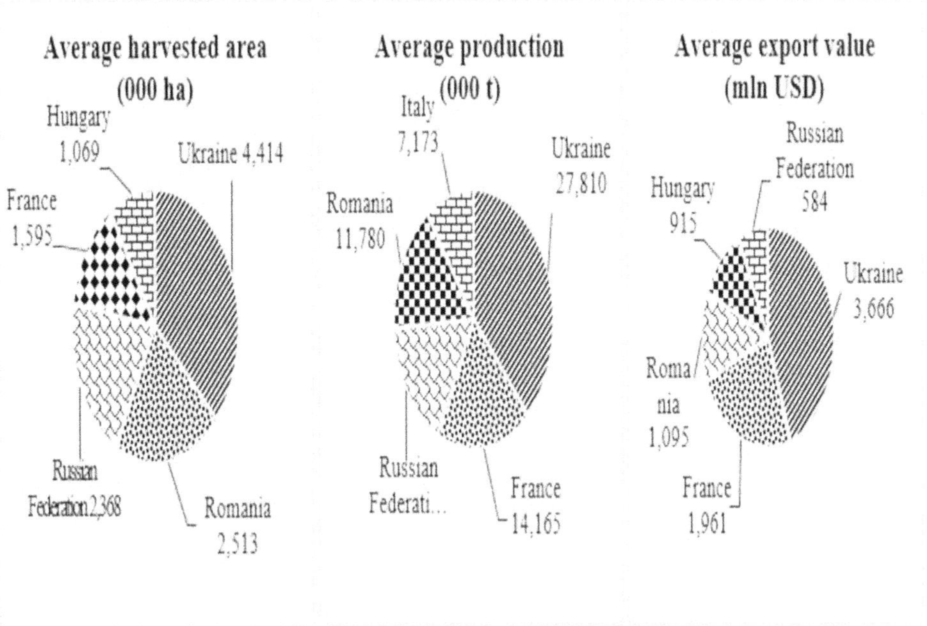

Source: Author's calculation based on FAOSTAT databases (Production and Trade of crops and livestock products)

In the graph above, we can see that Ukraine is the leading country when it comes to the average values of the observed variables, because from 2010 to 2022. had an average harvested area of 4,414 thousand hectares, a production of 27,810 thousand tons, and an export value of USD 3,666 million. Romania, France, Russian Federation, and Hungary stand out in the first five observed European countries.

Based on the previously presented and commented results, we can conclude that maize is a widespread vegetable crop, represented on all continents, successfully grown in all climate zones, has multiple purposes and is a daily subject of international trade exchange.

METHODOLOGY

This chapter was written to determine the changes in terms of harvested area (ha), production (t) and export value of maize (thousand USD) in the period from 2010 to 2022 on the example of selected European countries. However, this time series is not complete when analyzing the average share of arable land in agricultural land of the world, by continent, and for first ten European countries, because FAOSTAT did not publish the data of the observed categories for 2022 during our research.

The following European countries were included by this analysis: Austria, Belgium, Bosnia and Herzegovina, Bulgaria, Croatia, Czechia, Denmark, France, Germany, Greece, Hungary, Italy, Lithuania, Luxembourg, Moldova, Netherlands, North Macedonia, Poland, Portugal, Romania, Russia, Serbia, Slovakia, Slovenia, Spain, Switzerland and Ukraine. These countries are included in the analysis because there are statistical data according to the analyzed variables in the observed period (2010-2022). The basic source of data for the detailed analysis was the FAOSTAT Database, in the area of Production and Trade of plant products. Searching in TRADE MAP Database from Harmonized system with list of exporters by quantity and by value involved group analysis 1005 Maize or corn. Also, the relevant literature of other researchers dealing with agronomic and agroeconomic issues was used.

The following methods were used during the research:

a) The scientific description was carried out on empirical statistical data using the method of descriptive statistics (qualitative and quantitative);
b) The desk research method was also used during the research;
c) Methods of analysis and synthesis helped us to see the purpose of growing maize in certain countries (for own needs or for export);
d) The methods of induction and deduction were used for the conclusion;
e) The research results are adequately commented on.

The goal of writing the chapter is to determine the changes that occurred in the observed maize indicators, as well as the direction of movement of the analyzed economic countries (progression or regression).

The scientific justification of the research is reflected in the deepening and expansion of knowledge about current trends in selected agro - economic indicators of the state of maize in European countries. The social justification of the subject of research in this work is at a high level, because this plant crop is used daily in the nutrition of people, animals and industrial production (Dragomir et al., 2022; Kandil et al., 2020; Revilla et al., 2022).

Statistical processing of the collected data was carried out in the SPSS and Microsoft Excel program.

RESULTS AND DISCUSSION

In the methodological part of this chapter, it was pointed out that the primary source of data comes from the world database FAOSTAT in order to observe the changes that occurred in European countries from 2010 to 2022 in terms of harvested area, production and export value of maize. For these purposes, based on electronically collected data, average annual rates of change (abbr. AARC) and coefficients of variation (abbr. Cv) were calculated. The obtained results are displayed in table and expressed in percentages (Table 1.).

Table 1. Values of AARC and Cv of observed variables in selected European countries (in %), 2010-2022

Country	AARC, Area harvested	AARC, Production	AARC, Export value	Cv, Area harvested	Cv, Production	Cv, Export value
Austria	0.57	0.65	10.13	4.80	12.76	30.56
Belgium	0.05	-3.27	0.21	15.36	27.32	49.96
Bosnia and Herzegovina	-4.00	1.22	-5.44	12.09	27.61	88.02
Bulgaria	3.94	1.86	5.81	17.04	23.81	37.91
Croatia	-0.84	-1.90	17.38	8.42	17.13	70.90
Czechia	-2.06	-0.66	7.76	15.77	25.67	45.26
Denmark	-1.02	2.39	8.79	32.79	27.63	48.96
France	-0.69	-2.07	2.07	9.12	13.71	21.01
Germany	-0.18	-0.77	2.72	8.07	14.68	38.66
Greece	-3.97	-3.81	2.88	27.12	25.83	75.99
Hungary	-2.29	-7.43	-0.08	11.83	24.94	19.41
Italy	-4.06	-4.82	2.59	22.06	19.83	22.08
Lithuania	8.45	6.38	28.97	29.45	31.31	86.92
Luxembourg	-5.93	-9.75	7.79	51.27	66.00	30.80
Netherlands (Kingdom of the)	1.54	-0.89	8.44	25.69	25.91	31.16
North Macedonia	0.36	0.90	30.18	6.39	12.63	112.99
Poland	11.23	12.67	34.16	36.38	41.77	101.57
Portugal	-1.58	1.15	21.38	14.69	11.34	80.22
Republic of Moldova	2.08	-5.16	30.43	7.14	41.91	101.44
Romania	1.27	-0.98	11.76	6.19	31.22	39.46

continued on following page

Table 1. Continued

Country	AARC, Area harvested	AARC, Production	AARC, Export value	Cv, Area harvested	Cv, Production	Cv, Export value
Russian Federation	8.22	14.62	24.94	22.84	31.62	43.52
Serbia	-2.07	-4.24	2.14	9.96	24.03	31.82
Slovakia	-0.40	-2.46	13.60	9.56	26.73	54.81
Slovenia	1.10	-0.94	16.80	4.81	16.59	71.94
Spain	-0.02	0.64	3.31	10.97	11.04	14.37
Switzerland	-2.37	-1.12	6.02	13.68	20.84	46.33
Ukraine	3.76	6.75	22.86	17.01	27.57	42.43

Source: Author's calculation based on FAOSTAT databases (Production and Trade of crops and livestock products).

It was observed that there are positive and negative values by analyzing the AARC given variables. The highest average annual growth rates were achieved by: Poland, Russia, and Ukraine. Luxembourg and Hungary have the lowest negative average annual rates of change. The results of the analysis showed that the harvested area under maize in Poland increased by 11.23%, production by 12.67% and export value by 34.16%. In Luxembourg, the harvested area under maize decreased by -5.93% on average per year, production by -9.75%, while the value of exports increased by 7.79% on average per year. If we analyze only Serbia, we notice that in the observed period, the harvested area and the maize production decreased on average per year at the rate of -2.07% and -4.24%, while the value of the realized export of maize grew on average per year in the amount of 2.14%.

In the table above (Table 1.) are also displayed Cv values for the observed European countries according to the given variables. The results showed that the largest deviation from the average value of the harvested area under maize is recorded by Luxembourg, whose coefficient is 51.27%, followed by Poland with 36.38% and in third place is Denmark with a coefficient of variation of 32.79%. If we look at the realized production of maize, we notice that the biggest deviation from the average production was achieved by Luxembourg with 66%, followed by Moldova with 41.91% and in third place is Poland with a coefficient of variation of 41.77%. Indicators of the coefficient of variation in the realized value of maize exports show that the largest deviation from the average value was recorded in North Macedonia with 112.99%, followed by Poland with 101.57% and in third place is Moldova with a coefficient of variation of 101.44%. If we look only at Serbia, we notice that the values of the coefficient of variation show a deviation from the average value of harvested area by 9.96%, production by 24.03% and export value by 31.82%.

In the continuation of the research, we transited on to the analysis of variables from the aspect of applying descriptive statistics. In Table 2. the results of the descriptive statistics of the observed sample are given.

Table 2. Descriptive statistics of the analyzed variables of the observed sample

Variables	Mean	Std. Deviation	Cv (in %)
Area harvested (ha)	649681,18	1014868,176	156,2102
Production (t)	4231346,84	6348132,04	150,0263
Export Value (000 USD)	399212,67	835748,842	209,3493

Source: Author's calculation based on FAOSTAT databases. Output from SPSS software.

Based on the data displayed in Table 2. we see that, on the one hand, the variable with which we measured the value of maize exports recorded the largest coefficient of variation, and on the other hand, the smallest deviation from the arithmetic mean was achieved by maize production.

Below are the results of the Pearson correlation coefficient, which was calculated on the sample and represents an assessment of the association between variables in the population. In Table 3. the results of applying the Pearson correlation coefficient are presented (Table 3.).

Table 3. Pearson's correlation coefficient

Variables		Area harvested (ha)	Production (t)	Export Value (000 USD)
Area harvested (ha)	Pearson Correlation	1	.955**	.862**
	Sig. (2-tailed)		0,000	0,000
	N	351	351	351
Production (t)	Pearson Correlation	.955**	1	.897**
	Sig. (2-tailed)	0,000		0,000
	N	351	351	351
Export Value (000 USD)	Pearson Correlation	.862**	.897**	1
	Sig. (2-tailed)	0,000	0,000	
	N	351	351	351

Source: Author's calculation based on FAOSTAT databases. Output from SPSS software.

Pearson's correlation coefficient shows us that production and area harvested (.955), then export value and area harvested (.862), and finally expot value and production (.897) have the strongest correlation. Based on these results, we conclude that the observed variables have strong correlations.

The following graph (Figure 5) shows the dynamics of the movement in the form of a trend line of maize production in the observed period according to the analyzed European countries.

Figure 5. Trend line of maize production in the analyzed European countries, 2010 – 2022

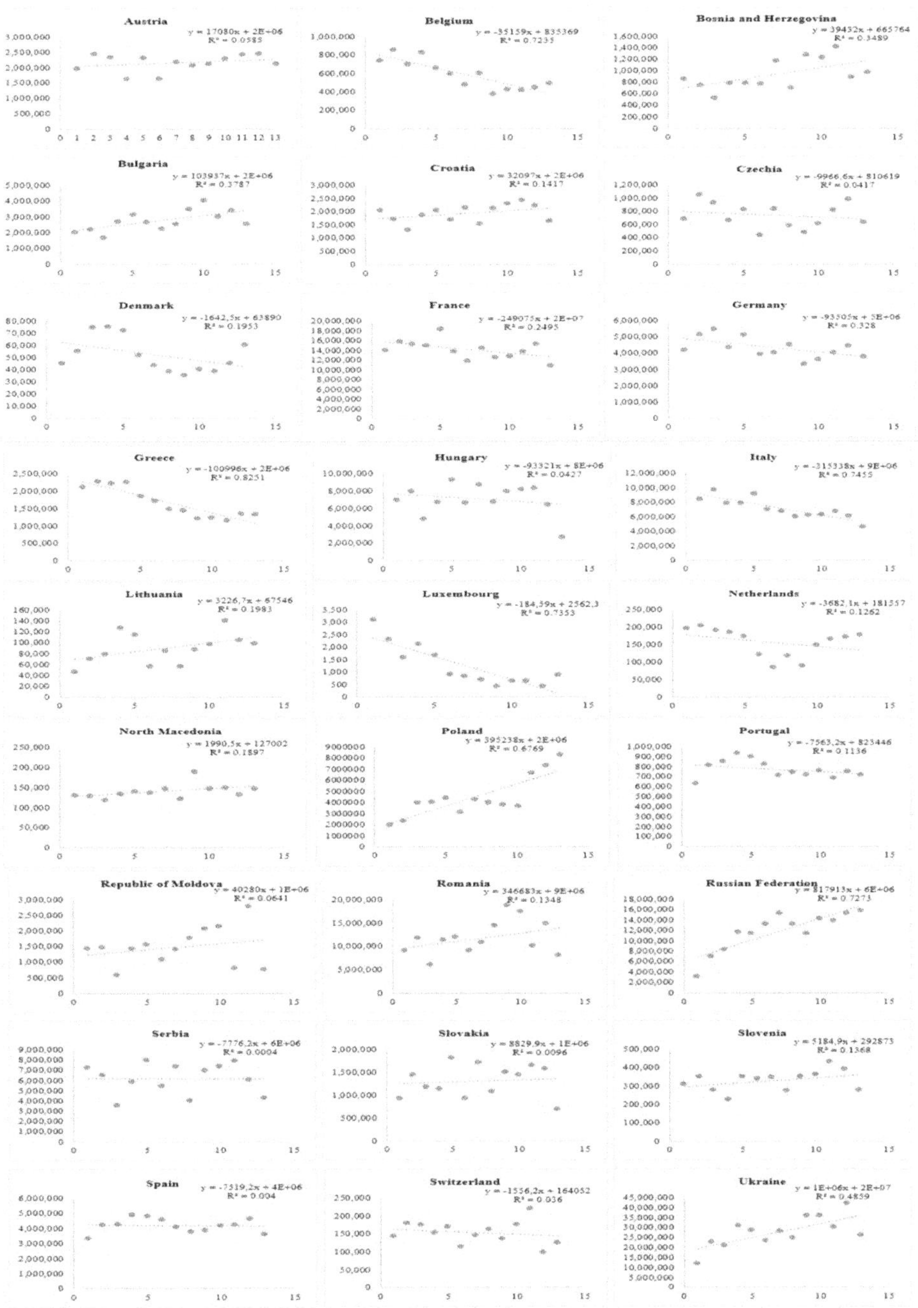

Source: Author's calculation based on FAOSTAT databases.

After showing the movement of the trend line of maize production in the analyzed period, we can conclude the following:

– Out of the total number of analyzed fourteen European countries (52%) countries achieved a negative trend in corn production;
– The biggest decrease in maize production in the past period was recorded in Luxembourg, Italy, Greece, and Belgium;
– A slight increase in maize production was observed in Slovakia and Slovenia;
– The largest increase in maize production was achieved by the Russian Federation, Poland, and Ukraine.

In general, maize production remains the leading plant crop in the cereal group, and these changes in the volume of production were mostly influenced by micro-climatic and social changes (bad weather conditions, the emergence of the COVID-19 pandemic, the beginning of the war in Ukraine, and others).

THE IMPACT OF THE COVID-19 PANDEMIC ON THE AGRICULTURAL PRODUCTION, TRADE, AND CONSUMPTION

We can say that the consequences of the COVID-19 pandemic are enormous and have affected all segments of society. It is equally important to look at the consequences of the pandemic in the past period of time, because we believe that they are still visible. All the measures adopted by the Governments of the countries at the world level affected and continue to affect the changes in the consumption of the population, legal entities and the economy as a whole (Elleby et al., 2020). The onset of the pandemic led to economic shifts in various economic sectors. During the duration of the pandemic, the agricultural and industrial sectors became inefficient over time, which caused fears about the emergence of an insufficient amount of food produced (Jambor et al., 2020; Sridhar et al., 2023). Also, international organizations showed concern, primarily the Food and Agricultural Organization (abbr. FAO), and the International Food Policy Research Institute (abbr. IFPRI), which constantly tried to keep their market open (Pu and Zhong, 2020).

This is supported by the fact that the pandemic has left the biggest mark on agriculture, because only this sector involves the production of food that is used both in human nutrition and in animal nutrition. Also, agricultural production, in all its stages of development, employs labor force, which was also affected by the epidemic, which rightly refers to the restrictions on the movement of people that were introduced and were in force in different periods, which mostly depended on the specific country which introduces them (Workie et al., 2020). Because of this, many countries have faced a shortage of seasonal labor which is extremely important for primary agricultural production. According to the FAO (2020), the biggest problem in the movement of labor was observed in the USA, Canada and Europe, which employed about 1 million workers originating from Eastern Europe and African countries.

Food prices during the pandemic depended on the country's policy and the way in which the prices of agricultural products were adjusted to the new situation. In general, food prices increased, while the author Siche (2020) considered that a significant increase in prices would be visible for high-value products. Thus, a group of authors (Hernandez et al., 2020; Elleby et al., 2020) pointed out that in India basic life products increased by more than 15% compared to the period before the pandemic, and in some African countries by more than 40% (Kubatko et al., 2023), while in Kenya, the amount of goods offered was reduced, and sales were also reduced by 97% (Kunyanga et al., 2023).

Many countries globally have experienced rising prices of domestic products, increased poverty and experienced a weakening of their domestic currency (Paudel et al., 2023; Khan et al., 2022). After the COVID-19 pandemic, there was a decrease in consumer demand for agricultural products, which was caused by an increase in prices, but there was also a change in the structure of industrial production. world-wide inflation occurred. It is believed that the main reason for this is the increase in the price of energy and energy products (Kubatko et al., 2023).

If we analyze food consumption, the author Mengoub (2020) states that research has shown that in the initial stages of the outbreak of the epidemic and the closing of the population in their homes, there was an increased consumption of food, especially packaged food. The population feared that there might be a shortage of certain food items, so larger purchases meant stocking packaged food on home shelves (Mengoub, 2020; Poudel et al., 2020).

The limited movement of people during the pandemic, especially in terms of the engagement of seasonal labor and the reduced volume of agricultural production, also reflected in the prices of agricultural products (FAO, 2020a). Blockades across the country caused people to involuntarily stop doing their jobs, return home, while small agricultural producers returned rented equipment (Dev, 2020). Also, it is considered that the world markets are integrated and interconnected, where the biggest role is played by Chinese markets and Chinese economy. Therefore, every economic change in the world market causes changes in the Chinese market as well, and these spill over into the economies of individual countries (FAO, 2020a).

There were significant changes in the market in terms of maize production, turnover and consumption at the beginning of the COVID-19 pandemic and during 2020 (Lin & Zhang 2020). These changes were mainly the result of disruptions in the supply chain between producers and buyers, restrictions on transportation, declines in consumption and economic uncertainty. For better understanding of the mentioned problems, we decided to analyze in more detail the key limitations that existed.

Due to *restrictions on transportation and logistics* travel restrictions and social distancing measures were applied in many coutries in aim to curb the spread of the virus. No one was prepared for these measures, so there was a problem in transportation globally and in terms of transporting goods (Bochtis et al., 2020). Also, the constraints on logistics caused delays in the traffic supply of maize, which led to changes in the plans of agricultural producers and traders. Also, the limitations in transport affected the lack of available labor force, as well as disruptions in the availability of inputs, and in order to reach certain markets, it was necessary to increase corn prices (Nchanji et al., 2021; Azra et al., 2021; Ceballos et al., 2021)

With the lockdown measures and economic uncertainty, there have been changes in *food consumption*. Restaurants, hotels, and other hospitality sectors faced a significant drop in demand, while demand for products used at home, including maize and maize products, even increased. This was influenced by the need of the population to create unnecessary stocks (Jámbor et al., 2020). Some countries such as Russia, Kazakhstan and Serbia have temporarily banned the export of key foodstuffs in order to build up stocks, reduce the spread of panic among citizens and ensure the security of the food supply during the pandemic (Pulighe & Lupia 2020; Jámbor et al., 2020).

Quarantine measures had the effect of reducing the available labor, both permanent and seasonal. The limitation of labor availability affected agricultural production. Primarily in the difficulty of carrying out agricultural work such as sowing, crop maintenance and harvesting.

During the COVID-19 pandemic, governments around the world intervened in world markets. The governments of the world's countries tried to adequately respond to the economic challenges caused by the pandemic through various support measures (Pan et al., 2020; Lopez-Ridaura et al., 2021). These measures included subsidies to farmers, changes in customs policies, and other interventions that affected the production and trade of maize.

We conclude that the impacts of the COVID-19 pandemic on maize production and trade were specific to each country and region, depending on a number of factors, including economic conditions, pandemic containment measures, and the structure of the domestic agricultural sector. The situation has changed during the different phases of the pandemic, with changes in global trade still possible as new circumstances emerge.

Finally, we can mention some positive changes caused by the COVID-19 epidemic in terms of agricultural production and food availability. Many conclusions have been drawn that are consistent with this topic, and we single out some of them:

– Greater consumption of vegetables in the human diet (Harris et al., 2020);
– Consumption of healthier food (Larson et al., 2021);
– More attention is on health (Glabska et al., 2020);
– Reduced consumption of tobacco and alcohol (Shrestha et al., 2020);
– Increasing representation and development of e-commerce (Ji and Zhang, 2022).

Certainly, the financial losses suffered by agricultural farms, especially those with low incomes, are unavoidable (Ellias and Jambor, 2021), so we can conclude that the COVID-19 pandemic has brought many more problems than benefits and that more research will be conducted on this topic. research in the following years so that the results are still comparable.

CONCLUSION

In global food production maize has a key part as it can be grown in all parts of the world under different microclimatic conditions. The high yields of maize and the ability to adapt to different conditions are important factors that make this cereal extremely important in global agriculture and widely present in the world.

The research conducted in the aim of writing this chapter led us to the following conclusions:

– In terms of quantity and value the largest exporter of maize is the USA looking globally;
– The largest exporters are the Russian Federation and Ukraine ranking the European countries;
– At the level of the world, there is an equally distribution of countries according to the shown intervals of the average share of arable land in agricultural land in the observed period;
– There are three European countries that rank among the top ten countries in the world according to the level of participation of agricultural land in arable land;
– We determined that Ukraine is the leading country by analyzing all three variables;
– Positive and negative rates of change of observed variables were recorded;
– We determined that the strongest correlation exists between production and area harvested by applying Pearson's correlation coefficient;

– Due to the emergence of the COVID-19 pandemic, the war in Ukraine, bad weather conditions and the like, more and more European countries are recording a negative trend in maize production.

In general, as a result of modification in food consumption, quarantine, problems in transportation, etc., there have been huge changes in the maize market in terms of production, turnover and consumption. Some countries haven't recovered yet from the losses caused by the aforementioned social changes, which is the reason for continued recording negative rates of movement of the observed parameters.

ACKNOWLEDGMENT

Chapter is a part of research financed by the Ministry of Science, Technological Development and Innovation of the Republic of Serbia and agreed in decision no. 451-03-66/2024-03/200054, 451-03-66/2024-03/200009, and research results on project U 01/2023 Green economy in the era of digitization, Faculty of Finance, Banking, and Auditing, Alpha BK University in Belgrade, Republic of Serbia.

REFERENCES

Aghaei, S., Alavijeh, M. K., Shafiei, M., & Karimi, K. (2022). A comprehensive review on bioethanol production from corn stover: Worldwide potential, environmental importance, and perspectives. *Biomass and Bioenergy*, 161, 106447. 10.1016/j.biombioe.2022.106447

Anđelković, V., Ignjatović-Mićić, D., Vančetović, J., & Babić, M. (2012). Integrated approach to improve drought tolerance in maize. *Plant breeding and Seed Production,18*(2), 1-18.

Azra, M. N., Kasan, N. A., Othman, R., Noor, G. A. G. R., Mazelan, S., Jamari, Z. B., Sarà, G., & Ikhwanuddin, M. (2021). Impact of COVID-19 on Aquaculture Sector in Malaysia: Findings from the First National Survey. *Aquaculture Reports*, 19, 100568. 10.1016/j.aqrep.2020.100568

Bhadru, D., Swarnalatha, V., Mallaiah, B., Sreelatha, D., Kumar, M. V., & Reddy, M. L. (2020). Study of genetic variability and diversity in maize (Zea mays L.) inbred lines. *Current Journal of Applied Science and Technology*, 39(38), 31–39. 10.9734/cjast/2020/v39i3831093

Bochtis, D., Benos, L., Lampridi, M., Marinoudi, V., Pearson, S., & Sørensen, C. G. (2020). Agricultural workforce crisis in light of the COVID-19 pandemic. *Sustainability (Basel)*, 12(19), 8212. 10.3390/su12198212

Brankov, M., Simić, M., Dragičević, V., & Kresović, B. (2017). Integrisani sistem suzbijanja korova u kukuruzu-značaj plodoreda, hibrida kukuruza i herbicida. *Acta herbologica, 26*(2), 95-101.

Brankov Papić, T., Jovanović, M., & Grujić, B. (2013). *Aflatoxin Standards And Maize Trade, Economics of Agriculture, N° 3/2013, Institute of Agricultural Economics*. Serbia.

Broocks, A., Rolf, M., & Place, S. (2016). *Corn as cattle feed vs. human food.* Oklahoma Cooperative Extension Service.

Ceballos, F., Kannan, S., & Kramer, B. (2020). Impacts of a National Lockdown on Smallholder Farmers' Income and Food Security: Empirical Evidence from Two States in India. *World Development*, 136, 105069. 10.1016/j.worlddev.2020.105069

Courtois, F., Lebert, A., Duquenoy, A., Lasseran, J. C., & Bimbenet, J. J. (1991). Modelling of drying in order to improve processing quality of maize. *Drying Technology*, 9(4), 927–945. 10.1080/07373939108916728

Dev, S. M. (2020). Addressing COVID-19 impacts on agriculture, food security, and livelihoods in India. *IFPRI book chapters*, 33-35.

Dragomir, V., Ioan Sebastian, B., Alina, B., Victor, P., Tanasă, L., & Horhocea, D. (2022). An overview of global maize market compared to Romanian production. *Romanian Agricultural Research*, 39, 535–544. 10.59665/rar3951

Elleby, C., Domínguez, I. P., Adenauer, M., & Genovese, G. (2020). Impacts of the COVID-19 pandemic on the global agricultural markets. *Environmental and Resource Economics*, 76(4), 1067–1079. 10.1007/s10640-020-00473-632836856

Ellias, B. A., & Jambor, A. (2021). Food Security and COVID-19: A Systematic Review of the First-Year Experience. *Sustainability (Basel)*, 13(9), 5294. 10.3390/su13095294

FAO. (2020). *Crops and Livestock Products*. Food and Agriculture Organization. https://www.fao.org/faostat/en/#data/QCL

FAO. (n.d.). FAPSTAT Database: Land Use, Visualize Data. FAO. https://www.fao.org/faostat/en/#data/RL/visualize

Farooq, A., Farooq, N., Akbar, H., Hassan, Z. U., & Gheewala, S. H. (2023). A Critical Review of Climate Change Impact at a Global Scale on Cereal Crop Production. *Agronomy (Basel)*, 13(1), 162. 10.3390/agronomy13010162

Fisher, M., Abate, T., Lunduka, R. W., Asnake, W., Alemayehu, Y., & Madulu, R. B. (2015). Drought tolerant maize for farmer adaptation to drought in sub-Saharan Africa: Determinants of adoption in eastern and southern Africa. *Climatic Change*, 133(2), 283–299. 10.1007/s10584-015-1459-2

Foltz, J. D., Aldana, U. T., & Laris, P. (2012). *The Sahel's Silent Maize Revolution: Analyzing Maize Productivity in Mali at the Farm-Level (No. W17801)*. National Bureau of Economic Research. 10.3386/w17801

Food and Agriculture Organization of United Nations. (2020). *Migrant workers and the COVID-19 pandemic*. FAO. https://www.fao.org/3/ca8559en/CA8559EN.pdf,

Food and Agriculture Organization of United Nations. (2020a). *Q&A: COVID-19 pandemic – impact on food and agriculture*. FS Cluster. https://fscluster.org/sites/default/files/documents/fao_qa_impact_on_food_and_agriculture.pdf,

García-Lara, S., & Serna-Saldivar, S. O. (2019). *Corn history and culture*. 10.1016/B978-0-12-811971-6.00001-2

Glabska, D., Skolmowska, D., & Guzek, D. (2020). Population-Based Study of the Changes in the Food Choice Determinants of Secondary School Students: Polish Adolescents' COVID-19 Experience (Place-19) Study. *Nutrients*, 12(9), 2640. 10.3390/nu1209264032872577

Grujić Vučkovski, B., Paraušić, V., Jovanović Todorović, M., Joksimović, M., & Marina, I. (2022). Analysis of influence of value indicators agricultural production on gross value added in Serbian agriculture. *Custos e Agronegocio*, 18(4), 349–372.

Gwirtz, J. A., & Garcia-Casal, M. N. (2014). Processing maize four and corn meal food products. *Annals of the New York Academy of Sciences*, 1312(1), 66–75. 10.1111/nyas.1229924329576

Harris, J., Depenbusch, L., Pal, A. A., Nair, R. M., & Ramasamy, S. (2020). Food System Disruption: Initial Livelihood and Dietary Effects of COVID-19 on Vegetable Producers in India. *Food Security*, 12(4), 841–851. 10.1007/s12571-020-01064-532837650

Hernandez, M., Kim, S., Rice, B., Vos, R. (2020). *IFPRI's new COVID-19 Food Price Monitor tracks warning signs of stress in local markets.* International Food Policy Research Institute.

Iljkić, D., Efinger, I., Rastija, M., Stipešević, B., Stošić, M., & Varga, I. (2021). Yield, agronomic and morphological properties of maize from the different FAO groups. *Proceedings of 56th Croatioan and 16th international symposium on agriculture*, Vodice, Croatia.

Islam, S. M. Z., & Karim, Z. (2020). *World's Demand for Food and Water: The Consequences of Climate Change*. IntechOpen. 10.5772/intechopen.85919

Jámbor, A., Czine, P., & Balogh, P. (2020). The impact of the coronavirus on agriculture: First evidence based on global newspapers. *Sustainability (Basel)*, 12(11), 4535. 10.3390/su12114535

Ji, W., & Zhang, J. (2022). The Impact of COVID-19 on the E-commerce Companies in China. *Review of Integrative Business and Economics Research*, 11(1), 155–165. 10.58745/riber_11-1_155-165

Jiao, Y., Chen, H. D., Han, H., & Chang, Y. (2022). Development and Utilization of Corn Processing by-Products: A Review. *Foods*, 11(22), 3709. 10.3390/foods1122370936429301

Kandil, E. E., Abdelsalam, N. R., Mansour, M. A., Ali, H. M., & Siddiqui, M. H. (2020). Potentials of organic manure and potassium forms on maize (Zea mays L.) growth and production. *Scientific Reports*, 10(1), 8752. 10.1038/s41598-020-65749-932472061

Kaul, J., Jain, K., & Olakh, D. (2019). An overview on role of yellow maize in food, feed and nutrition security. *International Journal of Current Microbiology and Applied Sciences*, 8(2), 3037–3048. 10.20546/ijcmas.2019.802.356

Kaushal, M., Sharma, R., Vaidya, D., Gupta, A., Saini, H. K., Anand, A., Thakur, C., Verma, A., Thakur, M., Priyanka, , & Kc, D. (2023). Maize: An underexploited golden cereal crop. *Cereal Research Communications*, 51(1), 3–14. 10.1007/s42976-022-00280-3

Khan, S. A. R., Razzaq, A., Yu, Z., Shah, A., Sharif, A., & Janjua, L. (2022). Disruption in food supply chain and undernourishment challenges: An empirical study in the context of Asian countries. *Socio-Economic Planning Sciences*, 82, 101033. 10.1016/j.seps.2021.101033

Kubatko, O., Merritt, R., Duane, S., Piven, V. (2023). The impact of the COVID-19 pandemic on global food system resilience. *Mechanism of an economic regulation, 1*(99), 144-148.

Kunyanga, C. N., Byskov, M. F., Hyams, K., Mburu, S., Werikhe, G., & Bett, R. (2023). Influence of COVID-19 Pandemic on Food Market Prices and Food Supply in Urban Markets in Nairobi, Kenya. *Sustainability (Basel)*, 15(2), 1304. 10.3390/su15021304

Larson, N., Slaughter-Acey, J., Alexander, T., Berge, J., Harnack, L., & Neumark-Sztainer, D. (2021). Emerging Adults' Intersecting Experiences of Food Insecurity, Unsafe Neighbourhoods and Discrimination during the Coronavirus Disease 2019 (COVID-19) Outbreak. *Public Health Nutrition*, 24(3), 519–530. 10.1017/S136898002000422X33092665

Lin, B. X., & Zhang, Y. Y. (2020). Impact of the COVID-19 pandemic on agricultural exports. [Top of Form]. *Journal of Integrative Agriculture*, 19(12), 2937–2945. 10.1016/S2095-3119(20)63430-X

Lopez-Ridaura, S., Sanders, A., Barba-Escoto, L., Wiegel, J., Mayorga-Cortes, M., Gonzalez-Esquivel, C., Lopez-Ramirez, M. A., Escoto-Masis, R. M., Morales-Galindo, E., & García-Barcena, T. S. (2021). Immediate impact of COVID-19 pandemic on farming systems in Central America and Mexico. *Agricultural Systems*, 192, 103178. 10.1016/j.agsy.2021.10317836569352

Marina, I., Grujić Vučkovski, B., & Jovanović Todorović, M. (2023). Distribution of Mechanization by Regions and Areas in the Republic of Serbia (Chapter 6). In *Sustainable Growth and Global Social Development in Competitive Economies*. IGI Global.

Mengoub, F. E. (2020). *Ensuring food security during the COVID-19 pandemic: review of short-term responses in selected countries.*

Mohammadi Shad, Z., Venkitasamy, C., & Wen, Z. (2021). Corn distillers dried grains with solubles: Production, properties, and potential uses. *Cereal Chemistry*, 98(5), 999–1019. 10.1002/cche.10445

Nchanji, E. B., Lutomia, C. K., Chirwa, R., Templer, N., Rubyogo, J. C., & Onyango, P. (2021). Immediate impacts of COVID-19 pandemic on bean value chain in selected countries in Sub-Saharan Africa. *Agricultural Systems*, 188, 103034. 10.1016/j.agsy.2020.10303433658743

Okoruwa, A. (1997). *Utilization and processing of maize.* (IITA research guide, no. 35). HDL. https://hdl.handle.net/20.500.12478/3924

Onumah, G., Dhamankar, M., Ponsioen, T., & Bello, M. (2021). Maize value chain analysis in Nigeria. *Report for the European Union, INTPA/F3*. Value Chain Analysis for Development Project.

Pan, D., Yang, J., Zhou, G., & Kong, F. (2020). The influence of COVID-19 on agricultural economy and emergency mitigation measures in China: A text mining analysis. *PLoS One*, 15(10), e0241167. 10.1371/journal.pone.024116733095814

Paudel, D., Neupane, R. C., Sigdel, S., Poudel, P., & Khanal, A. R. (2023). COVID-19 pandemic, climate change, and conflicts on agriculture: A trio of challenges to global food security. *Sustainability (Basel)*, 15(10), 8280. 10.3390/su15108280

Pejić, B., Bošnjak, Đ., Mačkić, K., Stričević, R., Simić, D., & Drvar, A. (2009). Response of maize (Zea mays L.) to soil water deficit at specific growth stages. *Annals of agronomy*, Faculty of agriculture, Novi Sad. *Serbia*, 33(1), 155–166.

Poudel, P. B., Poudel, M. R., Gautam, A., Phuyal, S., Tiwari, C. K., Bashyal, N., & Bashyal, S. (2020). COVID-19 and its global impact on food and agriculture. *Journal of Biology and Today's World*, 9(5), 221–225.

Pu, M., & Zhong, Y. (2020). Rising concerns over agricultural production as COVID-19 spreads: Lessons from China. *Global Food Security*, 26, 100409. Advance online publication. 10.1016/j.gfs.2020.10040932834954

Pulighe, G., & Lupia, F. (2020). Food first: COVID-19 outbreak and cities lockdown a booster for a wider vision on urban agriculture. *Sustainability (Basel)*, 12(12), 5012. 10.3390/su12125012

Revilla, P., Alves, M. L., Andelković, V., Balconi, C., Dinis, I., Mendes-Moreira, P., Redaelli, R., Ruiz de Galarreta, J. I., Vaz Patto, M. C., Žilić, S., & Malvar, R. A. (2022). Traditional foods from maize (Zea mays L.) in Europe. *Frontiers in Nutrition*, 8, 683399. 10.3389/fnut.2021.68339935071287

Ristić, D., Gošić-Dondo, S., Vukadinović, J., Kostadinović, M., Kravić, N., Kovinčić, A., & Mladenović Drinić, S. (2023). *Effect of abiotic and biotic stress on alteration of phytochemicals in maize leaf and grain - aftereffect on food quality and safety.* X Symposium of the Serbian association of plant breeders and seed producers and VII Symposium of the Serbian genetic society section of the breeding of organisms, Vrnjačka Banja.

Sharma, A., Sharma, S., Verma, S., & Bhargava, R. (2016). Production of biofuel (ethanol) from corn and co product evolution: A review. *Int. Res. J. Eng. Technol*, 3, 745–749.

Shrestha, C., Acharya, S., Sharma, R., Khanal, R., Joshi, J., Ghimire, C., Bhandari, P., & Agrawal, A. (2020). Changes and Compromises in Health Choices during COVID-19 Lockdown in Kathmandu Valley: A Descriptive Cross-Sectional Study. *JNMA; Journal of the Nepal Medical Association*, 58(232), 1046–1051. 10.31729/jnma.579034506372

Siche, R. (2020). What is the impact of COVID-19 disease on agriculture? *Scientia Agropecuaria*, 11(1), 3–6. 10.17268/sci.agropecu.2020.01.00

Srećkov, Z., Jan, B., Mrkonjić, Z., Bojović, M., Vukelić, I., Vasić, V., & Nikolić, O. (2023). Correlation analysis for grain yield of maize (Zea mays L.). *Thematic proceedings Biotechnology and modern approach in growing and breeding plants (Biotehnologija i savremeni pristup u gajenju i oplemenjivanju bilja).* Smederevdska Palanka, 190-197.

Sridhar, A., Balakrishnan, A., Jacob, M. M., Sillanpää, M., & Dayanandan, N. (2023). Global impact of COVID-19 on agriculture: Role of sustainable agriculture and digital farming. *Environmental Science and Pollution Research International*, 30(15), 42509–42525. 10.1007/s11356-022-19358-w35258730

Wallington, T. J., Anderson, J. E., Mueller, S. A., Kolinski Morris, E., Winkler, S. L., Ginder, J. M., & Nielsen, O. J. (2012). Corn ethanol production, food exports, and indirect land use change. *Environmental Science & Technology*, 46(11), 6379–6384. 10.1021/es300233m22533454

Workie, E., Mackolil, J., Nyika, J., & Ramadas S. (2020). Deciphering the impact of COVID-19 pandemic on food security, agriculture, and livelihoods: a review of the evidence from developing countries. *Curr Res Environ Sustain, 100014*. https:// doi.org/. crsust.2020.10001410.1016/j

Wossen, T., Menkir, A., Alene, A., Abdoulaye, T., Ajala, S., Badu-Apraku, B., Gedil, M., Mengesha, W., & Meseka, S. (2023). Drivers of transformation of the maize sector in Nigeria. *Global Food Security*, 38, 100713. 10.1016/j.gfs.2023.10071337752896

Compilation of References

Abdelhamied, H., Elbaz, A., Al-Romeedy, B., & Amer, T. (2023). Linking Green Human Resource Practices and Sustainable Performance: The Mediating Role of Job Satisfaction and Green Motivation. *Sustainability (Basel)*, 15(6), 4835. 10.3390/su15064835

Abiwu, L., & Nunoo, G. (2021). Green Recruitment Practices. In *Handbook of Research on Human Capital and People Management in the Tourism Industry* (pp. 73-93). https://doi.org/10.4018/978-1-7998-4522-5.ch005

Acquah-Sam, E. (2020). *The State as an Engine of Inclusive Sustainable Economic Growth and Development*. European Scientific Journal ESJ. 10.19044/esj.2020.v16n22p177

Adams, B. (2008). *Green Development: Environment and Sustainability in a Developing World* (3rd ed.). Routledge. 10.4324/9780203929711

Adjei-Bamfo, P., Maloreh-Nyamekye, T., & Ahenkan, A. (2019). The role of e-government in sustainable public procurement in developing countries: A systematic literature review. *Resources, Conservation and Recycling*, 142, 189–203. 10.1016/j.resconrec.2018.12.001

Afolabi, A. O., Tunji-Olayeni, P. F., Oyeyipo, O. O., & Ojelabi, R. A. (2017). The socio-economics of women inclusion in green construction. *Construction Economics and Building*, 17(1), 70–89. 10.5130/AJCEB.v17i1.5344

Afzal, F., Lim, B., & Prasad, D. (2017). An investigation of corporate approaches to sustainability in the construction industry. *Procedia Engineering*, 180, 202–210. 10.1016/j.proeng.2017.04.179

Agarwal, A., Srivastava, S., Gupta, A., & Singh, G. (2024). Food wastage and consumerism in circular economy: A review and research directions. *British Food Journal*, 126(6), 2561–2587. 10.1108/BFJ-04-2023-0272

Aggarwal, D. (2023). Green education for a sustainable future. *Journal of Environmental Impact and Management Policy (JEIMP)*, 27-30.

Aghaei, S., Alavijeh, M. K., Shafiei, M., & Karimi, K. (2022). A comprehensive review on bioethanol production from corn stover: Worldwide potential, environmental importance, and perspectives. *Biomass and Bioenergy*, 161, 106447. 10.1016/j.biombioe.2022.106447

Agrawal, S., & Pradhan, S. (2023). Employee green behavior in hotels: The role of green human resource management, green transformational leadership and value congruence. *Consumer Behavior in Tourism and Hospitality*, 18(2), 241–255. 10.1108/CBTH-11-2022-0191

Agyeman, J., Bullard, R. D., & Evans, B. (2002). Exploring the nexus: Bringing together sustainability, environmental justice, and equity. *Space and Polity*, 6(1), 77–90. 10.1080/13562570220137907

Ahenkan, A., & Osei-Kojo, A. (2014). Achieving sustainable development in Africa: Progress, challenges, and prospects. *International Journal of Development and Sustainability*, 3(1), 162–176.

Ahmad, B., Shafique, I., Qammar, A., Ercek, M., & Kalyar, M. N. (2022). Prompting green product and process innovation: Examining the effects of green transformational leadership and dynamic capabilities. *Technology Analysis and Strategic Management.*

Ahmadov, F., Zeynalova, R. A. U., Bayramova, R. A. U., & Quluzade, R. A. O. (2019). *Developmental Prospects of Women Entrepreneurs in Azerbaijan and an Analysis of the Problems They Face.*

Ahmadov, F., Zeynalova, U., Bayramova, U., & Mammadov, I. (2021). Analysis of educational impact on women entrepreneurs in sustainable social business: The case of Azerbaijan. [TURCOMAT]. *Turkish Journal of Computer and Mathematics Education*, 12(6), 1847–1856.

Ahmad, R., Nawaz, M. R., Ishaq, M. I., Khan, M. M., & Hafiz, A. A. (2023). Social exchange theory: Systematic review and future directions. *Frontiers in Psychology*, 13, 1015921. 10.3389/fpsyg.2022.101592136710813

Ahmad, S. (2015). Green human resource management: Policies and practices. *Cogent Business & Management*, 2(1), 1030817. 10.1080/23311975.2015.1030817

Aiyar, S., Malacrino, D., Mohommad, A., & Presbitero, A. (2022). *International trade spillovers from domestic COVID-19 lockdowns*. International Monetary Fund.

Akel, G., & Noyan, E. (2024). Exploring the criteria for a green and smart hotel: insights from hotel managers' perspectives. *Journal of Hospitality and Tourism Insights.*

Akerlof, G. A., & Kranton, R. E. (2000). Economics and identity. *The Quarterly Journal of Economics*, 115(3), 715–753. 10.1162/003355300554881

Akintunde, E. A. (2017). Theories and concepts for human behavior in environmental preservation. *Journal of Environmental Science and Public Health*, 1(2), 120–133. 10.26502/jesph.96120012

Akkaya, B. (2020). Review of leadership styles in perspective of dynamic capabilities: An empirical research on managers in manufacturing firms. *Yönetim Bilimleri Dergisi*, 18(36), 389–407. 10.35408/comuybd.681427

Akomea-Frimpong, I., Jin, X., & Osei-Kyei, R. (2022). Mapping studies on sustainability in the performance measurement of public-private partnership projects: A systematic review. *Sustainability (Basel)*, 14(12), 7174. 10.3390/su14127174

Alagöz, S. (2007). Yeşil pazarlama ve eko etiketleme. *Akademik Bakış*, (11), 1–13.

Albrow, M., & King, E. (1990). *Globalization, Knowledge and Society*. Sage Publications.

Ale Ebrahim, N., Ahmed, S., & Taha, Z. (2009). Innovation and R&D activities in virtual team. *European Journal of Scientific Research*, 34(3), 297–307.

Al-Ghazali, B. M., Gelaidan, H. M., Shah, S. H. A., & Amjad, R. (2022). Green transformational leadership and green creativity? The mediating role of green thinking and green organizational identity in SMEs. *Frontiers in Psychology*, 977998, 977998. 10.3389/fpsyg.2022.97799836211888

Ali, M., & Hassan, M. (2023). Green management practices and trust for green behavioral intentions and mediation of ethical leadership: An attribution theory perspective in tourism. *International Journal of Contemporary Hospitality Management*, 35(9), 3193–3215. 10.1108/IJCHM-04-2022-0506

AlKetbi, A., & Rice, J. (2024). The impact of green human resource management practices on employees, clients, and organizational performance: A literature review. *Administrative Sciences*, 14(4), 78. 10.3390/admsci14040078

Allen, I. E., Langowitz, N., & Minniti, M. (2007). Global entrepreneurship monitor. *2006 report on women and entrepreneurship, 3*(1), 54-88.

Almohamad, H., Knaack, A. L., & Habib, B. M. (2018). Assessing Spatial Equity and Accessibility of Public Green Spaces in Aleppo City, Syria. *Forests*, 9(11), 706. Advance online publication. 10.3390/f9110706

Alotaibi, A., & Abbas, A. (2023). Islamic religiosity and green purchase intention: A perspective of food selection in millennials. *Journal of Islamic Marketing*, 14(9), 2323–2342. 10.1108/JIMA-06-2021-0189

Alsaluli, A. (2023). A Modern Waste Management Strategy for Reducing Urban Air Pollution in Taif, Saudi Arabia. *International Journal of Environment and Waste Management*, 31(4), 514–524. 10.1504/IJEWM.2023.131147

Al-Serhan, A.F. (2020). Role of Green Transformational Leadership in Sustainable Business Development: Mediating Effect of Green Technology Innovation. *PalArch's Journal of Archaeology of Egypt/Egyptology,* 15178–15194.

Altuğ, T., & Akyol, A. (2018). Kurumsal yeşil imajın kurumsal web sitelerinde aktarımı: arçelik ve bosch örneği. *İnif E-Dergi, 3*(1), 194-212.

Amankwah-Amoah, J. (2020). Stepping up and stepping out of COVID-19: New challenges for environmental sustainability policies in the global airline industry. *Journal of Cleaner Production*, 271, 1–8. 10.1016/j.jclepro.2020.12300032834564

Amirian, P., Basiri, A., Gales, G., Winstanley, A., & McDonald, J. (2015). The next Generation of Navigational Services Using OpenStreetMap Data: The Integration of Augmented Reality and Graph Databases. *Lecture Notes in Geoinformation and Cartography*, 0(9783319142791), 211–228. 10.1007/978-3-319-14280-7_11

AMIS. (2024). Market Monitor is a product of the Agricultural Market Information System. *Market Monitor, 116.*

Amrutha, V., & Geetha, S. (2020). A systematic review on green human resource management: Implications for social sustainability. *Journal of Cleaner Production*, 247, 119131. 10.1016/j.jclepro.2019.119131

Anđelković, V., Ignjatović-Mićić, D., Vančetović, J., & Babić, M. (2012). Integrated approach to improve drought tolerance in maize. *Plant breeding and Seed Production,18*(2), 1-18.

Anderson, K. (2023). *What was the Industrial Revolution's environmental impact?* Greenly. https://greenly.earth/en-us/blog/ecology-news/what-was-the-industrial-revolutions environmental-impact Accessed 01.01.2024

Anderson, R. (2007). Thematic content analysis (TCA). *Descriptive presentation of qualitative data, 3*, 1-4.

Anderson, S. E., DeLeo, R. A., & Taylor, K. (2020). Policy entrepreneurs, legislators, and agenda setting: Information and influence. *Policy Studies Journal: the Journal of the Policy Studies Organization*, 48(3), 587–611. 10.1111/psj.12331

Andrei, J. V., Radulescu, I. D., Chivu, L., Erokhin, V., Nancu, D., Gao, T., & Vasic, M. (2022). A Short Descriptive Analysis of the European Evolutions of Input Price Indices of Agricultural Products between 2008-2017: Patterns, Trends, and Implications. *Strategic Management*, 27(3), 39–47. 10.5937/StraMan2200018A

Anguelovski, I., Connolly, J. J., Garcia-Lamarca, M., Cole, H., & Pearsall, H. (2018). New scholarly pathways on green gentrification: What does the urban 'green turn' mean and where is it going? *Progress in Human Geography*, 43(6), 1064–1086. 10.1177/0309132518803799

Antignac, T., Sands, D., & Schneider, G. (2016). Data Minimisation: A Language-Based Approach. *ArXiv*, abs/1611.05642. 10.1007/978-3-319-58469-0_30

Apostu, S. A., & Gigauri, I. (2023). Mapping the Link Between Human Resource Management and Sustainability: The Pathway to Sustainable Competitiveness. In *Reshaping Performance Management for Sustainable Development*, 31-59. 10.1108/S2051-663020230000008003

Armstrong, M. (2017). *Armstrong's Handbook of Performance Management: An Evidence-Based Guide to Delivering High Performance*. Kogan Page Publishers.

Arntzen, J. (2000). *Environmental Protection in the Context of Sustainable Development.* Research Gate.

Arponen, V. P. J. (2014). The cultural causes of environmental problems. *Environmental Ethics, Volume*, 36, 131–147.

Article 5 Main Environmental Principles, the Law of Georgia on Environmental Protection. Available at: https://matsne.gov.ge/en/document/view/33340?publication=21

AS. P., & TO, B. (2023, May). Corruption In Public Private. On *7th FEB International Scientific Conference* (p. 257). Research Gate.

Atasoy, H., Banker, R. D., & Pavlou, P. A. (2021). Information technology skills and labor market outcomes for workers. *Information Systems Research*, 32(2), 437–461. 10.1287/isre.2020.0975

Attfield, R. (2023). *Sustainability. The International Encyclopedia of Ethics*. Portico., 10.1002/9781444367072.wbiee033.pub2

Audretsch, D., Callejon, M., & Aranguren, M. J. (2008). Entrepreneurship, small firms and self-employment. In *High Technology, Productivity and Networks: A Systemic Approach to SME Development* (pp. 117–137). Palgrave Macmillan UK. 10.1057/9780230583726_6

Avery, G. (2005). *Leadership for Sustainable Futures*. Edward Elgar. 10.4337/9781845425494

Avolio, B. J., Bass, B. M., & Jung, D. I. (1999). Re-examining the components of transformational and transactional leadership using the Multifactor Leadership. *Journal of Occupational and Organizational Psychology*, 72(4), 441–462. 10.1348/096317999166789

Ayres, R. U., Turton, H., & Casten, T. (2007). Energy efficiency, sustainability, and economic growth. *Energy*, 32(5), 634–648. 10.1016/j.energy.2006.06.005

Aytan, O. A. (2021). Hareketli avcı-toplayıcı grupların yaşam biçimiyle yerleşik çiftçi toplulukların yaşam biçimi arasındaki insan-mekan ilişkisinin mukayesesi. *Kahramanmaraş Sütçü İmam Üniversitesi Sosyal Bilimler Dergisi*, 18(2), 979–1012. 10.33437/ksusbd.780605

Azra, M. N., Kasan, N. A., Othman, R., Noor, G. A. G. R., Mazelan, S., Jamari, Z. B., Sarà, G., & Ikhwanuddin, M. (2021). Impact of COVID-19 on Aquaculture Sector in Malaysia: Findings from the First National Survey. *Aquaculture Reports*, 19, 100568. 10.1016/j.aqrep.2020.100568

Backer, E., & Ritchie, B. W. (2017). VFR travel: A viable market for tourism crisis and disaster recovery? *International Journal of Tourism Research*, 19(4), 400–411. 10.1002/jtr.2102

Balbi, S., Bagstad, K. J., Magrach, A., Sanz, M. J., Aguilar-Amuchastegui, N., Giupponi, C., & Villa, F. (2022). The Global Environmental Agenda Urgently Needs a Semantic Web of Knowledge. *Environmental Evidence*, 11(1), 5. 10.1186/s13750-022-00258-y

Bandura, A. (1986). *Social foundations of thought and action*. APA.

Bandura, A. (1986). *Social foundations of thought and action: A social cognitive theory*. Prentice-Hall.

Bandyopadhyay, D., & Bandyopadhyay, D. (2018). Protection of traditional knowledge and indigenous knowledge. *Securing Our Natural Wealth: A Policy Agenda for Sustainable Development in India and for Its Neighboring Countries*, 59-70.

Bansode, S. (2022). Sustainable Development and Environment. *RESEARCH REVIEW International Journal of Multidisciplinary*, 7(6), 65–67. 10.31305/rrijm.2022.v07.i06.010

Barney, J. (1991). Firm Resources and Sustained Competitive Advantage. *Journal of Management*, 17(1), 99–120. 10.1177/014920639101700108

Barrena-Martínez, J., López-Fernández, M., & Romero-Fernández, P. M. (2019). Towards a configuration of socially responsible human resource management policies and practices. *International Journal of Human Resource Management*, 30(17), 2544–2580. 10.1080/09585192.2017.1332669

Bartniczak, B., & Raszkowski, A. (2018). Sustainable development in African countries: An indicator-based approach and recommendations for the future. *Sustainability (Basel)*, 11(1), 22. 10.3390/su11010022

Bass, B. M. (1995). *Leadership and Performance Beyond Expectations*. Free Press.

Bass, B. M. (1998). *Transformational leadership: Industrial, military, and educational impact*. Erlbaum.

Baştürk, Ş. (2001). Bir olgu olarak küreselleşme. *İş-Güç Endüstri İlişkileri ve İnsan Kaynakları Dergisi, 3*(2).

Baykal, H., & Baykal, T. (2008). Küresel Dünya'da çevre sorunları. *Mustafa Kemal Üniversitesi Sosyal Bilimler Enstitüsü Dergisi*, 5(9), 1–17.

Beder, S. (2000). Costing the earth: Equity, sustainable development, and environmental economics. *NZJ Envtl. L.*, 4, 227.

Been, V., Cunningham, M. K., Ellen, I. G., Parilla, J., Turner, M. A., Whitney, S. V., & Yowell, A. (2016). *Building environmentally sustainable communities: A framework for inclusivity*. Research Gate.

Begum, S., Ashfaq, M., Xia, E., & Awan, U. (2022). Does green transformational leadership lead to green innovation? The role of green thinking and creative process engagement. *Business Strategy and the Environment*, 31(1), 580–597. 10.1002/bse.2911

Behera, D. K. (2023). Promoting Sustainable Development Through Environmental Policy, Green Technologies, and Effective Waste Management: A Comprehensive Review. *Journal of Multidisciplinary Science: MIKAILALSYS*, 1(2), 179–198. 10.58578/mikailalsys.v1i2.1675

Bellamy, A. S. (2021). Seeds of Change: Establishing Frameworks for Understanding Global Environmental Changes. *Ambio*, 50(7), 1281–1285. 10.1007/s13280-021-01509-x33713292

Belmonte-Urena, L. J., Plaza-Ubeda, J. A., Vazquez-Brust, D., & Yakovleva, N. (2021). Circular Economy, Degrowth and Green Growth as Pathways for Research on Sustainable Development Goals: A Global Analysis and Future Agenda. *Ecological Economics*, 185, 107050. 10.1016/j.ecolecon.2021.107050

Beretta, I. (2014). *Becoming a European Green Capital: a way towards sustainability?* Emerald. .10.1108/S1047-004220140000014014

Berglund, T., & Gericke, N. (2018). Exploring the role of the economy in young adults' understanding of sustainable development. *Sustainability (Basel)*, 10(8), 2738. 10.3390/su10082738

Berrone, P., Ricart, J. E., Duch, A. I., Bernardo, V., Salvador, J., Piedra Peña, J., & Rodríguez Planas, M. (2019). EASIER: An evaluation model for public–private partnerships contributing to the sustainable development goals. *Sustainability (Basel)*, 11(8), 2339. 10.3390/su11082339

Bhadru, D., Swarnalatha, V., Mallaiah, B., Sreelatha, D., Kumar, M. V., & Reddy, M. L. (2020). Study of genetic variability and diversity in maize (Zea mays L.) inbred lines. *Current Journal of Applied Science and Technology*, 39(38), 31–39. 10.9734/cjast/2020/v39i3831093

Bobryshev, A., Chaykovskaya, L., Erokhin, V., & Ivolga, A. (2023). Sustaining Growth or Boosting Profit. Accounting Tools under Process-Based Management in a Transition Economy. *Journal of Risk and Financial Management*, 16(2), 92. 10.3390/jrfm16020092

Bochtis, D., Benos, L., Lampridi, M., Marinoudi, V., Pearson, S., & Sørensen, C. G. (2020). Agricultural workforce crisis in light of the COVID-19 pandemic. *Sustainability (Basel)*, 12(19), 8212. 10.3390/su12198212

Boeing, G. (2020a). A Multi-Scale Analysis of 27,000 Urban Street Networks: Every US City, Town, Urbanized Area, and Zillow Neighborhood. *Environment and Planning. B, Urban Analytics and City Science*, 47(4), 590–608. Advance online publication. 10.1177/2399808318784595

Bogdanova, E., Lobanov, A., Andronov, S. V., Soromotin, A., Popov, A., Skalny, A. V., Shaduyko, O., & Callaghan, T. V. (2023). Challenges of Changing Water Sources for Human Wellbeing in the Arctic Zone of Western Siberia. *Water (Basel)*, 15(8), 1577. 10.3390/w15081577

Bohmova, L., & Chudán, D. (2018). Analyzing Social Media Data for Recruiting Purposes. *Acta Informatica Pragensia*, 7(1), 4–21. 10.18267/j.aip.111

Bohnenberger, K. (2022). Greening work: Labor market policies for the environment. *Empirica*, 49(2), 347–368. 10.1007/s10663-021-09530-9

Bombiak, E. (2019). *Green human resource management – the latest trend or strategic necessity?* Entrepreneurship and Sustainability Issues., 10.9770/jesi.2019.6.4(7)

Borrero, J. D., & Yousafzai, S. (2024). Circular entrepreneurial ecosystems: A Quintuple Helix Model approach. *Management Decision*, 62(13), 188–224. 10.1108/MD-08-2023-1361

Bort, S. (2023). *The Environmental Commitment Of European Commercial Aviation: The Case Of Low-Cost Airlines*. Universitat Jaume. https://repositori.uji.es/xmlui/bitstream/handle/10234/203491/TFG_2023_Beltran_Bort_Sergio.pdf?sequence=1

Bortolini, M., Galizia, F. G., Gamberi, M., Mora, C., & Pilati, F. (2019). Enhancing stock efficiency and environmental sustainability goals in direct distribution logistic networks. *International Journal of Advanced Operations Management*, 11(1-2), 8–25. 10.1504/IJAOM.2019.098518

Bourdieu, P. (1986). The forms of capital. In J. Richardson (Ed.), *Handbook of Theory and Research for the Sociology of Education* (pp. 241-258). Greenwood.

Bourdieu, P. (1991). *Language and symbolic power*. Harvard University Press.

Brankov Papić, T., Jovanović, M., & Grujić, B. (2013). *Aflatoxin Standards And Maize Trade, Economics of Agriculture, N° 3/2013, Institute of Agricultural Economics*. Serbia.

Brankov, M., Simić, M., Dragičević, V., & Kresović, B. (2017). Integrisani sistem suzbijanja korova u kukuruzu-značaj plodoreda, hibrida kukuruza i herbicida. *Acta herbologica, 26*(2), 95-101.

Braun, P. (2010). Going green: Women entrepreneurs and the environment. *International Journal of Gender and Entrepreneurship*, 2(3), 245–259. 10.1108/17566261011079233

Broocks, A., Rolf, M., & Place, S. (2016). *Corn as cattle feed vs. human food*. Oklahoma Cooperative Extension Service.

Brouwer, F. (2023, May). A Resource Nexus Concept-Definition, design, and practice. In *EGU General Assembly Conference Abstracts (pp. EGU-3963)*. 10.5194/egusphere-egu23-3963

Brown, H., & Lee, J. (2019). The impact of linguistic proficiency on global intergroup relations. *International Journal of Intercultural Relations*, 45, 117–130.

Bukeviciute, L., Dierx, A., & Ilzkovitz, F. (2009). *The functioning of the food supply chain and its effect on food prices in the European Union*. European Commission.

Caldwell, L.K. (2007). *Principles of Sustainable Development.*

Carroll, A. B. (2009). *A History of Corporate Social Responsibility (A. Crane, D. Matten, A. McWilliams* (Moon, J., & Siegel, D. S., Eds.). Vol. 1). Oxford University Press., 10.1093/oxfordhb/9780199211593.003.0002

Castells, M. (1996). *The rise of the network society*. Blackwell Publishers.

Cavalieri, S., & Ghislandi, W. M. (2010). Understanding and using near misses' properties through a double-step conceptual structure. *Journal of Intelligent Manufacturing*, 21(2), 237–247. 10.1007/s10845-008-0193-2

Ceballos, F., Kannan, S., & Kramer, B. (2020). Impacts of a National Lockdown on Smallholder Farmers' Income and Food Security: Empirical Evidence from Two States in India. *World Development*, 136, 105069. 10.1016/j.worlddev.2020.105069

CESD. (2022). *COVID-19 and female entrepreneurs in Azerbaijan: Challenges and outcomes. CESD PRESS. Center for Economic and Social Development*. CESD.

Ceylan, U., & Kıpırtı, F. (2021). Turizm işletmelerinde yeşil pazarlama faaliyetleri: literatür incelemesi. *Socrates Journal of Interdisciplinary Social Studies*, 23-37. .10.51293/socrates.22

Chalkley, B. (2006). Education for sustainable development: Continuation. *Journal of Geography in Higher Education*, 30(2), 235–236. 10.1080/03098260600717307

Chamorro-Premuzic, T., & Akhtar, R. (2019). Should companies use AI to assess job candidates? *Harvard Business Review*. https://hbr.org/2019/05/should-companies-use-ai-to-assess-job-candidates

Chan, G., Wang, B., Zhang, V., & Li, M. (2021). Predicting psychological benefit in green for airlines passengers affect organization corporate image to switching decision. [IJSSR]. *International Journal of Social Science Research*, 3(4), 183–200.

Chang, C. T. (2013). The disappearing sustainability triangle: Community level considerations. *Sustainability Science*, 8(2), 227–240. 10.1007/s11625-013-0199-3

Chatjuthamard, P., Sarajoti, P., & Papangkorn, S. (2023). *Perspective Chapter: Sustainability and Corporate Innovation*. Chapters.

Cheba, K., Bąk, I., Szopik-Depczynska, K., & Ioppolo, G. (2022). Directions of green transformation of the European Union countries. *Ecological Indicators*, 136, 1–15. 10.1016/j.ecolind.2022.108601

Chênes, C., Giuliani, G., & Ray, N. (2021). Modelling Physical Accessibility to Public Green Spaces in Switzerland to Support the SDG11. *Geomatics*, 1(4), 383–398. 10.3390/geomatics1040022

Cheng, T. C. E., Kamble, S. S., Belhadi, A., Ndubisi, N. O., Lai, K. H., & Kharat, M. G. (2021). Linkages between big data analytics, circular economy, sustainable supply chain flexibility, and sustainable performance in manufacturing firms. *International Journal of Production Research*. 10.1080/00207543.2021.1906971

Chen, Y., Han, Y., & Guo, L. (2021). Recent Development and Regional Disparity of the Rural Industries in China. *International Journal of Social Economics*, 48(5), 759–775. 10.1108/IJSE-07-2020-0481

Chen, Y.-S., & Chang, C.-H. (2013). The Determinants of Green Product Development Performance: Green Dynamic Capabilities, Green Transformational Leadership, and Green Creativity. *Business Ethics (Oxford, England)*, 107–119.

Chen, Y.-S., Chang, C.-H., & Lin, Y.-H. (2014). Green Transformational Leadership and Green Performance: The Mediation Effects of Green Mindfulness and Green Self-Efficacy. *Sustainability (Basel)*, 6(10), 6604–6621. 10.3390/su6106604

Chen, Y.-S., & Yan, X. (2022). The small and medium enterprises' green human resource management and green transformational leadership: A sustainable moderated-mediation practice. *Corporate Social Responsibility and Environmental Management*, 29(5), 1–16. 10.1002/csr.2273

Cherian, J. P., & Jacob, J. (2012). A Study of Green HR practices and its effective implementation in the organization: A review. *International Journal of Business and Management*, 7(21), 1–15. 10.5539/ijbm.v7n21p25

Chiang, F. F. T., & Birtch, T. A. (2012). The performance implications of financial and non-financial rewards: An Asian Nordic comparison. *Journal of Management Studies*, 49(3), 538–570. 10.1111/j.1467-6486.2011.01018.x

Chisika, S. N., & Yeom, C. (2021). Enhancing sustainable management of public natural forests through public private partnerships in Kenya. *SAGE Open*, 11(4), 21582440211054490. 10.1177/21582440211054490

Chomsky, N. (2001). *9-11*. Seven Stories Press.

Choudhary, A., & Gokarn, S. (2013). Green marketing: A means for sustainable development. *International Refereed Research Journal*, 4(3), 26–32.

Ciulla, J. B. (2020). The Importance of Leadership in Shaping Business Values. In *Corporate Ethics and Corporate Governance* (pp. 67–77). Springer Berlin Heidelberg New York.

Clark, R., Reed, J., & Sunderland, T. (2018). Bridging funding gaps for climate and sustainable development: Pitfalls, progress and potential of private finance. *Land Use Policy*, 71, 335–346. 10.1016/j.landusepol.2017.12.013

Conger, R. D., & Donnellan, M. B. (2007). An interactionist perspective on the socioeconomic context of human development. *Annual Review of Psychology*, 58(1), 175–199. 10.1146/annurev.psych.58.110405.08555116903807

Constantin, M., Radulescu, I. D., Andrei, J. V., Chivu, L., Erokhin, V., & Gao, T. (2021). A Perspective on Agricultural Labor Productivity and Greenhouse Gas Emissions in Context of the Common Agricultural Policy Exigencies. *Ekonomika Poljoprivrede*, 68(1), 53–67. 10.5937/ekoPolj2101053C

Çop, S., Olorunsola, V. O., & Alola, U. V. (2020). Achieving environmental sustainability through green transformational leadership policy: Can green team resilience help? *Business Strategy and the Environment*, •••, 1–12.

Cosgrove, W. J., & Loucks, D. P. (2015). Water management: Current and future challenges and research directions. *Water Resources Research*, 51(6), 4823–4839. 10.1002/2014WR016869

Courtois, F., Lebert, A., Duquenoy, A., Lasseran, J. C., & Bimbenet, J. J. (1991). Modelling of drying in order to improve processing quality of maize. *Drying Technology*, 9(4), 927–945. 10.1080/07373939108916728

Cropanzano, R., & Mitchell, M. S. (2005). Social Exchange Theory: An Interdisciplinary Review. *Journal of Management*, 31(6), 874–900. 10.1177/0149206305279602

Cross, K. W. (2023). A critical evaluation of inter-generational equity and its application in the climate change context. In *Feminist Frontiers in Climate Justice* (pp. 40–67). Edward Elgar Publishing. 10.4337/9781803923796.00007

Crystal, D. (2012). *English as a global language* (2nd ed.). Cambridge University Press. 10.1017/CBO9781139196970

Custers, B., Ursic, H., & Schermer, B. (2019). *Discrimination and Privacy in the Information Society: Data Mining and Profiling in Large Databases*. Springer.

Daily, B. F., & Huang, S. (2001). Achieving sustainability through attention to human resource factors in environmental management. *International Journal of Operations & Production Management*, 21(12), 1539–1552. 10.1108/01443570110410892

Dale, G. (2018). *The emergence of an ecological Karl Marx: 1818-2018.*

Dale, G. (2019). Climate, communism and the Age of Affluence. *Review of FALC.*

Darvishi, Y., Karami, H., & Goodarzian, F. (2023). Sustainable development in oxygenated fuels. In *Advancement in Oxygenated Fuels for Sustainable Development* (pp. 315–330). Elsevier. 10.1016/B978-0-323-90875-7.00013-7

Das, N., Bera, P., & Panda, D. (2022). Can economic development & environmental sustainability promote renewable energy consumption in India?? Findings from novel dynamic ARDL simulations approach. *Renewable Energy*, 189, 221–230. 10.1016/j.renene.2022.02.116

Dean, T. J., & McMullen, J. S. (2007). Toward a theory of sustainable entrepreneurship: Reducing environmental degradation through entrepreneurial action. *Journal of Business Venturing*, 22(1), 50–76. 10.1016/j.jbusvent.2005.09.003

Deci, E. L., & Ryan, R. M. (1985). *Intrinsic motivation and self-determination in human behavior*. Plenum. 10.1007/978-1-4899-2271-7

Demirel, P., Li, Q. C., Rentocchini, F., & Tamvada, J. P. (2019). Born to be green: New insights into the economics and management of green entrepreneurship. *Small Business Economics*, 52(4), 759–771. 10.1007/s11187-017-9933-z

Demir, M., & Günaydın, Y. (2023). A digital job application reference: How do social media posts affect the recruitment process? *Employee Relations*, 45(2), 457–477. 10.1108/ER-05-2022-0232

DeNisi, A. S., & Murphy, K. R. (2017). Performance Appraisal and Performance Management: 100 Years of Progress? *The Journal of Applied Psychology*, 102(3), 421–433. 10.1037/apl000008528125265

Dev, S. M. (2020). Addressing COVID-19 impacts on agriculture, food security, and livelihoods in India. *IFPRI book chapters*, 33-35.

Devi Kalpana, J. K. (2018). Influence of Green HRM practices on employees performance level – a study with reference to literature review. [IJRAR]. *International Journal of Research and Analytical Reviews*, 5(3), 329–333.

Diener, E., Oishi, S., & Lucas, R. E. (2003). Personality, culture, and subjective well-being: Emotional and cognitive evaluations of life. *Annual Review of Psychology*, 54(1), 403–425. 10.1146/annurev.psych.54.101601.14505612172000

Djurić, Z. (2019). *Ekološka održivost poslovanja u hotelijerstvu*. Novi Sad: Biblioteka, Edukons univerzitet, Fakultet za sport i turizam.

Dong, K. (2002). Intergenerational Equity and Sustainable Development. *Journal of Yanan University*.

Dong, D., Xu, B., Shen, N., & He, Q. (2021). The Adverse Impact of Air Pollution on China's Economic Growth. *Sustainability (Basel)*, 13(16), 9056. 10.3390/su13169056

Doyle, E., & Perez Alaniz, M. (2021). Dichotomous impacts on social and environmental sustainability: Competitiveness and development levels matter. *Competitiveness Review*, 31(4), 771–791. 10.1108/CR-05-2019-0055

Dragomir, V., Ioan Sebastian, B., Alina, B., Victor, P., Tanasă, L., & Horhocea, D. (2022). An overview of global maize market compared to Romanian production. *Romanian Agricultural Research*, 39, 535–544. 10.59665/rar3951

Dubey, R., Gunasekaran, A., & Papadopoulos, T. (2017). Green supply chain management: Theoretical framework and further research directions. *Benchmarking*, 24(1), 184–218. 10.1108/BIJ-01-2016-0011

Dumitriu, M. L. I. (2021). The Principles of Environmental Protection. *Perspective Politice*, 14(1-2), 125. 10.25019/perspol/21.14.10

Duru, M., & Şua, E. (2013). Yeşil pazarlama ve tüketicilerin çevre dostu ürünleri kullanma eğilimleri. *Ormancılık Dergisi*, 9(2), 126–136. 10.54452/jrb.993685

Du, Y., & Yan, M. (2022). Green Transformational Leadership and Employees' Taking Charge Behavior: The Mediating Role of Personal Initiative and the Moderating Role of Green Organizational Identity. *International Journal of Environmental Research and Public Health*, 19(7), 4172. 10.3390/ijerph1907417235409857

Eagan, P. D., & Joeres, E. (1997). Development of a facility-based environmental performance indicator related to sustainable development. *Journal of Cleaner Production*, 5(4), 269–278. 10.1016/S0959-6526(97)00044-9

Eckerberg, K., & Bjärstig, T. (2022). Collaborative approaches for sustainable development governance. In *Handbook on the governance of sustainable development* (pp. 175–189). Edward Elgar Publishing.

Edmonds, R. (1999). The Environment in the People's Republic of China 50 Years on. *The China Quarterly*, 159, 640–649. 10.1017/S030574100000339820101811

Effelsberg, D., Solga, M., & Gurt, J. (2014). Transformational Leadership and Follower's Unethical Behavior for the Benefit of the Company: A Two-Study Investigation. *Journal of Business Ethics*, 120(1), 81–93. 10.1007/s10551-013-1644-z

Einarsson, S. F. (2019). *What is the link between Circular Economy (CE) and the Sustainable Development Goals (SDGs)?* LinkedIn. https://www.linkedin.com/pulse/what-link-between-circular-economy-ce-sustainable-goals-einarsson/

Ekvall, G. (1996). Organizational climate for creativity and innovation. *European Journal of Work and Organizational Psychology*, 5(1), 105–123. 10.1080/13594329608414845

Elder, G. H.Jr, & Caspi, A. (1988). Economic stress in lives: Developmental perspectives. *The Journal of Social Issues*, 44(4), 25–45. 10.1111/j.1540-4560.1988.tb02090.x

Elleby, C., Domínguez, I. P., Adenauer, M., & Genovese, G. (2020). Impacts of the COVID-19 pandemic on the global agricultural markets. *Environmental and Resource Economics*, 76(4), 1067–1079. 10.1007/s10640-020-00473-632836856

Ellias, B. A., & Jambor, A. (2021). Food Security and COVID-19: A Systematic Review of the First-Year Experience. *Sustainability (Basel)*, 13(9), 5294. 10.3390/su13095294

Environmental Protection Agency. (2023). *Ministry of Environmental Protection Republic of Serbia*. EPA. http://www.sepa.gov.rs/#

Environmental Protection Law of. 1999, No. 678–IQ, Azerbaijan (1999). https://www.fao.org/faolex/results/details/en/c/LEX-FAOC032661/

Erbaşlar, G. (2012). Yeşil pazarlama. *Mesleki Bilimler Dergisi*, 1(2), 94–101.

Erdős, L. (2019). Al Gore – The Climate Crusader. *Green Heroes*, 207–211, 207–211. 10.1007/978-3-030-31806-2_41

Erkızan, H. N. (2002). Küreselleşmenin tarihsel ve düşünsel temelleri üzerine. *Doğu Batı Dergisi*, 5(18), 65–66.

Erokhin, V., Gao, T., Chivu, L., & Andrei, J.V. (2022). Food Security in a Food Self-Sufficient Economy: A Review of China's Ongoing Transition to a Zero Hunger State. *Agricultural Economics – Czech, 68*(12), 476-487. .10.17221/278/2022-AGRICECON

Erokhin, V., Ivolga, A., & Heijman, W. (2014). Trade Liberalization and State Support of Agriculture: Effects for Developing Countries. *Agricultural Economics – Czech, 60*(11), 524-537. .10.17221/137/2013-AGRICECON

Erokhin, V. (2017a). Factors Influencing Food Markets in Developing Countries: An Approach to Assess Sustainability of the Food Supply in Russia. *Sustainability (Basel)*, 9(8), 1313. 10.3390/su9081313

Erokhin, V. (2017b). Self-Sufficiency versus Security: How Trade Protectionism Challenges the Sustainability of the Food Supply in Russia. *Sustainability (Basel)*, 9(11), 1939. 10.3390/su9111939

Erokhin, V. (2020). Produce Internationally, Consume Locally: Changing Paradigm of China's Food Security Policy. In Jean Vasile, A., Subic, J., Grubor, A., & Privitera, D. (Eds.), *Handbook of Research on Agricultural Policy, Rural Development, and Entrepreneurship in Contemporary Economies* (pp. 273–295). IGI Global. 10.4018/978-1-5225-9837-4.ch014

Erokhin, V., Diao, L., Gao, T., Andrei, J.-V., Ivolga, A., & Zong, Y. (2021a). The Supply of Calories, Proteins, and Fats in Low-Income Countries: A Four-Decade Retrospective Study. *International Journal of Environmental Research and Public Health*, 18(14), 7356. 10.3390/ijerph1814735634299805

Erokhin, V., Endovitsky, D., Bobryshev, A., Kulagina, N., & Ivolga, A. (2019). Management Accounting Change as a Sustainable Economic Development Strategy during Pre-Recession and Recession Periods: Evidence from Russia. *Sustainability (Basel)*, 11(11), 3139. 10.3390/su11113139

Erokhin, V., Esaulko, A., Pismennaya, E., Golosnoy, E., Vlasova, O., & Ivolga, A. (2021b). Combined Impact of Climate Change and Land Qualities on Winter Wheat Yield in Central Fore-Caucasus: The Long-Term Retrospective Study. *Land (Basel)*, 10(12), 1339. 10.3390/land10121339

Erokhin, V., & Gao, T. (2022a). Renewable Energy as a Promising Venue for China-Russia Collaboration. In Khan, S. A. R., Panait, M., Puime Guillen, F., & Raimi, L. (Eds.), *Energy Transition. Industrial Ecology* (pp. 73–101). Springer. 10.1007/978-981-19-3540-4_3

Erokhin, V., & Gao, T. (2022b). New Eurasian Land Bridge: The Connectivity-Inputs-Growth Triangle. *Rivista Internazionale di Economia dei Trasporti*, XLIX(2), 207–229. 10.19272/202206702004

Erokhin, V., Gao, T., Andrei, J. V., & Ivolga, A. (2020a). Transformation of Agricultural Land Distribution Patterns in Russia. *Ekonomika Poljoprivrede*, 67(3), 863–879. 10.5937/ekoPolj2003863E

Erokhin, V., Gao, T., & Ivolga, A. (2020b). Structural Variations in the Composition of Land Funds at Regional Scales across Russia. *Land (Basel)*, 9(6), 201. 10.3390/land9060201

Erokhin, V., Gao, T., & Ivolga, A. (2021c). Cross-Country Potentials and Advantages in Trade in Fish and Seafood Products in the RCEP Member States. *Sustainability (Basel)*, 13(7), 3668. 10.3390/su13073668

Erokhin, V., Li, D., & Du, P. (2020c). Sustainability-Related Implications of Competitive Advantages in Agricultural Value Chains: Evidence from Central Asia – China Trade and Investment. *Sustainability (Basel)*, 12(3), 1117. 10.3390/su12031117

Erokhin, V., Samygin, D., Tuskov, A., & Ivolga, A. (2023). Mitigating Spatial Disproportions in Agriculture through Revealing Competitive Advantages. *Ekonomika Poljoprivrede*, 70(4), 1157–1170. 10.59267/ekoPolj23041157E

Esaulko, A., Sitnikov, V., Pismennaya, E., Vlasova, O., Golosnoi, E., Ozheredova, A., Ivolga, A., & Erokhin, V. (2023). Productivity of Winter Wheat Cultivated by Direct Seeding: Measuring the Effect of Hydrothermal Coefficient in the Arid Zone of Central Fore-Caucasus. *Agriculture*, 13(1), 55. 10.3390/agriculture13010055

Espitia, A., Mattoo, A., Rocha, N., Ruta, M., & Winkler, D. (2021, February). Pandemic Trade: Covid-19. *World Bank Policy Research Working Paper*, PAPERS9. 10.1596/1813-9450-950833821085

Esposito, P., & Dicorato, S. L. (2020). Sustainable development, governance and performance measurement in public private partnerships (PPPs): A methodological proposal. *Sustainability (Basel)*, 12(14), 5696. 10.3390/su12145696

Etim, N. N., & Djekic, I. (2022). An overview of the interactions between food production and climate change. *The Science of the Total Environment*, 838(Pt 3), 156438. 10.1016/j.scitotenv.2022.15643835660578

European Union. (2014). Directive 2014/95/EU of the European Parliament and of the Council of 22 October 2014 amending Directive 2013/34/EU as regards disclosure of non-financial and diversity information by certain large undertakings and groups. *Official Journal of the European Union, L 330*, 1-9. https://eur-lex.europa.eu/legal-content/EN/TXT/?uri=celex%3A32014L0095

European Union. (2022). Directive (EU) 2022/2464 of the European Parliament and of the Council of 14 December 2022 amending Directive 2013/34/EU, Directive 2004/109/EC, Directive 2006/43/EC and Regulation (EU) No 537/2014, as regards corporate sustainability reporting. *Official Journal of the European Union, L 322*, 15-57. https://eur-lex.europa.eu/legal-content/EN/TXT/?uri=CELEX%3A32022L2464

Eurostat. (2020). *Waste statistics*. Eurostat. https://ec.europa.eu/eurostat/web/waste/data/database

Evans, L., & Nobes, C. (2021). Harmonization relating to auditor independence: The Eighth Directive, the UK and Germany. *European Accounting Review*, 7(3), 493–516. 10.1080/096381898336394

Fairfield, K. D. (2018). Educating for a sustainability mindset. *Journal of Management for Global Sustainability*, 6(1), 4. 10.13185/JM2018.06102

FAO. (2020). *Crops and Livestock Products.* Food and Agriculture Organization. https://www.fao.org/faostat/en/#data/QCL

FAO. (n.d.). FAPSTAT Database: Land Use, Visualize Data. FAO. https://www.fao.org/faostat/en/#data/RL/visualize

Farinelli, F., Bottini, M., Akkoyunlu, S., & Aerni, P. (2011). Green entrepreneurship: The missing link towards a greener economy. *Atdf Journal*, 8(3/4), 42–48.

Farooq, A., Farooq, N., Akbar, H., Hassan, Z. U., & Gheewala, S. H. (2023). A Critical Review of Climate Change Impact at a Global Scale on Cereal Crop Production. *Agronomy (Basel)*, 13(1), 162. 10.3390/agronomy13010162

Farooq, U., Wen, J., Tabash, M. I., & Fadoul, M. (2024). Environmental regulations and capital investment: Does green innovation allow to grow. *International Review of Economics & Finance*, 89, 878–893. 10.1016/j.iref.2023.08.010

Farrukh, M., Ansari, N., Raza, A., Wu, Y., & Wang, H. (2022). Fostering employee's pro-environmental behavior through green transformational leadership, green human resource management and environmental knowledge. *Technological Forecasting and Social Change*, 179, 121643. 10.1016/j.techfore.2022.121643

Fathi, B., Ansari, A., & Ansari, A. (2023). Green Commercial Aviation Supply Chain—A European Path to Environmental Sustainability. *Sustainability (Basel)*, 15(8), 1–14. 10.3390/su15086574

Fedotova, G., Kapustina, Y., Romadikova, V., Dzhancharova, G., Churaev, A., & Novikov, M. (2023). Green strategies for the sustainable growth of food security. In *E3S Web of Conferences* (Vol. 390, p. 04014). EDP Sciences. 10.1051/e3sconf/202339004014

Feist, A., Plummer, R., & Baird, J. (2020). The inner workings of collaboration in environmental management and governance: A systematic mapping review. *Environmental Management*, 66(5), 801–815. 10.1007/s00267-020-01337-x32734324

Filho, W.L., Ribeiro, P.C.C., Setti, A.F.F., Azam, F.M.S., Abubakar, I.R., Castillo-Apraiz, J., Tamayo, U., Özuyar, P.G., & Frizzo, K. (2023). *Toward food waste reduction at universities.*

Fischer, M. (2023). The Concept of Sustainable Development. *SpringerBriefs in business*. Springer. 10.1007/978-3-031-25397-3_2

Fisher, M., Abate, T., Lunduka, R. W., Asnake, W., Alemayehu, Y., & Madulu, R. B. (2015). Drought tolerant maize for farmer adaptation to drought in sub-Saharan Africa: Determinants of adoption in eastern and southern Africa. *Climatic Change*, 133(2), 283–299. 10.1007/s10584-015-1459-2

Fitzmaurice, M. (2021). Biodiversity and Climate Change. *International Community Law Review*, 23(2-3), 230–240. 10.1163/18719732-12341473

Foltz, J. D., Aldana, U. T., & Laris, P. (2012). *The Sahel's Silent Maize Revolution: Analyzing Maize Productivity in Mali at the Farm-Level (No. W17801).* National Bureau of Economic Research. 10.3386/w17801

Fontana, G., & Sawyer, M. (2023). The Macroeconomics of Near Zero Growth of GDP in a World of Geopolitical Risks and Conflicts. *Journal of Environmental Management*, 351, 119717. 10.1016/j.jenvman.2023.11971738042081

Fonte, C. C., Patriarca, J. A., Minghini, M., Antoniou, V., See, L., & Brovelli, M. A. (2019). Using OpenStreetMap to Create Land Use and Land Cover Maps: Development of an Application. In *Geospatial Intelligence* (Vol. 2). Concepts, Methodologies, Tools, and Applications. 10.4018/978-1-5225-8054-6.ch047

Food and Agriculture Organization of United Nations. (2020). *Migrant workers and the COVID-19 pandemic*. FAO. https://www.fao.org/3/ca8559en/CA8559EN.pdf,

Food and Agriculture Organization of United Nations. (2020a). *Q&A: COVID-19 pandemic – impact on food and agriculture*. FS Cluster. https://fscluster.org/sites/default/files/documents/fao_qa_impact_on_food_and_agriculture.pdf,

Franca, V. (2012). The Strength of the Employer Brand: Influences and Implications for Recruiting. *Journal of Marketing Management*, 3, 78.

Freitas, W. R. S., Caldeira-Oliveira, J. H., Teixeira, A. A., Stefanelli, N. O., & Teixeira, T. B. (2020). Green human resource management and corporate social responsibility: Evidence from Brazilian firms. *Benchmarking*, 27(4), 1551–1569. 10.1108/BIJ-12-2019-0543

Frenkel, S., Mamic, I., & Greene, L. (2016). *Global supply chains in the food industry: insights from the Asia-Pacific region*. International Labour Organization; ILO DWT for East and South-East Asia and the Pacific.

Friedman, T. L. (2005). *The world is flat: A brief history of the twenty-first century*. Farrar, Straus and Giroux.

Fulwari, A. (2017). Role of education for sustainable development. *International Education and Research Journal*, 3(5), 546–549.

Gable, S. L., & Haidt, J. (2005). What (and Why) Is Positive Psychology? *Review of General Psychology*, 9(2), 103–110. 10.1037/1089-2680.9.2.103

Gakh, D. (2023). Societal Patterns Evolution Model in Development of Economy,Society, and Environment. https://doi.org/10.20944/preprints202305.0632.v1

Galindo-Martín, M. A., Castano-Martinez, M. S., & Méndez-Picazo, M. T. (2020). The relationship between green innovation, social entrepreneurship, and sustainable development. *Sustainability (Basel)*, 12(11), 4467. 10.3390/su12114467

Gao, T., Erokhin, V., & Arskiy, A. (2019). Dynamic Optimization of Fuel and Logistics Costs as a Tool in Pursuing Economic Sustainability of a Farm. *Sustainability (Basel)*, 11(19), 5463. 10.3390/su11195463

Gao, T., Erokhin, V., Arskiy, A., & Khudzhatov, M. (2021). Has the COVID-19 Pandemic Affected Maritime Connectivity? An Estimation for China and the Polar Silk Road Countries. *Sustainability (Basel)*, 13(6), 3521. 10.3390/su13063521

Gao, T., Ivolga, A., & Erokhin, V. (2018). Sustainable Rural Development in Northern China: Caught in a Vice between Poverty, Urban Attractions, and Migration. *Sustainability (Basel)*, 10(5), 1467. 10.3390/su10051467

Garcia, E., Liu, S., Mitchell, R., & Smith, Y. (2021). Interdisciplinary perspectives on globalization: Understanding the interconnectedness of economics, culture, and society. *The Global Studies Journal*, 13(4), 1–22.

García-Lara, S., & Serna-Saldivar, S. O. (2019). *Corn history and culture*. 10.1016/B978-0-12-811971-6.00001-2

García, O., & Wei, L. (2014). *Translanguaging: Language, bilingualism and education*. Palgrave Macmillan. 10.1057/9781137385765

Gardner, H. (1983). *Frames of mind: The theory of multiple intelligences*. Basic Books.

Gardner, W. L., & Avolio, B. J. (1998). The charismatic relationship: A dramaturgical perspective. *Academy of Management Review*, 23(1), 32–58. 10.2307/259098

Garner, R. (2013). Politics and sustainable development. In *The Sustainability Curriculum* (pp. 208–217). Routledge.

Gedik, Y. (2020). Yeşil pazarlama stratejileri ve işletmelerin amaçlarına etkisi. *Sosyal Bilimler Dergisi*, 6(2), 46–65.

Gerhart, B. (2005). Human resources and business performance: Findings, unanswered questions, and an alternative approach. *Management Review*, 174–185.

Giddens, A. (1984). *The constitution of society: Outline of the theory of structuration*. Polity Press.

Gigauri, I., Palazzo, M., & Ferri, M. A. (Eds.). (2023). *Handbook of Research on Achieving Sustainable Development Goals With Sustainable Marketing*. IGI Global. 10.4018/978-1-6684-8681-8

Gilbert, B. C. (2007). *Collaborative synergy in resource and environmental management*.

Gilovich, T., Griffin, D., & Kahneman, D. (Eds.). (2002). *Heuristics and biases: The psychology of intuitive judgment*. Cambridge University Press. 10.1017/CBO9780511808098

Giovannoni, E., & Fabietti, G. (2013). What is sustainability? A review of the concept and its applications. *Integrated reporting: Concepts and cases that redefine corporate accountability*, 21-40.

Glabska, D., Skolmowska, D., & Guzek, D. (2020). Population-Based Study of the Changes in the Food Choice Determinants of Secondary School Students: Polish Adolescents' COVID-19 Experience (Place-19) Study. *Nutrients*, 12(9), 2640. 10.3390/nu1209264032872577

Gligorić, M., & Jovanović Gavrilović, B. (2017). Circular economy as the backbone of sustainable development of the economy of Serbia. *Economic perspectives. Society of Belgrade Economists, Belgrade*, 22(4), 119–132.

Global Reporting Initiative. (2021). *Integrating the SDGs into corporate reporting: A practical guide*. Global Reporting. https://www.globalreporting.org/media/mlkjpn1i/gri-sasb-joint-publication-april-2021.pdf

Global Sustainable Tourism Council. (2013). *Criteria for Hotels and Tour Operators. Washington.* Global Sustainable Tourism Council.

Gnoni, M. G., & Saleh, J. H. (2017). Near miss management systems and observability-indepth: Handling safety incidents and accident precursors in light of safety principles. *Safety Science*, 91, 154–167. 10.1016/j.ssci.2016.08.012

Gnoni, M. G., Tornese, F., Guglielmi, A., Pellicci, M., Campo, G., & De Merich, D. (2022). Near miss management systems in the industrial sector: A literature review. *Safety Science*, 150, 105704. 10.1016/j.ssci.2022.105704

Gnoni, M., & Lettera, G. (2012). Near-miss management systems: A methodological comparison. *Journal of Loss Prevention in the Process Industries*, 25(3), 609–616. 10.1016/j.jlp.2012.01.005

Goddek, S., Joyce, A., Kotzen, B., & Burnell, G. M. (2019). *Aquaponics Food Prodaction Systems*. Springer Nature Switzerland AG. 10.1007/978-3-030-15943-6

Goleman, D. (1995). *Emotional intelligence: Why it can matter more than IQ*. Bantam Books.

Gomółka, K. (2021). The Self-employment of Women in Azerbaijan. *Studia Europejskie-Studies in European Affairs*, 25(2), 171–190. 10.33067/SE.2.2021.8

Gong, Y., Huang, J.-C., & Farh, J.-L. (2009). Employee learning orientation, transformational leadership, and employee creativity: The mediating role of employee creative self-efficacy. *Academy of Management Journal*, 52(4), 765–778. 10.5465/amj.2009.43670890

Gorkina, T. И. (2023). Features of the energy transition in Asian countries. Journal of the Moscow University. Series 5. *Geography (Sheffield, England)*, (3), 18–29.

Government of Azerbaijan. (2020). *Energy potential of Karabakh and surrounding regions, Ministry of Energy of the Republic of Azerbaijan*. Government of Azerbaijan. https://minenergy.gov.az/en/xeberler-arxivi/dagliq-qarabag-ve-etraf-regionlarin-enerji-potensiali

Government of Azerbaijan. (2024). *Azərbaycanda bərpa olunan enerji mənbələrindən istifadə [Utilization of renewable energy sources in Azerbaijan]*. Ministry of Energy of the Republic of Azerbaijan. Government of Azerbaijan. https://minenergy.gov.az/en/alternativ-ve-berpa-olunan-enerji/azerbaycanda-berpa-olunan-enerji-menbelerinden-istifade

Graddol, D. (2006). *English next: Why global English may mean the end of 'English as a Foreign Language*. British Council.

Gradinac, O., & Jegdić, V. (2016). Inter-destination cooperation as a factor in strengthening the competitiveness of a tourist destination. *Business Economics (Cleveland, Ohio)*, 10(2), 284–300.

Grahek, M. S., Thompson, A. D., & Toliver, A. (2010). The character to lead: A closer look at character in leadership. *Consulting Psychology Journal*, 62(4), 270–290. 10.1037/a0022385

Greenland, S. J. (2019). Future sustainability, innovation, and marketing: A framework for understanding impediments to sustainable innovation adoption and corporate social responsibility. In *The Components of Sustainable Development: Engagement and Partnership* (pp. 63-80). Springer Singapore. 10.1007/978-981-13-9209-2_5

Grin, F. (2003). *Language policy evaluation and the European Charter for Regional or Minority Languages*. Palgrave Macmillan. 10.1057/9780230502666

Grosclaude, J. Y., Pachauri, R. K., & Tubiana, L. (Eds.). (2014). *Innovation for sustainable development. The Energy and Resources Institute*. TERI.

Grujić Vučkovski, B., Paraušić, V., Jovanović Todorović, M., Joksimović, M., & Marina, I. (2022). Analysis of influence of value indicators agricultural production on gross value added in Serbian agriculture. *Custos e Agronegocio*, 18(4), 349–372.

Guerci, M., Montanari, F., Scapolan, A., & Epifanio, A. (2016). Green and nongreen recruitment practices for attracting job applicants: Exploring independent and interactive effects. *International Journal of Human Resource Management*, 27(2), 129–150. 10.1080/09585192.2015.1062040

Guillot-Soulez, C., Saint-Onge, S., & Soulez, S. (2022). Green certification and organizational attractiveness: The moderating role of firm ownership. *Corporate Social Responsibility and Environmental Management*, 29(1), 189–199. 10.1002/csr.2194

Gull, S., & Idrees, H. (2022). Green training and organizational efficiency: Mediating role of green competencies. *European Journal of Training and Development*, 46(1/2), 105–119. 10.1108/EJTD-10-2020-0147

Günaydın, D. (2018). Türkiye'de Dördüncü Sanayi Devrimini Beklerken: Çerkezköy Organize Sanayi Bölgesi'nde Bir Araştırma. *Istanbul Management Journal*, 73-106.

Gupta, H. (2018). Assessing organizations performance on the basis of GHRM practices using BWM and Fuzzy TOPSIS. *Journal of Environmental Management*, 226, 201–216. 10.1016/j.jenvman.2018.08.00530119045

Gürlek, S. (2001). *Küreselleşme ve milli devletin geleceği bağlamında Türk milliyetçiliğini yeniden düşünmek.* Türkiye ve Siyaset, Küreselleşme ve Milliyetçilik Özel Sayısı, Kasım-Aralık, 27.

Gusenbauer, M., & Haddaway, N. R. (2020). Which academic search systems are suitable for systematic reviews or meta-analyses? Evaluating retrieval qualities of Google Scholar, PubMed, and 26 other resources. *Research Synthesis Methods*, 11(2), 181–217. 10.1002/jrsm.137831614060

Gwirtz, J. A., & Garcia-Casal, M. N. (2014). Processing maize four and corn meal food products. *Annals of the New York Academy of Sciences*, 1312(1), 66–75. 10.1111/nyas.1229924329576

H&M Group. (2020, October 1). *H&M has received a decision from the regional Data Protection Authority in Hamburg, Germany.* H&M Group. https://hmgroup.com/news/hm-has-received-a-decision-from-the-regional-data-protection-authority-in-hamburg-germany/?s=regional

Haase, D., Kabisch, S., Haase, A., Andersson, E., Banzhaf, E., Baró, F., Brenck, M., Fischer, L. K., Frantzeskaki, N., Kabisch, N., Krellenberg, K., Kremer, P., Kronenberg, J., Larondelle, N., Mathey, J., Pauleit, S., Ring, I., Rink, D., Schwarz, N., & Wolff, M. (2017). Greening cities–To be socially inclusive? About the alleged paradox of society and ecology in cities. *Habitat International*, 64, 41–48. 10.1016/j.habitatint.2017.04.005

Hagmann, C., Semeijn, J., & Vellenga, D. (2015). Exploring the green image of airlines: Passenger perceptions and airline choice. *Journal of Air Transport Management*, 43(4), 37–45. 10.1016/j.jairtraman.2015.01.003

Halder, P., Hansen, E. N., Kangas, J., & Laukkanen, T. (2020). How national culture and ethics matter in consumers' green consumption values. *Journal of Cleaner Production*, 265, 121754. 10.1016/j.jclepro.2020.121754

Hallegatte, S., Heal, G., Fay, M., & Treguer, D. (2012). *From growth to green growth-a framework (No. w17841)*. National Bureau of Economic Research. 10.3386/w17841

Hall, J. K., Daneke, G. A., & Lenox, M. J. (2010). Sustainable development and entrepreneurship: Past contributions and future directions. *Journal of Business Venturing*, 25(5), 439–448. 10.1016/j.jbusvent.2010.01.002

Handayani, I. P., & Prawito, P. (2010). Indigenous soil knowledge for sustainable agriculture. *Sociology, organic farming, climate change and soil science*, 303-317.

Hands, V., & Anderson, R. (2018). *Local sustainability indicators and their role in the implementation of the sustainable development goals in the HE sector. Handbook of Sustainability Science and Research.* Springer. 10.1007/978-3-319-63007-6_16

Hanson, A. (2019). *Ecological Civilization in the People's Republic of China: Values, Action, and Future Needs*. Asian Development Bank., 10.22617/WPS190604-2

Harris, J., Depenbusch, L., Pal, A. A., Nair, R. M., & Ramasamy, S. (2020). Food System Disruption: Initial Livelihood and Dietary Effects of COVID-19 on Vegetable Producers in India. *Food Security*, 12(4), 841–851. 10.1007/s12571-020-01064-532837650

Hartman, C. L., Hofman, P. S., & Stafford, E. R. (2002). Environmental collaboration: potential and limits. In *Partnership and leadership: Building alliances for a sustainable future* (pp. 21–40). Springer Netherlands. 10.1007/978-94-017-2545-3_2

Hartmann, P., & Apaolaza-Ibáñez, V. (2009). Green advertising revisited. *International Journal of Advertising*, 28(4), 715–739. 10.2501/S0265048709200837

Hart, S. L. (1995). A natural-resource-based view of the firm. *Academy of Management Review*, 20(4), 986–1014. 10.2307/258963

Harvey, R. J. (1991). Job analysis. In Dunnette, M. D., & Hough, L. M. (Eds.), *Handbook of industrial and organizational psychology* (2nd ed., pp. 71–163). Consulting Psychologists Press.

Hasewend, B., & Jokic, T. (2020). How the European green deal promotes sustainable energy research and innovation. In *Solar Energy Conversion in Communities: Proceedings of the Conference for Sustainable Energy (CSE) 2020* (pp. 455-456). Springer International Publishing. 10.1007/978-3-030-55757-7_32

Hecht, A. D., & Fiksel, J. (2020). Sustainability and Sustainable Development. In *Landscape and Land Capacity* (pp. 411-417). CRC Press. 10.1201/9780429445552-52

Heikinheimo, V., Tiitu, M., & Viinikka, A. (2023). Data on Different Types of Green Spaces and Their Accessibility in the Seven Largest Urban Regions in Finland. *Data in Brief*, 50, 109458. 10.1016/j.dib.2023.10945837600595

He, L., Wang, B., Xu, W., Cui, Q., & Chen, H. (2022). Could China's Long-Term Low-Carbon Energy Transformation Achieve the Double Dividend Effect for the Economy and Environment? *Environmental Science and Pollution Research International*, 29(14), 20128–20144. 10.1007/s11356-021-17202-134729713

Herfort, B., Lautenbach, S., Porto de Albuquerque, J., Anderson, J., & Zipf, A. (2023). A Spatio-Temporal Analysis Investigating Completeness and Inequalities of Global Urban Building Data in OpenStreetMap. *Nature Communications*, 14(1), 3985. 10.1038/s41467-023-39698-637414776

Hernandez, M., Kim, S., Rice, B., Vos, R. (2020). *IFPRI's new COVID-19 Food Price Monitor tracks warning signs of stress in local markets.* International Food Policy Research Institute.

Heyat, F. (2020). Women and the culture of entrepreneurship in Soviet and post-Soviet Azerbaijan. In *Markets and Moralities* (pp. 19–31). Routledge. 10.4324/9781003085966-3

Hidayati, S. N., Suyono, J., & Hartomo, D. D. (2022, December). The role of budgeting in realizing a green economy and economic growth. [). IOP Publishing.]. *IOP Conference Series. Earth and Environmental Science*, 1114(1), 012077. 10.1088/1755-1315/1114/1/012077

Hilliard, A., Kazim, E., Koshiyama, A., Zannone, S., Trengove, M., Kingsman, N., & Polle, R. (2022). Regulating the robots: NYC mandates bias audits for AI-driven employment decisions. *SSRN*. Retrieved from https://ssrn.com/abstract=408318910.2139/ssrn.4083189

Hofstede, G. (1980). *Culture's consequences: International differences in work-related values.* Sage Publications.

Hooper, P. D., & Greenall, A. (2005). Exploring the Potential for Environmental Performance Benchmarking in the Airline Sector. *Benchmarking*, 12(2), 151–165. 10.1108/14635770510593095

Hordofa, T. T., Vu, H. M., Maneengam, A., Mughal, N., & Liying, S. (2023). Does eco-innovation and green investment limit the CO2 emissions in China? Economic research-. *Ekonomska Istrazivanja*, 36(1), 634–649. 10.1080/1331677X.2022.2116067

Hörisch, J., Kollat, J., & Brieger, S. A. (2017). What influences environmental entrepreneurship? A multilevel analysis of the determinants of entrepreneurs' environmental orientation. *Small Business Economics*, 48(1), 47–69. 10.1007/s11187-016-9765-2

Hronová, Š., & Špaček, M. (2021). Sustainable HRM practices in corporate reporting. *Economies*, 9(2), 75. 10.3390/economies9020075

Huang, J., Wei, W., Cui, Q., & Xie, W. (2017). The Prospects for China's Food Security and Imports: Will China Starve the World via Imports? *Journal of Integrative Agriculture*, 16(12), 2933–2944. 10.1016/S2095-3119(17)61756-8

Huang, J., & Yang, G. (2017). Understanding Recent Challenges and New Food Policy in China. *Global Food Security*, 12, 119–126. 10.1016/j.gfs.2016.10.002

Huelgas, S.M. & Arellano, V.A. (2021). Green Transformational Leadership, Green Human Resource Management and Green Innovation: Key to Environmental Performance of Selected Port Management Offices of Philippine Ports Authority. *IOER International Multidisciplinary Research Journal*, 48–58.

Hülsmann, S., & Jampani, M. (2020). The nexus approach as a tool for resources management in resilient cities and multifunctional land-use systems. In *A Nexus Approach for Sustainable Development: Integrated Resources Management in Resilient Cities and Multifunctional Land-Use Systems* (pp. 1–13). Springer International Publishing.

Humphrey, J., & Memedovic, O. (2006). *Global value chains in the agrifood sector, United Nations* [UN]. Industrial Development Organization.

Huntington, S. P. (1996). *The clash of civilizations and the remaking of world order*. Simon & Schuster.

Hu, P., Jeong, H., & Haque, P. S. (2022). An Empirical Study on Environmental Kuznets Curve in China. *Journal of China Area Studies*, 9(1), 227–256. 10.34243/JCAS.9.1.227

Husgafvel, R. (2021). Exploring social sustainability handprint—part 2: Sustainable development and sustainability. *Sustainability (Basel)*, 13(19), 11051. 10.3390/su131911051

Hu, Z., Wu, Q., & Li, J. (2023). The Localization of SDGs in China: System Construction, Status Assessment and Development Reflection. *Ecological Indicators*, 154, 110514. 10.1016/j.ecolind.2023.110514

Hwang, B. G., Zhu, L., & Tan, J. S. H. (2017). Green business park project management: Barriers and solutions for sustainable development. *Journal of Cleaner Production*, 153, 209–219. 10.1016/j.jclepro.2017.03.210

Hwang, J., & Lyu, S. (2019). Relationships among green image, consumer attitudes, desire, and customer citizenship behavior in the airline industry. *International Journal of Sustainable Transportation*, 1–11. 10.1080/15568318.2019.1573280

Idowu, O. O. (2013). Challenges of urbanization and urban growth in Nigeria. *American Journal of Sustainable Cities and Society*, 2(1), 79–95.

Ilić, B., Stojanovic, D., & Pavicevic, N. (2018). Green financing for environmental protection and sustainable economic growth–a comparison of Indonesia and Serbia. *Progress in Economic Sciences*, (5).

Ilic, S., Petrovic, T., & Djukic, G. (2022). Eco-innovation and sustainable development. *Problemy Ekorozwoju, 17*(2).

Iljkić, D., Efinger, I., Rastija, M., Stipešević, B., Stošić, M., & Varga, I. (2021). Yield, agronomic and morphological properties of maize from the different FAO groups. *Proceedings of 56th Croatioan and 16th international symposium on agriculture*, Vodice, Croatia.

IMF. (2022, April). World economic outlook, WEO, Occasional paper, World economic and financial surveys. *World Economic Outlook.*

Imperatives, S. (1987). Report of the World Commission on Environment and Development: Our common future. *Accessed Feb, 10*(42,427).

Ioannou, A. E., & Laspidou, C. S. (2023). Cross-mapping important interactions between water-energy-food nexus indices and the SDGs. *Sustainability (Basel)*, 15(10), 8045. 10.3390/su15108045

Iraegui, E., Augusto, G., & Cabral, P. (2020). Assessing Equity in the Accessibility to Urban Green Spaces According to Different Functional Levels. *ISPRS International Journal of Geo-Information*, 9(5), 308. 10.3390/ijgi9050308

Isaak, R. (2017). *Green logic: Ecopreneurship, theory and ethics.* Routledge. 10.4324/9781351283168

Islam, M. T. (2023). Newly developed green technology innovations in business: Paving the way toward sustainability. *Technological Sustainability*, 2(3), 295–319. 10.1108/TECHS-02-2023-0008

Islam, S. M. Z., & Karim, Z. (2020). *World's Demand for Food and Water: The Consequences of Climate Change*. IntechOpen. 10.5772/intechopen.85919

Isopescu, D. N. (2018, August). The impact of green building principles in the sustainable development of the built environment. [). IOP Publishing.]. *IOP Conference Series. Materials Science and Engineering*, 399(1), 012026. 10.1088/1757-899X/399/1/012026

Izugbara, C., Sebany, M., Wekesah, F., & Ushie, B. (2022). "The SDGs are not God": Policy-makers and the queering of the Sustainable Development Goals in Africa. *Development Policy Review*, 40(2), e12558. 10.1111/dpr.12558

Jacobs, M. (2012). *Far from being a drag on growth, environmental policy can actually help drive it.* British Politics and Policy at LSE.

Jámbor, A., Czine, P., & Balogh, P. (2020). The impact of the coronavirus on agriculture: First evidence based on global newspapers. *Sustainability (Basel)*, 12(11), 4535. 10.3390/su12114535

James, K., Murry, A., & Pacheco, D. (2013). Strong communities: Integrating environmental, economic, and social sustainability. In *Social Sustainability* (pp. 54–78). Routledge.

Jamil, S., Zaman, S. I., Kayikci, Y., & Khan, S. A. (2023). The role of green recruitment on organizational sustainability performance. *Sustainability (Basel)*, 15(21), 15567. 10.3390/su152115567

Jenkins, H. (2006). *Convergence culture: Where old and new media collide*. New York University Press.

Jenkins, J. (2014). *Global Englishes: A resource book for students* (3rd ed.). Routledge. 10.4324/9781315761596

Jiang, K., Fu, B., Luo, Z., Xiong, R., Men, Y., Shen, H., Li, B., Shen, G., & Tao, S. (2022). Attributed Radiative Forcing of Air Pollutants from Biomass and Fossil Burning Emissions. *Environmental Pollution*, 306, 119378. 10.1016/j.envpol.2022.11937835500713

Jiao, Y., Chen, H. D., Han, H., & Chang, Y. (2022). Development and Utilization of Corn Processing by-Products: A Review. *Foods*, 11(22), 3709. 10.3390/foods1122370936429301

Ji, W., & Zhang, J. (2022). The Impact of COVID-19 on the E-commerce Companies in China. *Review of Integrative Business and Economics Research*, 11(1), 155–165. 10.58745/riber_11-1_155-165

Jonas, A. E., Gibbs, D., & While, A. (2011). The new urban politics as a politics of carbon control. *Urban Studies (Edinburgh, Scotland)*, 48(12), 2537–2554. 10.1177/004209801141195122081834

Jones, A., & Garcia, S. (2018). Economic decision-making and the role of social psychology: Exploring cognitive biases and social influences. *Behavioral Economics Review*, 6(2), 54–67.

Jordan, A. (1994). Managing. *Sustainable Development.*

Jovanović Gavrilović, B. (2013). Economic development with a human face. Center for publishing activities of the Faculty of Economics, Belgrade.

Ju, B., Shi, X., & Mei, Y. (2022). The Current State and Prospects of China's Environmental, Social, and Governance Policies. *Frontiers in Environmental Science*, 10, 999145. 10.3389/fenvs.2022.999145

Ju, Y., Dronova, I., & Delclòs-Alió, X. (2022). A 10 m Resolution Urban Green Space Map for Major Latin American Cities from Sentinel-2 Remote Sensing Images and OpenStreetMap. *Scientific Data*, 9(1), 586. 10.1038/s41597-022-01701-y36153342

Kachru, B. B. (1985). Standards, codification and sociolinguistic realism: The English language in the outer circle. In Quirk, R., & Widdowson, H. G. (Eds.), *English in the world: Teaching and learning the language and literatures* (pp. 11–30). Cambridge University Press.

Kahneman, D. (2011). *Thinking, fast and slow*. Farrar, Straus and Giroux.

Kain, T. (2023). *What Are The Biggest Environmental Problems?* Sigma Earth. https://sigmaearth.com/the-biggest-environmental-problems/

Kamakia, A. (2015). A Discussion on Sustainable Development. *SSRN* 2653722.

Kandil, E. E., Abdelsalam, N. R., Mansour, M. A., Ali, H. M., & Siddiqui, M. H. (2020). Potentials of organic manure and potassium forms on maize (Zea mays L.) growth and production. *Scientific Reports*, 10(1), 8752. 10.1038/s41598-020-65749-932472061

Kang, Y., Hsiao, H. S., & Ni, J. Y. (2022). The Role of Sustainable Training and Reward in Influencing Employee Accountability Perception and Behavior for Corporate Sustainability. *Sustainability (Basel)*, 14(18), 11589. 10.3390/su141811589

Kantrow, A. M. (1985). *Sunrise-sunset which changes the mhytos of the industrial becoming old.* New York, John Wiley and His Sons.

Karakuş, G. (2023). Türk Hava Yolları sürdürülebilirlik raporları üzerine bir araştırma. *Aerospace Research Letters (ASREL). Dergisi*, 2(2), 86–113. 10.56753/ASREL.2023.2.4

Kaul, J., Jain, K., & Olakh, D. (2019). An overview on role of yellow maize in food, feed and nutrition security. *International Journal of Current Microbiology and Applied Sciences*, 8(2), 3037–3048. 10.20546/ijcmas.2019.802.356

Kaur, G., & Mehndroo, M. (2022). Education and enlightenment for sustainable development. *International Journal of Health Sciences*, (II), 7525–7530. 10.53730/ijhs.v6nS2.6810

Kaushal, M., Sharma, R., Vaidya, D., Gupta, A., Saini, H. K., Anand, A., Thakur, C., Verma, A., Thakur, M., Priyanka, , & Kc, D. (2023). Maize: An underexploited golden cereal crop. *Cereal Research Communications*, 51(1), 3–14. 10.1007/s42976-022-00280-3

Keane, E. (2018). The GDPR and Employee's Privacy: Much Ado but Nothing New. *King's Law Journal : KLJ*, 29(3), 354–363. 10.1080/09615768.2018.1555065

Keleş, R. (2010). Türkiye'de kentleşme kime ne kazandırıyor? İdeal Kent Kent Araştırmaları Dergisi. *Sayı*, 1, 28–31.

Kennedy, C., Zhong, M., & Corfee-Morlot, J. (2016). Infrastructure for China's Ecologically Balanced Civilization. *Engineering (Beijing)*, 2(4), 414–425. 10.1016/J.ENG.2016.04.014

Key, G. (2023). *Unlocking sustainability in the hospitality industry.* Greenkey. https://www.greenkey.global

Keyman, E. F. (2002). Kapitalizm-oryantalizm ekseninde küreselleşmeyi anlamak: 11 Eylül, modernite, kalkınma ve öteki sorunsalı. *Doğu Batı Dergisi*, 5(18), 31–53.

Khan, O., & Hinterhuber, A. (2024). Antecedents and consequences of procurement managers' willingness to pay for sustainability: A multi-level perspective. *International Journal of Operations & Production Management*, 44(13), 1–33. 10.1108/IJOPM-02-2023-0135

Khan, S. A. R., Razzaq, A., Yu, Z., Shah, A., Sharif, A., & Janjua, L. (2022). Disruption in food supply chain and undernourishment challenges: An empirical study in the context of Asian countries. *Socio-Economic Planning Sciences*, 82, 101033. 10.1016/j.seps.2021.101033

Khatter, A., White, L., Pyke, J., & McGrath, M. (2021). Barriers and drivers of environmental sustainability: Australian hotels. *International Journal of Contemporary Hospitality Management*, 33(5), 1830–1849. 10.1108/IJCHM-08-2020-0929

Kibera, M. (n.d.). *Mapping Nairobi's Informal Settlements*. Map Kibera. https://www.mapkibera.org/

Koç, E. (2023). Green marketing strategies and climate change awareness in sustainable transportation: The case of airline companies. *Marine Science and Technology Bulletin*, 12(4), 459–472. 10.33714/masteb.1375842

Kochhar, K. (2022). Green Finance: An approach towards Sustainable Development Goals (SDGs). *Asian Journal of Management*, 13(1), 17–20. 10.52711/2321-5763.2022.00004

Kohn, M. (2020). *Digital transformation and public services: Societal impacts in Sweden and beyond*. Routledge.

Kong, Y., & Ding, H. (2023). Tools, Potential, and Pitfalls of Social Media Screening: Social Profiling in the Era of AI-Assisted Recruiting. *Journal of Business and Technical Communication*, 38(1), 33–65. 10.1177/10506519231199478

Korah, P. I., Akaateba, M. A., & Bernard, A. A. A. (2024). Spatio-Temporal Patterns and Accessibility of Green Spaces in Kumasi, Ghana. *Habitat International*, 144, 103010. 10.1016/j.habitatint.2024.103010

Kotler, P., & Armstrong, G. (2018). *Pazarlama İlkeleri (Çeviri Editörü:A. Ercan Gegez)*. Beta.

Krashen, S. (1982). *Principles and practice in second language acquisition*. Pergamon Press.

Krefeld-Schwalb, A., & Gabel, S. (2023). Empowering a Sustainable Future: Fostering Sustainable Behavior with Targeted Interventions. 10.31234/osf.io/nc2bh

Krueger, R., & Gibbs, D. (Eds.). (2007). *The sustainable development paradox: urban political economy in the United States and Europe*. Guilford Press.

Kubatko, O., Merritt, R., Duane, S., Piven, V. (2023). The impact of the COVID-19 pandemic on global food system resilience. *Mechanism of an economic regulation, 1*(99), 144-148.

Kubota, J. (2016). China's Environmental Problems and Prospects for Japanese Cooperation. *Journal of Contemporary East Asia Studies*, 5(1), 3–10. 10.1080/24761028.2016.11869088

Kumar, S., & Rathore, K. (2023). Renewable Energy for Sustainable Development Goal of Clean and Affordable Energy. *International Journal of Materials Manufacturing and Sustainable Technologies, 2*(1), 1–15. , 1.10.56896/ijmmst

Kunyanga, C. N., Byskov, M. F., Hyams, K., Mburu, S., Werikhe, G., & Bett, R. (2023). Influence of COVID-19 Pandemic on Food Market Prices and Food Supply in Urban Markets in Nairobi, Kenya. *Sustainability (Basel)*, 15(2), 1304. 10.3390/su15021304

Kwok, L., & Lin, M. S. (2023). Green food packages' effects on consumers' pre-to post-consumption evaluations of restaurant curbside pickup service. *International Journal of Contemporary Hospitality Management*.

Kyvelou, S., Marava, N., & Kokkoni, G. (2011). Perspectives of local public-private partnerships towards urban sustainability in Greece. *International Journal of Sustainable Development*, 14(1-2), 95–111. 10.1504/IJSD.2011.039640

La Torre, M., Sabelfeld, S., Blomkvist, M., & Dumay, J. (2020). Rebuilding trust: Sustainability and non-financial reporting and the European Union regulation. *Meditari Accountancy Research*, 28(4), 701–725. 10.1108/MEDAR-06-2020-0914

Lafferty, W. M., & Meadowcroft, J. (2000). *Implementing sustainable development: Strategies and initiatives in high consumption societies*. OUP Oxford. 10.1093/0199242011.001.0001

Landers, R. N., & Schmidt, G. B. (2016). *Social Media in Employee Selection and Recruitment: Theory, Practice, and Current Challenges*. Springer. 10.1007/978-3-319-29989-1

Larson, N., Slaughter-Acey, J., Alexander, T., Berge, J., Harnack, L., & Neumark-Sztainer, D. (2021). Emerging Adults' Intersecting Experiences of Food Insecurity, Unsafe Neighbourhoods and Discrimination during the Coronavirus Disease 2019 (COVID-19) Outbreak. *Public Health Nutrition*, 24(3), 519–530. 10.1017/S136898002000422X33092665

Lawson, R. (2006). An overview of green economics. *International Journal of Green Economics*, 1(1-2), 23–36. 10.1504/IJGE.2006.009335

Lee, C., & Wang, C. (2022). Does Natural Resources Matter for Sustainable Energy Development in China: The Role of Technological Progress. *Resources Policy*, 79, 103077. 10.1016/j.resourpol.2022.103077

Levit, T. (1983). The globalisation of markets. *Harvard Business Review*, 61(3), 92–102.

Liao, H., Wei, Y., Ali, S., Uktamov, K., & Ali, N. (2023). Natural Resources Extraction and Industrial Expansion: Natural Resources a Curse or blessing for the Industrial Sector of China? *Resources Policy*, 85, 103986. 10.1016/j.resourpol.2023.103986

Liao, Y., Zhou, Q., & Jing, X. (2021). A Comparison of Global and Regional Open Datasets for Urban Greenspace Mapping. *Urban Forestry & Urban Greening*, 62, 127132. 10.1016/j.ufug.2021.127132

Liddle, B. (2017). Urbanization and inequality/poverty. *Urban Science (Basel, Switzerland)*, 1(35), 1–7.

Lievens, F., & Chapman, D. (2010). Recruitment and selection. In S. Zedeck (Ed.), *APA handbook of industrial and organizational psychology, Vol 2: Selecting and developing members for the organization* (pp. 267-290). American Psychological Association. 10.4135/9780857021496.n9

Li, F., Fang, L., & Wu, F. (2023). A Roadmap for Sustainable Agricultural Soil Remediation Under China's Carbon Neutrality Vision. *Engineering (Beijing)*, 25, 28–31. 10.1016/j.eng.2022.08.010

Lin, B. X., & Zhang, Y. Y. (2020). Impact of the COVID-19 pandemic on agricultural exports. [Top of Form]. *Journal of Integrative Agriculture*, 19(12), 2937–2945. 10.1016/S2095-3119(20)63430-X

Liu, J., Hull, V., Godfray, H. C. J., Tilman, D., Gleick, P., Hoff, H., Pahl-Wostl, C., Xu, Z., Chung, M. G., Sun, J., & Li, S. (2018). Nexus approaches to global sustainable development. *Nature Sustainability*, 1(9), 466–476. 10.1038/s41893-018-0135-8

Liu, Q., Ullah, H., Wan, W., Peng, Z., Hou, L., Rizvi, S. S., Haidery, S. A., Qu, T., & Muzahid, A. A. M. (2020). Categorization of Green Spaces for a Sustainable Environment and Smart City Architecture by Utilizing Big Data. *Electronics (Basel)*, 9(6), 1028. 10.3390/electronics9061028

Liu, Y., Li, X., Zhu, X., Lee, M., & Lai, P. (2023). The Theoretical Systems of OFDI Location Determinants in Global North and Global South Economies. *Humanities & Social Sciences Communications*, 10(1), 130. 10.1057/s41599-023-01597-y37007733

Liu, Y., Qian, Y., & Lin, H. (2020). Green training and development for employees: A systematic literature review. *Journal of Cleaner Production*, 258, 120701.

Lopatnikov, D., & Gorbanyov, V. (2020). China on the Way to "Green Civilization": First Results. *Regional Environmental Issues, 4*, 85-94. https://doi.org/10.24411/1728-323X-2020-14085

Lopes, P., Fonte, C., See, L., & Bechtel, B. (2017). Using OpenStreetMap Data to Assist in the Creation of LCZ Maps. In *In 2017 Joint Urban Remote Sensing Event*. JURSE. 10.1109/JURSE.2017.7924630

López-Concepción, A., Gil-Lacruz, A. I., & Saz-Gil, I. (2022). Stakeholder engagement, CSR development, and SDGs compliance: A systematic review from 2015 to 2021. *Corporate Social Responsibility and Environmental Management*, 29(1), 19–31. 10.1002/csr.2170

Lopez-Ridaura, S., Sanders, A., Barba-Escoto, L., Wiegel, J., Mayorga-Cortes, M., Gonzalez-Esquivel, C., Lopez-Ramirez, M. A., Escoto-Masis, R. M., Morales-Galindo, E., & García-Barcena, T. S. (2021). Immediate impact of COVID-19 pandemic on farming systems in Central America and Mexico. *Agricultural Systems*, 192, 103178. 10.1016/j.agsy.2021.10317836569352

Ludwig, C., Hecht, R., Lautenbach, S., Schorcht, M., & Zipf, A. (2021). Mapping Public Urban Green Spaces Based on OpenStreetMap and Sentinel-2 Imagery Using Belief Functions. *ISPRS International Journal of Geo-Information*, 10(4), 251. 10.3390/ijgi10040251

Luo, H., & Lin, X. (2022). Dynamic Analysis of Industrial Carbon Footprint and Carbon-Carrying Capacity of Zhejiang Province in China. *Sustainability (Basel)*, 14(24), 16824. 10.3390/su142416824

Luthar, S. S., Cicchetti, D., & Becker, B. (2000). The construct of resilience: A critical evaluation and guidelines for future work. *Child Development*, 71(3), 543–562. 10.1111/1467-8624.0016410953923

Luxen, D., & Vetter, C. (2011). Real-Time Routing with OpenStreetMap Data. In *GIS:Proceedings of the ACM International Symposium on Advances in Geographic Information Systems*. ACM. 10.1145/2093973.2094062

Majerník, M., Chovancová, J., Drábik, P., & Štofková, Z. (2023). Environmental technological innovations and the sustainability of their development. *Ecological Engineering & Environmental Technology, 24.*

Majid, F., Raziq, M. M., Memon, M. A., Tariq, A., & Rice, J. L. (2023). Transformational leadership, job engagement, and championing behavior: Assessing the mediating role of role clarity. *European Business Review*, 35(6), 941–963. 10.1108/EBR-01-2023-0028

Malavisi, A. (2018). The urgency of the greening of ethics. *Australasian Journal of Logic*, 4(3), 593–609. 10.26686/ajl.v15i2.4872

Malik, P., Malik, P. K., Singh, R., & Gehlot, A. (2023). Sustainable Development, Renewable Energy and Environment. In *Micro-Electronics and Telecommunication Engineering: Proceedings of 6th ICMETE 2022* (pp. 455–463). Springer Nature Singapore. 10.1007/978-981-19-9512-5_42

Malos, S. B. (1998). Current legal issues in performance appraisal. In Smither, J. W. (Ed.), *Performance appraisal: State of the art in practice* (pp. 49–94). Jossey-Bass.

Mansoor, A., Farrukh, M., Lee, J. K., & Jahan, S. (2021). Stimulation of employees' green creativity through green transformational leadership and management initiatives. *Sustainability (Basel)*, 13(14), 7844. 10.3390/su13147844

Margerum, R. D., & Robinson, C. J. (Eds.). (2016). *The challenges of collaboration in environmental governance: Barriers and responses*. Edward Elgar Publishing. 10.4337/9781785360411

Marina, I., Grujić Vučkovski, B., & Jovanović Todorović, M. (2023). Distribution of Mechanization by Regions and Areas in the Republic of Serbia (Chapter 6). In *Sustainable Growth and Global Social Development in Competitive Economies*. IGI Global.

Markus, H. R., & Kitayama, S. (1991). Culture and the self: Implications for cognition, emotion, and motivation. *Psychological Review*, 98(2), 224–253. 10.1037/0033-295X.98.2.224

Martin, R., & Sunley, P. (2015). On the notion of regional economic resilience: Conceptualization and explanation. *Journal of Economic Geography*, 15(1), 1–42. 10.1093/jeg/lbu015

Martins, F., Cezarino, L., Liboni, L., Hunter, T., Batalhao, A., & Paschoalotto, M. A. C. (2023). Unlocking the potential of responsible management education through interdisciplinary approaches. *Sustainable Development*.

Masten, A. S. (2001). Ordinary magic: Resilience processes in development. *The American Psychologist*, 56(3), 227–238. 10.1037/0003-066X.56.3.22711315249

Mathews, J. A. (2013). Greening of development strategies. *Seoul Journal of Economics*, 26(2), 147–172.

Matten, D., & Moon, J. (2008). Implicit and explicit CSR: A conceptual framework for a comparative understanding of corporate social responsibility. *Academy of Management Review*, 33(2), 404–424. 10.5465/amr.2008.31193458

Mayer, R., Ryley, T., & Gillingwater, D. (2014). The role of green marketing: Insights from three airline case studies. *The Journal of Sustainable Mobility*, 1(2), 46–72. 10.9774/GLEAF.2350.2014.no.00005

McDougall, N., Wagner, B., & MacBryde, J. (2019). An empirical explanation of the natural-resource-based view of the firm. *Production Planning and Control*, 30(16), 1366–1382. 10.1080/09537287.2019.1620361

McKinney, M. L. (2006). Urbanization as a major cause of biotic homogenization. *Biological Conservation*, 127(3), 247–260. 10.1016/j.biocon.2005.09.005

McKinsey, Q. (2017). *Mapping the benefits of a circular economy*. McKinsey. https://www.mckinsey.com/capabilities/sustainability/our-insights/mapping-the-benefits-of-a-circular-economy

Mengoub, F. E. (2020). *Ensuring food security during the COVID-19 pandemic: review of short-term responses in selected countries.*

Merlin, M., & Chen, Y. (2022). Impact of green human resource management on organizational reputation and attractiveness: The mediated-moderated model. *Frontiers in Environmental Science*, 10, 1561. 10.3389/fenvs.2022.962531

Mert, A., & Pattberg, P. H. (2018). How Do Climate Change and Energy-related Partnerships Impact Innovation and Technology Transfer?: Some Lessons for the Implementation of the UN Sustainable Development Goals. In *The Cambridge Handbook of Public-Private Partnerships, Intellectual Property Governance and Sustainable Development* (pp. 289-307). Cambridge University Press.

Messina, G. (2021). The role of the committee of the regions (CoR) to implement the Green Deal at the local level: An overview of Italy. *AIMS Geosciences*, 7(4), 613–622. 10.3934/geosci.2021037

Middleton, P. (2018). Sustainable living education: Techniques to help advance the renewable energy transformation. *Solar Energy*, 174, 1016–1018. 10.1016/j.solener.2018.08.009

Midilli, A., Dincer, I., & Ay, M. (2006). Green energy strategies for sustainable development. *Energy Policy*, 34(18), 3623–3633. 10.1016/j.enpol.2005.08.003

Mihailović, B., Radić Jean, I., Popović, V., Radosavljević, K., Chroneos-Krasavac, B., Bradić-Martinović, A. (2020). Farm Differentiation Strategies and Sustainable Regional Development. *Sustainability, 12*(17), 1-18. 10.3390/su12177223

Mihailović, B., Radosavljević, K., & Popović, V. (2023). The role of indoor smart gardens in the development of smart agriculture in urban areas. *Ekonomika Poljoprivrede*, 70(2), 453–468. 10.59267/ekoPolj2302453M

Mikhno, I., Koval, V., Shvets, G., Garmatiuk, O., & Tamošiūnienė, R. (2021). *Green economy in sustainable development and improvement of resource efficiency*.

Ministry of Ecology and Environment of the People's Republic of China. (1994). *Report on China's Agenda 21*. MEE. https://english.mee.gov.cn/Events/Special_Topics/AGM_1/1994agm/meetingdoc94/201605/t20160524_345213.shtml

Mishra, P. (2017). Green human resource management. *The International Journal of Organizational Analysis*, 25(5), 762–788. 10.1108/IJOA-11-2016-1079

Mitrović, Đ. (2015). Transition from linear to circular economy. *Thematic collection of papers Economic policy and development* (pp. 111-113). Belgrade: Center for publishing activities of the Faculty of Economics.

Mittal, S., & Dhar, R. L. (2016). Effect of green transformational leadership on green creativity: A study of tourist hotels. *Tourism Management*, 57, 118–127. 10.1016/j.tourman.2016.05.007

Mohammadi Shad, Z., Venkitasamy, C., & Wen, Z. (2021). Corn distillers dried grains with solubles: Production, properties, and potential uses. *Cereal Chemistry*, 98(5), 999–1019. 10.1002/cche.10445

Mohsin, M., Iqbal, N., & Iram, R. (2023). *The Nexus Between Green Finance and Sustainable Green Economic Growth. Energy RESEARCH LETTERS, 4*. Early View.

Molina, M. J., & Molina, L. T. (2004). Megacities and Atmospheric Pollution. *Journal of the Air & Waste Management Association*, 54(6), 644–680. 10.1080/10473289.2004.1047093615242147

Molnar, E., & Mulvihill, P. (2003). Sustainability-focused Organizational Learning: Recent Experiences and New Challenges. *Journal of Environmental Planning and Management*, 46(2), 167–176. 10.1080/0964056032000070990

Moore, N. (2018, July 5). *Analysing desk research*. Facet eBooks. 10.29085/9781856049825.012

Morssy, A. (2012). Green growth, innovation and sustainable development. *International Journal of Environment and Sustainability*, 1(3). 10.24102/ijes.v1i3.94

Moser, E., Prskawetz, A., & Tragler, G. (2013). Environmental regulations, abatement and economic growth. In *Green growth and sustainable development* (pp. 87–111). Springer Berlin Heidelberg. 10.1007/978-3-642-34354-4_5

Mpofu, F. Y. (2022). Green Taxes in Africa: Opportunities and challenges for environmental protection, sustainability, and the attainment of sustainable development goals. *Sustainability (Basel)*, 14(16), 10239. 10.3390/su141610239

Mubera, S., & Jules, N. (2018). Nestor Uwitonze (2018) Energy Sector Development in Sub Saharan Africa: Case Study of Rwanda. *J Fundam Renewable Energy Appl*, 8(250), 2.

Muhammad, A., Ibitomi, T., Amos, D., Idris, M., & Ahmad Ishaq, A. (2023). Comparative Analysis of sustainable finance initiatives in Asia and Africa: A Path towards Global Sustainability. *Glob. Sustain. Res*, 2(3), 33–51. 10.56556/gssr.v2i3.559

Mulders, H., van Ruitenbeek, G., Wagener, B., & Zijlstra, F. (2022). Toward more inclusive work organizations by redesigning work. *Frontiers in Rehabilitation Sciences*, 3, 861561. 10.3389/fresc.2022.86156136189072

Muralidharan, E., & Pathak, S. (2018). Sustainability, transformational leadership, and social entrepreneurship. *Sustainability (Basel)*, 10(2), 567. 10.3390/su10020567

Mustapha, M. A., Manan, Z. A., & Alwi, S. R. W. (2017). Sustainable Green Management System (SGMS)–An integrated approach towards organisational sustainability. *Journal of Cleaner Production*, 146, 158–172. 10.1016/j.jclepro.2016.06.033

Mutangadura, G. B. (2005). Sustainable development in Southern Africa: Progress in addressing the challenges. *Journal of Sustainable Development in Africa*.

Mu, Z., Bu, S., & Xue, B. (2014). Environmental Legislation in China: Achievements, Challenges and Trends. *Sustainability (Basel)*, 6(12), 8967–8979. 10.3390/su6128967

Mwita, K., & Kinemo, S. (2018). The role of green recruitment and selection on performance of processing industries in Tanzania: A case of Tanzania Tobacco Processors Limited (TTPL). *International Journal of Human Resource Studies*, 8(4), 35. Advance online publication. 10.5296/ijhrs.v8i4.13356

Najafizadeh, M. (2016). Social entrepreneurship, social change, and gender roles in Azerbaijan. In *Routledge Handbook of Entrepreneurship in Developing Economies* (pp. 278–294). Routledge.

Narassimhan, E., Koester, S., & Gallagher, K. S. (2022). Carbon pricing in the US: Examining state-level policy support and federal resistance. *Politics and Governance*, 10(1), 275–289. 10.17645/pag.v10i1.4857

Nassiry, D. (2018). *The role of fintech in unlocking green finance: Policy insights for developing countries* (No. 883, ADBI working paper).

National Bureau of Statistics of China. (2024). *National Data.* NBSC. https://data.stats.gov.cn/english/easyquery.htm?cn=C01

Nchanji, E. B., Lutomia, C. K., Chirwa, R., Templer, N., Rubyogo, J. C., & Onyango, P. (2021). Immediate impacts of COVID-19 pandemic on bean value chain in selected countries in Sub-Saharan Africa. *Agricultural Systems*, 188, 103034. 10.1016/j.agsy.2020.10303433658743

Neighbours East, E. U. (2024.). *You can too: How the EU supports women entrepreneurs in Azerbaijan.* EU Neighbours East. https://euneighbourseast.eu/news/explainers/you-can-too-how-the-eu-supports-women-entrepreneurs-in-azerbaijan/

Nickerson, R. S. (1998). Confirmation bias: A ubiquitous phenomenon in many guises. *Review of General Psychology*, 2(2), 175–220. 10.1037/1089-2680.2.2.175

Nidumolu, R., Ellison, J., Whalen, J., & Billman, E. (2014). The collaboration imperative. *Harvard Business Review*, 92(4), 76–84.24830283

Niesten, E., Jolink, A., de Sousa Jabbour, A. B. L., Chappin, M., & Lozano, R. (2017). Sustainable collaboration: The impact of governance and institutions on sustainable performance. *Journal of Cleaner Production*, 155, 1–6. 10.1016/j.jclepro.2016.12.085

Nightingale, A. (2009). A guide to systematic literature reviews. [Oxford]. *Surgery*, 381–384.

Nisbett, R. E., & Masuda, T. (2003). Culture and point of view. *Proceedings of the National Academy of Sciences of the United States of America*, 100(19), 11163–11170. 10.1073/pnas.193452710012960375

Nittala, R., & Moturu, V. (2023). Role of pro-environmental post-purchase behaviour in green consumer behaviour. *Vilakshan-XIMB Journal of Management*, 82-97.

Niu, S.-Y., Liu, C.-L., Chang, C.-C., & Ye, K.-D. (2016). What are passenger perspectives regarding airlines' environmental protection? An empirical investigation in Taiwan. *Journal of Air Transport Management*, 55, 84–91. 10.1016/j.jairtraman.2016.04.012

Norris, F. H., Stevens, S. P., Pfefferbaum, B., Wyche, K. F., & Pfefferbaum, R. L. (2008). Community resilience as a metaphor, theory, set of capacities, and strategy for disaster readiness. *American Journal of Community Psychology*, 41(1-2), 127–150. 10.1007/s10464-007-9156-618157631

Norton, B. (2013). *Identity and language learning: Extending the conversation* (2nd ed.). Multilingual Matters. 10.21832/9781783090563

Novack, T., Wang, Z., & Zipf, A. (2018). A System for Generating Customized Pleasant Pedestrian Routes Based on Openstreetmap Data. *Sensors (Basel)*, 18(11), 3794. 10.3390/s1811379430404175

Nurwahdah, A. & Muafi (2022). The influence of green transformational leadership and green attitude on green organisational citizenship behaviour mediated by emotional intelligence. *International Journal of Research in Business and Social Science,* 99–111.

Nussbaum, M. C. (2010). *Not for profit: Why democracy needs the humanities*. Princeton University Press.

O'Riordan, T., Jacobs, G., Ramanathan, J., & Bina, O. (2020). Investigating the future role of higher education in creating sustainability transitions. *Environment*, 62(4), 4–15. 10.1080/00139157.2020.1764278

OECD. (2013). *OECD Due Diligence Guidance for Responsible Supply Chains of Minerals from Conflict-Affected and High-Risk Areas* (2nd ed.). OECD Publishing.

OECD. (2022). Agricultural Policy Monitoring and Evaluation 2022. *Reforming Agricultural Policies for Climate Change Mitigation*. OECD.10.1787/7f4542bf-en

OECD. (2023). Agricultural Policy Monitoring and Evaluation 2023. *Adapting Agriculture to Climate Change*. OECD. https://www.oecd.org/publications/agricultural-policy-monitoring-and-evaluation-22217371.htm

Öğretmenoğlu, M., Akova, O. & Göktepe, S. (2022). The mediating effects of green organizational citizenship on the relationship between green transformational leadership and green creativity: evidence from hotels. *Journal of Hospitality and Tourism Insights*, 734–751.

Okoruwa, A. (1997). *Utilization and processing of maize*. (IITA research guide, no. 35). HDL. https://hdl.handle.net/20.500.12478/3924

Öktem, B., & Karabınar, S. (2022). SASB Raporu Yayınlayan Şirketlerin Finansal Başarısızlıkları ile Sürdürülebilirlik Raporları Arasındaki İlişkinin Analizi. *Istanbul Journal of Economics/ İstanbul Iktisat Dergisi, 72*(2).

Olk, S. (2021). The effect of self-congruence on perceived green claims' authenticity and perceived greenwashing: The case of EasyJet's CO2 promise. *Journal of Nonprofit & Public Sector Marketing*, 33(2), 114–131. 10.1080/10495142.2020.1798859

Omer, A. M. (2021). Sustainable development in low carbon, cleaner and greener energies, and the environment. *Sinergi*, 25(3), 329–342. 10.22441/sinergi.2021.3.010

Onumah, G., Dhamankar, M., Ponsioen, T., & Bello, M. (2021). Maize value chain analysis in Nigeria. *Report for the European Union, INTPA/F3*. Value Chain Analysis for Development Project.

Organisation for Economic Co-operation and Development. (2024). *Green Growth in Action: China*. Organisation for Economic Co-operation and Development. https://www.oecd.org/fr/chine/greengrowthinactionchina.htm

Osipov, V. I. (2019). Sustainable Development: Environmental Aspects. *Herald of the Russian Academy of Sciences*, 89(4), 396–404. 10.1134/S1019331619040087

Özcan, H., & Özgül, B. (2019). Yeşil pazarlama ve tüketicilerin yeşil ürün tercihlerini etkileyen faktörler. *Türkiye Mesleki ve Sosyal Bilimler Dergisi*, 1(1), 1–18. 10.46236/jovosst.562230

Özdemir, M. (2010). Nitel veri analizi: Sosyal bilimlerde yöntembilim sorunsalı üzerine bir çalışma. *Eskişehir Osmangazi Üniversitesi Sosyal Bilimler Dergisi*, 11(1), 323–343.

Özgül, B., & Zehir, C. (2023). How Managers' Green Transformational Leadership Affects a Firm's Environmental Strategy, Green Innovation, and Performance: The Moderating Impact of Differentiation. *Sustainability (Basel)*, 15(4), 3597. 10.3390/su15043597

Paauwe, J. (2009). HRM and Performance: Achievements, Methodological Issues and Prospects. *Journal of Management Studies*, 46(1), 129–142. 10.1111/j.1467-6486.2008.00809.x

Pacheco, D. F., Dean, T. J., & Payne, D. S. (2010). Escaping the green prison: Entrepreneurship and the creation of opportunities for sustainable development. *Journal of Business Venturing*, 25(5), 464–480. 10.1016/j.jbusvent.2009.07.006

Padilla, E. (2002). Intergenerational equity and sustainability. *Ecological Economics*, 41(1), 69–83. 10.1016/S0921-8009(02)00026-5

Paillé, P., Valéau, P., & Renwick, D. W. (2020). Leveraging green human resource practices to achieve environmental sustainability. *Journal of Cleaner Production*, 260, 121137. 10.1016/j.jclepro.2020.121137

Pallarès-Blanch, M., Tulla, A. F., & Vera, A. (2015). Environmental capital and women's entrepreneurship: A sustainable local development approach. *Carpathian Journal of Earth and Environmental Sciences*, 10(3), 133–146.

Panait, M., Erokhin, V., Andrei, J. V., & Gao, T. (2020). Implication of TNCs in Agri-Food Sector – Challenges, Constraints and Limits – Profit or CSR? *Strategic Management*, 20(4), 33–43. 10.5937/StraMan2004033P

Panait, M., Gigauri, I., Hysa, E., & Raimi, L. (2023). Corporate Social Responsibility and Environmental Performance: Reporting Initiatives of Oil and Gas Companies in Central and Eastern Europe. In Machado, C., & Paulo Davim, J. (Eds.), *Corporate Governance for Climate Transition* (pp. 123–140). Springer. 10.1007/978-3-031-26277-7_6

Pan, D., Yang, J., Zhou, G., & Kong, F. (2020). The influence of COVID-19 on agricultural economy and emergency mitigation measures in China: A text mining analysis. *PLoS One*, 15(10), e0241167. 10.1371/journal.pone.024116733095814

Pandey, D. J., & Ghasiya, P. R. (2023). Sustainable economic development and environment. *International Journal of Applied Research*, 9(5), 32–35. 10.22271/allresearch.2023.v9.i5a.10785

Pattberg, P., Biermann, F., Chan, M., & Mert, A. (2007). Partnerships for Sustainable Development: An Appraisal Framework. In *International Studies Association 48th Annual Convention.*

Patwary, A. K., Rasoolimanesh, S. M., Hanafiah, M. H., Aziz, R. C., Mohamed, A. E., Ashraf, M. U., & Azam, N. R. A. N. (2024). Empowering pro-environmental potential among hotel employees: insights from self-determination theory. *Journal of Hospitality and Tourism Insights.*

Paudel, D., Neupane, R. C., Sigdel, S., Poudel, P., & Khanal, A. R. (2023). COVID-19 pandemic, climate change, and conflicts on agriculture: A trio of challenges to global food security. *Sustainability (Basel)*, 15(10), 8280. 10.3390/su15108280

Peat, D. (2005). On building local partnerships. *The Health Service Journal*, 115(5941), 27.15795982

Pejić, B., Bošnjak, Đ., Mačkić, K., Stričević, R., Simić, D., & Drvar, A. (2009). Response of maize (Zea mays L.) to soil water deficit at specific growth stages. *Annals of agronomy*, Faculty of agriculture, Novi Sad. *Serbia*, 33(1), 155–166.

Peng, H., Luo, X., & Zhou, C. (2018). Introduction to China's Green Finance System. *Journal of Service Science and Management*, 11(1), 94–100. 10.4236/jssm.2018.111009

Peng, J., Yin, K., Hou, N., Zou, Y., & Nie, Q. (2020). How to facilitate employee green behavior: The joint role of green transformational leadership and green human resource management practice. *Acta Psychologica Sinica*, 52(9), 1105–1120. 10.3724/SP.J.1041.2020.01105

Perez, J. A. E., Ejaz, F., & Ejaz, S. (2023). Green Transformational Leadership, GHRM, and Proenvironmental Behavior: An Effectual Drive to Environmental Performances of Small- and Medium-Sized Enterprises. *Sustainability (Basel)*, 15(5), 4537. 10.3390/su15054537

Peters, J. C., & Hertel, T. W. (2017). Achieving the Clean Power Plan 2030 CO2 target with the new normal in natural gas prices. *The Energy Journal (Cambridge, Mass.)*, 38(5), 39–66. 10.5547/01956574.38.5.jpet

Petushkova, V. (2022). Experience and Perspectives of Sustainable Development in China. *Bulletin of the Russian Academy of Sciences. Physics*, 92(4), 384–393. 10.31857/S0869587322040065

Pham, D., & Paillé, P. (2019). Green recruitment and selection: An insight into green patterns. *International Journal of Manpower*, 41(3), 258–272. 10.1108/IJM-05-2018-0155

Phillipson, R. (1992). *Linguistic imperialism*. Oxford University Press.

Phimister, J. R., Oktem, U., Kleindorfer, P. R., & Kunreuther, H. (2003). Near miss incident management in the chemical process industry. *Risk Analysis*, 23(3), 445–459. 10.1111/1539-6924.0032612836838

Piketty, T. (2014). *Capital in the twenty-first century*. Harvard University Press. 10.4159/9780674369542

Pimonenko, T., Bilan, Y., Horák, J., Starchenko, L., & Gajda, W. (2020). Green brand of companies and greenwashing under sustainable development goals. *Sustainability (Basel)*, 12(4), 1–15. 10.3390/su12041679

Pinho, M., & Gomes, S. (2023). What Role Does Sustainable Behavior and Environmental Awareness from Civil Society Play in the Planet's SustainableTransition. *Resources*, 12(3), 42. 10.3390/resources12030042

Pinto, L. V., Carla, S. S. F., Inácio, M., & Pereira, P. (2022). Urban Green Spaces Accessibility in Two European Cities: Vilnius (Lithuania) and Coimbra (Portugal). *Geography and Sustainability*, 3(1), 74–84. 10.1016/j.geosus.2022.03.001

Pinto, L., Ferreira, C. S. S., & Pereira, P. (2021). Environmental and Socioeconomic Factors Influencing the Use of Urban Green Spaces in Coimbra (Portugal). *The Science of the Total Environment*, 792, 148293. 10.1016/j.scitotenv.2021.14829334147815

Piwowar-Sulej, K., & Iqbal, Q. (2023). Leadership styles and sustainable performance: A systematic literature review. *Journal of Cleaner Production*, 382, 134600. 10.1016/j.jclepro.2022.134600

Pociovălişteanu, D. M., Silvestre, B., Novo-Corti, I., & Răbonţu, C. I. (2016). Innovation for sustainable development. *Journal of Cleaner Production*, 100(133), 389–390. 10.1016/j.jclepro.2016.05.152

Podsakoff, P. M., MacKenzie, S. B., & Bommer, W. H. (1996). Transformational leader behaviors and substitutes for leadership as determinants of employee satisfaction, commitment, trust, and organizational citize. *Journal of Management*, 22(2), 259–298. 10.1016/S0149-2063(96)90049-5

Polanyi, K. (1944). *The Great Transformation: The political and economic origins of our time*. Farrar & Rinehart.

Porter, M. E. (1985). *Competitive advantage: Creating and sustaining superior performance*. Free Press.

Potluri, S., & Phani, B. V. (2020). Women and green entrepreneurship: A literature based study of India. *International Journal of Indian Culture and Business Management*, 20(3), 409–428. 10.1504/IJICBM.2020.107675

Poudel, P. B., Poudel, M. R., Gautam, A., Phuyal, S., Tiwari, C. K., Bashyal, N., & Bashyal, S. (2020). COVID-19 and its global impact on food and agriculture. *Journal of Biology and Today's World*, 9(5), 221–225.

Prakash, S., Sharma, V. P., Singh, R., Vijayvargy, L., & Nilaish, . (2023). Adopting green and sustainable practices in the hotel industry operations-an analysis of critical performance indicators for improved environmental quality. *Management of Environmental Quality*, 34(4), 1057–1076. 10.1108/MEQ-03-2022-0090

Prensky, M. (2001). Digital natives, digital immigrants. *On the Horizon*, 9(5), 1–6. 10.1108/10748120110424816

Priyadarshi, A., & Prasad, D. (2023). An evaluation of green marketing policies on millennial customers towards the environment. *SSRN*, 1-12. 10.2139/ssrn.4400380

Pulakos, E. D. (2009). *Performance Management: A New Approach for Driving Business Results*. Wiley. 10.1002/9781444308747

Pulighe, G., & Lupia, F. (2020). Food first: COVID-19 outbreak and cities lockdown a booster for a wider vision on urban agriculture. *Sustainability (Basel)*, 12(12), 5012. 10.3390/su12125012

Pu, M., & Zhong, Y. (2020). Rising concerns over agricultural production as COVID-19 spreads: Lessons from China. *Global Food Security*, 26, 100409. Advance online publication. 10.1016/j.gfs.2020.10040932834954

Putnam, R. D. (2000). *Bowling alone: The collapse and revival of American community*. Simon & Schuster.

Pyatachkova, A., Potashev, N., & Smirnova, V. (2022). *Green Agenda in China's Policy*. Russian Internartional Affairs Council.

Qi, G., Jia, Y., & Zou, H. (2021). Is institutional pressure the mother of green innovation? Examining the moderating effect of absorptive capacity. *Journal of Cleaner Production*, 278, 123957. 10.1016/j.jclepro.2020.123957

Qin, Y., & Li, J. (2023). Research on sustainable development of China's Green Enterprise Economy. *American Journal of Economics and Business Innovation*, 2(2), 86–92. 10.54536/ajebi.v2i2.1891

Quan, L., Koo, B., & Han, H. (2023). Exploring the factors that influence customers' willingness to switch from traditional hotels to green hotels. *Journal of Travel & Tourism Marketing*, 40(3), 185–202. 10.1080/10548408.2023.2236649

Radosavljević, K. (2017). *Marketing channels of agricultural products*. Institute of Economic Sciences.

Radosavljević, K., & Mihailović, B. (2023). *Contemporary management problems in the hotel industry*. Belgrade Banking Academy. Faculty of Banking, Insurance and Finance.

Radulescu, I. D., Andrei, J. V., Chivu, L., Erokhin, V., Gao, T., & Nancu, D. (2022). A Short Review on European Developments in Agricultural Output Price Indices during 2008-2017: Are There Significant Changes? *Ekonomika Poljoprivrede*, 69(1), 107–117. 10.5937/ekoPolj2201107R

Raharjo, K. (2019). The Role of Green Management in Creating Sustainability Performance on the Small and Medium Enterprises. *Management of Environmental Quality*, 30(3), 557–577. 10.1108/MEQ-03-2018-0053

Ramos, T. B., & Caeiro, S. (2009). Meta-performance evaluation of sustainability indicators. *Ecological Indicators*, 10(2), 157–166. 10.1016/j.ecolind.2009.04.008

Raut, R. D., Luthra, S., Narkhede, B. E., Mangla, S. K., Gardas, B. B., & Priyadarshinee, P. (2019). Examining the performance oriented indicators for implementing green management practices in the Indian agro sector. *Journal of Cleaner Production*, 215, 926–943. 10.1016/j.jclepro.2019.01.139

Raza, A., Tong, G., Erokhin, V., Bobryshev, A., Chaykovskaya, L., & Malinovskaya, N. (2023a). Sustaining Performance of Wheat Rice Farms in Pakistan: The Effects of Financial Literacy and Financial Inclusion. *Sustainability (Basel)*, 15(9), 7045. 10.3390/su15097045

Raza, A., Tong, G., Sikandar, F., Erokhin, V., & Tong, Z. (2023b). Financial Literacy and Credit Accessibility of Rice Farmers in Pakistan: Analysis for Central Punjab and Khyber Pakhtunkhwa Regions. *Sustainability (Basel)*, 15(4), 2963. 10.3390/su15042963

Rehman, A., & Yaqub, M. S. (2021). Determining the influence of green transformational leadership, green innovation and green hrm practices on environmental performance of hospitality industry of pakistan: A moderating role of individual employee behaviour under COVID-19. [BBE]. *Bulletin of Business and Economics*, 10(2), 100–114.

Renfors, S. M. (2024). Education for the circular economy in higher education: An overview of the current state. *International Journal of Sustainability in Higher Education*, 25(9), 111–127. 10.1108/IJSHE-07-2023-0270

Ren, S., Tang, G., & Jackson, S. (2018). Green human resource management research in emergence: A review and future directions. *Asia Pacific Journal of Management*, 35, 769–803. 10.1007/s10490-017-9532-1

Renwick, D. W. S., Redman, T., & Maguire, S. (2013). Green human resource management: A review and research agenda. *International Journal of Management Reviews*, 15(1), 1–14. 10.1111/j.1468-2370.2011.00328.x

Ren, Y., Zhang, B., Chen, X., & Liu, X. (2023). Analysis of Spatial-Temporal Patterns and Driving Mechanisms of Land Desertification in China. *The Science of the Total Environment*, 909, 168429. 10.1016/j.scitotenv.2023.16842937967628

Revilla, P., Alves, M. L., Andelković, V., Balconi, C., Dinis, I., Mendes-Moreira, P., Redaelli, R., Ruiz de Galarreta, J. I., Vaz Patto, M. C., Žilić, S., & Malvar, R. A. (2022). Traditional foods from maize (Zea mays L.) in Europe. *Frontiers in Nutrition*, 8, 683399. 10.3389/fnut.2021.68339935071287

Rezaei, N. & Millard-Ball, A. (2023). Urban Form and Its Impacts on Air Pollution and Access to Green Space: A Global Analysis of 462 Cities. *PLoS ONE18*. .10.1371/journal.pone.0278265

Ricci, F. (2007). Channels of transmission of environmental policy to economic growth: A survey of the theory. *Ecological Economics*, 60(4), 688–699. 10.1016/j.ecolecon.2006.11.014

Ristić, D., Gošić-Dondo, S., Vukadinović, J., Kostadinović, M., Kravić, N., Kovinčić, A., & Mladenović Drinić, S. (2023). *Effect of abiotic and biotic stress on alteration of phytochemicals in maize leaf and grain - aftereffect on food quality and safety*. X Symposium of the Serbian association of plant breeders and seed producers and VII Symposium of the Serbian genetic society section of the breeding of organisms, Vrnjačka Banja.

Robertson, J. L. (2018). The nature, measurement and nomological network of environmentally specific transformational leadership. *Journal of Business Ethics*, 151(4), 961–975. 10.1007/s10551-017-3569-4

Robertson, J. L., & Barling, J. (2013). Greening organizations through leaders' influence on employees' pro-environmental behaviors. *Journal of Organizational Behavior*, 34(2), 176–194. 10.1002/job.1820

Robertson, J. L., & Barling, J. (2017). Toward a new measure of organizational environmental citizenship behavior. *Journal of Business Research*, 75, 57–66. 10.1016/j.jbusres.2017.02.007

Robertson, R. (1999). *Küreselleşme Toplum Kuramı ve Küresel Kültür (Çev. Ümit Hüsrev Yolsal)*. Bilim ve Sanat Yayınları.

Ronald, K., Callixte, K., & Tushabe, E. (2019, April). Environmental Conservation and its Influence on Tourism Development in Rwanda: Case Study of Rwanda Environment Management Authority (REMA). In *International Conference on the Future of Tourism (ICFT)* (pp. 1-23). The Open University of Tanzania.

Rosol, M., Béal, V., & Mössner, S. (2017). Greenest cities? The (post-)politics of new urban environmental regimes. *Environment & Planning A*, 49(8), 1710–1718. 10.1177/0308518X17714843

Rosskopf, M., Lehner, S., & Gollnick, V. (2014). Economic-environmental trade-offs in long-term airline fleet planning. *Journal of Air Transport Management*, 34, 109–115. 10.1016/j.jairtraman.2013.08.004

Ryan, R. M., & Deci, E. L. (2000). Self-determination theory and the facilitation of intrinsic motivation, social development, and well-being. *The American Psychologist*, 55(1), 68–78. 10.1037/0003-066X.55.1.6811392867

Saadaoui, S., & Belmouffeq, B. (2023). Systematic Literature Review on social media in Employee Recruitment and Selection (2018-2022). *International Journal of Innovation and Scientific Research*, 67(2), 190–201.

Sachs, J. (2015). *The age of sustainable development*. Columbia University Press. 10.7312/sach17314

Salancik, G. R., & Pfeffer, J. (1978). A social information processing approach to job attitudes and task design. *Administrative Science Quarterly*, 23(2), 224–253. 10.2307/239256310307892

Sambou, O., Riniwati, H., & Fanani, Z. (2019). Socio-economic and Environmental Sustainability of Ecotourism Implementation: A Study in Ubud Monkey Forest-Bali, Indonesia. *Journal of Indonesian Tourism and Development Studies*, 7(3), 200–204. 10.21776/ub.jitode.2019.007.03.09

Sawitri, D. R., Hadiyanto, H., & Hadi, S. P. (2015). Pro-environmental behavior from a socialcognitive theory perspective. *Procedia Environmental Sciences*, 23, 27–33. 10.1016/j.proenv.2015.01.005

Schaaf, T. (1995). Near miss reporting in the chemical process industry: An overview. *Microelectronics and Reliability*, 35(9-10), 1233–1243. 10.1016/0026-2714(95)99374-R

Schaltenbrand, B., Foerstl, K., Azadegan, A., & Lindeman, K. (2018). See what we want to see? The effects of managerial experience on corporate green investments. *Journal of Business Ethics*, 150(4), 1129–1150. 10.1007/s10551-016-3191-x

Schaper, M. (2016). Understanding the green entrepreneur. In *Making ecopreneurs* (pp. 7–20). Routledge. 10.4324/9781315593302

Schneider, B., & Konz, A. (1989). Strategic job analysis. *Human Resource Management*, 28(1), 51–63. 10.1002/hrm.3930280104

Schroeder, P., Anggraeni, K., & Weber, U. (2018). *The relevance of circular economy practices to the sustainable development goals*. Institute of Development Studies, University of Sussex.

Schultz, M., Voss, J., Auer, M., Carter, S., & Zipf, A. (2017). Open Land Cover from OpenStreetMap and Remote Sensing. *International Journal of Applied Earth Observation and Geoinformation*, 63, 206–213. 10.1016/j.jag.2017.07.014

Schumpeter, J. (1934). *The theory of economic development*. Harvard University Press.

Schunk, D. H., & DiBenedetto, M. K. (2020). Motivation and social cognitive theory. *Contemporary Educational Psychology*, 60, 101832. 10.1016/j.cedpsych.2019.101832

Schwartz, S. H. (1992). Universals in the content and structure of values: Theoretical advances and empirical tests in 20 countries. *Advances in Experimental Social Psychology*, 25, 1–65. 10.1016/S0065-2601(08)60281-6

Scoones, I., Newell, P., & Leach, M. (2015). The Politics of Green Transformations. I. (Editors) Scoones, P. Newell, & M. Leach içinde, *The Politics of Green Transformations* (s. 1-24). London and New York: Routledge.

Scott, D. (2006). Climate change and sustainable tourism in the 21st century, in: *Tourism Research: Policy, Planning, and Prospects* (J. Cukier, ed.) Waterloo, Department of Geography Publication Series, University of Waterloo.

Sebestyén, V., Trájer, A. J., Domokos, E., Torma, A., & Abonyi, J. (2024). Objective Well-Being Level (OWL) Composite Indicator for Sustainable and Resilient Cities. *Ecological Indicators*, 158, 111460. 10.1016/j.ecolind.2023.111460

Segovia, V. M. (2010). *Transforming mindsets through education for sustainable development.*

Seligman, M. E. P. (1990). *Learned optimism: How to change your mind and your life*. Knopf.

Seligman, M. E. P., & Csikszentmihalyi, M. (2000). Positive psychology: An introduction. *The American Psychologist*, 55(1), 5–14. 10.1037/0003-066X.55.1.511392865

Sen, A. (1999). *Development as freedom.* Oxford University Press.

Šestović, M., Radosavljević, K., & Chroneos-Krasavac, B. (2017). The importance of EU pre-accession funds for agriculture and their influence on country's competitiveness. *Economics of enterprise, 65*(7-8), 506-517.

Setiawan, H. H., & Wismayanti, Y. F. (2023). The green economy to support women's empowerment: social work approach for climate change adaptation toward sustainability development. In *Climate Change, Community Response and Resilience* (pp. 225-240). Elsevier. 10.1016/B978-0-443-18707-0.00012-6

Shah, A.K., Jintian, Y., Sukamani, D. & Kusi, M. (2020). How green transformational leadership influences sustainability? Mediating effects of green creativity and green procurement. *Journal on Innovation and Sustainability*, 69–87.

Shah, M., Shuaibu, M. S., AbdulKareem, H. K. K., Khan, Z., & Abbas, S. (2023). Inequality Consequences of Natural Resources, Environmental Vulnerability, and Monetary-Fiscal Stability: A Global Evidence. *Environmental Science and Pollution Research International*, 30(8), 22139. 10.1007/s11356-023-25365-236650371

Shaikh, Z. A. (2017). Towards sustainable development: A review of green technologies. *Trends in Renewable Energy*, 4(1), 1–14. 10.17737/tre.2018.4.1.0044

Sharma, A., Sharma, S., Verma, S., & Bhargava, R. (2016). Production of biofuel (ethanol) from corn and co product evolution: A review. *Int. Res. J. Eng. Technol*, 3, 745–749.

Sharma, S., & Ruud, A. (2003). On the path to sustainability: Integrating social dimensions into the research and practice of environmental management. *Business Strategy and the Environment*, 12(4), 205–214. 10.1002/bse.366

Sharma, T., & Chen, J. S. (2023). Expected green hotel attributes: visit intentions in light of climate change and COVID-19 double whammy. In *Advances in Hospitality and Leisure* (pp. 155–176). Emerald Publishing Limited. 10.1108/S1745-354220220000018009

Shi, J., & Yang, X. (2022). Sustainable Development Levels and Influence Factors in Rural China Based on Rural Revitalization Strategy. *Sustainability (Basel)*, 14(14), 8908. 10.3390/su14148908

Shiller, R. J. (2015). *Irrational exuberance* (3rd ed.). Princeton University Press. 10.2307/j.ctt1287kz5

Shi, S., & Yin, J. (2023). Trends in the Evolution of Sustainable Development Research in China: A Scientometric Review. *Environmental Science and Pollution Research International*, 30(20), 57898–57914. 10.1007/s11356-023-26515-236973622

Shrestha, C., Acharya, S., Sharma, R., Khanal, R., Joshi, J., Ghimire, C., Bhandari, P., & Agrawal, A. (2020). Changes and Compromises in Health Choices during COVID-19 Lockdown in Kathmandu Valley: A Descriptive Cross-Sectional Study. *JNMA; Journal of the Nepal Medical Association*, 58(232), 1046–1051. 10.31729/jnma.579034506372

Shu, C., Zhou, K. Z., Xiao, Y., & Gao, S. (2016). How green management influences product innovation in China: The role of institutional benefits. *Journal of Business Ethics*, 133(3), 471–485. 10.1007/s10551-014-2401-7

Shyshchenko, P., Havrylenko, O., & Tsyhanok, Y. (2021). "Accessibility of Green Spaces in the Conditions of a Compact City: Case Study of Kyiv." *Visnyk of V.N. Karazin Kharkiv National University, Series Geology. Geography.Ecology*, (55), 245–256. 10.26565/2410-7360-2021-55-18

Siche, R. (2020). What is the impact of COVID-19 disease on agriculture? *Scientia Agropecuaria*, 11(1), 3–6. 10.17268/sci.agropecu.2020.01.00

Sidney, M. T., Wang, N., Nazir, M., Ferasso, M., & Saeed, A. (2022). Continuous Effects of Green Transformational Leadership and Green Employee Creativity: A Moderating and Mediating Prospective. *Frontiers in Psychology*, 13, 840019. 10.3389/fpsyg.2022.84001935645899

Sikandar, F., Erokhin, V., Shu, W. H., Rehman, S., & Ivolga, A. (2021). The Impact of Foreign Capital Inflows on Agriculture Development and Poverty Reduction: Panel Data Analysis for Developing Countries. *Sustainability (Basel)*, 13(6), 3242. 10.3390/su13063242

Sikandar, F., Erokhin, V., Xin, L., Sidorova, M., Ivolga, A., & Bobryshev, A. (2022). Sustainable Agriculture and Rural Poverty Eradication in Pakistan: The Role of Foreign Aid and Government Policies. *Sustainability (Basel)*, 14(22), 14751. 10.3390/su142214751

Simon, D. (1987). Our Common Future: Report of the World Commission onEnvironment and Development (Book Review). *Third World Planning Review*, 9(3), 285. 10.3828/twpr.9.3.x4k73r2p72w22402

Singh, R. L., & Singh, P. K. (2017). Global Environmental Problems. In: Singh, R. (eds) *Principles and Applications of Environmental Biotechnology for a Sustainable Future* (p. 13-41). Springer, Singapore. 10.1007/978-981-10-1866-4_2

Sin, N. L., & Lyubomirsky, S. (2009). Enhancing well-being and alleviating depressive symptoms with positive psychology interventions: A practice-friendly meta-analysis. *Journal of Clinical Psychology*, 65(5), 467–487. 10.1002/jclp.2059319301241

Sipahi, E. B. (2010). Küresel çevre sorunlarına kolektif çözüm arayışları ve yönetişim. Selçuk Üniversitesi Sosyal Bilimler Enstitüsü Dergisi. *Sayı*, 24, 331–344.

Si, T. (2022). Opportunities and Challenges for Foreign Undertakings in China's PPPs Market. *Eur. Procurement & Pub. Private Partnership L. Rev.*, 17(1), 33–43. 10.21552/epppl/2022/1/7

Skutnabb-Kangas, T. (2000). *Linguistic genocide in education or worldwide diversity and human rights?* Lawrence Erlbaum Associates.

Smith, L., & Johnson, M. (2020). English as a lingua franca in global communication: Bridging cultural divides. *Language and Intercultural Communication*, 20(3), 237–252.

Sobaih, A. E. E., Hasanein, A., Gharbi, H., & Abu Elnasr, A. E. (2022). Going Green Together: Effects of Green Transformational Leadership on Employee Green Behaviour and Environmental Performance in the Saudi Food Industry. *Agriculture*, 12(8), 1100. 10.3390/agriculture12081100

Sourani, A., & Sohail, M. (2011, December). Barriers to addressing sustainable construction in public procurement strategies. []. Thomas Telford Ltd.]. *Proceedings of the Institution of Civil Engineers. Engineering Sustainability*, 164(4), 229–237. 10.1680/ensu.2011.164.4.229

Southwick, S. M., & Charney, D. S. (2012). *Resilience: The science of mastering life's greatest challenges*. Cambridge University Press. 10.1017/CBO9781139013857

Sowah, J. K.Jr, & Kirikkaleli, D. (2022). Investigating Factors Affecting Global Environmental Sustainability: Evidence from Nonlinear ARDL Bounds Test. *Environmental Science and Pollution Research International*, 29(53), 80502–80519. 10.1007/s11356-022-21399-035725872

Spijkers, O. (2018). Intergenerational equity and the sustainable development goals. *Sustainability (Basel)*, 10(11), 3836. 10.3390/su10113836

Srećkov, Z., Jan, B., Mrkonjić, Z., Bojović, M., Vukelić, I., Vasić, V., & Nikolić, O. (2023). Correlation analysis for grain yield of maize (Zea mays L.). *Thematic proceedings Biotechnology and modern approach in growing and breeding plants (Biotehnologija i savremeni pristup u gajenju i oplemenjivanju bilja).* Smederevdska Palanka, 190-197.

Sridhar, A., Balakrishnan, A., Jacob, M. M., Sillanpää, M., & Dayanandan, N. (2023). Global impact of COVID-19 on agriculture: Role of sustainable agriculture and digital farming. *Environmental Science and Pollution Research International*, 30(15), 42509–42525. 10.1007/s11356-022-19358-w35258730

Srour, C. K. G. E. K., Kheir-El-Din, A., & Samir, Y. M. (2020). The effect of green transformational leadership on organizational citizenship behavior in Egypt. *Academic Journal of Interdisciplinary Studies*, 9(5), 1–16. 10.36941/ajis-2020-0081

Stan, S. E. (2023). Measuring Supply Chain Performance from ESG Perspective. *International conference Knowledge-Based Organization*. Sciendo. 10.2478/kbo-2023-0026

State Council of the People's Republic of China. (2024a). *Guidelines Promote Greener China.* State Council of the People's Republic of China. https://english.www.gov.cn/policies/policywatch/202403/21/content_WS65fb9595c6d0868f4e8e54e0.html

State Council of the People's Republic of China. (2024b). *Xi Calls for Solid Efforts to Further Development of Central Region.* State Council of the People's Republic of China. https://english.www.gov.cn/news/202403/22/content_WS65fd5482c6d0868f4e8e5585.html

Steger, M. B. (2017). *Globalization: A very short introduction* (4th ed.). Oxford University Press.

Stern, P. C., Dietz, T., Abel, T., Guagnano, G. A., & Kalof, L. (1999). A value-belief-norm theory of support for social movements: The case of environmentalism. *Human Ecology Review*, •••, 81–97.

Stiglitz, J. E. (2002). *Globalization and its discontents.* W. W. Norton & Company.

Stojanović, D. (2020). Sustainable economic development through green innovative banking and financing. *Economics of Sustainable Development*, 4(1), 35–44. 10.5937/ESD2001035S

Sumathi, K., Anuradha, T. S., & Akash, S. B. (2014). Green Business as a Sustainable Career for Women Entrepreneurs in IndiaAn Opinion Survey. *Advances in Management*, 7(5), 46.

Sun, J., Chen, X., & Zhang, S. (2017). A Review of Research Evidence on the Antecedents of Transformational Leadership. *Education Sciences*, 7(1), 15. 10.3390/educsci7010015

Sun, X. (2018). Integrating Sustainability into Construction Engineering Projects: Perspective of Sustainable Project Planning. *Sustainability (Basel)*, 10(3), 784. 10.3390/su10030784

Sun, X., El Askary, A., Meo, M. S., & Hussain, B. (2022). Green transformational leadership and environmental performance in small and medium enterprises. *Ekonomska Istrazivanja*, 35(1), 5273–5291. 10.1080/1331677X.2021.2025127

Suparna, G., Yasa, N. N. K., Giantari, I. G. A. K., Sukaatmadja, I. P. G., & Setini, M. (2021). Green transformational leadership to build value, innovation and competitive advantage in era digital. *Webology*, 18(Special Issue 04), 102–115. 10.14704/WEB/V18SI04/WEB18117

Tekin, M., & Zerenler, M. (2012). *Pazarlama.* Günay Ofset.

Terrapon-Pfaff, J., Fink, T., Viebahn, P., & Jamea, E. M. (2019). Social impacts of large-scale solar thermal power plants: Assessment results for the NOORO I power plant in Morocco. *Renewable & Sustainable Energy Reviews*, 113, 109259. 10.1016/j.rser.2019.109259

Texier, M. L., Schiel, K., & Caruso, G. (2018). The Provision of Urban Green Space and Its Accessibility: Spatial Data Effects in Brussels. *PLoS One*, 13(10), e0204684. 10.1371/journal.pone.020468430332449

Thaler, R. H., & Sunstein, C. R. (2008). *Nudge: Improving decisions about health, wealth, and happiness.* Yale University Press.

The Hamburg Commissioner for Data Protection and Freedom of Information. (2020). *Hamburg Commissioner Fines H&M 35.3 Million Euro for Data Protection Violations in Service Centre.* Europea. https://www.edpb.europa.eu/news/national-news/2020/hamburg-commissioner-fines-hm-353-million-euro-data-protection-violations_en

Tian, H., Siddik, A. B., Pertheban, T. R., & Rahman, M. N. (2023). Does fintech innovation and green transformational leadership improve green innovation and corporate environmental performance? A hybrid SEM–ANN approach. *Journal of Innovation & Knowledge*, 8(3), 100396. 10.1016/j.jik.2023.100396

Tien, N. H., Hiep, P. M., Dai, N. Q., Duc, N. M., & Hong, T. T. K. (2020). Green entrepreneurship understanding in Vietnam. *International Journal of Entrepreneurship*, 24(2), 1–14.

Timur, T. (2000). *Küreselleşme ve Demokrasi Krizi*. İmge Kitabevi.

Tirno, R. R., Islam, N., & Happy, K. (2023). Green HRM and eco-friendly behavior of employees: Relevance of proecological climate and environmental knowledge. *Heliyon*, 9(4), e14632. 10.1016/j.heliyon.2023.e1463237082624

Tosun, C., Parvez, M. O., Bilim, Y., & Yu, L. (2022). Effects of green transformational leadership on green performance of employees via the mediating role of corporate social responsibility: Reflection from North Cyprus. *International Journal of Hospitality Management*, 103, 103218. 10.1016/j.ijhm.2022.103218

Triandis, H. C. (1995). *Individualism & collectivism*. Westview Press.

Trojanek, R., Gluszak, M., & Tanas, J. (2018). The Effect of Urban Green Spaces on House Prices in Warsaw. *International Journal of Strategic Property Management*, 22(5), 358–371. 10.3846/ijspm.2018.5220

Trotter, D. (2012). *Towards a green economy.*

Tubridy, F. (2020). Green climate change adaptation and the politics of designing ecological infrastructures. *Geoforum*, 113, 133–145. 10.1016/j.geoforum.2020.04.020

Tubridy, F. (2021). The green adaptation-regeneration nexus: Innovation or business-as-usual. *European Planning Studies*, 29(2), 369–388. 10.1080/09654313.2020.1757625

Tuncdogan, A., Acar, O. A., & Stam, D. (2017). Individual differences as antecedents of leader behavior: Towards an understanding of multi-level outcomes. *The Leadership Quarterly*, 28(1), 40–64. 10.1016/j.leaqua.2016.10.011

Tundys, B., & Wiśniewski, T. (2023). Triple bottom line aspects and sustainable supply chain resilience: A structural equation modelling approach. *Frontiers in Environmental Science*, 11, 1161437. 10.3389/fenvs.2023.1161437

Turkle, S. (2015). *Reclaiming Conversation: The Power of Talk in a Digital Age*. Penguin Press.

Turok, I. (2013). Green Cities of Europe. *European Planning Studies*, 21(2), 281–283. 10.1080/09654313.2012.745261

Tversky, A., & Kahneman, D. (1974). Judgment under uncertainty: Heuristics and biases. *Science*, 185(4157), 1124–1131. 10.1126/science.185.4157.112417835457

Tversky, A., & Kahneman, D. (1981). The framing of decisions and the psychology of choice. *Science*, 211(4481), 453–458. 10.1126/science.74556837455683

Umoh, S. U. (2024). Green Hotels and Green Practices in South Africa. In *Future Tourism Trends* (Vol. 1, pp. 91–98). Emerald Publishing Limited. 10.1108/978-1-83753-244-520241007

Unal Cilek, M., & Uslu, C. (2022). Modeling the Relationship between the Geometric Characteristics of Urban Green Spaces and Thermal Comfort: The Case of Adana City. *Sustainable Cities and Society*, 79, 103748. 10.1016/j.scs.2022.103748

UNESCO. (2019). *Global education monitoring report 2019: Migration, displacement and education: Building bridges, not walls*. UNESCO Publishing.

United Nations Conference on Trade and Development. (2024). *Data Centre*. UN. https://unctadstat.unctad.org/datacentre/

United Nations General Assembly. (1987). *Report of the World commission on environment and development: Our common future. Oslo, Norway:* United Nations General Assembly, Development and International Co-operation. *Environment*.

United Nations. (1992). *United Nations Conference on Environment and Development, Rio de Janeiro, Brazil, 3-14 June 1992*. UN. https://www.un.org/en/conferences/environment/rio1992

United Nations. (2024). *Sustainable Development Goals*. UN. https://www.un.org/sustainabledevelopment/sustainable-development-goals/

Uslu, Y. D., Hancıoğlu, Y., & Demir, E. (2015). Applicability to green entrepreneurship in Turkey: A situation analysis. *Procedia: Social and Behavioral Sciences*, 195, 1238–1245. 10.1016/j.sbspro.2015.06.266

Vandermaesen, T., Humphries, R., Wackernagel, M., Murthy, A., & Mailhes, L. (2019). *Living beyond nature's limits*. World Wide Fund for Nature.

Vassileva, A. G. (2022). Green Public-Private Partnerships (PPPs) as an Instrument for Sustainable Development. *Journal of World Economy: Transformations & Transitions*, 2(5).

Venkatesh, G. (2014). A critique of the European Green City Index. *Journal of Environmental Planning and Management*, 57(3), 317–328. 10.1080/09640568.2012.741520

Venter, Z. S., Barton, D. N., Gundersen, V., Figari, H., & Nowell, M. (2020). Urban Nature in a Time of Crisis: Recreational Use of Green Space Increases during the COVID-19 Outbreak in Oslo, Norway. *Environmental Research Letters*, 15(10), 104075. 10.1088/1748-9326/abb396

Venter, Z. S., Shackleton, C. M., Van Staden, F., Selomane, O., & Masterson, V. A. (2020). Green Apartheid: Urban Green Infrastructure Remains Unequally Distributed across Income and Race Geographies in South Africa. *Landscape and Urban Planning*, 203, 103889. 10.1016/j.landurbplan.2020.103889

Vetráková, M., Hitka, M., Potkány, M., Lorincová, S., & Smerek, L. (2018). Corporate sustainability in the process of employee recruitment through social networks in conditions of Slovak small and medium enterprises. *Sustainability (Basel)*, 10(5), 1670. 10.3390/su10051670

Vieira do Nascimento, D. (2016). Exploring climate finance for tourism adaptation development: An overview. *Worldwide Hospitality and Tourism Themes*, 8(5), 593–605. 10.1108/WHATT-06-2016-0036

Viinikka, A., Tiitu, M., Heikinheimo, V., Halonen, J. I., Nyberg, E., & Vierikko, K. (2023). Associations of Neighborhood-Level Socioeconomic Status, Accessibility, and Quality of Green Spaces in Finnish Urban Regions. *Applied Geography (Sevenoaks, England)*, 157, 102973. 10.1016/j.apgeog.2023.102973

Voronovsky, I., Ashmarina, T., Jiang, C., & Xiao, Y. (2022). Vector of Development of Ecological Civilization in China. *Law and Management, 10*, 219-225. 10.24412/2224-9125-2022-10-219-225

Vygotsky, L. (1978). *Mind in society: The development of higher psychological processes.* Harvard University Press.

Walcott, H. F. (1994). *Transforming qualitative data: Description, analysis and interpretation.* SAGE Publications.

Wallace, M., Lings, I., Cameron, R., & Sheldon, N. (2014). Attracting and retaining staff: The role of branding and industry image. In Harris, R., & Short, T. (Eds.), *Workforce Development* (pp. 19–36). Springer. 10.1007/978-981-4560-58-0_2

Wallington, T. J., Anderson, J. E., Mueller, S. A., Kolinski Morris, E., Winkler, S. L., Ginder, J. M., & Nielsen, O. J. (2012). Corn ethanol production, food exports, and indirect land use change. *Environmental Science & Technology*, 46(11), 6379–6384. 10.1021/es300233m22533454

Wang, D., Huangfu, Y., Dong, Z., & Dong, Y. (2022). Research Hotspots and Evolution Trends of Carbon Neutrality - Visual Analysis of Bibliometrics Based on CiteSpace. *Sustainability (Basel)*, 14(3), 1078. 10.3390/su14031078

Wang, J., Wang, S., Xue, H., Wang, Y., & Li, J. (2018). Green image and consumers' word-of-mouth intention in the green hotel industry: The moderating effect of Millennials. *Journal of Cleaner Production*, 181, 426–436. 10.1016/j.jclepro.2018.01.250

Wang, L., Weng Wong, P. P., & Elangkovan, N. A. (2020). The Influence of Religiosity on Consumer's Green Purchase Intention Towards Green Hotel Selection in China. *Journal of China Tourism Research*, 16(3), 319–345. 10.1080/19388160.2019.1637318

Wang, Q., Gazi, M., Sobhani, F., Masud, A., Islam, M., & Akter, T. (2023). Green human resource management and job pursuit intention: Mediating role of corporate social responsibility and organizational reputation. *Environmental Research Communications*, 5(7), 075001. 10.1088/2515-7620/acda81

Wang, X., Zhou, K., & Liu, W. (2018). Value Congruence: A Study of Green Transformational Leadership and Employee Green Behavior. *Frontiers in Psychology*. Frontiers.

Waris, I., Iqbal, A., Ahmed, R., Hashim, S., & Ahmed, A. (2023). Values and information publicity shape tourists' intentions to visit green hotels: An application of the extended value-belief norms theory. *Management of Environmental Quality*.

Wasaya, A., Prentice, C., & Hsiao, A. (2023). Norms and consumer behaviors in tourism: A systematic literature review. *Tourism Review*.

Weber, O. (2023). Financial sector sustainability regulations and guidelines. In *Encyclopedia of Business and Professional Ethics* (pp. 902–907). Springer International Publishing. 10.1007/978-3-030-22767-8_40

Weber, P., & Haklay, M. (2008). OpenStreetMap: User-Generated Street Maps. *IEEE Pervasive Computing*, 7(4).

Weigand, M., Wurm, M., Droin, A., Stark, T., Staab, J., Rauh, J., & Taubenböck, H. (2023). Are Public Green Spaces Distributed Fairly? A Nationwide Analysis Based on Remote Sensing, OpenStreetMap and Census Data. *Geocarto International*, 38(1), 2286305. Advance online publication. 10.1080/10106049.2023.2286305

Weiss Brown, E. (1990). In fairness to future generations. *Environment*, 32(3), 6–31. 10.1080/00139157.1990.9929015

Wen, W. (2022). Communication channels for the rule of law and environmental sustainability: Reflections from a green economy perspective. *Journal of Environmental and Public Health*, 2022, 2022. 10.1155/2022/1811896361O5517

Wettestad, J., & Gulbrandsen, L. H. (Eds.). (2017). *The evolution of carbon markets: Design and diffusion*. Routledge. 10.4324/9781315228266

Whitelock, V. G. (2019). Multidimensional environmental social governance sustainability framework: Integration, using a purchasing, operations, and supply chain management context. *Sustainable Development (Bradford)*, 27(5), 923–931. 10.1002/sd.1951

WHO-World Health Organization. (2023). *Household air pollution*. WHO. https://www.who.int/news-room/fact-sheets/detail/household-air-pollution-and-health

Widisatria, D., & Nawangsari, L. C. (2021). The influence of green transformational leadership and motivation to sustainable corporate performance with organizational citizenship behavior for the environment as a mediating: Case study at PT Karya Mandiri Sukses Sentosa. *European Journal of Business and Management Research*, 6(3), 118–123. 10.24018/ejbmr.2021.6.3.876

Wielewska, I., Kacprzak, M., Król, A., Czech, A., Zuzek, D., Gralak, K., & Marks-Bielska, R. (2023). Green human resource management. *Ekonomia i Środowisko - Economics and Environment*. https://doi.org/10.34659/eis.2022.83.4.496

Wolf, S., Teitge, J., Mielke, J., Schütze, F., & Jaeger, C. (2021). The European Green Deal—More than climate neutrality. *Inter Economics*, 56(2), 99–107. 10.1007/s10272-021-0963-z33840826

Workie, E., Mackolil, J., Nyika, J., & Ramadas S. (2020). Deciphering the impact of COVID-19 pandemic on food security, agriculture, and livelihoods: a review of the evidence from developing countries. *Curr Res Environ Sustain, 100014*. https://doi.org/. crsust.2020.10001410.1016/j

World Bank. (2022, December 8). *Azerbaijan Can Accelerate Its Green Economic Transformation, a World Bank Report Shows How* [Press release]. Woeld Bank. https://www.worldbank.org/en/news/press-release/2022/12/08/azerbaijan-can-accelerate-its-green-economic-transformation-a-world-bank-report-shows-how

Wossen, T., Menkir, A., Alene, A., Abdoulaye, T., Ajala, S., Badu-Apraku, B., Gedil, M., Mengesha, W., & Meseka, S. (2023). Drivers of transformation of the maize sector in Nigeria. *Global Food Security*, 38, 100713. 10.1016/j.gfs.2023.10071337752896

Wu, H.-C., Cheng, C.-C., & Ai, C.-H. (2018). An empirical analysis of green switching intentionsin the airline industry. *Journal of Environmental Planning and Management*, 61(8), 1438–1468. 10.1080/09640568.2017.1352495

Xiao, Y., & Watson, M. (2019). Guidance on Conducting a Systematic Literature Review. *Journal of Planning Education and Research*, 39(1), 93–112. 10.1177/0739456X17723971

Xiaoyi, W. (2013). Building a Fair and Conservation-Oriented Society. *Social Sciences in China*, 34(4), 171–179. 10.1080/02529203.2013.849097

Xi, J. (2017). *The Governance of China II*. Foreign Languages Press.

Xin, Y., & Senin, A. B. A. (2022). Features of environmental sustainability concerning environmental regulations, green innovation, and social distribution in China. *Higher Education and Oriental Studies, 2*(1).

Xing-ling, W. (2005). Construction and Realization of Green Values. *Journal of Southern Yangtze University*.

Xiu, J., Zang, X., Piao, Z., Li, L., & Kim, K. (2023). China's Low-Carbon Economic Growth: An Empirical Analysis Based on the Combination of Parametric and Nonparametric Methods. *Environmental Science and Pollution Research International*, 30(13), 37219–37232. 10.1007/s11356-022-24775-y36567394

Xue, B., Han, B., Li, H., Gou, X., Yang, H., Thomas, H., & Stückrad, S. (2023). Understanding Ecological Civilization in China: From Political Context to Science. *Ambio*, 52(12), 1895–1909. 10.1007/s13280-023-01897-237442892

Xu, G., Zang, L., Schwarz, P., & Yang, H. (2023). Achieving China's Carbon Neutrality Goal by Economic Growth Rate Adjustment and Low-Carbon Energy Structure. *Energy Policy*, 183, 113817. 10.1016/j.enpol.2023.113817

Xu, Y. (2023). Financial development, financial inclusion and natural resource management for sustainable development: Empirical evidence from Asia. *Geological Journal*, 58(9), 3288–3300. 10.1002/gj.4825

Xu, Z., Assenova, A., & Erokhin, V. (2018). Renewable Energy and Sustainable Development in a Resource-Abundant Country: Challenges of Wind Power Generation in Kazakhstan. *Sustainability (Basel)*, 10(9), 3315. 10.3390/su10093315

Yafi, E., Tehseen, S., & Haider, S. A. (2021). Impact of green training on environmental performance through mediating role of competencies and motivation. *Sustainability (Basel)*, 13(10), 5624. 10.3390/su13105624

Yang, Y., Jiang, L., & Wang, Y. (2023). Why do hotels go green? Understanding TripAdvisor GreenLeaders participation. *International Journal of Contemporary Hospitality Management*, 35(5), 1670–1690. 10.1108/IJCHM-02-2022-0252

Yeldan, E. (2002). *Küreselleşme Sürecinde Türkiye Ekonomisi*. İletişim Yayınları.

Yıldırım, A., & Şimşek, H. (2003). *Sosyal Bilimlerde Nitel Araştırma Yöntemleri*. Seçkin Yayınları, Ankara. https://www.worldairlineawards.com/worlds-top-10-airlines-2023/,

Yıldırım, S., & Yıldırım, D. Ç. (2020). Achieving sustainable development through a green economy approach. In *Advanced integrated approaches to environmental economics and policy: Emerging research and opportunities* (pp. 1–22). IGI Global. 10.4018/978-1-5225-9562-5.ch001

Yin, J., Fu, P., Cheshmehzangi, A., Li, Z., & Dong, J. (2022). Investigating the Changes in Urban Green-Space Patterns with Urban Land-Use Changes: A Case Study in Hangzhou, China. *Remote Sensing (Basel)*, 14(21), 5410. 10.3390/rs14215410

Yin, J., Qian, L., & Singhapakdi, A. (2018). Sharing Sustainability: How Values and Ethics Matter in Consumers' Adoption of Public Bicycle-Sharing Scheme. *Journal of Business Ethics*, 149(2), 313–332. 10.1007/s10551-016-3043-8

Yip, C. M. (2018). On the labor market consequences of environmental taxes. *Journal of Environmental Economics and Management*, 89, 136–152. 10.1016/j.jeem.2018.03.004

Yong, J., & Mohd-Yusoff, Y. (2016). Studying the influence of strategic human resource competencies on the adoption of green human resource management practices. *Industrial and Commercial Training*, 48(7), 416–422. 10.1108/ICT-03-2016-0017

Yong, J., Yusliza, M., & Fawehinmi, O. (2019). Green human resource management. *Benchmarking*, 26(3), 782–804. 10.1108/BIJ-12-2018-0438

Youssef, C. M., & Luthans, F. (2007). *Positive organizational behavior in the workplace: The impact of hope*. APA.

Yusif Asgarov, M. (2022). *"Avropa yaşıl sövdələşmə"nin əhəmiyyəti və əsas elementləri*. Scientific Work.

Yu, Y., & Huo, B. (2019). The impact of environmental orientation on supplier green management and financial performance: The moderating role of relational capital. *Journal of Cleaner Production*, 211, 628–639. 10.1016/j.jclepro.2018.11.198

Yu, Z., & Deng, X. (2022). Assessment of Land Degradation in the North China Plain Driven by Food Security Goals. *Ecological Engineering*, 183, 106766. 10.1016/j.ecoleng.2022.106766

Zafar, A., Nisar, Q.A., Shoukat, M. & Ikram, M. (2017). Green Transformational Leadership and Green Performance: The mediating role of Green Mindfulness and Green Self-efficacy. *International Journal of Management Excellence,* 1059–1066.

Zakaria, W. F. A. W., & Buaben, J. M. (2021). The Theory of Post-Industrial Society. *Akademika*, 91(1), 139–149. 10.17576/akad-2021-9101-12

Zhang, S., Liu, Y., & Huang, D. (2021). Understanding the Mystery of Continued Rapid Economic Growth. *Journal of Business Research*, 124, 529–537. 10.1016/j.jbusres.2020.11.023

Zhang, W., Xu, F., & Wang, X. (2020). How Green Transformational Leadership Affects Green Creativity: Creative Process Engagement as Intermediary Bond and Green Innovation Strategy as Boundary Spanner. *Sustainability (Basel)*, 12(9), 3841. 10.3390/su12093841

Zhang, X., Wu, H., Li, Z., & Li, X. (2023). Spatial-Temporal Evolution Characteristics and Driving Factors of Rural Development in Northeast China. *Land (Basel)*, 12(7), 1407. 10.3390/land12071407

Zhao, W., Zhou, A., & Yin, C. (2023). Unraveling the Research Trend of Ecological Civilization and Sustainable Development: A Bibliometric Analysis. *Ambio*, 52(12), 1928–1938. 10.1007/s13280-023-01947-937907802

Zhao, X., Jiang, M., & Zhang, W. (2022). The Impact of Environmental Pollution and Economic Growth on Public Health: Evidence From China. *Frontiers in Public Health*, 10, 861157. 10.3389/fpubh.2022.86115735419328

Zhou, J., Sawyer, L., & Safi, A. (2021). Institutional pressure and green product success: The role of green transformational leadership, green innovation, and green brand image. *Frontiers in Psychology*, 12, 704855. 10.3389/fpsyg.2021.70485534671290

Zhou, S., Zhang, D., Lyu, C., & Zhang, H. (2018). Does seeing "mind acts upon mind" affect green psychological climate and green product development performance? The role of matching between green transformational leadership and individual green values. *Sustainability (Basel)*, 10(9), 3206. 10.3390/su10093206

Zhou, Y., Shu, C., Jiang, W., & Gao, S. (2019). Green management, firm innovations, and environmental turbulence. *Business Strategy and the Environment*, 28(4), 567–581. 10.1002/bse.2265

Ziaul, I. M., & Shuwei, W. (2023). Environmental Sustainability: A Major Component of Sustainable Development. *International Journal of Environmental, Sustainability, and Social Science*, 4(3), 900–907. 10.38142/ijesss.v4i2.296

Zi, H. (2023). Role of green financing in developing sustainable business of e-commerce and green entrepreneurship: Implications for green recovery. *Environmental Science and Pollution Research International*, 30(42), 95525–95536. 10.1007/s11356-023-28970-337550481

Zilincikova, M., & Stofkova, J. (2022). Integration Of Sustainable Development Measures in The Field of Eco-Schools. In *INTED2022 Proceedings* (pp. 7380- 7387). IATED. 10.21125/inted.2022.1863

Zorlu, P. (2018). *Transforming the financial system for delivering sustainable development: A high-level overview.* Institute for Global Environmental Strategies.

Zwolińska, K., Lorenc, S., & Pomykała, R. (2022). Sustainable development in education from students' perspective—Implementation of sustainable development in curricula. *Sustainability (Basel)*, 14(6), 3398. 10.3390/su14063398

About the Contributors

Andrei Jean Vasile is full professor at Petroleum-Gas University of Ploiesti, Department of Business Administration and Ph.D mentor in economics at Bucharest University of Economic Studies, Romania. He is co-founder and scientific coordinator of the Research Network on Resources Economics and Bioeconomy. Andrei Jean-Vasile holds a Ph.D. in Economics from the National Institute of Economics Research – Romanian Academy of Sciences. He has earned a BA degree in Administrative Sciences (2005) and in Banks and Finances (2007) from the Petroleum-Gas University of Ploiesti. He has an MA degree in Economics, Administrative and Business Management (2007) earned at the same university. Jean Andrei is also Associate Editor of Economics of Agriculture (Serbia), scientific reviewer and committee member for numerous international conferences. He is member of scientific organizations: The Balkan Scientific Association of Agrarian Economists, Serbia (2008), DAAAM Vienna and Information Resources Management Association (2011). Issues like: agricultural economics and rural development, energy and resource economics and business economics are among his research and scientific interests.

Mile Vasic obtained his MA and PhD in the field of Human Resources Management. He has acted as a Dean of Faculty of Technical Sciences, Dean of Faculty of Economics and Management, Vice-Rector of PIM University and Vice-Rector and Rector of Slobomir P University. He was a guest lecture in Greece, Romania, Slovenia, Serbia, and the United Kingdom. Besides academic work, his passion is the implementation of scientific knowledge and skills in practice. He has been consulting and providing in-company training worldwide and most important clients were Coca-Cola, Renault, BH Mont Trade Srl., Johnson & Johnson, McDonald's, OMV. Between 2015 and 2018 professor Vasic served as an Ambassador Extraordinary and Plenipotentiary of Bosnia and Herzegovina to Romania. Dr. Mile Vasic is currently President of European Marketing and Management Association (EUMMAS).

Luminiţa Chivu is senior researcher in Economics (since 1992) and currently the general director and President of the Scientific Council of the National Institute for Economic Research "Costin C. Kiriţescu" - Romanian Academy (since 2011). She is author of 18 books in foreign and national publishing houses and more than 200 articles in economics. Member of the Consultative Council for Research, Development and Innovation of the Ministry of Research, Innovation and Digitization in Romania. She holds expertise on agricultural models and agricultural policies and competitiveness, sustainable rural development, labour market, industrial relations, working conditions, economic growth and restructuring and European integration. Experience in managing and coordinating more than 15 international and 20 national projects working with multidisciplinary teams of research experts. Co-chair of the Scientific Council of the international conference "Economic Scientific Research-Theoretical, Empirical and Practical Approaches" – ESPERA, editions 2013-2023.

About the Contributors

Boris Kuzman should especially emphasize the projects on organization and start-up of the APV Development Fund, a series of presentations of Vojvodina's economy, active participation in the development of the development strategy of the Municipality of Beočin, participation in the development of the Belgrade agricultural development strategy, activities in the development of an action plan for the cross-border cooperation program. In his previous work he served as a member of the Supervisory Board of the Center for Social Work in Novi Sad. He was the representative of the capital of the Republic of Serbia at the Assembly of the Development Fund of the Autonomous Province of Vojvodina. He served as the chairman of the supervisory board of PE Fruška Gora National Park, Performed the function of a member of the working group for the promotion of rural tourism and rural development at the Ministry of Trade and Tourism of the Republic of Serbia, Acting as a member of the Council of the Faculty of Agriculture in Zemun in front of the Government of the Republic of Serbia, He served as a member of the Board of Directors of the Institute for Agricultural Economics, Belgrade, Acts as a Council Member at the College of Business, Novi Sad, in front of the APV Government. He is the Chairman of the Supervisory Board of the Society of Agricultural Economists of Serbia (DAES). In recent years he has written two books in the field of strategic and business planning and three monographs, while co-authoring a number of publications of the Development Fund of the Autonomous Province of Vojvodina. He is a reviewer of scientific papers for the scientific journals Agricultural Economics and Agroeconomics. He also participated in several international symposiums where he presented scientific papers in the fields of agro-industry, markets, management and marketing. He has published more than 40 scientific and professional papers so far as author and co-author in national and international scientific journals. He was hired as a mentor, commentator and committee member in the preparation of several doctoral and master's theses.

***

Zeinab Afshar Bakeshlo is hardworking researcher who is interested in organizational behavior especially subjects related to the ethical and unethical behavior. She has 7 years of experience as a HR executive. She has been graduated from Kharazmi University with master of business administration in human resource and organizational behavior since 2021 and then have been active as a researcher. She is interested to cooperate with other researchers on subjects related to organizational behavior, human resource, Leadership, ethical and unethical behavior, pro-social and pro-environmental behavior and CSR.

Munir Ahmad, Ph.D. in Computer Science, brings over 24 years of invaluable expertise in the realm of spatial data development, management, processing, visualization, and quality assurance. His unwavering commitment to open data, big data, crowdsourced data, volunteered geographic information, and spatial data infrastructure has solidified him as a seasoned professional and a trusted trainer in cutting-edge spatial technologies. With a profound passion for research, Munir has authored more than 30 publications in his field, culminating in the award of his Ph.D. in Computer Science from Preston University Pakistan in 2022. His dedication to propelling the industry forward and sharing his extensive knowledge defines his mission.

Aleksandr Arskiy is a Russian scientist and associate professor of the university. Specialization: logistics systems of the Russian Federation and the EAEU; customs regulation and customs policy in the Russian Federation; problems of organizing educational clusters; problems of continuing professional education. Co-author of 6 textbooks on marketing and logistics. The author of more than 50 scientific papers on logistics and customs regulation. Thesis: "The mechanism of interaction between customs authorities and participants in foreign economic activity using the services of transport and logistics companies" (Russian Customs Academy, 2011). He teaches logistics and customs regulation: 1. Russian academy of personnel support for the agro-industrial complex 2. RUDN University

Zarina Burkadze is a distinguished scholar with a keen interest in political dynamics, specializing in comparative politics, democratization, and political violence. She earned her doctoral degree in Political Science at the University of Zurich (2014 -2018). During her time there, she delved deep into the intricacies of political systems, fostering a profound understanding of democratic processes and mechanisms. Burkadze's scholarly pursuits led her to the United States as a Fulbright Postdoctoral Scholar at the Elliot School of International Affairs at George Washington University. Her tenure as a Fulbright scholar from 2019 to 2020 was marked by a rigorous exploration of democracy promotion and autocracy promotion, resulting in the book publication with Rochester University Press (2022). Her scholarly contributions have significantly advanced the understanding of democratization processes, shedding light on the dynamics of political violence and the intricate interplay between democratic and autocratic forces. With an unwavering dedication to academic excellence, she continues to push the boundaries of knowledge in her field, employing rigorous methodologies and innovative approaches to address pressing questions in contemporary politics.

Abhijit Pramod Chandratreya is currently working as Deputy Director in the Department of Post Graduate Research Centre at SCES's Indira Institute of Management, Pune for the past 16 years. He joined IIMP after working in various Industries for 17 years. He graduated in Production Engineering from Birla Vishwakarma Mahavidyalaya (Sardar Patel University), Anand, Gujarat, India. He secured a Master of Business Administration in Human Resource Development from IGNOU. He has been awarded a Ph.D. in the field of Marketing Management from Savitribai Phule Pune University, India. He has presented several papers in National and International Journals, conferences, and Symposiums and has published 15 research papers both in referred and SCOPUS / ABDC-listed Journals. He has published three patents. He is a certified trainer of CSCP, CPTP, CLDM, MTF, and CID certified by MiddleEarth HR. His main areas of interest include Marketing, HRM, SCM, Statistics, Business Analytics, and Research Methodologies. ORCID ID; https://orcid.org/0000-0001-9403-2094 ; SCOPUS ID: 58695471800 Google Scholar ID: jJN5ZcQAAAAJ

Vasilii Erokhin is Associate Professor at Harbin Engineering University, School of Economics and Management, Polar Development and Northeast Asian Economic Research Center (PAERC). His spheres of research interests: international trade, globalization, trade integration and liberalization, sustainable development, economies in transition, food security issues. Dr. Erokhin is an author of over 150 research works in international economics, international trade, sustainable rural development and regionalization. Vasily Erokhin is a member of editorial review boards of several international journals: International Journal of Sustainable Economies Management (IJSEM); Economies; Journal of World Economic Research; Economics of Agriculture (Ekonomika poljoprivrede), editor of international book projects "Global Perspectives on Trade Integration and Economies in Transition" (IGI Global, USA, 2016) and "Establishing Food Security and Alternatives to International Trade in Emerging Economies" (IGI Global, USA, 2017). He is a holder of the honorary awards from the Ministry of Agriculture of the Russian Federation (2010), Ministry of Education and Science of the Russian Federation (2012).

Iza Gigauri received her PhD in Business Administration (Summa Cum Laude) from Ivane Javakhishvili Tbilisi State University (Georgia). She holds an MBA from Business School Netherlands and an MBA with highest honors from the American University for Humanities (Georgia). She is a graduate with highest honors from Ilia State University (Georgia) and from Ruhr-University Bochum (Germany). She delivers lectures and teaches seminars at all three levels of higher education. She is an expert, opponent, and supervisor of dissertations. She won a number of international scholarships and awards in the field of her academic specialization. Her research interests include corporate responsibility, marketing, sustainability, entrepreneurship, HRM, and leadership. She has participated in 38 international scientific conferences and published over 80 peer-reviewed papers, 2 books, and 18 book chapters. She is a scientific committee member and keynote speaker at international conferences, a guest editor, an editorial board member and a reviewer at international journals within Emerald, Springer, IGI Global, Frontiers, Taylor & Francis, Elsevier, Wiley, and Inderscience.

About the Contributors

Biljana Grujic Vuckovski graduated 2010 on the Faculty of Agriculture, University of Belgrade. Doctoral thesis degree 2017 at the Faculty of Business Studies, Megatrend University (John Naisbitt University), and gained title a Ph.D. of Economic Sciences. She is employed in the Insitute of Agricultural Economics in Belgrade from 2011. She was also involved in numerous projects of Institute and strategies of local community development as a member of the research team.

Nargiz Uzeir Hajiyeva is the distinguished Ph.D Research Fellow, Swiss Federal Excellence Scholarship Holder, University of Michigan, Weiser Award holder, political scientist, and academic instructor. Currently, she is the "Director of Organization of Scientific Activities" Unit and the Chair of Women Researchers Council - Research Center and a part-time academic instructor on "Political Science", and "Political Leadership and Organizational Behavior"courses at Azerbaijan State University of Economics (UNEC). Dr. Hajiyeva is the first female political scientist from Azerbaijan serves also as the Co-Director of "Empirical Methods" Working Group at the Swiss Political Science Association in Bern, Switzerland. She is a research fellow and a member of Democracy NET - Scholar Network of the Department of Political Science at the University of Zurich, Switzerland. Mrs. Hajiyeva is an honored graduate student at Vytautas Magnus University and Institute D'etudes de Politique de Grenoble, Sciences PO. She got a bachelor degree with the merit diploma at Baku State University from International Relations and Diplomacy program. Her main research fields concern on international security and foreign policy issues, energy security, cultural and political history, global political economy, and international law. She worked as an independent researcher at Corvinus University of Budapest, Cold War History Research Center. She was also a successful participator of International Student Essay Contest, Stimson Institute, on how to prevent the proliferation of the world's most dangerous weapons, held by Harvard University, Harvard Kennedy School and an honored alumnus of European Academy of Diplomacy in Warsaw Poland. She is a holder of different academic scholarships and grants in Europe. She served as an Advisor and the First Responsible Chairman in International and Legal Affairs at the Executive Power of Ganja. At that time, she was defined to the position of Chief Economist at the Heydar Aliyev Center. Since June 2017, Ms. Hajiyeva has been working as an independent diplomatic researcher at International Relations Institute of Prague under the Czech Ministry of Foreign Affairs in the Czech Republic. In 2019, Mrs. Hajiyeva has also served as a juror at Innovation in Politics İnstitution based in Vienna, Austria. She speaks Azerbaijani, English, French, German, Russian, Turkish and a bit Lithuanian.

Mehmet Emin Kalgı was born in 1989 in Yumrutepe village of Siverek district of Şanlıurfa, and completed his primary education in his village and his secondary education in Siverek. In 2011, he completed his bachelor's degree in classroom teaching at Kilis 7 Aralık University. In 2014, he completed his master's degree in the Department of Classroom Teaching at Zirve University, Faculty of Education. He completed his doctorate at Çukurova University, Department of Philosophy and Religious Sciences (Psychology of Religion) in 2020. After working as a teacher and administrator in various schools, he started working as a faculty member at Ardahan University, Faculty of Theology, Department of Psychology of Religion in 2022. He became an associate professor in 2023.

Güzide Karakuş is an Assistant Professor at Necmettin Erbakan University, department of Aviation Management. He holds a bachelor's degree in Industrial Engineering from Kocaeli University (1999) and an MBA degree from Gebze Institute of Technology. (2002). She completed her PhD in Production Management and Marketing at Selçuk Universitiy 2014. Prior joining academia, she worked in consulting about quality management systems, CE marking and project management. She teaches Innovation Management, Technology Management, Project Management, Quality Management and Supply Chain Management courses at both undergraduate and graduate levels. She continues her academic studies on Industry 4.0 and digital transformation, as well as sustainability and green transformation.

Saida Khalil is a dynamic academic and finance professional, currently serving as the Director of the Bloomberg Financial Laboratory at Azerbaijan State University of Economics. With a diverse array of interests and expertise, Khalil is at the forefront of research and innovation in finance, specializing in green economy, circular economy, green finance, fintech, digitalization of finance, and gender studies. Khalil's academic journey culminated in the attainment of her Ph.D. in Finance from Dokuz Eylul University in Turkey, where she developed a comprehensive understanding of circular economy and practices. Her doctoral research laid the foundation for her subsequent exploration of cutting-edge topics in circular economy, positioning her as a thought leader in emerging fields such as circular economy and green economy. In addition to her role as Director of the Bloomberg Financial Laboratory, Khalil is a dedicated lecturer at Azerbaijan State University of Economics, where she imparts her knowledge and expertise to the next generation of finance and economic professionals. Her commitment to education and mentorship underscores her passion for fostering talent and driving positive change within the financial industry.

Irina Marina graduated 2020 on the Faculty of Agriculture, University of Belgrade, Department of Agricultural machinery. She completed her master stud- ies in 2021 at the Faculty of Agricultural, University of Belgrade, Department of Biotechnical and information engineering. After that, in the year 2021, PhD studies are enrolled at the Agricultural faculty in Belgrade, University of Belgrade, Department of Biotehnology. She is employed in the Institute of Agricultural Economics in Belgrade from 2022, on possition Research Trainee. The main area of research is agricultural mechanization, biotechnology sustainable agriculture and precision agriculture.

Branko M. Mihailović PhD (in Economics) is Scientific Adviser at the Institute of Agricultural Economics in Belgrade, Serbia. In master's work, doctoral dissertation, monographs and papers published in domestic and foreign professional journals and presented at scientific meetings of national and international importance, he deals with consulting, enterprise restructuring, transition and agrarian economics. Based on previous scientific research, the Ministry of Science and Technological Development of the Republic of Serbia assigned him a category of researchers A1.

|Mohammadsadegh Omidvar - Contributing Author| Mohammadsadegh is a passionate researcher specifically in the field of CSR and consumer behavior who has 9 years of work experience in sales management, marketing, and advertising. He also cooperation with Iran's top newspapers as an economic analyst, and also has a teaching experience as a teaching assistant at Kharazmi University. He received his master's in strategic management from Kharazmi University in 2020. several papers and business projects, two book translations, and more works under progression are among his resume.

Sinan Özyurt, who was born in Erzurum in 1981, graduated from Alparslan Anatolian Teacher High School as the valedictorian in 1999 and successfully graduated from the Middle East Technical University (METU) Department of English Language Teaching in 2004. From this date until December 28, 2008, he actively participated in English speaking clubs and courses in institutions such as National Education institutions, American Language Culture College and Language Schools, and in 2008, he started working at Gaziantep University School of Foreign Languages. He continued to work as a Lecturer at this institution from the specified date until May 16, 2022. After successfully completing his doctorate in English Language Teaching (ELT) on September 17, 2021, he started working as an Assistant Professor in the Department of English Translation and Interpretation at Gaziantep Islam Science and Technology University / School of Foreign Languages on May 16, 2022 and continues his career there. Sinan Özyurt, who is married and the father of three children, speaks foreign languages such as Persian and French at an intermediate level.

About the Contributors

Sabyasachi Pramanik is a professional IEEE member. He obtained a PhD in Computer Science and Engineering from Sri Satya Sai University of Technology and Medical Sciences, Bhopal, India. Presently, he is an Associate Professor, Department of Computer Science and Engineering, Haldia Institute of Technology, India. He has many publications in various reputed international conferences, journals, and book chapters (Indexed by SCIE, Scopus, ESCI, etc). He is doing research in the fields of Artificial Intelligence, Data Privacy, Cybersecurity, Network Security, and Machine Learning. He also serves on the editorial boards of several international journals. He is a reviewer of journal articles from IEEE, Springer, Elsevier, Inderscience, IET and IGI Global. He has reviewed many conference papers, has been a keynote speaker, session chair, and technical program committee member at many international conferences. He has authored a book on Wireless Sensor Network. He has edited 8 books from IGI Global, CRC Press, Springer and Wiley Publications.

Katica Radosavljević PhD (in Economics) is Senior Research Associate. She was born on July 16, 1975 in Gothenburg, Sweden. Since 2000, she has been employed at the Faculty of Economics, University of Belgrade and at the Institute of Agricultural Economics in Belgrade. She defended the doctoral thesis with the topic: The strategy of marketing channel development in agribusiness of the Republic of Serbia.Katica Radosavljević managed two projects related to the valuation of corporate capital. She also assisted on numerous projects.

Fatma Selin Sak received her bachelor's degree from the Department of Civil Air Transportation Management in 2010 and her master's degree from the department of aviation management in 2015 with her thesis "Analyzing the profiles and preferences of airline passengers traveling for holiday purposes with geographical information systems: Antalya example". It is understood that she graduated from Anadolu University, Institute of Social Sciences, Department of Civil Aviation Management in 2020 with his thesis "The role of experience in the effect of customer value co-creation behavior on customer satisfaction: the example of Sabiha Gökçen Airport". Besides having sector experience in the field of Civil Aviation, she also has various studies on airline and airport marketing.

Denis Samygin is a Doctor of Economic Sciences, Professor at Penza State University. Areas of scientific interests: strategic planning and forecasting of the agricultural sector, project management and financing in agriculture, food security modeling, financial management in agricultural business, planning budget allocations for agriculture, control and analysis of the use of subsidies in the agricultural economy. Author of more than 200 scientific and educational works, of which more than 100 in journals recommended by the Higher Attestation Commission of the Russian Federation, more than 15 publications in publications indexed by the international citation databases Scopus / WoS, more than 10 textbooks, including 3 with the UMO stamp, more than 10 monographs in central publishing houses, of which 5 are in a foreign language. Head of scientific projects: (1) Grant of the President of the Russian Federation No. MK-5177.2016.6 "Strategic planning and forecasting of the agri-food sector: project approach", 2016-2017; (2) RSF grant 23-28-10277 "Territorial planning of the agri-food sector in the context of ensuring the physical and economic accessibility of products", 2023-2024.

Index

H

I

L

N

O

P

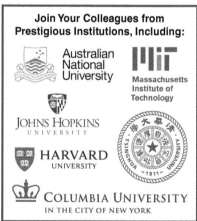

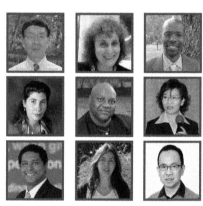

Milton Keynes UK
Ingram Content Group UK Ltd.
UKHW052235120824
446789UK00009B/124

9 798369 334393